**THE
ILLUSTRATED
DICTIONARY
OF
TWENTIETH
CENTURY
DESIGNERS**

THE
DICTIONARY
TWENTIETH

ILLUSTRATED OF CENTURY DESIGNERS

INTRODUCTION BY PETER DORMER

HEADLINE

A QUARTO BOOK

First published in Great Britain in 1991
by HEADLINE BOOK PUBLISHING PLC

British Library Cataloguing in Publication Data
The Illustrated dictionary of twentieth century designers
1. Design, history, Biographies. Collections
I. Dormer, Peter
745.44922

ISBN 0-7472-0268-0

This book was designed and produced by
Quarto Publishing plc
The Old Brewery
6 Blundell Street
London N7 9BH

Senior Editor   Cathy Meeus
Copy Editor   Christine Shuttleworth

Assistant Art Director   Chloë Alexander
Designers   Michelle Stamp and Alun Jones

Picture Manager   Joanna Wiese
Picture Researchers   Ellie Trelawny, Deirdre O'Day

Publishing Director   Janet Slingsby
Art Director   Moira Clinch

Manufactured in Hong Kong by Regent Publishing Services Ltd
Typeset by ABC Typesetting Ltd, Bournemouth
Printed in Hong Kong by Leefung-Asco Printers Ltd.

HEADLINE BOOK PUBLISHING PLC
Headline House
79 Great Titchfield Street
London W1P 7FN

Special thanks to Crucial Books, London

CONTENTS

CONTRIBUTORS

INTRODUCTION by Peter Dormer

Peter Dormer is a well-known writer and critic with far-ranging interests and enthusiasms in the area of design and applied arts. His books include *The New Furniture, The New Ceramics, The New Jewellery,* and *Meanings in Modern Design* (all published by Thames & Hudson). He is a visiting tutor at the Royal College of Art, London, a consultant to the College of Art and Design, Oslo, and an external examiner in Fine Art at Newcastle Polytechnic. He has organized a number of international exhibitions, including "Fast Forward" (ceramics) at the ICA, London; "British Design" in Vienna; and "The New Spirit" in London and Los Angeles. In 1987 he co-founded Design Analysis International Ltd. (DAI), dedicated to providing top level design research and project management to companies and cultural institutions.

ARCHITECTURE

Tim Clarke is a journalist specializing in architecture. Formerly the architecture correspondent of *The Independent*, he now contributes to a variety of architecture and design publications.

Fay Sweet is a writer on architecture and design. She is a regular contributor to *The Designer's Journal, The Architects Journal, The Independent, Design Week* and *Design Magazine*. She also co-wrote with Rod Hackney *The Good, The Bad and The Ugly* (Muller, 1990).

TEXTILES

Chloë Colchester is a researcher and writer in the fields of textiles and crafts, and her work has been published in *The Sunday Times Magazine* as well as in specialist journals.

FASHION

Amy de la Haye is currently Assistant Curator at the Hove Museum and Art Gallery, Sussex, and also lectures on design and dress history at Brighton Polytechnic. She is the author of the *Fashion Source Book* (Macdonald Orbis, 1988).

INDUSTRIAL AND PRODUCT DESIGN

Hugh Aldersey-Williams is a design and technology writer. He is the European Editor of the American magazine *International Design*, and was author of *New American Design* (Rizzoli).

Anne Massey is senior lecturer in design history at Southampton Institute of Higher Education. She is the author of *Twentieth Century Interior Design* (Thames & Hudson, 1990).

Catherine McDermott teaches at the Faculty of Design at Kingston Polytechnic. She also works as a freelance design writer and exhibition organizer. She has written various publications including *Street Style,* a survey of British Design.

Emma Platt, a former writer on *Design Week,* is currently assistant editor on *Design magazine.*

Mary Powell is a former features editor on *Design Week.* She now writes freelance on design for magazines such as *Designer's Journal, Design Magazine, IQ* and *Creative Review.*

GRAPHICS

Liz McQuiston, a former head of the post-graduate course in typography at the London College of Printing, was also Head of the Department of Graphic Art and Design at the Royal College of Art (1985–7). She has written *Women in Design: A Contemporary View* (Trefoil, 1988), and co-authored the *Graphic Design Source Book* (Macdonald Orbis, 1987).

DECORATIVE ARTS

Patricia Bayer has written extensively on the decorative arts of the 19th and 20th centuries. She co-authored the recently published *Lalique* and was author of the *Art Deco Source Book* (Phaidon, 1988). She was a contributor to *Jewellery* (Thames & Hudson).

TWENTIETH CENTURY DESIGNERS

INTRODUCTION

Milestones of modern design

1874	**1876**	**1877**	**1878**	**1879**
Isaac Cole (USA) patents a chair whose back, seat and front support were made from a continuous sheet of bent plywood. Typewriter introduced in USA.	First refrigerator devised by Karl von Linde (Germany).	Thomas Edison (USA) introduces phonograph.	Microphone invented. First commercial telephone exchange opens in Connecticut, USA. First effective carbon filament light by Swan (UK).	Thomas Edison develops his own electric lamp.

Designers are usually conservative in their approach to their work. Their job is to provide people with what they want, and most people want the familiar. Occasionally designers do invent but generally design follows in the wake of earlier traditions, styles and fashions. Early railway locomotives looked little more than water-pumping machines on wheels and the carriages they drew looked exactly like the stage coaches they were replacing. This was not just because of the limited technology and skills available at the time; it was essentially because the imagination of the designers concerned could not – as our own imaginations cannot – stretch much beyond the known. Not even Henry FORD, the great American automobile designer, could make the mental leap from a Model T to a streamlined saloon without running boards. Like everything else, design evolves. Of course, from time to time, designers, flirting with the most recent developments in late-20th-century art, experiment with "outrageous" design – especially in furniture and interior furnishings. But the price the designer frequently pays for this is to be ignored by the consumer.

On 20 July 1969 the first men landed on the moon. The Apollo 11 mission was a triumph for American design and technology, yet in terms of its impact on everyday life somewhat of an anti-climax.

This entrapment within an evolutionary rather than a revolutionary process is not a problem for designers; it is something they have learned to accept. If pressed, however, most designers will admit to wanting to be a little bit different. Even though they are dealing with the ephemeral, they hope to snatch a little professional fame for themselves through being identified with this rather than that style. Such fame, like that of television celebrities, is apt to be fleeting. Yet the work of designers, the bric-à-brac of consumption, is even now being collected by museums: design has become the folk art of the 20th century. This art may not be profound but, in the glimpses it provides of our own times, it is extremely interesting.

The reader must, however, be warned that the way those glimpses should be read is currently a matter of debate. So far the history of design, written by design critics, has tended to avoid politics, economics and the issues of class and gender. But there is now a growing body of design writing that is challenging that anodyne history and, in particular, challenging the essentially male view of design which has predominated until recently. As in all history, the facts simply will not speak for themselves; an understanding of context is required.

What is a designer? In this book, the term "designer" has been interpreted broadly to include those who design for manufacture – whether mass-produced consumer products, such as furniture and clothing, or larger "one off" items, such as buildings. Also included are a number of craftspeople (for example, potters and jewellers) who, although their output may not have been designed for industrial manufacture, have by their vision greatly influenced other designers and thereby the look of a much wider range of industrial products.

Designers differ from artists, who have been excluded from this book. The differences between the two are at least fourfold. First, the main concern of an artist is usually to please himself or herself, whereas a designer needs to please others, notably the client and the client's customers. Second (a point related to the first), contemporary artists do not like being told what form their work should take, but industrial designers, on the other hand, have to be briefed, because their role is to provide a service. Third, artists do not need to be in tune with society's values (on the contrary, much art criticizes or subverts those values), but it is essential for designers to be in sympathy with the times, or at least to echo them, because much of the designer's usefulness to a manufacturer lies in his or her ability to identify current popular taste. Fourth, the artist is usually creating a one-off product, whereas the designer is concerned with products that can be economically mass-produced. This means that the designer has to take account in his or her work of the methods and costs of production.

Profitability is an obvious constraint on the designer, but not all design activities are directly quantifiable in terms of increased profits for the client. One example of this is corporate design. Corporate design can, for a large manufacturing company, be a colossal undertaking, affecting the livery of the company's vehicles, its stationery, its signage (informational and directional signs), its reception areas and the design of its internal communications. Designers specializing in this complex service justifiably claim that it improves the company's image, both with the public and with its own employees, and helps the company clarify its ideas about what it is hoping to achieve.

Increasingly, design is as much about talking as it is about drawing and modelling. Leaders in corporate design argue that the most important part of recreating a company's corporate identity is the questions they ask of management and of other employees about how they think the company performs, what quality of service it provides and how the company sees itself. This is because corporate identity and company performance are often linked: a low-quality signage system, inadequate reception areas and poorly designed stationery usually indicate a lack of attention within the company to service, and lack of such attention always leads to commercial failure.

An emphasis on talking is a feature not only of the corporate design process, but of most design commissions. For example, a manufacturer of kitchen furniture who commissions a designer to produce a new range will probably have only a hazy idea of what he or she wants, and before the designer can be briefed designer and manufacturer will have to explore the subject together. Sometimes this exploration is entirely verbal but often it involves rough drawings and even rough mock-ups before the brief – and the real work of designing – is finalized. Determining the brief can take two or three meetings and constitutes 80 per cent of the designer's creative work.

Misha BLACK, a Russian-born designer who worked in Britain, described the design process as having four

The impact of the personal computer during the 1980s was comparable to that of the automobile in the 1920s. Fears among skilled workers that computers would render their jobs obsolete were largely dispelled once the benefits of the new technology began to be felt.

1892

First trunk telephone line opened (between New York and Chicago). General Electric Company established (USA). Diesel engine constructed by Rudolf Diesel (Germany).

1895

Petrol engine introduced by Gottlieb Daimler and Karl Benz (Germany).

1897

Charles Rennie Mackintosh (Britain) designs first of the Glasgow tearooms. Secession building in Vienna designed by Joseph Olbrich (Austria).

1898

Work begins on Charles Rennie Mackintosh's Glasgow School of Art building (finished 1907). Otto Wagner (Austria) creates Karlsplatz underground station in Vienna.

1900

Ferdinand von Zeppelin begins work on prototypes that lead to the Zeppelin airships. Kodak Box Brownie camera first marketed. First radio transmission using Morse code sent.

basic stages: accumulating information; analysing facts relevant to the design problem; producing hypotheses based on analysis of the facts; and verifying the hypotheses. Black said the third stage, producing hypotheses, is both rational and intuitive – the intuitive part perhaps being the ability to see new relationships between existing technology and existing needs. It is noteworthy that the design process outlined by Black depends on a team of people; it is a co-operative, communal activity, because no one discipline has all the facts relevant to the design of, for example, a railway locomotive, a desk-top computer or a hand-held video game. Black himself said: "If we accept a co-operative role for the designer, the element of magic recedes and the designer appears as not fundamentally different from any other skilled practitioner who is concerned with innovation."

There are many anecdotes (some originating from the veteran pioneer of design, the French-born American Raymond LOEWY) that suggest designers plan their creations on the backs of envelopes. In view of the responsibilities of a designer, this cavalier approach is probably more fiction than fact. What is true is that most designers, whether in clothing, automobile, ceramic, graphic or product design, think through drawing (increasingly by using a computer) and making rough mock-ups. There are exceptions to

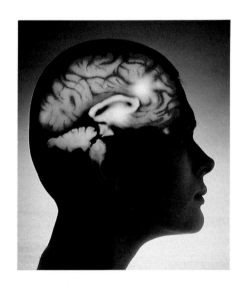

We tend to compare the brain to the computer but attempts to replicate human intelligence and creativity artificially by taking the computer as a model have yet to yield substantial fruits.

this, especially where design abuts onto engineering. The British engineer and designer Barnes WALLIS, for example, said that in his experience the conception and development of true three-dimensional work is essentially a mental process, which in its highest expression is carried out in the mind itself, quite independently of that special co-ordination of hand and eye revealed by a natural ability to draw or paint. Thus his R100 airship was shaped, not by a drawing or a model, but by a mathematical equation.

Wallis's approach may be valid but the immediate drawback to wholly mental designing is that it cannot usually be communicated to the client; designers find that very few clients can even understand technical drawings or plans, let alone read an algebraic statement and see it in the mind's eye as a three-dimensional form. This is not a flippant point: pivotal to the work of designing is communication between the designer and the client that enables the former to "sell" the design concept. From this point of view designing is a *service* industry.

Broadly speaking, design work concerns styling and packaging. For although each innovation – the Sony Walkman, the personal computer, the pocket calculator, the telefax machine, the home video recorder – creates a market without difficulty to begin with, once each market is saturated the only way to renew it is for designers to keep recasting the product in successive models, each incorporating minor improvements on, and looking rather different from, the last. It is now possible to use computers to design products, and there are fears that this will de-skill designers. Accordingly, we are beginning to see new claims made about designers and designing which echo the arguments put forward earlier this century by men and women who wanted a handicraft revival to counteract the dehumanizing aspects of mass

1901	1902	1903	1904	1905
Hubert Cecil Booth (Britain), invents first vacuum cleaner.	Reginald Fessenden (USA) transmits human voice via radio waves over distance of one mile.	Wilbur and Orville Wright (USA) make first successful powered flight near Kitty Hawk, North Carolina. Wiener Werkstätte (Austria) established by Josef Hoffmann and Koloman Moser.	Radio valve invented by Sir John Ambrose Fleming (Britain). Frank Lloyd Wright's (USA) Larkin administrative building begun (completed 1905).	Antoni Gaudí (Spain) designs Casa Mila, Barcelona (completed 1910), noted for inventive use of concrete in organic, flowing style.

manufacture. Recently, for example, Michael and Katherine McCoy, of CRANBROOK Academy of Art, have argued: "Designers who design like machines will be replaced by machines. It is not the digital but the intuitive, not the measurable but the poetic, and not the mechanical but the sensual, which provide the essential humanization of design."

At one level this is special pleading for the sake of job protection, but at another it is true enough that an important part of a designer's work is to make sure that purchasers like using what he or she has designed, and appealing to the senses and imagination plays a key role in such popularity. This does not mean, however, that the designer is free to assert the "intuitive" over the measurable or the "poetic" over the mechanical. The core of good design is function and performance, and these depend on facts not poetry. Often, however – and this was Barnes Wallis's view – the right facts in the right alignment make poetry of their own.

As well as designers whose work is intended for mass production, there are those who create one-off products. Their work may be just as innovative and disciplined as that of designers working for a large market. The calligraphy of Irene WELLINGTON, for example, achieves beauty through the complexity of its design and merits every bit as much attention as more obviously "progressive" innovations such as, for example, the bare, angular lettering that was produced by Constructivist graphic designers in Russia after the Revolution. The jeweller Wendy RAMSHAW, although designing mass-produced jewellery, knitted textiles and ceramic ware, also makes one-off pieces of jewellery, and these two sides of her work have fed each other. Functional crafts, such as pottery and making furniture by hand, have a high design input and satisfy the human need for variety and texture in design.

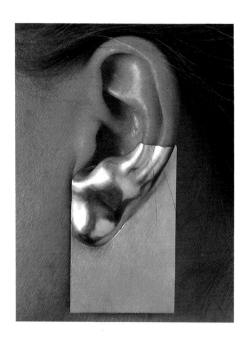

This silver earring by the German avant-garde jeweller Gerd Rothman demonstrates a high degree of craftsmanship. Rothman came to prominence in the 1980s by relating jewellery to the newly-fashionable performance art.

Assumptions that some areas of design are less technical than others are not always correct. For example, there is a relationship between the "bias cut" in dressmaking and rocket construction. As Professor J E Gordon, an expert in materials and structures has explained, when the French dress designer VIONNET invented the bias cut in 1922, she solved a major technical problem. If the weave of the cloth is disposed at 45 degrees to the vertical, the considerable lateral contraction of the material that results can be used to produce a clinging effect. The connection with rocketry is that a similar structural solution was used in the construction of rocket cases in the 1950s – and the idea, says Gordon, "stemmed from the bias-cut nighties which were around at the time".

Design is obviously not an activity peculiar to the 20th century. What is peculiar to the 20th century is design as a business in its own right, separate from manufacture. Design as a hived off enterprise of this kind sprang up in Europe, notably in Britain, Germany, Denmark and Sweden, but flourished particularly in the United States. By the early 1900s the United States was a leading industrial power. With its ever-

1906

Auguste Perret (France) produces concrete-framed six-storey block of flats in Paris. Weimar School of Arts and Crafts established by Henri van de Velde, providing a bridge between Jugendstil (the later German form of Art Nouveau) and Modernism. Frank Lloyd Wright designs Unity Temple, Oak Park, Chicago.

1907

Pablo Picasso completes *Les Demoiselles d'Avignon,* the painting that launched Cubism. Formation of German Werkbund. Belgian-born Leo Baekeland (USA) invents Bakelite.

1908

Adolf Loos (Austria), architect and writer publishes his essay, *Ornament and Crime.* AEG factory redesigned by Peter Behrens (Germany) in modern functionalist style.

1909

Evinrude outboard motor manufactured (USA). Model T Ford appears. Futurist Manifesto launched by Filippo Marinetti (Italy). Peter Behrens designs an electric kettle for AEG.

increasing population of pioneers opening up the North American continent in fields as diverse as oil and leisure (films, phonographs, magazines) the nation offered a great opportunity to designers. The breakthrough, for the profession of design, was when the designer set up independent studios. Among the pioneers in this field were Henry DREYFUSS, Walter Dorwin TEAGUE and Raymond Loewy. Because the American home market was large, there developed a diversity of thriving manufacturing companies which could buy the services of independent design studios. Of course, companies had to be persuaded that they needed designers and it was not until the late 1920s that design was recognized by manufacturers as a force for generating profits.

Vladimir Tatlin's 1919 "Tower" (a reconstruction is pictured here) remains for many designers and architects the archetypal 20th century assertion of faith in technological progress. Others see a closer parallel with the tower of Babel or Pisa.

The technological culture It is far from true that all the major technological breakthroughs of the 20th century have been American but, as will be discussed, a case can be made for asserting that the dominant culture of the 20th century has been technological and that America has dominated that culture. In non-technological culture, however, Europe has led the way and – with the exception of streamlining, Hollywood and the contribution of the American Abstract Expressionists – the major aesthetic (and ideological) contributions to design have been European-led. Among the most influential movements have been Arts and Crafts (Vienna, Berlin, London, Glasgow), Art Nouveau (Paris, Vienna, Brussels, Glasgow, London), Modernism (Dessau, Paris), Constructivism (Moscow), De Stijl (the Netherlands), Art Deco (Paris), Organic Modernism (Stockholm, Helsinki, Copenhagen), Rationalism (Ulm), Pop art (London), Post-modernism (Milan).

Throughout these movements, leading practitioners from Europe have visited or emigrated to America, finding there both a welcome for new ideas and a willingness to put them into production. Putting things into production has been something that the United States is extraordinarily good at.

In the 19th century, first Britain, then Germany, led the world in technology and rapidly industrialized not only manufactures such as textiles, iron-making and pottery but also hitherto non-industrial areas such as agriculture. But by the mid-1800s America was doing everything Europe was doing, and doing it better.

John A Kouwenhoven in his book *Made In America* points out that the pioneers "had to become familiar with the nature of materials and the use of tools" and that they had to relearn a truth that Europeans could get along without – the truth of function. By this Kouwenhoven means that there was in Europe a modern division between those who plan and those who do; whereas. in pioneering the exploitation of a continent, practically everyone had to do as well as plan. And those who have to do as well as plan have a particular vested interest in the quality and performance of their technology. Moreover, it makes them receptive to anything that saves manual effort. It can be argued that the real truth of function is known only to those who use a tool.

1911

Fagus shoe-last factory opened, designed by German architects Walter Gropius and Adolf Meyer. Frederick Winslow Taylor (USA) publishes *The Principles of Scientific Management*. Auguste Perret uses concrete for the

1913

Théâtre des Champs-Elysées (completed 1914).

Formica, the rigid decorated laminated plastic, invented (USA). Frank Lloyd Wright creates The Midway Gardens, Chicago.

1914

Le Corbusier (Switzerland) designs his "little Dom-Ino" house. Deutsche Werkbund exhibition opens in Cologne. Model T Ford manufactured on mass-assembly methods.

1915

Christine Frederick publishes *Household Engineering*. Design and Industries Association formed in Britain as equivalent to German Werkbund with slogan "Fitness for purpose".

One of the successes of modern technology, to which all industrial nations have contributed, is accuracy and fine measurement. (Today if one discusses an industrial product with a designer – for example, the Italian specialist in plastics Anna Castelli FERRIERI – one is quickly drawn into an examination of the quality of the moulds or presses that produced the casing or components of the product. The designer looks for clean lines and accurate fitting.) By 1850 the Americans were capable of more precise manufacturing than, for example, the British, especially in armaments. When, in 1853, Britain wanted to produce the Enfield rifle in great numbers, it awarded the contract for the machine tools – the jigs, fixtures and gauges – to Robbins and Lawrence of Vermont.

The late Reyner Banham, an astute commentator on design, noted in 1965 the importance of what he called the "gizmo" in American society. He said that the most typical American way of improving the human situation has been by means of such "crafty and usually compact little devices". In their ideal form "you peel off the packaging, fix four bolts and press the go button". As an example, Banham cited the Evinrude outboard motor, first devised in 1909. Fitting an inboard motor to a boat is a very difficult task but the Evinrude, ordered from a catalogue, could be attached easily with the two clamps that came with it. The purchaser added fuel, pulled the starter and off he went. (The main feature of American inventions, however, is their robustness – they had to get by without constant attention or the life support system of maintenance shops: the adjustment or repair of machines had to be capable of being done by ordinary people, not specialized craftsmen.)

The Canon EOS-1 camera. In industrial nations the camera is almost as commonplace as the television set. Photography is a popular and vastly lucrative leisure enterprise which has been designed to satisfy every level of consumer interest. As cameras themselves become more advanced, less skill is needed to operate them successfully (aside from any artistic merit in the resulting photographs).

In American society technology was regarded as unquestionably good, and children, especially boys, were given books and toys which celebrated the machine. The route to children was, as Cecilia Tichi, an American professor of literature says, through the mother. In America the promoters of Erector, a kit of parts from which children could make buildings or machines, told mothers that the toy would help prepare their sons for the business world. A similar toy, Meccano, was available in Germany and Britain, and in both countries, as in France, there were plenty of books describing the wonders of technology.

But in extolling America's triumphant contribution to technological culture (the heart of modern design) one should not ignore European contributions. European steel, for example, was better than the American product, as Henry Ford discovered. The European steel was an alloy of vanadium. Ford first used the new steel in the Model N because it made the car lighter, stronger and faster.

The Model T Ford was the Model N's successor. What was special about the Model T was not that it was a harbinger of change but a response to the needs that changes were creating: people were ready for a cheap car that was easy for the owner to service himself, and after several attempts Ford got it right. Ford's car was made of relatively few components and most were cheap enough to be replaced.

1916	**1917**	**1918**	**1919**	**1920**
Edward Johnston's sans-serif alphabet first used for London Transport (Britain).	Wilhelm Kåge (Sweden) designs "workers'" dining set. First issue of *De Stijl* (Netherlands), Russian Suprematism comes to fore, succeeded by Constructivism.	Gerrit Rietveld (Netherlands) produces his Red/Blue chair.	Bauhaus opens in Weimar (Germany). First two-way crossing of the North Atlantic by R34 airship.	Tatlin's tower, a model for an intended monument to the Third International, is constructed. Gunnar Asplund (Sweden) starts work on the Stockholm Library (completed 1928).

Robert Lacey in his book *Ford* explains that technically the Model T contained many advances. It was, for example, the first car to have a "modern" engine – a single cylinder block and a separate bolt-down cylinder head. When the car appeared it was not the cheapest on the market but it was very good value: it had a semi-automatic gearbox and a magneto system which did away with dry-storage batteries. The car also had suspension, which meant it could be driven over uneven surfaces without too much discomfort.

The production line The principles of mass production that were eventually used by Ford to produce the Model T and that form the foundations of modern industrialism are sometimes referred to as Fordism. It is now fashionable to refer to the 1990s as an era of post-Fordism because it is assumed that new methods of computerized production and organization of labour are ending the traditional assembly-line approach to industrial manufacture.

The practice of mass assembly, introduced into the Ford factories in 1914, was to place the most basic component of an assembly on an elevated way or rails, then carry or push it past successive stationary groups of workers who fixed the various components of the assembly to the basic part. All the components were perfectly gauged and absolutely interchangeable, each piece could be affixed in a pre-determined time and the whole assembly could be moved along the rails at a uniform rate.

Ford was not the first person to recognize the importance of the standardization of parts, nor was he the first to understand the principles of the conveyor belt and the breaking down of labour into units (these had their roots in the slaughterhouses of Cincinnati). He simply perfected these developments. By standardizing and minimizing the number of components necessary for a product to be effective and by employing people to work like the machines they were making, the manufacturer made assembly quicker and cheaper.

Assembly-line manufacturing of the 20th century is rooted directly in the principles of slaughtering and butchering perfected in the American abattoirs of the mid 19th century. However, the division of labour had been practised in the textile industries of medieval Europe.

In 1911 an American, Frederick Winslow Taylor, published *The Principles of Scientific Management*, a book aimed at making workforces efficient. Many entrepreneurs, especially in the United States and Germany, were taken with the book's idea of using a workforce like a machine.

Speed and travel Speed, as a selling point, has played an important role in industrial design this century. It has mainly taken the form of ensuring that the controls of products are quick and easy to use and of constantly increasing the speed of operation of existing products (faster-boiling kettles, faster-working computers), but it has also been incorporated metaphorically into the styling of a wide variety of products from cars to electric irons.

Speed is a 20th-century obsession. In this, the invention of cinematography may have played a part, for it altered people's attitudes to time. In the cinema, mass audiences

1921	1922	1923	1924	1925
Einstein Tower completed, designed by Erich Mendelsohn (Germany).	Stanley Morison (Britain) starts the journal *The Fleuron* and joins the Monotype Corporation as a designer. Work begins on Auguste Perret's (France) war memorial church of Notre Dame, Le Raincy, Paris.	Le Corbusier publishes his book *Towards an Architecture*.	Rayon manufactured (USA). Mart Stam (Germany) designs first cantilevered tubular steel chair (not made until 1926).	Bauhaus moves to Dessau. Sonia Delaunay (France) sets up the Boutique Simultanée with Jacques Heim. Exposition des Arts Décoratifs opened in Paris from which Art Deco style emerges.

were treated to a vision of their world cut and elided into impossibly short time frames, especially in newsreels. The acts of royalty, politicians and film stars were compressed into segments measured in mere minutes and seconds, and the exploits of a succession of record-breakers on the race track, on water and in the air were regularly celebrated.

Raymond Loewy was rapturous about speed, and about America, which he identified with speed's associated qualities such as change and exhilaration. In describing one of his designs for a streamlined steam locomotive his feelings for design, motion and America fuse into a veritable paean:

"I waited for the S1 to pass through at full speed. I stood on the platform and saw it coming from the distance at 120 mph. It flashed by like a steel thunderbolt, the ground shaking under me, in a blast of air that almost sucked me into its whirlwind. I felt shaken and overwhelmed by an unforgettable feeling of power, by a sense of pride at the sight of what I had helped to create in a quick sketch six inches wide on a scrap of paper. I realized I had, after all, contributed something to a great nation that had taken me in and that I loved so deeply."

Travel and speed are at the heart of American culture. This is not the result simply of a desire to see new places, seek wealth or leave old debts behind. There is also the intoxication of travel and speed as ends in themselves; speed gives many people a physical and mental "high".

This preoccupation with travel and change reached new levels in the 1960s through the ready availability of cheap air travel, which climaxed in the development of the BOEING 747. But in the early decades of the 20th century, although many more people than before were moving around by rail, sea and road, they were not doing so at great speed and they understood its fascination only at second hand.

Industrial designers gave these ordinary consumers who did not fly or race cars a surrogate feeling of speed by streamlining designs as a metaphor for speed. In the 1930s and 1940s almost any object – whether a locomotive, a cigarette lighter or a camera – would be designed to wear a sleek, flowing-formed sheath. This was made possible by manufacturing processes which enabled thin sheet metal to be stamped out in such forms. This pressed-metal streamlining influenced automobile design more than the analysis of an automobile's optimum shape tested in a wind tunnel.

Raymond Loewy was a giant of 20th century design. He led the profession into convincing manufacturers that increased attention to design and styling was not simply a matter of aesthetics, but would also lead to an increase in profits.

Function, style and meaning There is no clear dividing line between function and style. This is because there are close links between the function of an object and how people feel about it, what it means to them. If one were invited to redesign a field telephone (a piece of communication equipment used by the army and police) it might be possible to design it in the form of a Mickey Mouse telephone, without any loss of durability or reliability. However, the design would be rejected, mainly because its image would subvert the importance of the soldier's or policeman's job and would not enhance his view of himself.

To take the point a stage further, consider the field of graphic design or, as it might reasonably be called, the arts of propaganda and information. The propaganda arts include advertising and packaging design. In these practices the skill is to present one reality and suppress others, and the graphic designer, the illustrator, the photographer, the directors and camera operators put their talents to that end.

Some graphic design work, however, is not overtly propagandist but conveys values in a more subtle way. Signage, whose efficacy depends mainly on the choice of suitable lettering, is an example. An institution that wishes to convey solidity, dignity and tradition – a bank or university, for example – can go some way to achieving this simply by choosing for its signage a classical serif lettering (such as one based on that on Trajan's Column in Rome).

By contrast, in the period of revolutionary design in the USSR from 1917 to the mid-1920s, we see letter forms, as well as other graphic devices, given a sharp, geometrical dynamism which rejects classicism, cuts out all clutter and stresses energy and change. Designers such as the Russians El LISSITZKY and Alexander RODCHENKO were especially important here. Their poster and book cover designs punch at the eye, and the

Perhaps the biggest visible contribution made by designers is through the graphic and propaganda arts of packaging, signage and posters. These constitute the decorative art of our time. This example is by the Dutch designer Gert Dumbar, whose "human" approach to graphics has enlivened corporate design since the 1980s.

machine, using Bakelite as the sheath material. BBC begins experimental television service. Vladimir Zworykin produces the first satisfactory tube for television reception. Mies van der Rohe designs German

Pavilion for the International Exhibition, Barcelona. Henry Dreyfuss (USA) sets up his New York studio. Alvar Aalto (Finland) begins work on his Paimo Sanatorium, Finland (completed 1932).

Norman Bel Geddes (USA) starts to design a pioneering range of metal furniture for Simmons Co., Chicago.

Stockholm Exhibition. Henry Dreyfuss designs the classic model 300 table telephone for Bell. Mies van der Rohe succeeds Hannes Meyer as director of the Bauhaus.

Eric Gill publishes *An Essay on Typography*. Walter Gropius designs Adler Limousine.

layouts, though compositionally well organized, have no repose – there is the aura of a battle about them. Similarly, the De Stijl design movement, which emerged in the Netherlands at around the same time as the Russian experiments in art and design and which was loosely based on the flat, geometrical paintings of Piet Mondrian, developed a plain, brutal graphic style intended to be redolent of the new age.

The 20th century, with its constant striving for the new and its emphasis on the technical, has generated typefaces and letterforms to match the spirit of the age. For example, this century has seen the design and widespread use of sans serif typefaces, the first one designed by a craftsman, the British letterer and calligrapher Edward JOHNSTON. Sans serif faces look business-like and are alleged to be more readable in public places by people in a hurry than are letters with serifs. Hence the adoption of sans serif faces by airports and transport authorities. One of the formative designers of sans serif lettering was Herbert BAYER, a Bauhaus typographer, one of whose typefaces was called Universal. This whole style of lettering could in fact be called universal, since modern travellers see it everywhere they go.

It might seem that the consumers, "us", are entirely in the hands of the designers, "them", who appear to control both meaning and function. In this respect architects are often regarded as the greatest "culprits". But the following example shows that consumers can obstinately resist what has been decided for them from above.

Judy Attfield, a British design historian, has studied the interiors of houses in Harlow, a new town in England, built in the early 1950s. There were two special features about this new housing. The kitchens were at the front of the house, not the back; and instead of having two rooms for living in – a dining room and a sitting room – there was one large, open-plan room.

An English working class family c. 1954.

The idea of placing the kitchen at the front was to enable whoever was working in it to see what was going on in the world. But since the street had neither workplaces nor shops there was little of interest to see. The open-plan living area was unpopular, too. Traditionally, the British working class (and indeed the greater part of the middle class) liked to keep the "front room" for best occasions and to have it on display at the front of the house, while it relaxed in the "back room", unwatched by the world outside. The combined, open-plan room destroyed this traditional division.

The architects of the Harlow houses had assumed their inhabitants would want airiness and light, but in fact what they most wanted was privacy – they blocked off their large windows by curtaining – and they set about creating a cosy clutter, which was absolute anathema to the architects. The houses often came to be loved by their tenants but not until they had been converted into something approximating to what the tenants wanted; until such a desired layout and décor had been achieved the houses did not effectively function for their occupants as homes.

1932

Eliel Saarinen (Finland) becomes President of Cranbrook Academy of Art (USA). Bauhaus moves to Berlin. Stanley Morison designs Times New Roman typeface. The International Style exhibition opens at the Museum of Modern	Art, New York (USA). Philip Johnson and Henry Russell Hitchcock publish *The International Style,* which examined the rise of the modern undecorated building. Le Corbusier's Cité de Refuge started	(completed 1933). *L'Architecture d'Aujourd'hui* first published (France). Norman Bel Geddes publishes *Horizons,* his view of the future of industrial design.	**1933** Bauhaus closed down by Nazis. Boeing 247 commercial airliner and Douglas DC1 enter service, both aircraft using new integrated monocoque structures with streamlined forms. Richard Buckminster Fuller develops a three-	wheeled automobile version of the Dymaxion. Serge Chermayeff's De la Warr Pavilion started at Bexhill-on-Sea (completed 1935). Alvar Aalto patents his method for bending wood for stools. Walter

Consumers, then, are not always passive. Given an opportunity, they will want their say. For example, earlier this century women in Britain actively contributed to the design of new electrical gadgets. Between the World Wars two associations were founded: The Women's Engineering Society (1919) and the Electrical Association for Women (1924). It should be pointed out, however, that there are products whose design has so strong an appeal that the consumer in his or her desire to purchase the product, is willing to discount faults in construction and performance. One obvious example is the French CITROËN 2CV automobile, which had a cult following despite the fact that the vehicle had poor acceleration, offered little protection in a crash and rusted easily.

Rationalists and stylists In spite of the interrelationship of function and style there has been an attempt by design historians, and designers themselves, to split design into two camps: the rationalists and the stylists.

We can caricature rationalists as being obsessed with function and a distaste for ornament. They belong to what is called the modernist movement and include such architects and furniture designers as the Germans Annie ALBERS, Marcel BREUER, Ludwig MIES VAN DER ROHE and Walter GROPIUS, the French Charlotte PERRIAND, and the Irish Eileen GRAY.

The physical effort expended on domestic chores – such as those shown in this illustration of a French kitchen c. 1900 – was diminished by the increasing availability of electrical appliances. However, the amount of time spent on domestic tasks barely diminished throughou 20th century.

Design writers and historians characterized these designers as being interested in the essence of things and in truth to materials. But they were also concerned with the spirit of rationalism itself and with such developments as time-and-motion studies, in which the aim was to minimize the effort required to perform certain tasks. These studies influenced design in the home. For example, in 1912 an American, Christine Frederick, applied work-study analysis to the kitchen and in 1915 published a book called *Household Engineering*.

On the other hand, stylists – who include two practitioners of art deco, the American interior designer of the 1930s Donald DESKEY and the French decorator and furniture designer of the 1920s and 1930s Jacques-Emile RUHLMANN – jazzed up the plain line and simple geometry. They did this with clever lighting and rich rich colour or with glitzy, reflective materials, such as chrome and mirror glass, or with very expensive veneers, lacquers and exotic leathers. It was not easy to tell, looking at the work of the "two camps", if one was being more true to materials than the other or if one was producing more functional wares than the other. It was all style and the choice depended on the consumer's own values and self-image.

It is interesting that such a young profession as design so quickly asserted itself as an authority on taste and values. This phenomenon is partly to do with the connections design has with architecture and partly the result of many industrialists and architects sharing the same values and beliefs as designers. All three have had a common view of what an up-to-date interior befitting the technological age ought to look like: ordered and uncluttered. But there is no logical or utilitarian necessity which dictates that every office

Dorwin Teague (USA) designs Baby Brownie Camera for Kodak. London Passenger Transport Board (Britain) formed under direction of Frank Pick, who created a good public service via design, good

management and propaganda, and the London Underground topographic map, designed by Harry Beck, put into production. The streamlined and fast "Flying Hamburger" diesel-electric railcar, designed

by Count Kruckenberg, enters service (Germany).

Fiat Zero A, prototype of Fiat 500, appears, designed under direction of Dante Giacosa. Henry Dreyfuss begins designing for the Hoover company. "The City of Salina" begins operation – the USA's first streamlined

train. Terry anglepoise lamp designed by George Carwardine (Britain). The uncommercial but ultimately influential Chrysler Airflow was manufactured, designed largely by Chrysler engineer Carl Breer.

should look like a factory or every kitchen like a laboratory. If the clean, plain style has been chosen for interiors it has been because of the meaning it conveys.

The designer's name Every profession has its larger-than-life characters whose names have meanings and functions of their own, and design perhaps has more than most. For, despite the fact that designers are in the main servants to clients, designers enjoy marketing themselves. Intellectually, they may accept the words of Gottfried Semper, a 19th-century German architect, who said that designs are shaped by the society, the time and the place in which they are made. But emotionally, designers want to take individual credit for their work and perhaps it is almost instinctive in Western society to want to give it to them.

A well-known name adds provenance to an object and provenance adds value to it. In the worlds of fine art and antiques, where money is made on "other values" (these being anything other than function, utility or performance), much depends on who did what. Design, even more than fine art and antiques, is business- and profit-orientated, and in the market place, as the British design critic Deyan Sudjic has observed, it benefits business if the myth of the designer as superstar is encouraged.

The German painter and sculptor Georg Baselitz, one of the artistic celebrities of the 1980s. Designers came to envy artists their status and their irresponsibility and the 1980s saw a number of designers making art out of design.

In his book *Cult Heroes* Sudjic notes: "The exploitation of key names has become an important part of the way the economy works." We have become accustomed to leading designers lending their names to things they have never touched and barely seen. They get a percentage as a fee and the manufacturer has the benefit of association with someone known for his or her taste and judgement.

Sudjic reckons that the American clothing designer Ralph LAUREN is the richest of all the American fashion names. In 1987 he sold $625 million worth of Lauren-branded goods including furniture and scent. The French fashion designer Pierre CARDIN's name is also valuable: in 1987, 800 licensees in 93 countries yielded a royalty of $75 million.

Most interesting of all, perhaps, is Sudjic's case study of the Italian fashion designer Giorgio ARMANI. (Sudjic points out that Armani even looks like a film star.) Apart from the clothes that Armani designs himself, the many other products that bear his name are not literally his. Sudjic says: "Armani's involvement is limited to approval. He simply sells his signature, and the licensees, provided that they meet his standards, bask in the reflected Armani glory. Sometimes there may be an Armani sketch, translated into detailed instructions by one of his assistants. But the point about an Armani product is not what it is, but who it is signed by."

And name-exploitation is not limited to fashion designers. There is the star French designer Philippe STARCK, who was first known for designing furniture and now gets asked to design almost everything. This

1935

The Douglas DC3 entered service which revolutionized air transport.

1936

BBC begins first regular television broadcasting service in the world, using both Baird system and the superior EMI system. Frank Lloyd Wright designs Johnson Wax administration building and Falling Water house,

Pittsburgh, which exploits expressiveness of natural concrete as engineering. Stanley Morison publishes *First Principles of Typography.*

1937

Raymond Loewy's streamlined locomotive for the Penn Railroad Company appears. Harley Earl, car stylist (USA) produces first of his dream cars for General Motors – the Buick Y.

1938

Hans Coray (Switzerland) produces classic aluminium chair, the Spartana. Piet Zwart (Netherlands) designs Bruynzeel modular kitchen. Volkswagen car factory opens to produce the people's car, known after the

is not quite the same as simply selling one's signature but in terms of the way Starck describes how he works it is close. For Starck says he just draws and leaves the working out of the "how" to others. Then there are architects, such as the Americans Richard MEIER, Michael GRAVES and Robert VENTURI, who design tea kettles, plates and furniture for companies such as the Italian ALESSI or the American KNOLL International.

The French furniture designer Philippe Starck became an international name with the standing of a major pop star. Like many design "superstars" his interests and creativity now extend into almost every field of design.

Such designers, who have their names promoted as a part of the "meaning" of what they design, have usually been men, but there are examples of companies building up products around star women designers. One example is the British ceramic tableware designer Susie COOPER, whose work for WEDGWOOD bore her name, a rare accolade which other ceramic designers have also deserved but not received.

Smart machines, "dim" users The most useful task that a product designer can perform is to make sure that the product is easy to use, this being as necessary to safety as to any pleasure to be had from the product. Electronics companies have for some years been building more and more functions into their products but this has resulted in confused purchasers who do not know how to work their machines. Video recorders are a notorious example. A television critic, failing to record TV programmes for later review, wrote: "Eventually I figured it out. With the 'on' times, the 'off' times and the channel numbers all present and correct, I pressed the timer button. A little clock-face appeared but it was flashing on and off, which didn't seem right . . . . Three days later I found out why the little clock-face had been flashing. It was trying to tell me there was no tape in the machine."

Currently, designers and engineers are working on three approaches to such problems:

1. Designers are trying to make objects explain themselves – so a telephone-answering machine with diary and memory functions is designed to look like an electronic book. The desire to make objects explain themselves is a noble one because it underlines the sense that design is a service, one that requires the designer to imagine another person using the object. There is a trend (it began in the mid-1980s and looks set to flower in the 1990s) towards making printers, answering machines, and the like look like other more familiar objects, such as books, to help users feel more at ease with these pieces of equipment, but this is only a trend – not a once-and-for-all answer. The only advantage in having an answering machine that looks like a book is if you feel more comfortable with books than with gadgets. If not, then a sensibly laid-out sequence of switches on a simple box is just as good.

1939

Second World War as the Beetle, designed by Ferdinand Porsche (Germany).

Norman Bel Geddes produces model of a "teardrop"-shaped bus. New York's World Fair opens, dominated by its futuristically designed buildings, including Walter Dorwin Teague's DuPont building. Nylon stockings appear on the market.

1940

Walter Dorwin Teague publishes *Design This Day*. Charles Eames (USA) and Eero Saarinen (Finland) collaborate on systems storage units and win organic furniture design competition.

1942

Earl Tupper (USA) begins producing Tupperware (thin-walled polythene containers). First atomic reactor made to work at Chicago.

2. Rationalist designers of a new breed who call their discipline "product semantics" are investigating the relation between function and meaning – which in essence, so far, has meant putting switches in the right places (where "right" means "most likely to make sense to a human being of average intelligence". One of the leaders of this movement is Professor Reinhart F H Butter of Ohio State University who says he and his team are looking at design in a systematic way in order to take chance out of it.

3. Japanese engineers are concentrating on making the machine do *all* the thinking for you. They have developed a new generation of machines that control themselves. And this revolution has been brought about, not by design, but by a theory called "fuzzy logic". This provides those who are programming the machines (for these will obviously incorporate microchips) with an input language which resembles that with which ordinary people deal with the world – that is, a language which is not precise but which makes constant use of such approximations as "about", "most" and "often". Fuzzy logic is resulting in some remarkable, if extravagant, machines. For example, two technology journalists, the American Richard Ernsberger Jr and the Japanese Yuriko Hoshiai, in describing the Aisaigo Day Fuzzy washing machine, note that this machine tests how dirty the clothing is by adding water to the clothes and then sensing to what degree, and how quickly, the water is saturated with dirt. All in all, the washing machine has 600 different cycles, and it decides for you which one should be used.

Unlike some manufacturers, those who make and sell cameras have long solved the problem of how to produce "idiot proof" designs. Pictured here, is a Brownie 127, c.1955, a popular successor to the classic Box Brownie that demystified photography for ordinary people in the 1930s.

There are some areas of manufacture, especially those aimed at the amateur, where designers have been adept at creating machines that are very easy to use and that look after themselves. The most notable is photography. In 1900 the Kodak Box Brownie camera made snapshot photography simple for everyone, and 48 years later the Land Polaroid camera enabled amateurs to take instant pictures. Other major developments have included the 35mm slide and projector, the home movie camera and most recently the hand-operated video camera. Many of the more sophisticated cameras, of course, "think things out for themselves": sensors and microchips remove the need for human calculation – if you want them to.

There is, however, a caveat to all of this: we may want things to be easy to understand but we do not necessarily like delivering ourselves entirely into the hands of the designer and the engineer. We may not want or need to understand how a machine, especially an electronically driven machine, works but we might well want a greater say in how the machine is repaired – and this is an area of design neglected since Henry Ford. In the 1950s in the United States and in the 1960s in Western Europe ordinary intelligent people were first irritated by, and then reluctantly came to accept, the phenomenon whereby when a small part broke you could not buy a replacement but had to buy the whole unit. This was because product engineers, the people who translate the designer's final ideas into manufacture, were concerned with efficient assembly in the factory, not with ease of maintenance by the individual purchaser.

1943	**1944**	**1945**	**1946**	**1947**
IKEA, the Swedish furniture retailing firm, founded, offering simple, modern design at good prices.	Walter Dorwin Teague becomes first President of the American Society of Industrial Designers.	Wells Coates (Britain) designs the almost circular Ekco radio, model A22, in Bakelite. First atomic bombs dropped in hostilities.	Eero Saarinen produces "Womb Chair", made with fibreglass with a metal rod support. Eames chair designed by Charles Eames and his wife Ray for Herman Miller Inc.	Vespa scooter first produced in Italy. Christian Dior (France) launches his New Look fashion style. Jan Tschichold (Switzerland) redesigns Penguin Books house style.

Undoubtedly the personal computer is a powerful, flexible tool of great creative potential. It is a prime example of a machine that is used by vast numbers of people in all kinds of contexts but whose workings are understood by comparatively few.

However, increasingly more people are resenting having to throw away an iron or radio or computer because of a single broken component – they would like to be able to buy a replacement part and slot it in. This is not just because of the personal savings they could make but because of growing concern about the environment and conserving resources. The influential American designer Bill STUMPF has been a campaigner for better design of this kind. It presents an interesting, if not especially glamorous, challenge to industrial designers.

The avant-garde There are terms which, like dustbin liners, can be stuffed with any old rubbish. One such, in design, is avant-garde, which should be reserved to mean anything that is genuinely innovative and pioneering but which is constantly misused to describe anything that is merely new. For example, in fashion design, the highly structured clothing of the Japanese Issey MIYAKE or the allusions to the costume of sexual bondage by Vivienne WESTWOOD, British designer, are both examples of avant-garde; but a high-technology ski boot is simply new.

Industry, whether it be producing motor vehicles or mass footwear, is not interested in the avant-garde unless or until it becomes more commonly accepted; industry cannot afford to upset people. The avant-garde is often awkward: it usually seeks to extend the boundaries of art and of people's sensibilities, and sometimes its intention is to subvert, or at least oppose, the ruling ideas and conventions of the day.

New materials or new methods of doing things can be pressed into service by the avant-garde because they have no history of use and tradition to get in the way of fresh thinking. Plastic, for example, found favour with the European "new jewellery" movement of the late 1970s and early 1980s, in which young jewellers rejected the use of precious materials and adopted plastic as their basic material. Plastic was not associated with what these designers considered to be the grosser values of precious materials; plastic was democratic, and in its various types, especially in its colour ranges and different degrees of opacity, it was versatile.

The degree to which design and architecture can concern itself with the avant-garde as opposed to the new is not fixed. There are periods when experimentation is more widely tolerated than usual by those who subsidize the avant-garde.

The avant-garde as a group of people is also rather small: if you are opposing current conventions then you are bound to be in a minority. Thus, in the fashion world during the 1980s, although there was internationally lauded (but also jeered at) experimentation in jewellery and clothing – the work of the British designer Caroline BROADHEAD is one example, that of the Swiss Otto KÜNZLI another – the solid core of fashion design (by, for example, the Americans Ralph Lauren and Calvin KLEIN) was far from experimental or threatening to established design conventions.

1948	**1949**		**1950**	**1951**
Marcello Nizzoli (Italy) produces Lexicon 80 Typewriter for Olivetti.	Charles and Ray Eames design the LAR chair, the first to have a seat of moulded plastic. Alec Issigonis' (Britain) design for the Morris Minor launched. First flight of the prototype de Havilland Comet, the world's first jet	airliner. Hasselblad camera introduced to the marketplace.	Marcello Nizzoli (Italy) produces Lettera typewriter for Olivetti. Hochschule für Gestaltung founded in Ulm, Germany, with Max Bill as director.	Henry Dreyfuss designs interior for Lockheed Super G Constellation airliner. Festival of Britain. Max Braun (Germany) produces his model 550 electric shaver.

The most challenging designs in real life are in fashion and accessories, because a person who dresses differently, "oddly", is a challenge to any crowd. It still takes a brave woman or man to walk down the street wearing one of Caroline Broadhead's veils or one of Otto Künzli's more outrageous brooches. (What the public accepts in a colour photograph on the printed page and what it accepts in real life are often different things.) People who have worn avant-garde jewellery have been jeered at, had their hair pulled, been abused. Sometimes the motives are clear: there is a famous photograph taken in Paris in 1947 of some matronly women trying to tear the Christian DIOR-designed clothes off a young woman's back. Dior's extravagant use of costly material and the young woman's apparent profligacy were too much for those war-worn middle-aged women.

The fashion for aggressive anti-middle class dressing called Punk that emerged in Britain in the mid-1970s was quickly tamed by the media's cameras and many of its ideas absorbed into the mainstream of design.

When seeking to be confrontational, clothes designers or jewellers have in this century sometimes looked to the avant-garde in fine art. The famous Italian clothes designer Elsa SCHIAPARELLI hired such artists as Jean Cocteau and Salvador Dali to design fabrics and accessories for her. She had opened her salon in 1929 and was for a while influenced by Surrealism: some of her hats were designed in the form of a shoe, an ice cream cone or a lamb cutlet. Of course, much of her work, though inventive, was less extreme; even so, most ordinary people were unlikely ever to want to buy a Schiaparelli because even a conservative example of her work was radical. Schiaparelli's influence over the use of details such as buttons or zips has parallels in the "new jewellery" movement of the 1970s and 1980s.

Surrealism has been influential on avant-garde applied arts and fashion partly because its most obvious recipe – the juxtaposing of any two incongruous objects – is relatively easy to copy. However, the creative "fringe" areas of clothing, of which "new jewellery" and "conceptual clothing" are examples, have not been dependent upon fine art for their energy. Rather the reverse; for a period between the early 1970s and the mid-1980s the "new jewellers" explored ornamenting and dressing the body with a freshness that had not been seen since the experimental street theatre of the Russian avant-garde in the early 1920s.

Of course, one of the distinctions between being new and being avant-garde lies in the practicality or lack of it exhibited by a design. The explosion in magazines, illustrated books and television has encouraged an avant-garde whose images are intended to look good in photographs but which in real life are disappointing. Photography has thus furthered the ephemeral nature of the modern avant-garde, and the printed media, with its considerable demand for new ideas and new pictures every week, has fuelled experimentation; inevitably, much of this is banal.

Exhibitions are another form used by the avant-garde to state an argument. In an exhibition nothing has to work, nothing has to withstand the rigours of use and wear and tear. On the same lines, there was a fashion in Italy from about the late 1960s for design and theory studios. These studios, such as ARCHIZOOM, STUDIO ALCHYMIA and MEMPHIS, were loose structures – affiliations between friends, held together by joint

1951–2	**1953**	**1954**	**1955**	**1956**
Harry Bertoia (USA) completes design of his diamond lattice shell chair.	Arne Jacobsen (Denmark) designs Ant Chair for Fritz Hansen. Fiat 1100 launches a modern-style small car. Routemaster bus, designed by Douglas Scott (Britain), introduced in London.	Ford Thunderbird sports car launched in USA. Prototype Boeing 707 jet airliner flown.	Henry Dreyfuss publishes his *Designing for People*. Mary Quant opens Bazaar fashion store in London. ICI launch Terylene. Citroën DS19 motor car launched.	Henry Dreyfuss designs the John Deere 720 Tractor. World's first nuclear power station opened at Calder Hall, Britain.

projects such as exhibitions. Like exotic mushrooms, they tended to appear quite quickly and then fade, leaving rather little behind except an enhanced reputation for their leading participants.

Architecture has generated avant-garde theory and philosophy that has influenced design, but, as noted earlier, architectural theory, once it is built in the form of houses, is not inviolable – it is adapted, changed and subverted by its users. Architects have not, on the whole, come to terms with that lesson.

Modern architecture Architecture is, perhaps, one of the areas (others include graphics and furniture design) where the new and the avant-garde become fused.

No single person can be credited as a prime mover of what we understand as modern architecture. None the less, individuals do stand out. One of the contributors to the development of the skyscraper was the American architect Louis SULLIVAN, whose masterpiece is the Guaranty Building (1894–5). This structure is still interesting because it combines modernity with decoration. It looks as contemporary as the AT&T building (1987) in New York, by another American Philip JOHNSON, which got critics excited because it too had some decorative elements, notably a broken pediment as its crown.

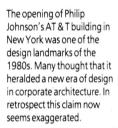

The opening of Philip Johnson's AT & T building in New York was one of the design landmarks of the 1980s. Many thought that it heralded a new era of design in corporate architecture. In retrospect this claim now seems exaggerated.

A lack of decoration has been one of the features of modern architecture. Decoration was rejected partly because of its association with the past – the modern impulse has been to break with the past – and partly because, as buildings became ever larger, dispensing with frills became an easy way to reduce costs. (New construction methods also cut the cost of erecting large buildings. An iron or steel frame supporting a glass curtain wall or lightweight concrete or stone slabs made it possible to achieve both height and breadth in an economic way.)

Apart from Louis Sullivan, the early stars of modern architecture were the American Frank Lloyd WRIGHT, the Germans Ludwig Mies van der Rohe, Walter Gropius and Peter BEHRENS, the Austrians Josef HOFFMANN and Otto Wagner, the Dutchman J P Oud and the Swiss LE CORBUSIER and Auguste PERRET. Running as a theme throughout their work (a theme much clearer with hindsight) is the notion of the "machine aesthetic". Put very simply, this means that architects, designers and artists have used forms that echo those in machines – they used them because the forms were both beautiful and looked contemporary. Whereas 60 years ago an architect might have wanted to respond in his or her work to the contemporary excitement of pistons or aircraft or pylons, so today, in the same fervour of wanting to be up to date, young architects in Japan borrow imagery from microchips and computers.

The machine aesthetic as an ideology had largely disappeared from architecture by the start of the Second World War, although, as it happens, after that War buildings became very much more machine-*like*. For

1957	1958		1959	1960
World's first artificial satellite, Sputnik 1, launched by USSR. Eero Saarinen's tulip chairs and tables produced by Knoll International. Fiat 500 motor car introduced. Jack Kilby (USA) devises first silicon chip.	Univers typeface designed by Adrian Frutiger for Deberny and Peignot launched. Helvetica typeface designed by Max Meidinger for Haas, launched. Honda launches the 50cc moped, one of the most	successful motor vehicles of all time. PH5 light-fitting by Poul Henningsen (Denmark) launched. This became a much imitated classic.	Morris Mini Minor, designed by Alec Issigonis, launched in Britain.	Vico Magistretti (Italy) begins working for Cassina. Henry Dreyfuss publishes his human engineering charts under the generic title *The Measure of Man*. First laser action developed in USA by Theodore Maiman.

example, from the 1950s to the 1980s there was a huge programme of prefabricated and systems-designed housing in Europe (both East and West). A substantial amount of this was in the public or state sector, and much of it was let down, not always by inherent flaws in design, but by poor workmanship in the manufacture of components and slack supervision on the building sites. Private housing built to systems-conceived designs fared much better because demands for quality were higher.

Buildings became machine-like in other ways as well. Office blocks, hospitals and hotels became designed around the ever more sophisticated services which enabled them to function: air conditioning, plumbing, service lifts and, increasingly, cabling for electronics, as well as telecommunications.

However, it has become apparent that in some countries people do not want to live in a building that looks machine-like. And since almost every variation of housing design imposed by above has been tried with only partial success, the concept of "community involvement" is finding favour in Scandinavia, parts of the United States and Britain. It is not a soft option, and it remains to be seen how far communities can succeed as their own architects. They need the support of professional interest groups such as architects, politicians, planners and financiers, who might not see it to their own advantage to do more than pay lip service to the idea.

Other issues, such as racism, religion and sexism, are involved in community participation in architecture. For example, there have emerged in the 1980s groups such as Matrix, an affiliation of feminist designers and architects, who as well as designing buildings publish research aimed at redressing the imbalance of interests and knowledge between architects and the public, especially women. In 1984 Matrix published *Making Space: Women and the Man-made Environment*.

Man-made environment Although new forms in housing are being sought, occasionally in consultation with those who are to be housed, there is uncertainty about risking the avant-garde in housing. However, this has not meant that the avant-garde has disappeared from architecture. Take, for example, the London-based Iranian-born architect Zaha HADID. She is a brilliant painter and draughtswoman and her designs are light, airy, gravity-defying and radical in that they express a commitment to the contemporary world of science, new mathematics, rapid communications and change. But if or when she begins to get large-scale architectural commissions her buildings will, if their integrity survives planning laws, cost constraints and the conservatism of civil engineers, present a complete rupture with all architectural tradition. It is not an architecture for the masses and could not be attempted in tired cultures.

Zaha Hadid's view of architecture is optimistic in its commitment to the creative possibilities offered by science and technology.

Perhaps it might succeed in Japan. In an exhibition called Transfiguration, first displayed in 1989, six young Japanese architects displayed a theoretical architecture which took its cues from computers, the instant

1961
Archigram formed (UK) as group of Futurist architects, emphasizing use of technology. The Soviet cosmonaut, Yuri Gagarin, first man in space. Sony launch the first transistorized video recorder. Letraset developed.

1962
Sony develop 5-inch micro-television.

1964
Polypropylene stacking chair by Robin Day (Britain). Dora portable typewriter designed by Ettore Sottsass (Italy). First Habitat store opened in London.

1965
Earlybird, the world's first communications satellite, launched by USA. Ralph Nader (USA) publishes *Unsafe at any Speed*. The Bell Trimline telephone introduced, a radical departure from existing designs.

1966
Herbert Spencer publishes *The Visible Word*. Archizoom (Italy) founded. Ergon office chair developed by William Stumpf (USA) for Herman Miller. Pierre Cardin's (France) Space Age collection launched.

transfer of information, variety, videos and constant change – not from the traditions of either East or West. A spokesman of the new Japanese architecture and its philosophy, Riichi Miyake, wrote in the catalogue to the exhibition: "The computer has now put itself at the forefront of creation and materials have been completely overhauled. That is why architecture as we know it can no longer be enough. We must get rid of the notion of stylized architecture and go back to the essence of things."

Professor Ilrie, a Japanese architect, who put the exhibition together, also displays the 20th-century fascination with speed, for he says: "The speed of transport means we can go anywhere in the world in next to no time. Wishing to return with nostalgia to the styles of the past flies in the face of these characteristics of our era." It is tempting to be uncharitable and dismiss this as rhetorical nonsense, self-serving and familiar in its polemic, but it does underline the gap in values between the avant-garde in late 20th-century architecture and the ordinary individual in the street.

The handicrafts movement The intellectual avant-garde in design and architecture has posed one set of oppositions to mainstream values. But weaving in and out of the development of design this century, as in the previous one, there has been an opposition of a different sort – that of handicrafts.

Intelligent men and women in the handicraft movement have sought for an aesthetic and a range of sensibilities in design that industrial designers were not giving them. There have been two routes by which designer-makers, artist-craftspeople and studio craftspeople have made an impact. One has been by working freelance (this has worked for textile designers particularly well); the other has been to establish a workshop or studio and make small batches of products which are then sold in outlets such as craft shops or galleries.

Fine art has boomed since the war, but its meaning has become obscure. Popular taste is now better fulfilled by the design and media industries. Shown here is an environmental sculpture by Joseph Beuys, begun in 1958.

The handicraft movement has been used by some practitioners as a means of escape from the orthodoxies of modern life and by others, particularly women, as a route to success in mainstream design. The movement began to flower in its modern form in the early 1920s. Textiles and studio pottery were the two most successful areas, and they were joined by jewellery and metalwork in the 1960s, by furniture in the 1970s and by glass, in the 1950s in the USA, in the 1970s in Europe. This is not to be taken as meaning that all but pottery and textiles were dormant until after the last World War, only that they were less extensive.

As far as the relevance of craft design to contemporary consumers is concerned, the key areas are textiles and pottery. Fabrics and rugs can be produced by hand but in sufficient batch production to keep prices within the limits of luxury rather than art prices; and domestic tableware in particular has been invigorated by a number of talented designers, including the Englishman Wally Keeler, the Dane Lisbet DAEHLIN and the American Betty WOODMAN.

1967

Victor Papanek's *Design for the Real World* published (USA). *The Medium is the Message* published by Marshall McLuhan (USA).

1968

Sony Trinitron colour television introduced. The Hochschule für Gestaltung in Ulm closes.

1969

Valentine portable typewriter, in bright red plastic and aimed at youth, launched by Olivetti, designed by Perry King (Britain) and Ettore Sottsass. Americans Neil Armstrong and Edwin Aldrin become first

men to walk on the Moon. First flight of prototype Concorde, world's first supersonic airliner. First flight of Boeing 747 Jumbo jet airliner. Sony U-Matic colour video-cassette introduced. Frog design

studio, one of Germany's most powerful design consultancies, founded. Saab 99 motor car launched, designed by Sixten Sason and Bjorn Envall (Sweden).

If the USA during the period between the World Wars was the engine of industrial design, it is not stretching matters too far to say that Britain was the hub of the handicrafts revival in the same period. This is not to downplay the importance of crafts in the evolution of the BAUHAUS, that seminal German art and design school, but to draw attention to the individuality of the movement in Britain.

The British movement had a number of excellent polemicists, among them Ethel Mairet, an expert on textiles (especially weaving and dyeing) who was also the first woman to become a Royal Designer for Industry, Britain's most coveted design award. Mairet's *Hand Weaving Today*, published in 1939, was as important in re-awakening the possibilities of handcrafted textiles (and their relevance to modern interior design and industrial textiles) as Bernard LEACH's *A Potter's Book*, published in 1940, was in creating an ideology for non-industrially produced ceramics.

The opening chapter of *A Potter's Book*, Towards a Standard, was especially influential because it argues that common to all pots that are good and express human values are criteria that a potter could learn and that a buyer would recognize.

After the Second World War the handicrafts revival flowered in Western Europe, Scandinavia and the USA, although its success in penetrating the world of industrial design and mass production has often been hindered by the connotations of the word crafts, namely "old-fashioned" and "amateur".

It is disappointing but unsurprising (given what has been said about the designer as star and the importance of provenance in adding value to design) that European design-led manufacturers of domestic goods, such as Alessi, have turned not to craftspeople but to architects for the design of their products.

Stoneware dish by Michael Cardew. A founder of the 20th-century European handicraft pottery revival, Cardew's first interest was in English vernacular ware. Later he drew inspiration from his contact with the pottery traditions of West Africa.

Similarly, although there has been a resurgence in furniture design and making as a studio craft, it has proved very difficult for designer-makers to get their work into anything more than very limited batch production. Sometimes, as has been noted, this is because the designs fail the repeatability test – they are too expensive to make in quantity. But also, whenever a company like Vitra, CASSINA or Knoll International seeks to enliven its range it has always chosen to go to an architect. The craft movement remains stuck at the periphery of commercial design.

This isolation has been in part self-inflicted, but it is also the case that, insofar as handicrafts are identified with home and women, then the aesthetic, design and practical virtues of handicrafts have been ignored because of male prejudice. Another reason for their neglect has been the politics of fine art and fine art dealership. There is an overlap, aesthetically, between, on the one hand, fine art and, on the other, weaving, quilting, tapestry making, block printing and other craft activities, but by admitting practitioners of these through its portals fine art would lose its exclusivity. The German sculptor Joseph

1970

Zandra Rhodes (Britain) launches her Primavera look, a harbinger of the "back to nature" vogue of the 1970s.

1971

Issey Miyake (Japan) holds his first show in New York. Saab 900 series motorcar launched, designed by Bjorn Envall. Intel Corporation of California introduce microprocessor.

1972

Renault 5 motorcar launched. World's first pocket calculator designed and manufactured by Clive Sinclair (Britain).

1974

Volkswagen Golf motorcar launched.

1975

Site Architects (USA) design a radical building for the Best store group. Giorgio Armani (Italy) sets up as fashion consultant. Clive Sinclair launches first pocket television.

Beuys could exhibit several bundles of felt and a few half kilos of animal fat in a fine art museum but a studio pot is not thought worth accepting. One also cannot help wondering, perhaps in an over-simplified way: if instead of Mr P Mondrian painting it had been Ms P Mondrian doing tapestry of the same design, would she have been hailed, as he has been, as a pioneer of modernist aesthetics?

Design and the environment Practitioners of crafts have sometimes been caricatured for wanting to live and work in a way that celebrates nature or at least ruralism and is antithetical to conventional routines that divide work and workplace from leisure and home. It is thus assumed that craftspeople are the forerunners of the "green" movement. The caricature is partly justified but, even so, mainly irrelevant. In so far as craftspeople have sought alternative lifestyles (and many have not, preferring to live in cities and to use modern technology), they have done so on an amateur basis. And, in so far as they have opposed industrial excesses, they have done so from the periphery rather than the mainstream.

Green industrial design, if it is to be treated seriously, will need to be rooted in high technology. Until quite recently "greenness" was not regarded as chic by designers but now, after an explosion of green fashion-consciousness, there is already a risk that designers and consumers may soon become bored with "the environment".

Essentially, green design concerns itself with the rights of the consumer to a healthy, safe range of products, the rights of manufacturing employees to a working environment and practice not injurious to health, and the elimination of unnecessary waste and environmentally damaging materials. Some people believe that green design should also not use manufacturing processes which exploit people in poorer or non-industrial countries; and yet others believe it should avoid any abuse of the rights of animals – for example, that cosmetics and toiletries should not be tested on them.

The population bomb has exploded; there are now probably too many people for comfort. Unable to tackle this central issue, designers and their clients concentrate on safety and "green" design as we search for ways to improve the quality of life in the West.

One of the pioneers of environmental and health-and-safety-conscious design was the American Victor Papanek, author of *Design For the Real World* (1971). The book began: "There are professions more harmful than industrial design, but only a very few of them." This attention-grabbing beginning was, of course, hyperbole – one can say the same of many other professions. None the less, Papanek marshalled an impressive series of examples to make his attack. He was critical of, for example, the automobile industry, which he blamed for killing or maiming a million people a year, largely as a consequence of poor design. In the second edition of his book, published in 1985, the attack on design continues but with a greater emphasis on waste and pollution. Papanek was not the first critic of the automobile industry. Another American, Ralph Nader, had already campaigned against the General Motors Corvair in the mid-1960s, in particular its over-steering fault, and had launched a crusade with his *Unsafe at any Speed* (1965).

1977	1978	1979	1980	1981
Emilio Ambasz (Italy) launches innovative Vertebra chair. Apple I personal computer appears, soon followed by the Apple II computer.	The Centre Georges Pompidou, designed by Richard Rogers (Britain), The Ergonomi design group is set up in Stockholm. The Tizio lamp by Richard Sapper (Germany) appears. Sony launches its Walkman.	Studio Alchymia founded in Milan by architect Alessandro Guerriero. The Supporto chair by Fred Scott is launched by Hille, UK.	Memphis design studio formed in Milan by Ettore Sottsass.	Columbia, first reusable space vehicle (space shuttle) is launched.

A year after Papanek's book was first published, an American housewife was killed in a brand-new Ford Pinto car. A vehicle had driven into the back of the Pinto, rupturing its fuel tank. The car exploded. In the months and years that followed more Pintos suffered similar accidents, giving rise to many court cases. The problem was that Ford had wanted to build a car that was 2,000lb in weight and no more. To achieve this they eliminated the rear subframe members, the steel skeleton which as well as carrying a sheet metal skin protects the fuel tank. By the end of the Pinto's career the car had been strengthened considerably but it was a damaging period for the company. As Robert Lacey points out in his book *Ford*, the relationship between safety, innovation, price competitiveness and profit is extraordinarily complex to assess.

Taking weight out of cars in the 1970s was harder than it is now. The 1990s are seeing much lighter cars, owing to the development of new composite materials, often used in combination with aluminium. This results in energy savings, both in production and in the fuel used during the vehicle's life, and this is beneficial not only in cutting costs for manufacturer and consumer alike but in its effects on world fuel reserves. Robert Lacey quotes a stylist at Ford as saying: "We were not very good, in those days, at taking weight out of cars. It's an art. But, over the years, there had been a tendency in America not to be concerned with weight, because, frankly, we weren't concerned with fuel – and that generated one hell of a lot of bad habits..."

The B2 Stealth Bomber is a hugely expensive aircraft designed to hide from radar. At a time when the improvement in relations between the superpowers is meant to yield a "peace dividend" in terms of reduced defence expenditure, such weapons have become symbolic of the wasteful use of resources by industrialized nations. Unfortunately the dividend is perpetually postponed by new threats.

The 1970s saw the growth in the USA and Europe of consumer rights, increased safety of products and environmental pressure groups. However, the abuses of industrial power which these developments set out to remedy were not confined to the developed world. Much of Victor Papanek's attention is directed towards the Third World and to devising safer, simpler and less polluting tools. He has advocated a return to sailing ships (with the sails being trimmed by computers) and airships. Underlying many of Papanek's ideas is a rejection of man's love affair with speed. But essentially he is asking us to rethink what people need and what nature can tolerate. Just as the pioneering Americans of the 19th century rediscovered the real meaning of function and what constituted a necessary tool, so we too have to help emergent countries discover suitable functions and develop tools less elaborate and costly than ours. By doing this we can help to make them less dependent upon the industrial world's manufacturing and help to detach their economies from those of the West and Japan.

The designer's responsibilities Most design is about hiding something, whether it is the casing to protect the machine and keep the users safe or, more sinisterly, the packaging which pretends that things are different from what they actually are. The food industry, for example, has a lot to hide: the mass farming of animals is generally brutal and cruel, their slaughter painful. The drug industry involves all manner of unpleasant testing on animals. The chocolate bar has the hidden tyranny of the laboratory in the background

1982	1983	1984	1986	
Ricardo Bofill's (Spain) precast concrete classical housing, in form of amphitheatre, opens in Marne-la-Vallée near Paris. Ford Sierra motorcar launched in Europe in response to competition from Japan.	Michael Graves's (USA) public services building in Portland, Oregon, opens; it becomes one of the landmarks of post-modern architecture. Fiat Panda motorcar launched.	Issey Miyake's Bodyworks exhibition opened at the Victoria & Albert Museum, London.	Challenger space shuttle blows up. Lloyds Building, designed by Richard Rogers, opens in London. *The Material of Invention* by Ezio Manzini (Italy), perhaps the most important book about design of the decade, published.	Alan Sugar (Britain) launches Amstrad PCW 8256 personal computer/word-processor, successfully aimed at a new market of home users.

just as behind the burger lurks the abattoir. The function of design – graphic design, illustration, packaging – is to play its part in ensuring that these worlds of pain never intrude on the world of pleasure.

Papanek complained bitterly that when his book was first received he was ridiculed. Part of the problem was that he was attacking the values of capitalism. We can see now that his forceful, heartfelt attack on industrial design was a necessary corrective to the prevailing ethos of the time. One thing he pointed out was that the early founders of industrial design, such as the Americans Raymond Loewy, Norman BEL GEDDES, Russel WRIGHT, and Henry Dreyfuss, were from the fields of stage design or window display – and not, Papanek could have added, from engineering, physics or mathematics. He remarks in the 1985 edition of the book: "Honest design striving for true simplicity has recently become frighteningly rare..." Clearly he was not finding it in the new generation of Post-Modernist designers who had been let off the leash in the USA and in Europe by the architect Robert VENTURI.

The view that designers are not responsible for products gets short shrift from Papanek: "Designers often excuse themselves by explaining that it is all the fault of the front office, the sales department, market research and so forth. But of more than 200 mail-order, impulse buying items foisted on the public in 1983, a significantly large number were conceived, invented, planned, patented and produced by members of the design profession."

Papanek is not alone in what he is saying. Worldwide, several thousand scientists and thinkers have been warning us about the excesses and wrongheadedness of our technological culture. Gradually there is a critical political mass building up that will favour at least some of Papanek's thinking. However, predicting the future is impossible, and it is not clear how our culture will accommodate necessary change.

Throughout the West designers are organizing conferences with major manufacturers to discuss more environmentally sensitive approaches to manufacturing. Green design is being driven by public opinion and shaped by scientific research and will be impelled by legislation, but it is not an autonomous activity: it is not the sole or even the main job of designers to shoulder green responsibilities. The designer, in green matters, as in most others affecting his or her work, is a broker – a middleperson between the manufacturer's interests and society's values. Green design is a side issue compared to the major issue – green business.

An unstable aesthetic One of the more uncertain truisms about design and designing is that there is such a thing as classic design – design that will last for ever as a benchmark, a fixed standard.

Clearly, some design is so obviously bad that there can be no argument about it. The Ford Pinto car, with its fatal flaw, is an example. But is it so easy to state that any particular

The Austin Mini remains a brilliant post-war example of economical functionalism. It is a classic design that remains a powerful symbol of its time. Oddly enough, although it sold in its millions, nobody is sure whether it returned a real profit.

HUY 801

design is indisputably good? Take an example of a so-called classic of design, Raymond Loewy's repackaging of the Gestetner duplicator: it is mentioned in this book, every design manual shows it. Loewy took the old, messy printer and put it in a neat sheath that hid the mechanisms away. But today it is quite conceivable that a substantial number of people, offered a choice between the look of the old Gestetner and that of Loewy's, would choose the former. The old design is more "expressive" and, in the sense that it does not attempt to conceal, as Loewy's packaging does, one might say it is an honest or "innocent" design.

The way that design styles are in favour one year, out of favour the next, does tend to place concepts of classic design, good taste, bad taste and truth to materials in a less than certain light. This is not to suggest that all opinions as to what is good or bad design are equally valid or that everyone is a designer. But it is obvious that, in the absence of absolutes other than those of pure function, we should always bear in mind Misha Black's comment on the standard by which we should judge industrial design: "It is now clear, or should be, that all industrial design is ephemeral and disposable; it is concerned with an expendable aesthetic, it can be as exciting as designing a new automobile... but it is always concerned with solutions to immediate social/aesthetic etc problems and should be judged only in relation to immediacy and not against more exacting criteria."

Despite the fact that, in general, the design world is one of continual change, it is clear that in some areas of design, especially those overlapping with traditional crafts, there are some constants: perennial themes, familiar forms, fixed values. For example, despite the ideology of this or that design movement and the need for this or that corporate identity, you will often find that management and its executives, in government, the civil service or industry, try to make their offices domestic, like home. Again, it is of great significance that in the famous Lloyds building in London, that splendid piece of industrial baroque designed by the British architect Richard ROGERS, the executives meet in an 18th-century committee room, a genuine state room designed by Robert Adam and saved from demolition. The executives clearly wanted, amid all the modernity and minimalism around them, some contact with a familiar décor that combined tradition with opulence and an acknowledgement of the human dimension.

The boom in consumer spending in the 1980s, largely fuelled by the easy availability of credit, provided an impetus to designers to devise new products to satisfy demand.

Misha Black may be right that design, in the industrial sense, is dealing with immediacy. This idea of his was perhaps heightened because he saw design only in terms of its response to technology, which changes with disconcerting speed (one of the problems of a technology-led culture). The 1990s will see increased efforts to address the tensions caused by an excess of such change and, as a consequence, an excess of short-term thinking. If industrial and other designers can effectively contribute to a reassessment of broader human needs, then it may be said that the design profession will, finally, have matured.

A–Z OF DESIGNERS

AALTO Alvar 1898–1976 see page 38

AICHER Otl b.1922 German

`graphic designer`

Corporate identity and information systems.

Otl Aicher is a long-standing specialist in corporate identity, and much of his work is characterized by a commitment to pure line and geometric form – as employed, for example, in the design of pictograms. In 1967, he was consultant designer for the corporate identity of the 1972 Munich Olympic Games. This was followed by the development of a system of pictograms in 1968. However, over a long period from the mid-1950s into the 1980s, he also produced corporate identity systems for major German firms, including Braun, Lufthansa, Blohm &` Voss, Westdeutsche Landesbank, as well as designing the complex information system for Frankfurt airport.

Some have mistaken his pictograms and geometric style for the mere products of formulas and grids; the mark of a personality lacking sensitivity or imagination. But Aicher confounded his critics when, at the end of the 1970s, he produced a new identity (to encourage tourism) for the small German Alpine town of Isny. He created 120 images depicting features of the area – people, animals, landscape, etc. – all executed in his famous "stark" geometric style. However, instead of bearing the hardline qualities of severity and regimentation, the images were full of warmth, gaiety, sentiment and romance.

Aicher's contribution to the education world has been equally formidable. He was one of the founding members of the world-renowned Hochschule für Gestaltung at ULM in the late 1940s, head of its Visual Communications department for many years, and Director of the school from 1962 to 1964.

Otl Aicher, pictograms for the Munich Olympic Games, 1972.

ALAIA Azzedine b. c. 1935 Tunisian

`fashion designer`

Body-hugging knits (from late 1970s).

Alaia studied at the Ecole des Beaux Arts in Tunis; he then moved to Paris and worked for other designers – DIOR, Laroche and MUGLER – for many years. He started to produce his own collection from the late 1970s.

His name is associated with his tightly fitting, stretchy knits, which are produced in long and short lengths. His garments generally follow the exact contours of the body, but have also created curves where none exist and often reveal expanses of flesh. His collections are frequently presented in a seductive, camp style; since 1989 they have moved towards softer silhouettes and more fluid lines.

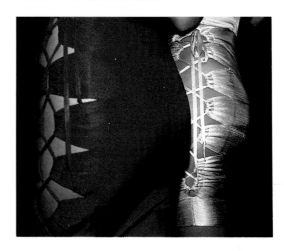

Azzedine Alaia, body-hugging laced dress, spring/summer 1986.

ALBERS Anni 1899–1981 German-American

`textile designer`

Influential theories of textile design based on Bauhaus principles.

Born in Berlin, Anni Albers (née Fleischmann) trained as an art student before joining the BAUHAUS in 1919 to study weaving under Georg Muche, Gunta STÖLZL and Paul Klee. When the Bauhaus moved to Dessau in 1925 she and her newly-wed husband, Josef Albers, were part of a group of Bauhaus students who were appointed teachers. Under the new directorship of Gunta Stölzl the weaving workshop changed its emphasis from artistic improvisation to the preparation of designs for industry. It now styled itself a research laboratory for experimentation, and mathematics and geometry were given precedence. Anni Albers contributed a considerable amount of research into new materials (she was the first designer to experiment with weaving cellophane). The couple emigrated to America in 1933 and began teaching at Black Mountain College of Art in North Carolina, where their experimental approach to design education soon made this school a lively centre for Bauhaus theories of design.

However, it is Anni Albers' writings, notably her classics, *On Weaving* (1965) and *On Design* (1959), and work as a designer and craftswoman, that have had the most enduring influence. Her theories on craft weaving went on to form the intellectual backbone of American fibre art theory in the post-war period. She held that for weaving to have relevance and artistic merit, it should be based upon a rigorous, holistic philosophy of design. She isolated the thread as the basic unit of construction from which the pattern should develop into an ordered and harmonious whole. She urged craftsmen not to impose patterns on the surface of the fabric, but let their designs emanate from the process of weaving itself. "It is better," she said, "that the material speaks than that we should speak ourselves."

STUDIO ALCHYMIA founded 1976 Italian
design studio

Experimental "anti-design" and research into decorated surfaces.

Studio Alchymia's full title is "Alchymia, the projection of images for the 20th century". It was founded in Milan by Alessandro and Adriana Guerriero with Alessandro MENDINI and attracted designers such as Ettore SOTTSASS and Michele de Lucchi (b.1951). Like ARCHIZOOM, this group was interested in urban culture and employed a quasi-scientific approach to its work, and saw what it did as "experiments" and "research".

The desire to explore artificial and theatrical aspects of youth culture encouraged the group to create stage sets in parking lots or exhibition halls – *The Labourer's Room,* Galleria d'Arte Moderna in Bologna, (1981) is an example. In the 1970s the work of the group was more art than design, but by the beginning of the 1980s the group was producing furniture and lighting designs for Ettore Sottsass, Andrea Branzi and Michele de Lucchi.

In the early 1980s Studio Alchymia undertook research into decorated surfaces for a group of manufacturers. The prototype furniture of Sottsass and the

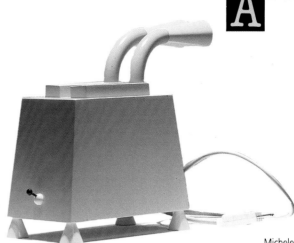

Michele de Lucchi, prototype toaster for Studio Alchymia, 1984.

others which Alchymia produced "tested" or showed the fruit of these "researches" and contributed to the 1980s fashion in product design for elaborately printed and decorated surfaces.

ALESSI founded 1922 Italian
manufacturing company

Superior-quality tableware and gifts.

Alessi's success was based on its products for the hotel and restaurant trade. In the early 1970s, however, it changed its range, producing tableware and giftware. Alessi began commissioning well-known designers and architects to produce "art-design" objects.

Among those recruited by the company were Richard MEIER, Aldo ROSSI, Michael GRAVES and Arata Isozaki. For example, in 1983 Michael Graves designed a silver coffee-service for Alessi; part of the quality of the design is that it contains historical references to earlier, 20th-century Viennese designs. The architect Richard Meier has also designed a silver set for Alessi (1983), and this too has art-historical references, this time to the Russian artist Kasimir Malevich. Aldo Rossi, another architect, designed a stainless-steel coffee-maker for Alessi in 1984.

▶ page 39

Robert Venturi, tray designed for Alessi, 1984.

AALTO

Alvar Aalto, Baker Dormitory, Massachusetts Institute of Technology, Cambridge, Massachusetts, 1947.

AALTO Alvar 1898–1976   Finnish

architect

Paimio Sanatorium, Villa Mairea, Baker Dormitory, Säynatsälo Town Hall, Imatra Church.

Alvar Aalto was a pioneering and highly influential modern architect with a prodigious output. His success was in fusing traditional and modern styles of building. He admired the classical architecture of ancient Greece and Rome, was preoccupied with the idea of architecture being close to nature and promoted the use of craftsmanship and quality materials.

Among his early major buildings was the Paimio Sanatorium, Finland (1929–32). The white-painted structure stands on high ground overlooking a landscape of trees and lakes and is composed of one long, rectangular, six-storey slab facing south, with large windows and balconies.

Aalto also produced beautiful small-scale work. He designed the Finnish Pavilion at the World's Fair (New York, 1939) – a towering, undulating and overhanging cliff-face of wooden slats, against which were suspended enormous photographs and underneath which were displayed Finnish crafts.

There were also charming buildings such as the Villa Mairea, Noormarkku (1938–9). This L-shaped building, although modern in its composition of cubic shapes, was built very much in the Finnish tradition, using local stone and woods and designed along the lines of traditional farmsteads, where buildings enclosed a courtyard.

While working as visiting professor at the Massachusetts Institute of Technology, Aalto designed the Baker Dormitory (1946–7). He demonstrated his skill and sensitivity in acknowledging local traditions by constructing the hall of residence in red brick. The long snaking wall of dormitories with uniform horizontal rows of square windows rose six floors and was given a flat roof. The building's undulating wall, a feature often used by Aalto, broke down the mass and gave students views over the nearby River Charles.

Aalto was adept at designing buildings which hugged the topography of the landscape as seen in his work for the town centre and town hall at Säynatsälo, Finland (1949–52). This collection of low-rise cubic buildings built of brick and wood was set amid a wooded landscape. The focus was the Town Hall, which was reached by passing the smaller structures and climbing the rising levels of land by a series of small flights of steps.

Aalto's admiration of Greek architecture displayed itself most clearly with the designs for the Otaniemi Institute of Technology, Finland (1955–64). This series of rectangular buildings was laid out in a grid enclosing small gardens; the dominant feature was the main lecture theatre, which was built in brick.

However, Aalto was at his best working on a small scale, and his Imatra Church, Finland (1957–9), since destroyed by a hurricane, was a beautiful example. The exterior was composed of three stepped blocks graduating in size and finished in white, with horizontal bands of glazing around the tops of the walls. Inside, it was white and peaceful with uneven-shaped walls. Decoration was kept to a minimum.

Aalto's forays into the white-finished, cubic modern style of building were not always successful; one of the most curious was the head offices of the Enso-Gutzeit company, Helsinki (1959–62). This five-storey stone building was harsh in its design, with walls composed of a grid of large inset square windows.

Aalto was also a most significant designer of furniture. He chose wood as his medium but sought constantly to design for mass production. His designs for bent plywood, especially his laminated birchwood chairs, influenced a generation of designers including Marcel BREUER and Charles and Ray EAMES.

His use of wood, especially plywood, which is a renewable resource, is an aspect of his work that is of increasing relevance to today's environment conscious designers.

Aalto's career spanned the birth and growth of modern architecture, and yet, while he adopted from and influenced the new movement, he retained and was greatly respected for his own distinctive style.

Alvar Aalto, furnishings for student accommodation at the Massachusetts Institute of Technology, early 1940s.

Alvar Aalto, vase for Iittala Glass, 1930.

In the 1980s Alessi became a leading vehicle for post-modern design experimentation. The company helped to revive the applied art of silverware by attaching it to the provenance of architecture, not handicraft – star architectural names gave silverware a new respectability with the intelligent, affluent and status-conscious consumer.

AMBASZ Emilio b.1943 — Argentinian

architect and designer

Vertebra chair; San Antonio Botanical Garden Conservatory, Texas.

Ambasz studied architecture at Princeton University, New Jersey. He was Curator of Design at the Museum of Modern Art, New York, from 1970 to 1976, and editor of the exhibition catalogue *Italy: The New Domestic Landscape,* which accompanied the highly influential exhibition of the same name held at MOMA in 1972. His design work has included some architecture and interior design – San Antonio Botanical Garden Conservatory, Texas (1982), for example – and systems furniture and lighting. His Vertebra chair of 1977 has become something of a classic. Stephen Bayley notes both the precociousness and the thoroughness of this designer and polemicist. He completed his under-graduate course in Princeton in one year, and when he designed Vertebra he carried out all the costings for production as well – correctly.

AMIES Hardy b.1909 — British

fashion designer

Dressmaker to Queen Elizabeth II; contributed to wartime utility clothing designs.

Amies was initially trained as a journalist and then as a salesman. Later he was apprenticed to Lachasse, a London company famous for women's quality sports clothing and tweed suits. It was during the Second World War that he first made his mark. He had joined the Army, but was soon released to design luxury couture clothing for the South American market, to earn much-needed dollars for Britain. During this period he also designed for the House of Worth and pecame a member of the Incorporated Society of London Fashion Designers, who were responsible for creating utility clothing in 1941. This clothing scheme sought to ensure that the nation was adequately

Hardy Amies.

A

Hardy Amies, ready-to-wear wool coat dress with dolman sleeves, spring/summer 1986.

clothed, while using the minimum quantity of fabric and manufacturing time, without sacrificing style. For the first time the majority of women wore garments directly designed by Britain's top couturiers.

In 1945 Amies opened his own couture house and became internationally famous for his understated tweed and wool suits and for his restrained but elegant evening dresses. Amies received his first order from the Queen, then Princess Elizabeth, in 1951, and was officially awarded the Royal Warrant in 1955. Amies states that, in his designs, "Nonchalance is the operative word. Elegant British style is countrified in town. It is restrained, it is disciplined, but in the end it must be relaxed." (*The Sunday Times*, 13 June, 1989.)

During the 1950s the couture trade declined internationally in favour of ready-to-wear clothing. Amies was one of the first both to move into this area in 1950 and to arrange licensing agreements. He now has licensees all over the world producing menswear, womenswear, underwear, luggage, umbrellas and household goods.

ARAD Ron b.1951   Israeli

furniture designer and architect

Furniture designs related to industrial themes.

Arad studied architecture at the Architectural Association in London, a private architectural school with a reputation for encouraging the avant-garde and a recent history of producing innovative designers or theoreticians rather than practising architects.

In 1981 Arad founded the One-Off design company, which became a focal point of alternative design in Britain, its very title opposing the orthodoxy of *mass* manufacture and implying a relationship between art and design. In 1981 Britain was in a deep economic recession and the smokestack industries of heavy engineering, coal-mining and iron and steel manufacturing were closing. This context of a rusting Britain provided the theme and the much-imitated aesthetic of Arad's work, which was, throughout the 1980s, coarse in its looks and usually made in metal. Most people find his furniture uncomfortable, but one exception is his most famous chair design to date, which uses seats taken from scrapped Rover cars. So successful was this recycled design that it featured in lifestyle television advertising in 1988 and 1989. Following the lead of Ron Arad (and that of Nigel COATES), the recycling of outmoded components from

Ron Arad, seated in his Big Easy Volume II – Stainless Steel

industry became a popular strategy among young, radical designers and artist craftspeople, culminating in the "New Spirit in Craft and Design" show at the Crafts Council, London, in 1987.

Arad has produced hi-fi systems in concrete, as well as an all-steel armchair that looks like a First World War tank. His 1980s aesthetic is already an idiosyncratic footnote in history, and examples of his work are appearing in sales at the international auction houses Sotheby's and Christie's.

ARAI Junichi b.1932   Japanese

weaver, textile designer and manufacturer

Experimental production processes with fibres to produce woven fabrics.

Junichi Arai is renowned for his experimental craft tradition. His spectacular fabrics link computer technology, contemporary materials and craft tradition.

Arai was born in Kiryu, a traditional weaving centre to the north of Tokyo. Like other designers of his generation, Arai has his roots in the Japanese folk crafts tradition. His travels after the war extended his knowledge of the ancient textiles of South America, India and Indonesia.

Arai's early fabrics used unorthodox combinations of materials such as celluloid, aluminium tape, metallic filament, silk and polyester. He then shifted his attention to the technology of weaving. Here, his

A

major innovation was to maximize the potential of punch cards used for jacquard weaving by making them on computer. This technique, which enabled him to produce woven patterns of a hitherto unimaginable complexity, was soon taken up by designers all over the world. Arai has subsequently explored the design potential of textile post-production processes, creating fabrics out of fibres that have different shrinkage rates and exposing them to extreme heat to create drawn thread, puckered or bubble effects. Arai has also used heat to fix synthetic fibres, and even lacerated film into complex weave structures.

In 1987 Arai was nominated a Royal Designer for Industry, but his manufacturing company, Anthologie, collapsed in the same year. He now operates as an independent designer through his retail company, Nuno, in Tokyo.

ARCHIZOOM ASSOCIATI founded 1966　　Italian

design studio

Urban-based experimental architectural and furniture design.

Archizoom was founded in Florence by Andrea Branzi, Gilberto Corretti, Paolo Deganello and Massimo Morrozzi. All trained as architects; all are designers and theorists. The late 1960s was a period of questioning the role of architects and planners. Archizoom, excited by television and the rapid growth of the media generally, sought to transform planning and architecture into "art" and "theatre". Believing that the only

Andrea Branzi, founder of Archizoom, Domestic Animals furniture, 1987.

20th century culture possible was an urban one, it had no time for alternative cultures based on nature, the land or countryside. The city ruled.

The group then moved on to industrial and furniture design, and to what was termed "dressing design", which was basically adding decoration to existing objects to enhance, alter or subvert the original meaning of that object. Archizoom contributed to the new domestic landscape exhibition held at the Museum of Modern Art, New York, in 1972.

As one of the leading protagonists of this and successive experimental design studios, Andrea Branzi has become one of Italy's best-known theorists and writers.

ARMANI Giorgio b.1935　　Italian

fashion designer

Loose, understated tailoring in fine fabrics.

Milan emerged as a capital of fashion in the mid-1970s, and has produced some of the 1980s most successful fashion designers; Basile, Cerruti, Fendi, Ferre, MISSONI, MOSCHINO, Soprani, VALENTINO and VERSACE. Most highly acclaimed of all is Giorgio Armani.

Armani initially studied medicine – a career he chose not to pursue – and then trained as a window-dresser for a department store. His first work as a clothing designer was with the menswear manufacturer Nino Cerruti, where he was employed from 1961 to 1974. He then worked for a brief period as a fashion consultant, before launching his own range of menswear in 1974 and a range of womenswear in 1975.

Armani is contemptuous of passing fashion fads. His own philosophy is that the designer should avoid "traumatic caprices, needless infatuations that are as sudden as they are fleeting, mass crazes that feed foolish consumerism without consolidating a market". (Armani, quoted in *Mattino*). He has created a sustaining, understated, loosely tailored style, which has exerted the strongest influence upon the design of men's clothing in the 1980s. During the early 1980s he used shoulder-pads, but has since moved towards a softer, natural line; he creates unstructured shapes, eliminating the superfluous, with the emphasis on a casual, abandoned elegance. His garments appear nonchalant and lived-in. To accentuate this, in 1982 he introduced a battered and crumpled look, the antithesis of traditional tailoring.

He is noted for injecting muted but colour-

Giorgio Armani.

ful tones – reds, browns and greens, as well as window-pane checks and stripes – into men's formerly sombre clothing. He has also expanded on the usual range of suitings, and uses soft and luxurious fabrics, such as velvets and corduroys, unusually textured weaves, herringbone tweeds, camel-hairs, cashmere, fine leathers and fake-fur fleece finishes.

Armani is particularly known for his spacious, three-button sports blazers and loosely cut suits with six-button double-breasted jackets with no defined waist and full, cuffed trousers, based on a revival of the 1960s Ivy League sack suit. Many of his jackets have dropped lapels. Armani has abandoned the traditional technique of gluing the jacket lining to the underside of the fabric.

Armani's wearable, smart womenswear is designed along the same lines as his men's clothing; he put women back in suits, and is responsible for the widespread adoption of tailored jackets worn with dresses and loose, wide-legged trousers. In the late 1980s he introduced a range of elegant evening wear for women in fine silks, georgettes and grosgrains.

Armani is the sole designer of each item of clothing that bears his label. In 1989 he produced a phenomenal 3,000 designs. Giorgio Armani SpA, a consultant company to Armani licensees, does not undertake any manufacturing and gains its revenues from royalties.

ARQUITECTONICA founded 1977 American

architectural practice

Creators of a brash, eclectic "Miami Modernism".

The practice was founded in 1977 by Hervin Romney and the husband-and-wife team of Laurinda Hope Spear and Bernardo Fort-Brescia, who now run it.

The Atlantis apartment block Miami (1978) made the practice famous and illustrates many of its trademarks. It uses a wide range of idiosyncratic detail drawn from the history of modernism – Russian Constructivism and De Stijl. Like other late modernist work, it reconsiders the design of the tall building; it has a dramatic "sky court" complete with palm cut into the middle of the building. The practice is avowedly modernist rather than Post-Modernist. But their use of allusion is deliberately populist/superficial.

The designs are wilful and arbitrary, but the practice is adept at meeting the needs of developers in Miami. They seem to have found a virtue in artificiality

and to be creating something which is authentic for Miami. The high-profile nature of their work has led them to design a house for Don Johnson, the star of *Miami Vice*!

There have been many other major commissions across America, and in Melbourne and Luxembourg. The Banco de Credito, Lima, Peru was completed in 1989 and shows some of the contradictions of Arquitectonica: the building is responsive to the landscape and even to Inca architecture, but because of import restrictions all the modernist elements had to be made locally.

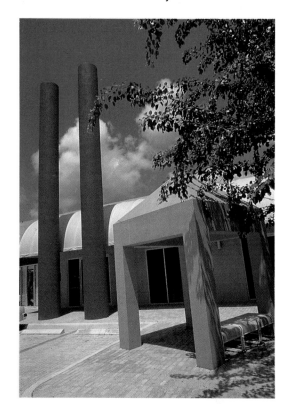

Arquitectonica, Decorative Arts Plaza, Miami, 1981.

ARTELUCE founded 1939 Italian

lighting design company

Adventurous modern lighting design.

Arteluce was one of the small-scale companies which contributed to the international success of Italian design during the 1950s. Founded in Milan just after the Second World War, the firm manufactured adventurous modern lighting designed by Gino Sarfatti. Inspired by the mobiles of Alexander Calder, these abstract forms of coloured Perspex and metal were in

Giorgio Armani, casual womenswear at the Milan shows, autumn/winter 1986–87.

Giorgio Armani, women's suit with padded shoulders, spring/summer 1986.

keeping with the flamboyant interiors of the time.

During the 1980s Arteluce continued to produce innovative lighting, mainly for the contract interior market. The Donald desk lamp by KING & MIRANDA featured a yellow eye-shade on the main lamp, which triggered associations with the Disney character Donald Duck. Jill, a slender halogen floor lamp with black enamelled stem and satined glass diffusor was designed by King & Miranda with G. Arnaldi in 1980 and remains in production today.

ASCHER Zika and Lida   Czechoslovakian–British
textile designers

Fashion-oriented screenprinted textile designs of the 1940s and 1950s.

Zika (b. 1910) and Lida Ascher emigrated to Britain at the outbreak of the Second World War and launched their screenprinting company in London in 1942. Though self-taught, Zika soon became an expert screenprinter and Lida's bold, gestural approach to pattern complemented this technique well. Together they created strong, vibrant prints in which brilliant colours such as tangerine, cyclamen and chartreuse were combined with navy blue and black. Their designs proved a dramatic contrast to most wartime fabrics.

The majority of Lida's wartime designs were essays in simplicity. Typical were her prints of roughly drawn dots or dashes and a striped print of mock calligraphy, usually printed on silk in two colours. What made these designs classic were their rhythm. By 1946 they had started to supply fashion designers in France, Italy and America. What cemented the Aschers' reputation, however, was their idea to commission artists such as Henri Matisse, Jean Cocteau and Henry Moore to create designs for a series of scarves – the Ascher Squares.

In the years after the war they strengthened their relationship with couturiers, for example, producing in 1952 cabbage rose prints for Christian DIOR that were to become a classic element of 1950s fashion.

D'ASCANIO Corradino 1891–1981   Italian
helicopter and vehicle designer

Vespa motor scooter.

During the 1920s Corradino d'Ascanio worked chiefly on the design of helicopters. His first helicopter design

appeared in 1926, but it was not until 1930 that a successful prototype was produced.

In 1934 d'Ascanio joined the Piaggio engineering company, for whom he designed a range of aircraft components. During and after the Second World War he also continued to work on helicopter design, his chief love.

The Vespa motor scooter (1947), for which d'Ascanio is principally known, was the original idea of Enrico Piaggio. Initially designed to appeal to women as a cheap means of transport over short distances, it was soon popular with men as well.

Corradino d'Ascanio, Vespa scooter, first produced in 1947.

ASHLEY Laura 1926-88   British
clothing, furnishing and product designer

Nostalgic countrified clothing and furnishing fabrics.

Laura Ashley was one of the first British designers to explore the idea of lifestyle marketing. Her romantic vision of 19th-century rural life, adapted to suit contemporary domestic realities, inspired a generation of middle-class Britons who went back to country life during the 1960s and 1970s.

Laura Ashley, née Mountney, was born in Merthyr Tydfil in Wales. She launched her business by silkscreening textiles and making up tea-towels on the kitchen table in her attic in Pimlico. With the technical support of her husband, Bernard Ashley, she formed a printing company, moving first to Kent and then to Carno in Wales. More of an assimilator than a designer Laura Ashley adapted the patterns of 18th- and 19th-century cotton dress fabrics for her own work. Her sprigged floral patterns, such as Wild Clematis, which

A

provided the basis for the company's success, edited in positive-negative monochrome colourways, challenged contemporary movements in textile design with their qualities of historicism and simplicity.

Starting with a cotton drill apron in 1961, Laura Ashley went on to develop a line of clothing. At a time when the succession of fashion styles had become increasingly frenetic and the 1930s "Vamp Look" was temporarily back in fashion, Ashley created an anti-style look of wholesome innocence. Her inexpensive tucked and frilled dresses in coarse cotton and her lacy white shirts with Edwardian leg-o'-mutton sleeves expressed the reassuring stability and ethical certainties of an imagined pre-industrial past. In 1968 the company opened its first London shop in Kensington. This was an immediate success, and as Laura Ashley outlets spread throughout England and Europe during the 1970s the retail side of the business was expanded to include a range of do-it-yourself home furnishings.

A model of the 1970s "superwoman", Ashley based her marketing ideas on her own experience, and they were therefore very relevant to contemporary domestic life. Her vision of the rural middle-class home, whose slate-tiled kitchen floors she envisaged "strewn with gumboots, dogs and children", appealed to thousands. Equipped with the latest digital technologies for garment handling and cutting, and with 450 shops throughout the world Laura Ashley proved herself the equal of Agatha Christie in constructing a popular fiction of British rural life.

Laura Ashley.

ASPLUND Gunnar 1885-1940   Swedish

architect

Stockholm City Library, an extension to the Goteborg Town Hall, the Stockholm Exhibition, and the Stockholm Crematorium.

Throughout the Scandinavian countries of Denmark, Finland and Sweden there was a wave of reaction against the heavy, elaborately decorated buildings which had been popular in the 19th century. In its place architects sought a calmer simplicity and created designs which were modern interpretations of the classical Greek and Roman styles. Among the influential pioneers of the emerging new style was Gunnar Asplund.

Asplund's Stockholm City Library (1920–8) was one of the earliest Swedish buildings to be completed in the new Modern idiom. It is composed of two

Gunnar Asplund, Stockholm Crematorium, 1935–40.

elements, having a rectangular, three-storey box for its base, topped by a circular drum used as a reading room. The exterior is stark and stripped of decoration; walls are flat and smooth, and light enters the building by alternate layers of widely spaced windows.

Asplund's skill was in taking inspiration from elements of classicism, such as the ideas on proportion and the use of Egyptian or Greek motifs, and then creating his own style.

Shortly after completing the library he went on to design buildings for the Stockholm Exhibition of 1930. Here he attracted international attention by incorporating large expanses of steel and glass into his designs. From this time onwards he became known as an International Modernist – a term coined in the 1930s for the style characterized by the use of plain, cubic shapes, asymmetrical composition of buildings and the frequent use of white rendering.

Asplund's monumental Stockholm Crematorium (1935–40) was one of his finest achievements. It comprises a series of low, cubic buildings fronted by a simple, temple-like portico with a flat roof supported on rows of square pillars. Before the buildings stands an enormous, entirely plain, stone cross.

ASTORI Antonia b.1940   Italian

furniture designer

Oikos and Kaos ranges of industrial and domestic systems furniture.

Antonia Astori works mainly for the Italian company Driade. She is a specialist in systems furniture for use in both the home and the office, whose work has been much copied. Astori's style is derived from the patterns of De Stijl painting (Piet Mondrian) and De Stijl design (Gerrit RIETVELD) of the inter-war years.

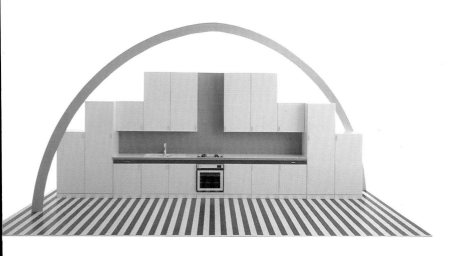

Antonia Astori, system-based kitchen designed for Driade, 1982.

Her most famous ranges are called Oikos and Kaos. A limited-edition book, privately published as a celebration of Astori's designs, describes Oikos thus: "The basic idea is to provide fixed structures to serve as containers and to define several spaces within the house and then to grant the user utmost freedom in completing those spaces at will by combining single pieces of furniture of his own choice."

The units are made in coated chipboard, and they are sold as flat-packed units. Unlike some systems these by Driade are well manufactured and detailed – for example, the final paint surfaces are applied and finished by hand.

Her first system, Driade 1, was launched in 1968; Oikos appeared in 1973, and soon spawned many imitators. Oikos is constantly updated to beat off the competition, and Driade has commissioned further ranges from Astori including Bri, designed in collaboration with Enzo Mari. Astori's technical collaborator is another woman, Fiorella Gussoni. Astori is a Compasso d'Oro prizewinner.

AUBOCK Carl b.1925 — Austrian

architect and designer

Versatile designer with emphasis on ergonomics and problem-solving.

Aubock studied at the Technische Universität, Vienna, and Massachusetts Institute of Technology, USA. Currently Professor of Architecture and Design at the Hochschule für Angewandte Kunst, Vienna, he has established an international reputation as a designer, especially of domestic items. He has designed prefabricated parts for buildings, scientific instruments, many houses and exhibitions. He is particularly interested in both craftsmanship and ergonomics.

Aubock's father, who, with Aubock's mother, was a student of the Weimar BAUHAUS, came from a family that had been involved in experimental craft movements such as the Wiener Werkstätte. Carl Aubock served a traditional apprenticeship as a metalworker at the family bronze casting workshops.

Many of Aubock's achievements in design are pure problem-solving. Thus his design for the Neopan research microscope in 1963 included adjustments to the focusing mechanism and a new approach to protective cladding that set the standard for future microscopes. His design for ski-boots improved the fastening mechanism; his design for skiwear pioneered the idea of using a simple design in bright colours to act as a signal on the slopes. His ceramic and metal tableware has won design awards and is commercially successful. In 1989–90 he was working on a range of oven-to-table ware.

AWATSUJI Hiroshi b.1929 — Japanese

print designer and manufacturer

Exploration of the potential of print using graphic texture.

Hiroshi Awatsuji was born in Kyoto. He studied printing at the Koyoto Municipal College of Arts, and opened his own textile design studio in 1958. His major commissions include decorating the Japanese government pavilion for the Japanese trade fair Expo 70 and creating tapestries for the Keiro Plaza. Awatsuji manufactures many of his own designs. He also designs for Fujie Textiles, one of the first Japanese companies to use its strong base of technology and design talent to make an impression on the international market.

Awatsuji's prints are often unorthodox, featuring large repeats printed on a giant scale, but he has always maintained that he is a designer of furnishing fabrics rather than an artist.

In the late 1960s Awatsuji created a series of giant fluorescent-coloured prints using bold graphic images inspired by the Japanese pop art movement. In the early 1980s he began experimenting with different bold graphic marks to construct decorative surfaces and has refined these experiments to form a sophisticated graphic language that explores visual texture. At the end of the 1980s he produced a remarkable collection of monochrome prints that explored the textural surfaces of the natural environment in close-up.

BACKSTROM Olaf b.1922   Finnish

Fiskars O-series general purpose scissors.

Backstrom, an electrical engineer by training, took up woodcarving in the 1950s and won a silver medal for wooden household objects at the Milan Triennale of 1957. He began working for Fiskars as a cutlery designer in 1958.

The famous Fiskars orange-coloured, plastic-handled scissors designed by Backstrom are a masterpiece of ergonomic design; they fit in the hand comfortably and their shape enables more efficient pressure to be applied and easier cutting. They are designed from the point of view that cutting cloth or paper is a one-handed operation; the other hand, of course, is guiding the paper or cloth along the path of the blades. The Fiskars project began in 1961 and was completed in 1967. The scissors are an excellent example of practical design making a genuine addition to comfort in utilitarian tasks.

A concern for more ergonomic design in such apparently basic objects as handles had been occupying the minds of several European designers in the period immediately following the Second World War. Backstrom's designs are anticipated to some extent by research and modelling of doorhandles and scissor handles by Zdenek Kovar, a Czechoslovak professor of design. There is a review of his work in *Design* (p.8, 13 March 1952).

BAHNSEN Uwe b.1930   German

Ford Sierra: a radical change to the design of mass-produced cars.

Uwe Bahnsen was born in Hamburg in 1930. He completed his education at the Academy of Fine Arts in Hamburg and during the 1950s worked with an assortment of companies in advertising, stage and film-set design.

Meanwhile his passion was motor-racing. Racing from the Scuderia Colonia stable, Bahnsen developed his skill in modelling one-off, fibreglass racing-car shells. His enthusiasm introduced him to a job with Ford Werke AG's Design Centre in Cologne in 1958. There Bahnsen was involved in the launch of the Ford P3 Taunus, or the "Cologne Egg" as it was known.

In 1976 Bahnsen was appointed Vice President

(Design) for Ford Europe. In this position Bahnsen was responsible for the Taunus/Cortina range, the Fiesta, the Granada, the Escort, the Cargo and the Sierra.

The Sierra, launched in 1982, set new standards in design, engineering and packaging of popular cars throughout the car industry. Under Bahnsen's direction, the Sierra became the foundation for the corporate style for Ford of Europe.

BAKKER Gijs b.1942   Dutch

Contemporary jewellery and furniture.

Bakker studied gold and silversmithing at the Amsterdam Art Academy and he is well known as a jeweller, sculptor, furniture designer and, to a lesser extent, industrial designer. He and his wife Emmy van Leersum (now dead) were leaders of a new wave in contemporary jewellery.

They began in the mid-1960s by designing and making collars and bracelets in aluminium. They liked the lightness and malleability of the material, but chose it primarily because it was non-precious and classless. As their work developed during the 1970s they took jewellery into art and performance and sculpture: the human body became an important part of the jewellery, and not just the thing upon which the jewellery was hung.

In the mid-1980s Bakker produced some vast neckpieces made up of colour photographs pressed between Perspex. These were funny and rather beautiful examples of lateral thinking.

Bakker has produced furniture designs since 1972, and he has also produced a number of product designs. His chairs include the strip chair (1974) and the

Gijs Bakker.

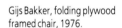

Gijs Bakker, folding plywood framed chair, 1976.

Gijs Bakker, aluminium bracelet for a man or woman, 1968.

finger chair (1979). In common with the mainstream of design consultants he has always resisted working for a single company. He argues: "In my opinion, the designer should be some-one who is outside the firm for which he works, who learns to understand it, but who remains detached."

BALENCIAGA Cristobal 1895–1972   Spanish

fashion designer

1950s loosely tailored suits and sculptural evening wear.

Balenciaga has often been hailed as the greatest of all *couturiers*. His introduction to fashion has become legendary: as a young boy of 13 years he admired in the street the dress of the Marquesa de Casa Torres and daringly asked if he could make her a suit. She later became one of his greatest customers, introduced him to the Parisian *couturier* Drecoll and encouraged him to open his own house in San Sebastian in 1916. He soon had branches in Madrid and Barcelona and earned a reputation as Spain's leading *couturier*, who was both master tailor and dressmaker. Balenciaga derived much of his inspiration from his Spanish heritage: his collections regularly included Spanish black lace, braids, fringing, ruffles and embroidery.

In 1938 Balenciaga left Spain, which was repressed under Franco, to open a couture house in Paris. During the late 1930s fashions in furnishings and dress saw a Victorian revival, and Balenciaga's first collection featured full, crinoline dresses. His influence was, however, most strongly felt during the 1950s: in 1952 he rebelled against Dior's New Look by introducing soft, tailored suits, which became widely adopted. These had loosely fitting jackets with indented waists, cutaway necks, rounded mounted collars and three-quarter-length sleeves. They were worn with the tiny pill-box hats, which he first designed in 1946. In contrast to the simplicity of his daytime styles, his evening dresses were dramatic, sculptural and made in strong colours. He created dresses that narrowed from wide shoulders to hobble skirts, and Princess dresses which, conversely, flowed from a narrow top to a wide hem. Balenciaga favoured crisp, heavy fabrics which he formed into garments which often stood independent of the body. In 1957 he abandoned shape and launched a series of sack dresses.

In 1968 he retired, recognizing that his luxu-

rious couture garments could no longer be supported. The house of Balenciaga was reopened in the 1970s under new ownership, and currently produces a range of clothing and costume jewellery in the spirit of the founder, designed by Michael Gomas, who previously worked at PATOU.

Balenciaga, luxurious draped and flounced evening gown, c.1955.

BALL Douglas b.1935   Canadian

industrial designer

Race office system.

Ball studied industrial design at the Ontario College of Arts, Toronto. He has won several Canadian Design Awards and is well known for his Race office system (1978) for Sunar Hauserman.

The Race system is elegant, but it is designed to fit into any one of a number of corporate offices. It is not bland, but it is self-effacing, and this is a characteristic that other designers of quality office furniture have striven for in order to attract the corporate market. The Race system was one of the first to tackle seriously the problem of wire management in the office – it contains well-designed ducting for cabling and wires. Ease of access and maintenance is a priority.

B

His other commissions include transportation and public seating systems, and also wheelchair designs for physically disabled users.

BALMAIN Pierre 1914–82 French

Elegant evening gowns and film costumes.

Balmain studied architecture at the Ecole des Beaux Arts in Paris, but did not complete his course as his heart lay in fashion. He started by selling drawings to the Paris *couturier* Piguet, then worked for Molyneux from 1934 to 1939 and for Lelong from 1939 to 1941, when he closed because of the war. Lelong soon enticed Balmain back with the promise that he and another young designer, Christian DIOR, could control the house style. Balmain left to open his own business and showed his first collection in 1945.

His first collection opened with a model wearing trousers, low-heeled shoes and a loose homespun brown jacket, and leading an Airedale dog. He also showed large woollen kimonos, which zipped at the shoulder. The rest of the collection revelled in opulent, costly furs and rich laces, embroideries, feathers and flowers, which provided a dramatic and welcome contrast to the austerity of wartime dress. Balmain built his reputation on the luxury of his fabrics and the simplicity and elegance of his styles, from simple tailored suits to ballgowns. He regularly travelled to the East, and his love of the Orient regularly enriched his collections. Soon he attracted a glamorous clientele, which included Queen Marie José of Italy. He also designed for the theatre and cinema, creating the wardrobes for some one hundred films, dressing leading stars including Marlene Dietrich, Brigitte Bardot and Sophia Loren.

Pierre Balmain.

Pierre Balmain, sketch for a tailored suit, autumn/winter 1979–80 (above); evening dress, c.1952 (right).

BARRON AND LARCHER founded c.1920 British

Use of traditional block-printing techniques to produce original designs.

Phyllis Barron (1890–1964) and Dorothy Larcher (1884–1952) were the foremost hand-block printers during the 1920s and 1930s.

Phyllis Barron studied painting under Henry Tonks and Wilson Steer at the Slade School of Art (1905–09). She taught herself the ancient crafts of dyeing and block-printing, using 18th- and 19th-century manuals for guidance. Despite her Arts and Crafts ideals she was visually a modernist, and began to exhibit her work with the London Group and at the Omega workshops.

In the early 1920s she was joined by the painter Dorothy Larcher, and together they established a small craft workshop in Hampstead, London. They created small, finely crafted, bold prints of sprigs, lozenges, dots and stripes printed on unbleached cotton, linen, velvet or silk, which they suggested could be used for fashion and interior furnishings. Their abstract patterns were suggested by natural forms and the materials and techniques of the printing process itself. During the 1920s, financial constraints restricted them to single-colour prints, but did not impede their experiments. Their experiments with traditional vegetable and mineral dyes such as indigo, quercitron, rose madder, walnut and iron black and buff led to some innovative results. At this time they received their major commission to provide all the furnishing fabrics for the Duke of Westminster's yacht *The Flying Cloud*. In 1930, in true Arts and Crafts tradition, they moved their workshop to the Cotswolds. Their prints of this time became more complex as they experimented with combinations of Larcher's floral designs with Barron's abstract geometric motifs.

BASS Saul b.1920 see page 50

BAUHAUS founded 1919 German
`school of arts, crafts and industrial design`

Highly influential school which brought together many outstanding European artists, designers and theorists.

The Bauhaus opened in 1919 in Weimar, directed by Walter GROPIUS, who had succeeded the architect Henry VAN DER VELDE as Director of the Art School and the School of Arts and Crafts at Weimar. Gropius, himself an architect, amalgamated the two schools in an effort to break down barriers between the disciplines of art and design. At first the new school was crafts-orientated, but in 1925 it was moved to Dessau, and an industrial design curriculum was introduced.

Bauhaus buildings at Dessau, designed by Walter Gropius, 1926.

Gropius secured the services of Paul Klee, Johannes Itten, Wassily Kandinsky, László MOHOLY-NAGY, Adolf Meyer and Marcel BREUER. It was a volatile mix which bred disagreements. Gropius resigned in 1928 and was replaced by Hannes MEYER, who was in turn replaced in 1930 by Ludwig MIES VAN DER ROHE. The Bauhaus moved to Berlin in 1932, and was dissolved by the Nazis in 1933. The New Bauhaus was reformed in Chicago under Moholy-Nagy in 1935, and became the Chicago Institute of Design.

The Bauhaus made an invaluable contribution to the modern movement in design between the two wars in Europe partly because it brought talented thinkers and practitioners together. Paul Klee, for example, did some of his work there, an analytical study of line, form and colour which became published as *The Thinking Eye*. But although men such as Breuer and Gropius, Mies van der Rohe and others espoused industrial techniques and mass production, it was largely the Americans who put design ideas of a Bauhaus origin into production. For example, it was the Chicago-based Howell Company that adapted Breuer's work for manufacture.

Originally the Bauhaus encouraged students to work with materials in workshops, but this was the cause of ideological differences within the Bauhaus, because some people maintained that by leaving the craft-based aesthetic intact, students were not being taught how to design for mass, standardized manufacturing processes.

The Bauhaus made important contributions to design teaching – and Johannes Itten's basic foundation course, which all students had to take, was adopted by many art schools throughout the world after the Second World War. Unfortunately the contemporary versions of Itten's original course are a pale shadow of the original, partly because while Itten (and Bauhaus teachers generally) espoused the importance of craft knowledge and skill-learning, modern Western art schools have disavowed skill-teaching.

BAYER Herbert 1900–85 Austrian-American
`graphic designer and typographer`

Innovative Bauhaus designer and teacher. Designed the Universal typeface.

Herbert Bayer was the last Bauhaus designer/teacher alive and active in the 1980s. Born in Haag, near Salzburg, in Austria, Herbert Bayer trained as an architect/designer. He became a student of the Bauhaus in Weimar (1921-3), studying under both Kandinsky and MOHOLY-NAGY. In 1923 he was commissioned by the State Bank of Thuringia to design banknotes: the notes were designed using bold sans serif type, a radical departure from the norm and very much a preview of things to come.

When the Bauhaus moved to Dessau in 1925, Herbert Bayer, Marcel BREUER, Joost Schmidt and Josef Albers (all former students) were appointed teachers. Bayer was put in charge of the typography workshop, ▶ page 52

BASS

Saul Bass & Associates, logo
for Quaker Oats Company,
1971.

BASS Saul b.1920   American

graphic designer and film director

Pioneer of modern film title.

Saul Bass is one of the great names in American graphic
design; his firm has covered the full range of the design
spectrum, including a plethora of corporate identities
from the 1960s onwards that fashioned the "corporate
face" of modern America. With a location on Sunset
Boulevard over the past 40 years, it is not surprising
that his life has also been inextricably linked with the
film industry, and, in fact, that is where he has done his
greatest pioneering work, for he is regarded by many
as the inventor of the modern film title. He has also
designed special sequences for films, and directed
short films and television commercials.

Bass grew up in the Bronx, and studied at the
Art Students League in Manhattan (1936–9) and under
György KEPES at Brooklyn College (1944–5). He worked
for a while as a freelance designer and art director in
New York, then in the late 1940s headed for Los
Angeles, where he worked on advertising for motion
pictures. He soon became known in the movie world as
a bright new talent and by 1955, he had gone into
business on his own.

His groundbreaking activities began in 1954
with the film *Carmen Jones,* for which he created
poster graphics that carried over into the opening
sequence of the film. But it was in 1955 that Bass really
caused a sensation, with the graphics and animated
titles for Otto Preminger's motion picture *The Man
with the Golden Arm.* Whereas motion pictures had
traditionally been publicized with pictorial poster
imagery, Bass took off in a totally new direction. He
devised an emotionally charged pictographic image (a

Saul Bass, "trademark" for
The Magnificent Seven,
1960.

jagged arm, symbolizing the heroin addiction of the
main character) to convey the theme or essence of the
film. It became the main feature in an animated title
sequence (accompanied by bars, abstract forms, and
typography that interacted with jazz music), and was
also the identifying "still" used on cinema marquees,
posters and other forms of advertising. When the film
opened on Broadway in New York, only the trademark
of the film (the jagged arm) appeared on the marquee;
there were no words at all – no title, and no mention of
the film's stars Frank Sinatra and Kim Novak (that in
itself was a first in movieland). The film's title sequence

a side of life you never expected to see on the screen!

COLUMBIA PICTURES PRESENTS CHARLES K. FELDMAN'S

WALK ON THE WILD SIDE

a new kind of love-story starring

LAURENCE HARVEY
CAPUCINE
JANE FONDA
ANNE BAXTER
and **BARBARA STANWYCK** as "JO"

HEAR BROOK BENTON SING "WALK ON THE WILD SIDE"

WITH JOANNA MOORE Screenplay by JOHN FANTE & EDMUND MORRIS Based on the novel by NELSON ALGREN Produced by CHARLES K. FELDMAN Directed by EDWARD DMYTRYK A BLC RELEASE

Saul Bass, poster for the motion picture *A Walk on the Wild Side* (1962).

was a pioneering step for the world of "moving graphics", showing a powerful translation of two-dimensional graphics into kinetic form. It also marked the beginning of a collaboration between Preminger and Bass that continued for decades.

Bass went on to design credits or special sequences for over 35 films, including *Around the World in 80 Days* (1956); *Bonjour Tristesse* (1958); *Vertigo* (1958); *Anatomy of a Murder* (1959); *North by North West* (1959); *Exodus* (1960); *Psycho* (on which he was also visual consultant, 1960); *Spartacus* (also visual consultant, 1960); *West Side Story* (also visual consultant, 1961); *A Walk on the Wild Side* (1962); *Grand Prix* (also visual consultant and editor of the racing sequences, 1966); and many more. Many of the titles have become Hollywood classics in themselves, and it must be said that, in some cases, the Bass titles were better than the films. His collaborations with Alfred Hitchcock on the film *Psycho* are now a part of Hollywood legend. Bass designed and shot the opening titles (a model of schizophrenia), as well as the unforgettable shower sequence; he matted in the accelerated, time-lapsed clouds that raced so menacingly in the sky above the Bates house on the hill; he storyboarded all, and filmed part, of the sequence in which Martin Balsam falls backwards down the stairway to his death.

He has also designed and directed film shorts, as well as the feature film *Phase IV* (1974) a beautifully shot science fiction thriller in which ants become a life-threatening force. Most celebrated is the 1968 documentary short Bass made with his wife Elaine, entitled *Why Man Creates*, commissioned by Kaiser Aluminum and receiver of an Academy Award in 1969.

His flair for devising a single graphic concept around which to build film titles and publicity transferred easily into the realm of corporate design. Bass was one of the earliest and most distinguished practitioners of corporate identity in America, and since the 1960s has been responsible for the public face of such notable corporations as Alcoa Aluminum, American Telephone and Telegraph (AT&T, formerly the Bell System), Rockwell International, Continental Airlines, United Airlines, Warner Communications, Exxon, Minolta and the Celanese Corporation – as well as much-loved American institutions such as Quaker Oats and Dixie Cups.

The office of Saul Bass Associates became Bass/Yager & Associates in 1978, with the addition of Bass's younger, marketing-trained partner Herb Yager. Still occupying its Sunset Boulevard premises, the firm draws clients from all over the world, and still handles a wide range of work, with special emphasis on corporate identity programmes, packaging and films. What is more, having attracted new young design talent travelling to the West Coast over the years, it can claim credit for having fostered a couple of generations of top-level designers (some stayed, and others moved on to start new firms), and has more or less become an American institution in itself.

Saul Bass & Associates, logo for American Telephone and Telegraph, 1971.

B

Herbert Bayer, cover of the first issue of the journal *Bauhaus*, 1928.

and in this role his innovations were profound. A strong advocate of the sans serif, he argued strongly for a single alphabet without capitals, with the result that in 1925 the Bauhaus abandoned the use of capital letters in its publications. In that same year he designed a minimal, single-alphabet, sans serif typeface, composed purely from straight lines and a few select curves (now known as his Universal typeface). He designed posters, ephemera and the journal *Bauhaus* (first issue dated 1928) and was responsible, to a great extent, for the graphic identity we associate with the Bauhaus.

In 1928 Bayer left the Bauhaus and set up a design studio in Berlin, handling advertising, editorial design, display design and typography, and making heavy use of photomontage. Although not a Surrealist as such, he became heavily influenced by the dream-orientated imagery of Surrealism in the 1930s.

He emigrated to America in 1938 and immediately became involved in the design and collation of the Bauhaus exhibition at the Museum of Modern Art in New York. After working as art director for J. Walter Thompson (1944) and Dorland International (1944–6) he moved to Aspen, Colorado, and from that time worked as a consultant. In addition to graphics, he designed theatres, factories, museums, churches and other public environments. One of his most famous consultancies was for the Container Corporation of America (1946 onwards). He played a key role in their Great Ideas of Western Man project in 1950.

BEALL Lester 1903–69   American

graphic and industrial designer

Poster series for the Rural Electrification Administration; work on corporate identity systems.

Lester Beall was born in Kansas City, Missouri, and studied engineering at Lane Technical School in Chicago and art history at the University of Chicago. His studies provide an early indication of the two passions that were to interact throughout his career in graphics – the artist's love of creative freedom and the designer's love of precision, organization and discipline.

He set up his office in Chicago in 1927, working as a freelance advertising artist, then in 1935 moved to the more international climate of New York. There Beall was heavily influenced by artistic developments in Europe – Constructivism, the BAUHAUS, etc. Drawing inspiration from their experiments with type and photography, he developed his own highly unconventional style, distinguished by the use of woodcuts, drawings, flat abstract shapes, directional arrows and

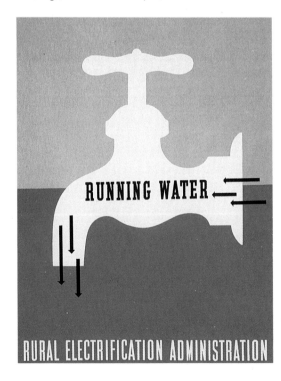

Lester Beall, poster design for the Rural Electrification Administration, 1937.

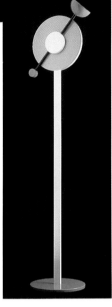

highly accentuated typographic devices, and all wielded with a freshness and liveliness that was still gently controlled. His famous poster series for the Rural Electrification Administration in the 1930s shows how his style enlivened the depiction of mundane objects, and at the same time overcame the constraints of limited colour.

In 1937 Beall's success was acknowledged when he became the first commercial designer to be honoured with a one-person exhibition at the Museum of Modern Art in New York. He continued to work independently in New York, designing a wide range of graphic material. Then, in 1951, he moved his design office to his farm in Connecticut, where he created an environment in which to pursue design as a total lifestyle; and there he remained until his death.

In addition to the Rural Electrification posters, Beall is well remembered for his designs for *Scope* magazine for the Upjohn Pharmaceutical Company; designs for *Collier's* and *Time* magazines; and his pioneering work in the area of corporate identity systems. Above all, he made a vital contribution to the development of American advertising design and corporate identity graphics, by demonstrating to industry that design made good business sense.

BECKER Friedrich b.1922   German

goldsmith

Design and craftsmanship of gold jewellery and church ware.

Professor Friedrich Becker is one of the world's most talented goldsmiths, who also works with precious stones. His designs include elaborate ornaments for the church. One example is a monstrance (a vessel for displaying the consecrated host) made in 1958. The vessel is supported by a sheaf of gold tubes which spring like fire from an ivory base and are jewelled with garnets, diamonds and rock crystal.

In his jewellery work Becker has explored several themes, but from the late 1960s onwards he has been especially interested in kinetic jewellery and sculpture. He has constructed geometric rings which have carefully weighted bars that rotate fluidly on micro-ballbearings. Sometimes the optical effect of a spinning surface is enhanced by the addition of precious stones set into the metal.

Becker's use of movement in goldsmithing has helped to revitalize an important decorative art.

Friedrich Becker.

Friedrich Becker, gold and diamond bracelet, 1981.

Through his work Becker was also one of those men in Germany who defended and expanded the skills of goldsmithing when fashion and the artistic avant-garde were hostile to the craft and its values.

BEDIN Martine b.1957   French

industrial designer

Vuitton luggage.

Bedin trained as an architect in Paris and went to Italy in 1978, working first with the group Super-studio, then with ALCHYMIA and, in 1981, the MEMPHIS group of Milan. Her work is as an industrial and product designer producing designs for furniture, lighting and accessories such as luggage for Louis Vuitton.

Martine Bedin, Charleston lamp for Memphis, 1984.

BEENE Geoffrey b.1927   American

fashion designer

Mens- and womenswear in soft, easy-care fabrics.

Beene studied at the Traphagen School of Design and then the Académie Julian in Paris. In 1963 the Geoffrey Beene Organization was founded, and became known for its crisp geometric garments and sophisticated Empire-line evening dresses. During the early 1970s Beene reassessed his design philosophy and has since become known for his fluid, comfortable, quality menswear and womenswear.

Beene designs many of his own textiles. He seeks to provide garments which require a minimum amount of care and has used fabrics which have inherent, woven wrinkles. He regularly uses mohair, which he admires because it is s ft, light and travels well, and wool jersey. Beene was one of the first designers to mix patterns and textures, and generally prefers dark and neutral colours.

Of his variously priced menswear collections, many are designed along the lines of sportswear, such as drawstring running trousers. His Beenebag Men range was introduced in 1971, and for this Beene has sought to break down the formality of men's work clothes. His garments are made in the conventional grey and navy of men's tailored suits, but the fabric is soft, malleable wool jersey.

Beene's 1989 and 1990 womenswear collections included elegant jumpsuits with candy-striped bodices, high-waisted trousers, quilted cotton bolero jackets and fitted jersey shift dresses.

Geoffrey Beene, evening dress with gold back and trim, spring/summer 1990.

BEHRENS

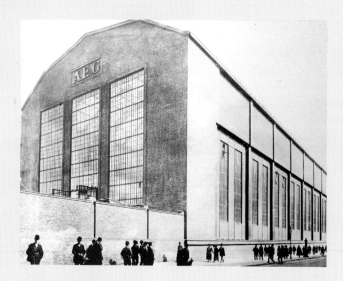

Peter Behrens, AEG factory, 1908–09.

BEHRENS Peter 1868–1940   German

architect and designer in various media

Designs for AEG electrical company.

Peter Behrens was born into an affluent Hamburg family. He studied painting in Karlsruhe and Düsseldorf before moving to Munich in 1890. He helped set up the Munich Vereinigte Werkstätten für Kunst im Handwerk in 1896, and three years later was invited to join the Mathildenhöhe artists' colony, established by Grand Duke Ernst Ludwig II von Hesse in Darmstadt. His Haus Peter Behrens at Darmstadt (1901) was widely acclaimed, and he exhibited at the 1902 Turin International Exhibition. While Director of the Düsseldorf Kunstgewerbeschule from 1903 to 1907, he supplied publicity and packaging designs to the Berlin electrical company AEG, and from 1907 to 1914 he was the firm's architect and all-round aesthetic adviser, designing their turbine factory in 1908–09 as well as a wide variety of functional objects. Together with other architects, designers and manufacturers, Behrens was closely associated with the Deutscher Werkbund, the organization committed to high-quality design for industry that was founded in 1907. From 1922 to 1936 he taught architecture at the Vienna Academy of Art, and later at the Berlin Academy.

During his long and rich career, which spanned curvilinear *Jugendstil* and rectilinear modernism, Behrens proved an eclectic, at times highly innovative industrial designer: foremost among his novel creations were electric kettles for AEG. These were offered in a number of different forms, based on varying combinations of a limited number of standardized elements in a range of materials and finishes. He was also a prolific designer of graphics, glass, fabric, jewellery, pottery, silverware, furniture, typefaces and book bindings. His early furniture and interiors tended to be in the gently curving *Jugendstil* mode, and some were even opulently neo-classical. But a confirmed sense of modernism imbued his 20th-century pieces and rooms, such as those for toy-maker W.J. Bassett-Lowke's Northampton house, New Ways, in the mid-1920s, which also recalled the Vienna Secession (Behrens was teaching in the Austrian capital at the time). Today he is best remembered for his crisp, proto-modern metalwork designs for AEG – eminently practical yet handsome examples of mass-production made to a high standard – as well as for being the employer-teacher of LE CORBUSIER, GROPIUS and MIES VAN DER ROHE.

Peter Behrens, electric kettle for AEG, 1908.

Peter Behrens, electric fan for AEG, 1908.

BEL GEDDES Norman 1893–1958 · American

industrial designer

Visionary ideas and "streamline" styling.

Norman Bel Geddes was one of the first designers to set up in practice as a consultant, and the first to achieve public recognition. He first caught the public's attention through the stage set he designed for a hit Broadway play in 1923.

Bel Geddes started his career as an artist and illustrator, and later worked in the theatre and as a window-display designer for New York shops; window display offered new opportunities to designers.

He began working as an industrial designer in the late 1920s, though few of his projects and ideas led to commercially produced designs. He is famous for his association with the design in 1929 of the Toledo Scale – a weighing-machine for shops commissioned by the Toledo Scale Company. But another designer, Harold VAN DOREN, designed the version of the scale that eventually went into production.

Bel Geddes also designed prototype cars for the Graham Paige company, radios for PHILCO and RCA and ship interiors. During the Second World War his consultancy made models of battles and military equipment.

His visions of the future were spelt out in two

Norman Bel Geddes and Otto Kuhler, model for the Super Airliner 4, 1929.

books – *Horizons* (1932) and *Magic Motorways* (1940). He foresaw the motorway system, and on the stand he designed for General Motors at the New York World's Fair (1939–40), he exhibited plans and models of the streamlined vehicles that were part of his scheme.

Bel Geddes is credited with popularizing streamlining. Streamlining – shaping vehicles with broad "noses" and narrow "tails" in order, as was hoped, to facilitate movement – is an idea that originated in aerodynamics research. Bel Geddes adopted the principles of streamlining to create new shapes and styles for cars, buses and ships.

Eliot NOYES, a designer who later achieved notoriety for his work with IBM, worked for Bel Geddes in the late 1940s.

BELLINI Mario b.1935 · Italian

industrial designer and architect

Typewriters (for Olivetti) and furniture (for Cassina, Vitra).

Mario Bellini studied architecture at Milan Politechnico, and still practises architecture along with the main focus of his career, which has been industrial and furniture design. In 1973, Bellini set up Studio Bellini in Milan for industrial design.

Since 1968 he has been consultant designer to Olivetti and has worked on a variety of products for the company, including the Logos and Divisumma calculators and numerous typewriters notably the ET 101 electronic typewriters, which established a new typeform. Bellini was one of the first to explore the possibilities of the new micro-circuitry and he designed strong, new sculptural forms that have been imitated the world over.

His working practice is unusual in that he does not draw his designs, but communicates them directly to his model-maker, who interprets his ideas in a three-dimensional form.

Among his more notable furniture designs is the Cab side chair for CASSINA (1977) – a steel frame completely covered in a stitched leather skin.

Bellini was among the first to seek to design a chair for the office which is technologically and ergonomically efficient but which does not look like a machine. His Figura chair is fabric-covered; levers have been banished and there are just release buttons under the seat. It is claimed to have been the first office chair to mould itself to each occupant.

Bellini has also worked in automotive design and has been a consultant to Renault since 1978. He says, "I'm not interested in considering an object as an isolated item. It is part of a wider system of objects, structures and spaces, that work together as part of our environment as a whole".

Since 1986 Bellini has been editor-in-chief of the Italian design and architecture magazine *Domus*.

Mario Bellini, leather and steel Corium 1 chair, first made by Matteo Grassi in 1978.

BENSON W.A.S. 1854–1924 · British

architect, metalwork and furniture designer

Director of Morris and Co. and co-founder of craft and design groups.

London-born William Arthur Smith Benson studied at Winchester and Oxford, and in 1878, his last year at

B

Oxford, he was articled to the architect Basil Champneys. The painter and etcher Heywood Sumner, with whom Benson shared lodgings, introduced him to the painter Edward Burne-Jones, through whom he met William Morris. The latter was the main impetus behind Benson's setting up a metal workshop in Hammersmith around 1880 and, some three years later, a larger factory in Chiswick, the Eyot works.

His Bond Street shop began trading in 1887, and his handsome, utilitarian pieces made of copper, brass, electroplate and occasionally silver – teapots, platters, chafing dishes, warming trays, jugs, andirons, lamps, fenders and the like – were sold there and elsewhere. Also in the 1880s, Benson designed furniture for art nouveau cabinetmakers J.S. Henry & Co. and for Morris and Co., as well as producing decorative metal mounts for the latter. His furniture designs were distinguished for their exotic-wood inlays and, not surprisingly, their elaborate metal hinges, pulls, etc. Metal fireplaces and grates were also made to Benson's design by the Falkirk and Coalbrookdale iron companies. Upon Morris's death in 1896, Benson was named a director of Morris and Co., and he continued to design furniture as well as wallpaper for the firm.

Unlike other Arts and Crafts exponents, Benson was not averse to machine production and was in fact quite interested in studying and advancing mechanical and engineering processes, especially in the production of his metalwork. Throughout his career, Benson was active in and committed to the advancement of crafts and design, and to the co-operation of artists and manufacturers, helping to found the Art-Workers' Guild in 1884, the Arts and Crafts Exhibition Society in 1888 and the Design and Industries Association (England's response to the Deutscher Werkbund) in 1914. He also wrote two books: *Elements of Handicraft and Design* (1893) and *Drawing, Its History and Uses* (published posthumously in 1925).

W. A. S. Benson, silver-plated gas lamp with silk shade, *c.*1900.

BERTOIA Harry 1915–78　　　　Italian-American

sculptor, jewellery and furniture designer

Diamond chair.

Bertoia, born in Italy, studied at the CRANBROOK Academy of Art, Bloomfield Hills, Michigan, in 1937. In 1939 he set up a metal workshop and taught metalsmithing and jewellery.

In 1943 he joined Charles EAMES (also a Cranbrook graduate) in California working on aircraft and

medical equipment for the Evans Product System, and together they experimented with moulded plywood seating. Bertoia set up a studio in Pennsylvania in 1950, working in collaboration with Florence and Hans KNOLL (founders of what is now known as Knoll International, a leading design-orientated furniture manufacturer). The most famous of the designs he produced there is the Diamond Chair, which is almost the motif of contemporary 1950s style – a sort of modernist *moderne.* This chair, of welded-steel latticework on a pivoting mechanism, appeared in 1952. It became popular with designers and architects because its open latticework made it look airy and light and wholly appropriate for open-plan interiors.

From the mid-1950s onwards, Bertoia concentrated upon sculpture.

Harry Bertoia, diamond-lattice chair for Knoll International, 1952.

BERTONE Flaminio b.1903　　　　see CITROEN

BERTONE Giuseppe ("Nuccio") b.1914　　　　Italian

car designer

Alfa Romeo Giulietta Sprint and Citroën BX.

Bertone became manager of his father's firm, a body shop, and from it created an automobile design studio. His early interest in motor-racing gave him invaluable insights into aerodynamics, coding and balance – knowledge that was later to contribute to his designs for high-performance cars. Among the apprentices of his studio have been Giorgio GIUGIARO, the designer of the famous 1974 Volkswagen Golf, and Marcello Gandini. Bertone's designs include the Alfa Romeo Giulietta Sprint (1954) of which 35,000 were produced, the Lamborghini Miura (1966), the Ferrari Dino 308 (1966) and the British Leyland Innocenti Mini (1974). He also produced the Citroën BX in 1982.

BILL Max b.1908   Swiss

painter, sculptor and architect

Student of the Bauhaus, criticized the development of modern design.

Born in Winterthur, Switzerland, Bill studied at the Zurich Art School and the BAUHAUS in Dessau (1927–9). He worked in private practice and lectured in Europe and in both north and south America.

In 1951 he became rector of the Hochschule für Gestaltung, Ulm, West Germany, an institution set up by a private foundation to revive the spirit and purpose of GROPIUS's original Bauhaus. Bill designed the school's buildings (1953–5) and ran it until his resignation in 1956.

Bill felt the contradiction between the rigorous principles of the BAUHAUS and designing for a consumer society. He was also critical of the way in which modernism had developed, and in a well-known lecture in 1954 he attacked what he saw as the stylistic formalism of contemporary Brazilian architecture. He defined architecture as a social art that should not be subject to "style".

He has designed private houses and offices. In 1985 he became the chairman of the Bauhaus Archive in Berlin, a post which he still holds.

Max Bill, design for his own house.

BLACK Misha 1910–1977   British

industrial designer

Exhibition design and design education.

Misha Black was born in Baku, Russia but moved to Britain as a young child. He trained as an architect and in his early career concentrated on exhibition design.

Black was an active member of the design community all his life. In the early 1930s he was a member of the Artists' International Association, an anti-war movement and in 1938 he was secretary to the Modern Architecture Research (MARS) Group.

Black designed radios and a television cabinet for E.K. Cole (EKCO), the pioneering manufacturing company that invited designers like Black, Serge CHERMAYEFF and Wells COATES to explore the possibilities of the new plastics.

During the Second World War, Black worked as an exhibition designer for the Ministry of Information. In 1943 Black and fellow Ministry designer Milner GRAY set up the Design Research Unit (DRU), which grew to be a hugely successful international design practice.

Black was chief exhibition designer for Britain Can Make It, a 1946 exhibition at the Victoria and Albert Museum and designed part of the Festival of Britain exhibition in 1951. He also designed the Kardomah cafés in London and Manchester, rolling stock and stations for the Victoria Line and the interiors of London buses.

In 1959 he became Professor of Industrial Design (Engineering) at the Royal College of Art and is credited with setting a model for design education. He was knighted in 1972.

Misha Black, cover design for the magazine *Everyman*.

BLAHNIK Manolo b.1940   Spanish-born

shoe designer

Luxurious and fantastical shoe designs.

Blahnik studied art and literature at Geneva University before briefly moving to Paris in 1968. He then prepared a portfolio of extravagant theatre designs, which he showed in London and New York. His shoe designs were much admired and Diana Vreeland, as editor of *Vogue*, put him in touch with an Italian shoemaker who produced his fantastical designs. Blahnik acknowledges a debt to the leading footwear designer Yanturni, whose elegant brocaded and buckled shoes he saw at an exhibition while a young boy.

He produced his first collection in 1971, the

B

year in which he opened his Chelsea shop, and has established an international reputation for his use of seductive, luxurious materials, such as soft leathers, silks and lace and ornate accessories, such as pearl and diamond buckles. His designs are provocative, inventive and highly influential. Some of his shoe clasps have been fashioned in the form of fruits and foliage. Others have shown the influence of Surrealism, such as the yellow and bright green leather glove shoes (1982) and his Siamese twin designs (1989). He has also had his shoes photographed in a surreal manner by Michael Roberts. Blahnik has designed for numerous leading fashion houses including Ossie CLARK, Jean MUIR, Zandra RHODES, Calvin KLEIN and Yves SAINT LAURENT .

BODY MAP founded 1982   British

fashion company

Bold, patterned, wearable fashions since 1984.

Body Map's founders Stevie Stewart and David Hollah (both b. 1958) set up their business from a market stall in London, selling old army-surplus clothes which they re-styled and dyed in strong colours. The money raised financed their first major collection, humorously called Cat in a Hat Takes a Rumble with a Techno Fish.

Body Map clothes are essentially eccentric but wearable, the design inspiration having evolved from their individual approach to pattern-cutting whereby they aim to re-invent shapes and sculpt materials. Their greatest influence lies in their leggings, mini-skirts, shorts, skirts that flare from the knee down, and T-shirts. The clothes are unstructured and multi-layered. Body Map's much-copied geometric and graphic printed textiles are designed by Hilde Smith. White, black and cream predominate, although forays into the realms of bad taste have exploited dayglo colours and Lurex. This was most apparent in the 1984 collection, Barbie Takes a Trip Around Nature's Cosmic Curves. Financial difficulties resulted in closure in 1986, but Body Map was back in business by 1987.

Body Map's monochrome fashion, spring/summer 1985.

BOEKHOUDT Onno b.1944   Dutch

jeweller and sculptor

Jewellery both for wearing and as art object.

Boekhoudt studied at the Vakschool, Schoonhoven, and the Kunst- und Werkschule, Pforzheim. He now teaches at the Rietveld Akademie.

Boekhoudt's jewellery is in the spirit of the De Stijl design movement, for, although it is not geometrical, it retains a natural quality which comes from keeping some of the attractiveness found in worked metal just before its edges and surfaces are finally honed up and polished. During the 1980s he has produced collections of small objects, and one object in each collection is a piece of jewellery for wearing. When it is not worn it retains its life as art object through its association with the other objects. This notion of keeping the jewellery object "alive" when it is not being worn has stimulated a great deal of thinking among modern jewellers. Typical of Boekhoudt's work are rings with objects in silver, copper and steel.

Boekhoudt remarked that his ambition was to "give the material so much value that it is swollen with vanity and begins to speak".

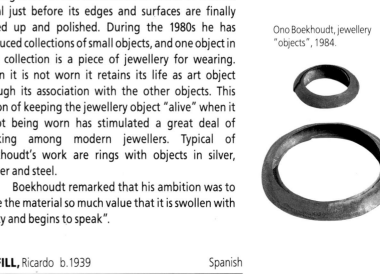

Ono Boekhoudt, jewellery "objects", 1984.

BOFILL, Ricardo b.1939   Spanish

architect

Xanadu, Barrio Gaudí, Les Arcades du Lac, Palace of Abraxas.

In the tradition of great Catalonians such as Salvador Dali and Antoni GAUDÍ, Ricardo Bofill produces work which is distinctly surreal. With his Taller de Arquitectura Bofill has worked on a number of massive public housing schemes in the 1970s and 1980s, most of which are in France. The structures resemble classical palaces and yet are constructed on modest budgets using concrete and glass.

Among Bofill's early work was the Barrio Gaudí at Reus, Spain (1964–70). This was a mini-city composed of housing clusters built in cubes on many different levels, some with pitched, tiled roofs and some with flat roofs providing walkways.

Ricardo Bofill, Palace of Abraxas, Marne la Vallée, 1978–82.

Also in the late 1960s, Bofill used the cluster idea again for a block of seaside apartments called Xanadu at Calpe, Spain (1967). Looking like a large version of "the house that Jack built", the stepped block is an irregular jumble of 17 apartments, complete with sloping tiled roofs on the top and over the rooms, which protrude at different angles and heights around the central core.

Bofill's mastery at creating something special from meagre resources was clearly demonstrated when, with the Taller, he designed a "pyramid" to mark the Spanish/French border at the Parc de la Marca Hispanica (1974–76). The monument was built using earth and materials left over from the construction of a new motorway. And again his ingenuity was shown at his own studio in Barcelona, housed in a converted cement factory (1972–6).

Bofill's recent work has been concentrated in the Paris suburbs with public housing schemes including Les Arcades du Lac (1974–81), the Palace of Abraxas (1978–82) and Les Echelles du Baroque (1983–6).

At a time when there was considerable public hostility to modern architecture Bofill received many commissions for his playful use of classicism. All his housing projects have borrowed heavily from the architecture of ancient Greece and Rome, and yet, while they appear to be enormous, stone-built palaces, complete with arcaded walk-ways, pilasters, rusticated stonework and neat, rectangular windows, they are in fact constructed of concrete.

STUDIO BOGGERI founded 1933   Italian

`graphic design firm`

Leading force in Italian graphic design from the 1930s.

In 1933 the graphic design firm Studio Boggeri was founded in Milan, and it has remained one of the great names in the Italian design world. Antonio Boggeri (b. 1900), its founder, is best known for leading the Studio from 1933 to 1981, as well as for his own experimental work in photography, reflected in the products of the studio. Under his leadership, Studio Boggeri was noted for its warm, elegant and humanist approach to design which contrasted heavily with the coldness and severity of the work of the Swiss/German schools of the same period.

Well-known Swiss and Italian designers who have worked within or collaborated with the Studio

include Walter Ballmer, Aldo Calabresi, Erberto Garboni, Franco GRIGNANI, Max Huber, Bruno Monguzzi, Bruno Munari, Bob Noorda and Roberto Sambonet (who often collaborates with Monguzzi in the area of exhibition design).

The Studio and its projects have been documented in a number of books, notably *Lo Studio Boggeri 1933–1973* (ed. Paolo Fossati, introduction by Herbert Bayer, Milan 1974) and *Lo Studio Boggeri 1933–1981* (ed. Bruno Monguzzi, with texts by Franco Origoni and Giovanni Anceschi, Milan 1981); it has also been the subject of many articles in international journals.

Studio Boggeri, promotional design for Olivetti by Xanti Schawinsky (above).

Studio Boggeri, promotional design for Bayer by Bruno Monguzzi (above left).

BONETTI Mattia b.1953   see GAROUSTE

BONETTO Rodolfo b.1929   Italian

`industrial designer`

Car design for Pininfarina and Fiat; innovatory use of plastic moulding.

Rodolfo Bonetto started his design career in the Pininfarina car design studio. He founded his own studio in 1958. Although Bonetto is best known among industrial designers for his work with automobiles, his work has embraced domestic appliances, furniture, and industrial machinery. His clients have included Driade, Siemens and Olivetti. He has won the Compaso d'Oro award several times, his first being gained in 1964 for the Sfericlock alarm clock for the Italian company Borletti.

He taught at the Hochschule für Gestaltung at

B

ULM (1961–5), the seat of functionalist design. Bonetto, however, tempers his rationalist approach with humour and colour. For example, he designed a plastic sectional table called the Quattroquarti which can be rearranged in different configurations. Produced between 1970 and 1978, it is brightly coloured and has a sinuous, graceful line.

Bonetto's particular talent is in the use of plastic moulding. He won much acclaim for the single-piece mouldings used in the interior he designed for the Fiat 132 Bellini.

Fiat 132 Bellini for which Rodolfo Bonetto designed the interior plastic mouldings.

BOTTA Mario b.1943   Swiss

architect

Staatsbank, Fribourg; Ransila 1 Building, Lugano.

Mario Botta was apprenticed to an architectural firm (Tita Carloni and Luigi Camenisch) when he was 15 and later studied architecture at the University Institute of Architecture in Venice. Botta was influenced by the ideas on "organic" architecture as developed by Bruno Zevi, an architect and critic who came to prominence in the early 1950s in Italy.

Botta's early buildings show a preference for materials such as rough hewn stone and later, even when his use of "natural" materials gave way to concrete and brick, Botta has continued to create lively surfaces. Some of his buildings, such as family houses designed in the 1960s, have strong echoes of Le Corbusier's work but gradually Botta developed his own style which includes a liking for the tower, the cylinder, the circle and the atrium.

During the 1980s Botta has had several major commissions (such as the Staatsbank in Fribourg) which have allowed him to experiment with the challenge of making a new building fit into and exploit an urban landscape. One of the most striking examples of this work is the Ransila 1 Building, Lugano (1985).

Botta has also ventured into furniture design in which he has favoured metal frames and metal lattices.

BRANDT Edgar 1880–1960   French

metalworker

Ornamental ironwork of the 1920s making use of modern techniques.

A Parisian with Alsatian roots, Brandt was a science student who at a young age became apprenticed to noted ironworker Emile Robert. Early creations included both silver jewellery and larger ironwork, for which he began winning recognition in the Paris Salons from 1905. In 1919 Brandt opened his own atelier (on the site of his father's old arms works), and the 1920s brought him numerous public and private commissions, and considerable acclaim as the premier *ferronnier* working in the art deco mode. His working methods were modern but meticulous, producing handsome, almost seamless products by means of new machines and technologies heretofore unavailable to the metalworker.

Brandt's workshops produced, among other pieces, radiator grilles and covers, firescreens, and-irons, mirror frames, console tables, pedestals, jardinières and table, floor and wall lamps. At the 1925 Exposition des Arts Décoratifs et Industriels Modernes in Paris, his many contributions included the Porte d'Honneur (which, because of its ephemerality, was made not of expensive wrought iron but of a cheap alloy with aluminium finish), gates for Ruhlmann's *Hôtel du Collectionneur,* and his own ornamental metal-filled showroom, which featured his master-work, *L'Oasis,* a five-panel wrought-iron and brass screen that was a veritable compendium of art deco motifs. In 1925–6 Brandt opened showrooms in both Paris and New York; the latter, Ferrobrandt, Inc., was run by Jules Bouy and the objects it displayed were to inspire many ornamental ironworkers in America.

Public projects included the Eternal Flame of the Tomb of the Unknown Soldier in Paris, the gate for the new French Embassy in Brussels and a staircase in the Louvre.

Edgar Brandt, wrought-iron wall lamp, c.1925.

BRAUN founded 1921   German

manufacturer of electrical products

One of the most influential arbiters of taste in modern consumer societies.

Braun was founded in 1921 by Max Braun for the manufacture of radios and record-players. However it was not until Braun's sons, Artur and Erwin, took over

Braun electric shaver.

the company in 1951 that the business began to assume its present identity.

In the same year Fritz Eichler (b. 1911), a former theatre designer, was appointed design director. His first initiative was to establish design as the Braun philosophy and identity. One of Eichler's first appointments was Otl AICHER, as consultant on graphics and exhibition design.

It was Eichler who introduced Braun to the work of the Hochschule für Gestaltung in ULM; this resulted in a fruitful collaboration, culminating in the 1955 Braun Phonosuper SK4 record player.

The designers of the Phonosuper were Hans GUGELOT, director of product design at Ulm, and Dieter RAMS. True to the design philosophy of Ulm, the SK4 was a pure expression of the function it was to perform and of the technology. Braun was henceforth credited with having created a new aesthetic for modern design, one that divorced itself from art.

Braun electrical appliances are designed as innovative instruments for domestic use which have a strong "family" resemblance. Rams, design director since 1956, comments that Braun products shed all that is superfluous to emphasize what is important.

BRETTEVILLE Sheila Levrant de b.1940   American
graphic designer and typographer

Publication design, typography, promotion of women's culture and creative expression.

Sheila Levrant de Bretteville, wall commemorating the life and work of Biddy Mason, 1990.

Sheila de Bretteville holds a master's degree in graphic design from Yale University's School of Art, and operates her own studio in Los Angeles. She has received many design and typography awards, but she com-

mands even greater respect as one of the few high-ranking American designers who has managed to combine social and political attitudes with design.

Feminism and a commitment to women's creative expression provided an early inspiration for graphic products, lectures, writings, and the development of programmes and facilities that previously didn't exist. In 1971 she created the Women's Design Program at the California Institute of the Arts – the first course of its kind, dedicated to exploring the relationship between feminism and design. Two years later she co-founded and directed the Woman's Building, a public centre for women's culture in Los Angeles. Within it, she created the Women's Graphic Center, providing teaching and print facilities to women who previously had had access to neither. Both facilities grew and prospered under her direction into the 1990s.

Much of her studio work has continued to deal with social themes. Women's rights, the multi-ethnic community, the plight of the elderly and other issues have appeared in a wide range of forms – from small personal projects to large public endeavours (such as her 1989 80ft-long poured concrete wall, to commemorate Biddy Mason – black woman/slave/midwife/philanthropist and extraordinary figure in the 19th-century history of Los Angeles). Her more recent educational work includes positions as Chair of Communication and Design at Otis/Parsons School of Design in Los Angeles (1982–90) and, from 1990, Director of Graduate Studies in Graphic Design at Yale University School of Art.

BREUER Marcel 1902–81   Hungarian-American
architect, furniture and industrial designer

Wassily tubular steel chair.

Born in Hungary, Breuer trained at the BAUHAUS (1920-5). He is known primarily as a designer of furniture, although during his time in America, where he lived from 1937, he worked as an architect and industrial designer. In 1955, for example, he designed a diesel railcar for the Budd Company. But it is for his chromium-plated tubular steel chairs of the 1920s such as his Wassily chair that he is most famous.

The Wassily chair has been copied and reproduced for 60 years, and its design roots are to be found in another designer's work – the Red and Blue Chair of Gerrit RIETVELD. Rietveld's chair (1917) was

Marcel Breuer.

B

built from wood slats and planks. Breuer's Wassily chair (designed for Wassily Kandinsky) uses leather sheets suspended between a tubular steel structure.

Similarly, Breuer adapted the ideas of another designer, those of Mart STAM, in a series of cantilevered chairs. The cantilevered chair was first conceived by Stam in 1924 and reworked by Ludwig MIES VAN DER ROHE in 1927; Breuer's final version appeared in 1928. This springy design, popular among designers and architects as a dining-chair, epitomizes for many people what the modern interior should contain.

Of Breuer's other furniture work, perhaps his laminated plywood chair, designed for the Isokon Furniture Company (UK) in 1935, is the most famous. It is a form of *chaise-longue,* and makes use of the ideas of Alvar AALTO.

Caroline Broadhead, Veil necklace/headpiece made from nylon monofilament, 1983.

BROADHEAD Caroline b.1950   British

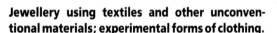
jewellery

Jewellery using textiles and other unconventional materials; experimental forms of clothing.

Caroline Broadhead studied at the Central School of Art in London. Her early work involved colouring ivory, but she became interested in less restrictive materials. By 1977 she was producing bound-cotton necklaces, and in 1978 she devised an influential design whereby a wearer pushed his or her hand through tufts of nylon held in place in a wood or silver frame.

Broadhead was one of the leaders of the new jewellery movement in Europe that flourished from around 1968 and petered out in the mid-1980s. It was a movement that employed design and art, and later performance art, to break the conventions of traditional jewellery. Exotic or traditionally valuable materials such as gold, silver and precious gems were rejected in favour of plastic, paper, rubber and cloth.

Broadhead was one of the first of the new jewellers in Europe to use textiles, and her use of bright colour can be seen as a continuation of the pioneering work of the West German avant-garde.

In the 1980s, with other young British women jewellers such as Catherine Mannheim and Susannah Heron, she produced a series of "wearables" – jewellery-cum-clothing-cum-wearable sculpture. One of her most famous and beautiful pieces is a veil or headpiece – a woven cylinder of light-coloured plastic thread. This work probably looks at its best when worn by a model and in a photograph.

None the less, much of Broadhead's work is ingenious, beautiful and flattering. As the 1980s progressed she produced less jewellery as such, and turned to "clothing" such as her "shirt with seven necks, shirt with seven sleeves". More recently she has stated: "My work has moved from jewellery to clothing. . .forms of clothing have a greater scope for expression. . ."

BRODOVITCH Alexey 1898–1971   American

graphic designer and magazine art director

Art director of *Harper's Bazaar* for 25 years.

Born in Russia, Alexey Brodovitch worked in Paris during the 1920s designing books, posters, furnishings and advertising. He emigrated to America in 1930 and, after a short period of teaching and advertising work, became art director of *Harper's Bazaar* magazine in New York. In this role from 1934 to 1958 he revolutionized American magazine design.

His work for *Harper's* was sensitive and intuitive; type, image and colour were handled with flair and artistic daring, rather than being subjected to the constraints of a stylistic or academic mould. But the real revolution was in the use of photography and type. Brodovitch commissioned photography from the European avant-garde with startling results; cropped photographs in a totally new way; encouraged his photographers to compose shots as full-frame pages; and made use of illusory effects such as size contrast to create a sense of depth within the page. Type was always sympathetic with the photography, but was allowed a movement and beauty of its own. Captions and paragraphs with absurdly ragged edges (creating

Alexey Brodovitch, advertising design, 1933.

long, stringlike wisps across the page) were one of his hallmarks. Issues of *Harper's Bazaar* that were produced during Brodovitch's regime have become a historical design study in themselves – haunting photographs by Man Ray are to be found there, as well as illustrations by a young Andy Warhol.

In 1950, in co-operation with Frank Zachery, Brodovitch also produced and designed another of the major magazine accomplishments of that era – a large-format showcase for graphic design entitled *Portfolio* (a sumptuous magazine, with no advertising).

Brodovitch taught and lectured in a number of schools including Yale, Pratt, etc., but his main educational role came in the teaching of a seminar course known as the Design Laboratory. The Laboratory existed in the Philadelphia Museum School of Industrial Art from 1936, then the New School for Social Research in New York in the 1940s, and other venues as time went on. Brodovitch's students included photographers Irving Penn, Richard Avedon and Art Kane.

BRODY Neville b.1957   British

graphic designer

Art director of *The Face* magazine.

Neville Brody rose to fame on the wave of "designerism" that marked the early to mid-1980s: a time when the economy was seen to be expanding; marketing, promotion and "cultural enterprise" were in the air; and youth culture was a money spinner. Within this media-conscious scenario Neville Brody became Britain's first international graphic design superstar.

Brody attended the London College of Printing from 1977 to 1980. He worked initially for Alex McDowell's design company Rocking Russian, then for Stiff Records and Fetish Records. From 1981 he was art director of *The Face,* one of the most important style magazines of the decade; it reached its heyday from 1983 to 1985. His hallmark was an unconventional and experimental use of type (influenced by the Constructivist work of LISSITZKY and RODCHENKO) and, in particular, the creation and use of specially drawn logos, symbols and typefaces, which acted as visual codes for the magazine's cult audience. Under Brody's art direction the magazine received international acclaim and his work initiated a typographic revolution among young designers in Britain, characterized by a new interest in the creative possibilities of type, as well as a growing breed of Brody imitators.

Neville Brody, poster for Touch, 1987.

In addition to *The Face* magazine, Brody also at that time designed record album sleeves for various rock groups; logos for organizations such as Red Wedge (a grouping of young people allied to the Labour Party) and Artists Against Apartheid; redesigns for *City Limits* and *New Socialist* magazines; and a host of other projects. His prolific output was placed on public view in1988, when he was honoured (at the age of 31) with a retrospective exhibition held at the Victoria & Albert Museum in London. At the same time he launched a book of his collected work, *The Graphic Language of Neville Brody* (Thames & Hudson), which became one of the best-selling art books of 1988.

Brody continues to run his own studio in London, and recent activities include art direction for *Arena* magazine; designs for Swatch watches (due for release in late 1990); the design of retail outlets for Post, a new agency which handles all forms of three-dimensional design, and which he co-partners; and a growing amount of work for clients in Japan, including corporate design and projects for fashion, music and publishing companies.

BURTIN Cipe Pineles b.1910   American

graphic designer and magazine art director

First woman to make her mark in magazine art direction in USA.

Cipe Pineles Burtin was born in Austria-Hungary, emigrated to America in 1923, and thereafter studied

Cipe Pineles Burtin.

B

at the Pratt Institute in New York. She embarked on a career in magazine art direction in the early 1930s, when the profession was almost totally populated by men.

Starting at Condé Nast in New York as assistant to the highly acclaimed Dr M. F. Agha, she worked on *Vogue* and *Vanity Fair*, both of which set new standards. On the basis of this work, she was admitted as first woman member of the Art Directors Club.

For over 20 years she directed a variety of magazines, including *Seventeen, Glamour, Charm* and *Mademoiselle.* She left publishing in 1959 and became an independent design consultant, and later the first art director for the Lincoln Center of the Performing Arts (1965–72). She was also a faculty member at Parsons School of Design in New York from 1963, and became their Director of Publication Design in 1970. Under her guidance, Parsons School of Design publicity material achieved great renown in the 1970s and 1980s, including the "fruit mailers" of 1980 for the Parsons branch in New York (The Big Apple), Los Angeles (The Big Orange), and at the American College in Paris (The Big Grape). Her editorial design class produced a book on New York's bread industry which was published in 1974 as the *Parsons Bread Book* by Harper and Row, and was chosen as one of the 50 best books of that year by the American Institute of Graphic Arts.

Will Burtin.

BURTIN Will 1908–72   American

graphic and exhibition designer

Educational exhibitions interpreting science to the public.

Will Burtin was born and educated in Germany, and trained as a typographer. He emigrated to America in 1938, working initially as a freelance designer in New York City. During the war he designed training manuals and other graphic material for the US Army Air Force and the Office of Strategic Services, and later became art director of *Fortune* magazine (1945–49). In his hands, *Fortune* became one of America's most distinguished magazines.

After 1949, Burtin opened his own office. Working for various industries, he embarked on the long-term personal mission of attempting to explain scientific theories and subjects to a broader audience (namely, the general public) – and ultimately, building a bridge between science and art. To this end, he became expert at communicating with scientists, and interpreting their knowledge in visual form. His efforts were displayed in the design of *Scope*, a magazine for physicians that broke new ground in the presentation of scientific data.

But the two-dimensional innovations soon became three-dimensional, and Burtin progressed to educational exhibitions – building giant models that made use of electronics, films, slides and other devices to aid communication. Most famous were a giant model of the human brain, showing how the brain functions; and a model of a human cell that was large enough to walk through.

Burtin's models were particularly remarkable in that they were not just enlargements of existing images or objects. They were the visualization of processes not perceivable to the eye – a product of his imagination, but informed by science.

BUTLER Nick b.1942   British

product designer

Founder of BIB Design Consultants, and designer of the Durabeam torch.

Nick Butler's reputation as an industrial designer has been bound up with the company he co-founded in 1967, BIB Design Consultants. He trained in industrial design at the Leeds School of Art and subsequently as a postgraduate at the Royal College of Art. His interest has always been to combine product aesthetic and functionality with a sound background in engineering. So when Butler founded BIB, he equipped the consultancy with the modelmaking facilities and the skills of specialists in material and production processes to ensure involvement in the design of the whole product, both inside and out.

Although BIB designs specialist products for medical and industrial fields, it is for products designed for the consumer market that BIB (and therefore Butler) has built its reputation. For instance, the Durabeam torch, which delivered Duracell a 30-per-cent share of the flashlight market, was for a long time presented by industry commentators as an example of good product design. Other examples of BIB's work for which Butler has been responsible include: the Minolta 7000 camera, Dunhill pens, the British Telecom Tribune telephone, JCB earth-moving equipment, the Agenda Electronic Diary and the Racal Decca range of electronic navigation equipment.

Will Burtin, Vision '65 and Vision '67 brochures.

C

CAPUCCI Roberto b.1919 — Italian

fashion designer

Adventurous designs during the 1960s; also a master of line and cut.

Capucci studied at the Accademia delle Belle Arti in Rome and then worked for the designer Emilio Schuberth. He opened his own house in 1951 and gained a reputation for his magnificent and daring fashions. In 1962 Capucci moved to Paris. He was at the peak of his profession throughout the 1960s when he became known for his flamboyant use of Mediterranean colours and his inventive work with fabrics and sculptural form: for example, he produced experimental garments which consisted of sealed plastic filled with coloured water. He was also respected for the skilful cut of his clothing.

In 1969 he returned to Rome, where his first collection was inspired by the Pre-Raphaelite painters, and a subsequent one consisted of garments made entirely of woven ribbons.

Roberto Capucci, sketches for sculptural cocktail dresses, spring/summer 1989.

CARDER Frederick 1863–1963 — British

glass designer

Founder of modern glass industry in USA.

Considered one of this century's greatest designer-craftsmen working in glass, Frederick Carder was born in Wordsley, Staffordshire. From 1881 to 1902 he worked with the engraver John Northwood as a designer at the Stevens & Williams glass works in Stourbridge, Worcestershire. In 1903 he left for the United States, ostensibly to observe glassmaking there, but soon after he set up the Steuben Glass Works in upstate Corning, New York, which was to become a major force in American – and international – glass, first making iridescent Aurene glass in the art nouveau style of Louis Comfort Tiffany. In 1918 Steuben was taken over by the massive CORNING Glass Works, but Carder remained his company's art director until 1933 not fully retiring until he was in his nineties.

Carder's design skills, combined with his vast technical knowledge, led to his development and the factory's production of various types of decorative coloured glassware besides Aurene, including the Calcite, Cintra, Cluthra, Intarsia, Ivrene, Moss Agate, Silverine and Verre de Soie lines. Carder also created glass in the art deco style in the 1920s and early 1930s, with geometric shapes, conventionalized flowers and the like, although he kept many of his earlier organic forms in production as well. Under his leadership, in the late 1920s, Steuben began to produce large pieces of architectural glass, such as lighting and panels for New York's Rockefeller Center. He experimented with a wide variety of old and new production methods and types of decoration, among them cased, cameo and bubbled glass and etching and enamelling on glass, and from the mid-1930s he worked in his own laboratory on, among other things, a method of casting glass in the lost-wax technique.

Much of Carder's output was firmly grounded in late 19th-century design and tech-niques – those which he had learned while still in England – but his adoption of curvilinear, organic art nouveau elements, and later more rectilinear and stylized art deco ones, evinced his willingness to implement change and go with the times, rather than stay within the comfortable confines of tradition.

A craftsman, designer, scientist and business-man *par excellence,* Carder was a member of numerous professional associations, including the Society of Glass Technology, the American Chemical Society and the American Ceramic Society. He was a member of the Hoover Commission which the American president appointed to review the 1925 Paris Exposition (in which the USA did not participate), as well as a Fellow of the Society of Arts in London and a member of the Metropolitan Museum of Art's Advisory Committee. After Louis Comfort TIFFANY (who in fact unsuccessfully took Carder to court in 1913 for infringement of method), Carder was the premier exponent of early 20th-century American art glass – and the unrivalled founder of that country's modern glass industry.

Frederick Carder, Aurene vase for Steuben Glass, c.1920–30.

C

CARDEW Michael 1901–83   British

potter

Studio pottery in traditional forms.

At the age of 22, Cardew persuaded the potter Bernard LEACH to accept him as a pupil. For three years Cardew worked with Leach and Shoji Hamada, the now famous Japanese potter. In 1926 he established his own pottery at Winchcombe, Gloucestershire. In 1939 he set up a pottery at Wenford in Cornwall, and in 1942 he accepted a job in Ghana to run a pottery at Achimota College. After six years he set up another at Vune, attempting to train West African potters in a new modern-cum-quasi-African tradition.

He returned to England in 1948, but in 1951 returned to Africa as pottery officer to the Nigerian Government. In 1965 he re-established himself in the pottery at Wenford Bridge.

Cardew was a founder of the 20th-century craft pottery movement which rediscovered traditional forms in pottery, such as harvest jugs and cider bottles, and slip-trailed decoration. In a sense this work was deeply reactionary, opposed to modern attitudes and production methods and its vigour largely derives from this. Cardew, like Leach, and like others who followed in their wake, provides an alternative aesthetic which gives a respite from the machine world for which many people are grateful.

Pierre Cardin, futuristic menswear, c.1974.

CARDIN Pierre b.1922   French

fashion designer

Futuristic fashions during the 1960s; mass-licensing of his own name.

Pierre Cardin trained at the Paris fashion houses of Paquin, SCHIAPARELLI and DIOR. In 1949, while still a trainee, he designed the costumes for Jean Cocteau's highly acclaimed Surrealist film *La Belle et La Bête*. He opened his own couture house in 1950 and showed his first collection in 1953.

By the 1960s, Cardin had earned a reputation for being one of Paris's most adventurous *couturiers*. In 1961 he moved into menswear. Challenging traditional men's tailoring, Cardin dressed his daring and often famous customers – including the Beatles – in brightly coloured and patterned garments, high-buttoned and collarless jackets and zipped smocks instead of coats. In 1964 he launched his futuristic fashions, designed for the Space Age, some of which, promoted as body

jewellery, were made entirely from metal and plastic. Cardin dressed his models in shiny vinyls, skin-tight catsuits, space helmets and high-legged leather boots. His collections are characteristically overstated and oversize. In the 1960s, when he used collars, they were enormous, his necklines plunged to the navel and his cut-outs were the most revealing on the catwalks. At the same time however, he was also known for the more subtle and clever cut of his garments, reviving VIONNET's cowl drape and bias-cut dresses. In 1965 he designed for the cinema again, reviving the Edwardian fashion for high-necked, lacy blouses in *Viva Maria*.

Today, the name Pierre Cardin is known worldwide, not because of his extravagant, trend-setting couture collections, but because of his monogrammed goods, produced by some 600 licensees.

Pierre Cardin.

CAROTHERS Dr. Wallace Hume 1896–1937   American

organic chemist

Pioneering research into synthetic fibres, inventor of nylon.

Nylon was the first and most famous synthetic fibre to be used in clothing and heralded the success of synthetics in this market. Wallace Carothers, an organic chemist, was the guiding genius behind its discovery. Carothers had started to analyse the structure and polymerization – the system by which two elements link together – of certain protein compounds whilst he was teaching at Harvard. In 1928 Du Pont Chemicals invited him to direct a fundamental research programme into organic chemistry at their plant in Seaford, Delaware, with a view to developing synthetic fibres. It took 13 years, a team of over a hundred chemists and engineers and the largest research and development budget that a textile company had ever invested to transform Carothers' academic research into a marketable product. Nylon was developed in 1935. In 1941, the first year of full scale commercial production, 64 million pairs of nylon stockings were sold. Coinciding with the rise of women's hemlines, which had greatly increased the demand for sheer stockings, "nylons" became a household name overnight.

Since the Second World War other synthetic fibres discovered on the basis of Carothers' research, such as polyester and Lycra, have had a lasting impact on the design of clothing and other domestic and industrial products.

CARTER Ronald b.1926 — British

furniture designer

Co-founder of Carter/Miles company, producing his own furniture designs.

Carter studied interior design at Birmingham College of Art, followed by furniture design at the Royal College of Art, London. He was awarded the title of Royal Designer for Industry in 1974. In 1980 he and a manufacturer called Peter Miles formed the Carter/Miles Company. The company produces a wide range of Carter's designs, many of which, such as the Witney dining chairs (1981), have become classics. Carter and Miles have completed many corporate commissions: BBC, Clore Gallery (Tate Gallery, London), and the British Airports Authority.

Carter's work is rooted in both Tudor and Shaker designs, which means that he is interested in simplicity, form and proportion. His designs, such as the Witney range, sometimes include details like chamfered legs – and for Carter the chamfer is like the serif on a letter form. Indeed, in Carter's work the closest analogy to another discipline is typography – just as a typographer is concerned with how the letters go together, so too is Carter concerned with how furniture sits together.

Ronald Carter, oak reception/dining chairs by Miles & Carter Ltd., 1988.

CARTIER Louis 1875–1942 — French

jeweller

Luxury designs in jewellery and timepieces; invention of the wrist-watch.

Louis Cartier, grandson of the House of Cartier founder, Louis-François (who set up the Paris firm in 1847), was responsible for bringing the greatest fame and acclaim to the family business, beginning in the early 1900s and continuing through the 1930s. In 1898 Louis became his father's partner, soon after opening an elegant shop in the rue de la Paix. The next two decades were a time of much expansion and success for the Cartiers.

Among Louis' many improvements and innovations were an increased use of platinum from around 1900, its soft, flexible settings ideal for Cartier's classically inspired, lace-like garland style of diamond-set jewellery; a greater usage of geometric, Cubist-inspired shapes in the art deco period, as well as a stunning black-and-white palette, for example, onyx or black lacquer against stark diamonds or rock crystal; and, influenced by the bold colour combinations of the Ballets Russes, the novel, equally bold juxtaposition of coloured stones with flat enamelled surfaces. Cartier was also inspired by Egyptian, Indian, Islamic and Far Eastern art, inspiration which richly manifested itself in, for instance, gold, lapis lazuli and coral cigarette and powder boxes, adorned with blue faience cats, coral-and-onyx lotus blossoms and etched hieroglyphics, and chinoiserie dragon-, pagoda-, Fu dog- and landscape-embellished clocks, bracelets, boxes, etc.

Cartier's stunning Mystery Clocks, introduced in 1913, contained an ingenious optical device which seemed to enable the hands to rotate on their faces without any visible works. Some of these clocks, designed in the art deco period, were unique works of sculpture as well as outstanding timepieces. Even earlier, Louis Cartier was responsible for inventing a supremely functional, largely non-decorative timepiece: the wrist-watch. His first such revolutionary creation was a practical, solid, handsome watch with a *"déployant"* strap and buckle in 1904 for a Brazilian friend, the aviator Albertos Santos-Dumont, who wanted to be able to tell the time without leaving his aeroplane's controls to retrieve his pocket watch (the Santos was marketed in 1911). In 1917 he designed the classic curved platinum and gold Tank watch, its shape inspired by the silhouette of American tanks of the First World War.

Louis Cartier.

Cartier Mystery Clock.

CASSANDRE

A. M. Cassandre, poster advertising Dubonnet, 1934.

CASSANDRE A. M. 1901–68   French

poster artist, type designer and stage designer

World-renowned poster designs.

Throughout the 1920s and 1930s A. M. Cassandre produced some of the most memorable poster images of this century. He is held in such high esteem that we now refer to "The three Cs of French poster design: Cassandre, Carlu and Colin" – but first and foremost, always Cassandre. More broadly speaking, he was one of the earliest and most successful "commercial artists", providing advertising images (some of which outlived their products) and a decorative style that have been emulated by designers and graphic artists ever since.

He was born Adolphe Jean-Marie Mouron in Kharkov, in the Ukraine, and, arriving in Paris in 1915, studied painting at the Académie Julian. His exposure to the various French art movements of the time (including Surrealism, Cubism and particularly the work of Picasso, Braque, Derain and Léger) had a profound influence on his poster work, which he first undertook to support his studies. From 1922 onwards he worked as an independent painter and commercial artist, signing his posters with the pseudonym "A. M. Cassandre". Although his graphic art received inspiration from his painting, he kept the two disciplines separate throughout his life. Cassandre believed that the painter expresses himself, whereas the poster designer does not – instead, he acts like a telegraph operator; his sole job is to communicate or transmit messages.

From 1923 to 1936 Cassandre produced a stream of stunning and highly significant posters. Their outstanding features included the reduction of people and objects to simple geometric shapes; a brilliant and painterly use of colour; the integration of the product (or service) name within the composition, as well as an overall unity between lettering and image; and a warm humour derived from the everyday occurrences of life, or from human character. Most of all, Cassandre had the ability to combine all of these to create an astounding sense of atmosphere, with a result most often described as enchanting or magical.

His railway posters were filled with the mystique of travel; his ocean liners gleamed with majesty and elegance. *Etoile du Nord* (1927), publicizing the Paris–Amsterdam train, must be one of the most popular posters of all time, with tracks reaching into the distance like long fingers, leading one on to unknown places far away. *Normandie* (1935) has a monumentality and haughtiness unmatched by any other poster to date. The classic 1934 poster of the Dubonnet man, filling himself up with the aperitif in three stages, *Dubo...Dubon...Dubonnet* (beautiful-...good...Dubonnet), conveys the warmth and quirkiness of the ordinary citizen and the French street café (the little Dubonnet man quickly became a national symbol). The famous poster for Nicolas wine merchants (1935) showing a walking man with wine bottles swinging in his hands, against a background of vibrating, patchwork patterns of red and yellow stripes, creates the searing, dizzying effect of sunlight on a summer morning, complete with roving, sharp shadows. It is said that Cassandre designed 95 posters in all, and about a third of them went unpublished.

From 1927 Cassandre was a founding partner, with Charles Loupot and Maurice A. Moyrand, of the Alliance Graphique advertising and poster agency in Paris, which produced his posters as well as those of

C

A. M. Cassandre, specimen
of Peignot typeface, 1937.

other French designers. But with the death of Moyrand (the administrator) in a car accident in 1934, the agency disbanded soon after. In the early 1930s Cassandre also conducted a small school of design which included Raymond Savignac, Bernard Villemot, and André François among its students; and he later taught at the Ecole des Arts Décoratifs (1934–5).

From the mid-1930s Cassandre designed three typefaces for his friend Charles Peignot of the Deberny and Peignot type foundries: Bifur (1929), Acier Noir (1930) and Peignot (1936). The typefaces reflect his adherence, in his poster work, to the use of sans serif type and capitals. In fact, up to the end of 1939 Cassandre restricted his typography almost exclusively to capitals, believing that capitals enhanced the modularity and the monumental qualities of his work, while also allowing proportional distortion without affecting legibility.

From the mid-1930s Cassandre became heavily involved in stage and costume design, mainly for well-known theatres in France, and pursued this career (as well as his painting) for the rest of his life. He also produced a typeface design shortly before his death in 1968 which was, in the end, never published; it was named "Cassandre" after his death.

CASSINA founded 1927   Italian

furniture design company

Pioneer in employing leading designers.

Cassina is one of several companies in Italy that have made a commercial success through employing leading designers to add value to their products, rather than either seeking to compete with other manufacturers on price or keeping to purely traditional designs. It can claim to be one of the pioneers in its field.

In 1950 the company began working with Gio PONTI, and one of the first fruits of this collaboration was the Superleggera chair. It went into production in 1957 and became a huge international success. The company has gone on to work with Vico MAGISTRETTI, Mario BELLINI and Paolo Deganello (of the ARCHIZOOM studio) and the Japanese designer Tokiyuki Kita, who produced the famous Wink chair, a very colourful, loosely upholstered chair with strong anthropomorphic qualities. In the 1980s the company started to manufacture design classics created by individuals such as LE CORBUSIER, Charlotte PERRIAND and Charles Rennie MACKINTOSH.

Cassina's Milan showroom, 1989.

CASTIGLIONI Achille b.1918   Italian

designer and architect

Mezzadro and Primate stools.

Achille Castiglioni studied architecture at the Milan Polytechnic and went on to practise industrial, furniture and exhibition design. He is an organizer and propagandist for design, and was prominent in getting the Milan Triennale into its position of influence. He has many notable designs to his credit, including Mezzadro, a little tractor-seat stool designed in 1957,

C

and Primate, a stool which you kneel into. This was designed in 1970, and anticipated by several years the famous Norwegian design of Peter OPSVIK, called the Balans chair, which you also kneel into.

Primate, like Balans, has an ergonomic theme and was the result of an "urge to strip the chair back to its ergonomic essentials". With Opsvik's chair you can rock to and fro; Castiglioni's chair is static, but the principle of kneeling to aid good posture is the same.

Castiglioni did a great deal of lighting design for the Flos company, and also designed a wide range of ceramic and other tableware, and small domestic appliances such as radios.

As an elder mandarin, Achille Castiglioni has taken a lofty view of design, and in *Blueprint* magazine he has said that design has become fashion- rather than ideas-orientated. He claims that new designs have to be justified by a need that is more than a desire for stylistic change. In this he has shown himself to be well abreast of contem-porary Italian design fashion, which now claims philosophy and theory as one of the functions of a designed object.

Achille Castiglioni, Gibigiana lamps, 1981.

CASTLE Wendell b.1932   American
furniture-maker and designer

Sculptural furniture using *trompe l'oeil* effects.

Wendell Castle studied sculpture at the University of Kansas and graduated with a master's degree in 1961. Castle is the USA's best-known independent furniture producer. In the 1960s he pioneered an approach to furniture-making in which he laminated stacks of wood which he carved into organic forms for use as chairs or settees. He then produced a range of *trompe l'oeil* pieces of sculptural furniture still lifes. These consisted of chairs which were perfectly real, but had a jacket or a hat carved on to the seat or the back. These wood sculptures are of a dazzling technical virtuosity, but have been superseded in the Castle genre by a series of grand pieces of furniture that are elaborately worked in expensive materials. They are imperialistic items which would be well suited to a post-modern reincarnation of, say, the Austro-Hungarian Empire.

Castle: "I'm continuing the furniture tradition using the same decorative vocabulary that's been around for 400 years, but keeping in step with the times." Castle's work both fascinates and repels Europeans. It represents a conceptual difference bet-ween European and American design thinking.

Wendell Castle, Ghost Clock, bleached mahogany, 1985.

Chanel, trouser suit, spring/ summer 1988.

CHANEL Gabrielle ("Coco") 1883-1971   French
fashion designer

The Garçonne Look, sports style fashion and classic suits.

Chanel came from a poor background and had no formal training. She was initially set up in business and introduced to fashionable society by her wealthy British lover, Boy Capel. She opened her first dress shop in 1914, but business was thwarted by the First World War. Chanel reopened in 1919 and recognized in the post-war years that women had begun to enjoy a wider variety of work and leisure activities outside the home. Many had worked for the first time during the War and had gained greater independence, both financially and socially. These women who had worked largely in comfortable and functional clothing were not ready to be squeezed again into restrictive clothing in the name of fashion. In response to this social trend, Chanel became famous for designing stylish, but practical, clothing for active women.

Chanel was among the leading advocates of sun- and sea-bathing during the early 1920s. Before this time, only working people, unavoidably exposed to the sun, were tanned. Hats, parasols and a leisured lifestyle protected the wealthy from the sun, and they prided themselves upon the whiteness of their com-plexions, which was a clear indicator of their social position. In 1924 Chanel designed wool jersey bathing-costumes for the dancers of Diaghilev's Ballets Russes to wear in their performance of *Le Train Bleu*. Similar costumes were widely adopted by men, women and children for beachwear until the early 1930s. For the first time women could swim unhindered by bulky swimming-costumes. Chanel also carried this practical

CHANEL

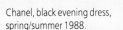

Chanel, black evening dress,
spring/summer 1988.

Chanel, ready-to-wear dress
with characteristic chunky,
fake jewellery, autumn/
winter 1985–6.

Coco Chanel in one of her
classic suits, 1929.

approach to design into her clothing and with her great rival, Jean PATOU, in 1925 created what became known as the Garçonne Look.

The Garçonne Look basically consisted of loose, tubular garments which hung from the shoulders and facilitated a freedom of movement previously denied to women of fashion. Chanel's garments were designed to be worn without corsets, and therefore to liberate women, although many continued to wear both corsets and breast-flattening brassières to achieve the fashionable slim and waistless ("boy") look. Many of Chanel's garments were derived from sports clothing and menswear, and included loose trousers, tweed jackets, blazers and trench-coats, which seemed revolutionary at the time. She also dressed her customers in knitted twinsets and knee-length knitted suits. Never before had women revealed so much of their legs. She immortalized the "little black dress" and was the first *couturier* to promote costume jewellery, such as ropes of artificial pearls and thick gilt chains.

Before the First World War, *haute couture* had been characterized by its use of the richest silks and finest satins. Many of Chanel's garments, in stark contrast, were made in fabrics such as wool jersey and corduroy, which had traditionally been confined to more humble usage. Her fashions were largely made in dark or neutral colours (especially beige), or occasionally in bright red. The Garçonne Look revolutionized women's dress, and not just that of the wealthy. It quickly filtered down to the cheapest levels of clothing production. The basic styling of Chanel's garments was easy to copy and cheap to manufacture, as it required only a small quantity of fabric and its straight, loose styling overcame sizing problems. It was ideal for the

lifestyle of ordinary women, as well as that of the wealthy patrons of *haute couture*.

Unlike most *couturiers*, Chanel was pleased that her clothing was widely copied, confident that the cut and quality of the original would always stand out. Her garment shapes may have been simple and many of her fabrics utilitarian, but her tubular evening dresses were intricately embellished with the most luxurious beading and embroidery and her trench-coats lined with the finest furs. Indeed, she was often credited with creating a "poverty de luxe".

When the Germans occupied France in June 1940, Chanel closed her doors. Taking an influential German as a lover, she bypassed the grinding poverty and shortages which most French people suffered during the Second World War. At the end of the hostilities, fearing reprisals, she escaped to Switzerland and it was not until 1954 that she returned.

At first some of the fashion press, still resentful of her collaboration with the Germans, boycotted her first show, but none the less her first collection was immensely successful. She had chosen the right time to reopen. After the tight-waisted and full-skirted New Look, created by Christian DIOR in 1947, Chanel's comfortable straight skirts, worn just below the knee with matching braid-trimmed jackets, held much appeal – in the same way as had her Garçonne Look some 30 years earlier.

Since her death in 1971, the House of Chanel has remained open under the direction of various designers, most notably Karl LAGERFELD, who took over in 1983, and continues to be one of the most successful fashion houses in Paris. The legendary perfume Chanel No. 5, introduced in 1921, remains one of the international top-selling scents.

Chanel, tailored suit and
coat, autumn/winter
1986–7.

C

CHERMAYEFF & GEISMAR founded 1960   American

design partnership

Graphic and exhibition design.

The New York design partnership of Brownjohn, Geismar and Chermayeff, founded in 1956, rapidly achieved fame for graphic work of great boldness and vitality. When Robert Brownjohn left for England in 1960, the office of Chermayeff and Geismar carried on to become one of the most important and influential design groups in America.

Partners Ivan Chermayeff and Thomas Geismar (both b. 1932) were products of Ivy League schools, both subsequently studied at Yale University School of Art, and both reaped the cultural benefits of an association with Chermayeff's father, Serge, a noted modernist architect. Their work has been intellectual in nature and rich in historical and artistic references. The influence of art movements both past and present can be seen in one of their hallmarks: a tendency to imbue ordinary objects, with significance and new meaning (à la Warhol and others). An example of this was the cover of the 1959 Pepsi-Cola Annual Report, where a bar chart of success was rendered as piles of bottle caps – a ground-breaking image for its time.

But they admit to no particular "style". Their design approach is based on the Bauhaus tradition of problem-solving – finding the appropriate solution for each client's problem – and their success at applying it to corporate design has been enormous. They have completed over 100 corporate identity programmes for such major US businesses as Mobil (with the famous red "o"), Xerox, Burlington Industries, the Chase Manhattan Bank, Pan American World Airways, the Museum of Modern Art in New York and others.

Their work extends to exhibition design and architectural graphics, and they have won many awards, both singly and together. In 1979 they both received the Gold Medal from the American Institute of Graphic Arts (its highest award), and in 1983 the First International Design Award by the Japan Foundation. Chermayeff's work as a designer, painter and illustrator has been exhibited throughout the USA and Europe while Geismar served as Chairman of the Advisory Committee on Transportation Related Signs and Symbols (US Department of Transportation). Under his leadership a new national system of standardized symbols was developed – an achievement for which he received one of the first Presidential Design Awards in 1985.

Chermayeff and Geismar, front cover of Pepsi Cola Company annual report for 1959.

CHIHULY Dale b.1941   American

studio glass artist

Founder of Pilchuck Glass School, Seattle, USA.

Chihuly is one of America's most esteemed glass artists. His vast oeuvre, including early environments of glass and later major architectural installations, plus his best-known series of blown vessels – Cylinders, Baskets, Sea Forms and Macchia – rank among the finest works of glass art of the 20th-century. Chihuly was born in Tacoma, Washington, and studied interior design architecture, with special interests in weaving and glass, at the University of Washington in Seattle. After graduation in 1965, he worked briefly as a designer for a Seattle architect, but in 1966 he received a scholarship to the University of Wisconsin at Madison. In Wisconsin he studied with glass master Harvey Littleton, soon developing into one of the latter's most gifted students. He received a Master of Science degree in 1967 and then took on a teaching assistantship at the Rhode Island School of Design (RISD), earning a Master of Fine Arts there in 1968.

In the same year Chihuly was awarded a Tiffany Foundation Grant and a Fulbright Fellowship to study in Italy, and became the first American glassblower to work at the VENINI glass factory in Murano. For four summers, from 1968, he taught at Haystack in Maine, as well as travelling extensively abroad. In 1969 Chihuly became Chairman of the Glass Department at RISD, a post he held until 1980 (he then became Artist-in-Residence there).

Chihuly's initial plans for setting up a glass school in his native Pacific Northwest became a reality in 1971, when he started the Pilchuck Glass School on a 40-acre tree farm (the land belonged to John and Anne Gould Hauberg, collectors and benefactors of contemporary glass and other art). Pilchuck is now a summer school of significant, even legendary, renown, and it has drawn talented international artists to its excellent workshops and facilities for some two decades.

From his Glass Forests of the early 1970s to his sensuous Sea Forms, begun in 1980, Dale Chihuly has drawn on nature as a major source of inspiration. Among his early blown vessels were the handsome Navajo Cylinders, thick-walled, iconic and monumental pieces inspired by the colours and patterns of Indian blankets, their designs achieved by rolling hot glass cylinders on coloured glass rods (Kate Elliott and Flora Mace provided the glass "drawings" that created the patterns on the vessels). From the late 1970s his works in the main have comprised multiple parts, such as the Pilchuck Baskets, inspired by Northwest Coast Native American baskets. Sea Forms are similar glass families, only their inspiration arises from the ocean and marine life.The Macchia (Italian for "spotted") groups, begun in 1981, above all emphasize colour over form; they are often blindingly vivid to behold. In 1986 Chihuly returned to his earlier methods of "drawing" on single forms, only this time soft, thin cylinders were the recipients of the designs; he also began making experimental hybrid pieces (Untitled New Forms), and he is continuing to work in new directions.

CITROËN founded 1919 French

automobile manufacturer

Traction Avant; 2CV; DS 19.

This car manufacturer has produced some of the world's most interesting, innovative cars for the mass market. For example, in 1934 Citroën launched the Traction Avant, which was revolutionary because it had front-wheel drive. It was also an early example of "niche" marketing because the three basic models were available in 21 different versions and three colours. The equally innovative Citroën 2CV – the *Deux Chevaux* – was launched in 1939, kept hidden from the Germans during the war and relaunched in 1949 as a front-wheel-drive car of pared-down simplicity and a 375-cc air-cooled flat twin engine. The 2CV was conceived by Pierre Boulanger (1886–1950). The 2CV's highly original and idiosyncratic shape was styled by Flaminio Bertone (b. 1903). The 2CV, like the German Volkswagen, was designed as rugged, basic transport.

Citroën DS, 1955.

Its geometric, chicken-shack styling was a product of simple, metal-bashing manufacturing and it remained in production, with modifications, until 1990.

But Citroën, before it was taken over by Peugeot (1975), was famous for more than the 2CV. In 1957 Citroën launched the DS 19. This was stylistically and technically a revolutionary vehicle. It too was designed by Flaminio Bertone. For a while, the vehicle was marketed almost as if it was a sculpture on wheels. It was a front-wheel-drive car, and made use of plastics, large areas of glass and almost surreal streamlining. The DS 19 has been celebrated in essays in France (by the late Roland Barthes, the literary and cultural critic, for example) and in England by the architects Peter and Alison SMITHSON.

CLARK Ossie b.1942 British

fashion designer

Youth fashions (1960s) and flowing and romantic evening wear (from 1967).

Clark studied at Manchester College of Art (1957–61) and at the Royal College of Art (1961–4), where many of the decade's leading fashion designers, including Zandra RHODES, Bill Gibb, Anthony PRICE, Marion Foale and Sally Tuffin, also trained under the direction of Janey Ironside. Clark graduated at the peak of the pop revolution, when London had established its lead in ready-to-wear youth fashion. Clark had designed for the boutique Woollands 21 Shop while he was a student, and his work was soon featured in *Vogue*.

In 1965, with his partner Alice Pollock, he set up his own company, Quorum, which became one of Chelsea's most successful boutiques. At this time Clark's fashion designs were influenced by the leaders of the op art movement.

Clark reached his peak during the late 1960s, when the fashion mood changed from futuristic to romantic design. He became famous for his crêpe, satin, jersey and chiffon evening wear, his slinky, plunge-back evening dresses, use of handkerchief points and flowing trouser-suits. The beautiful flower-printed textiles in which many of his garments were made up were designed by his wife Celia Birtwell.

In 1968 Radley bought Quorum, and Clark continued to design for the company until he started Ossie Clark Ltd., in 1977. In 1980 his new company was briefly acquired by MAK Industries and, following their withdrawal, went into liquidation.

Ossie Clark. Latin-inspired fashions for Quorum c.1967.

CLIFF

Clarice Cliff, hand-painted
Age of Jazz plaque.

CLIFF Clarice 1899–1972   British

ceramics decorator and designer

Original and colourful Bizarre range of dinner- and tea-sets.

In the 1920s and 1930s art deco period, the colourful and fanciful hand-painted Staffordshire pottery of Clarice Cliff stood out as a welcoming beacon in the commercial ceramics industry, a bright, rather un-English response to times that generally were dark and grey. The daughter of an iron-moulder and one of eight children, Cliff was born in Tunstall, one of the half-dozen pottery towns of Staffordshire. She left school at 13 to do an apprenticeship as an enameller at the earthenware factory Lingard Webster & Co., near to her home, where she learned to paint free-handedly on pottery. She then went to Hollinshead & Kirkham, also in Tunstall, to learn lithography (in this context, the technique by which transfer-printed designs are applied to pottery before firing), and at the same time she took evening painting classes at the Tunstall School of Art. Finally, at the age of 17 she was taken on as a lithographer at A.J. Wilkinson Ltd., the Royal Stafford-shire Pottery in Burslem, the firm with which she was associated for the rest of her life (its managing director, Colley Shorter, would later become her husband).

Up to around 1925, Cliff was engaged in learn-ing a variety of additional skills at Wilkinson's, includ-ing modelling, firing, gilding and keeping pattern and shape books, and in 1924–5 she took evening classes at the Burslem School of Art. Observing her interest in and obvious talent for painting designs on pottery, Shorter and his brother-in-law, the shop decorating manager Jack Walker, gave Cliff free rein to ex-periment on stock blanks in the adjacent Newport

Pottery (which Wilkinson's had acquired). After two months in 1927 studying sculpture at the Royal College of Art in London, she returned to an atelier she set up in the Newport factory, and in late 1928 some 60 dozen of her designs were unveiled and market-tested (much to the misgivings of several of the salesmen, who considered them too "extreme"). The medium-priced, brightly hand-painted wares she called Bizarre proved a success, however, and soon some of the blanks she was decorating assumed shapes as bold and unusual as her palette. Her colours included bright Tango orange, rich blues and yellows, bold reds, purples and greens, and shiny black, usually against a creamy, rather than stark-white, ground. The motifs ranged from stylized blossoms and puffy trees, to rectilinear, Cubist pat-terns, to perky castle- and house-dotted landscapes, to remarkable abstract designs, their varied hues creating painterly, "melted-wax" effects. Besides the tradi-tional crockery shapes, there were conical vases on geometric tripod bases; half-moon-shaped sugar-bowls on dainty cylindrical-tube feet, their lids topped with circular knobs; teacups with triangular (and somewhat unwieldy) handles; teapots with pyramidal spouts, and even rectangular dinner-plates, albeit with perfectly round recessed centres. Within the broad Bizarre range, there were a myriad patterns and shapes, many romantically or whimsically named, like Fantasque, Biarritz, Gayday, Peter Pan, Caprice, Le Bon Dieu, Delecia, Inspiration and Sunburst.

The years 1929 to 1935 marked the peak success period of Newport Wilkinson's Bizarre wares. In 1930 Cliff was appointed company art director, overseeing a host of mostly female decorators – some 150 employed in the decorating shop and trained by Cliff and two assistant teachers. Exhibitions and demonstrations of

Clarice Cliff, ginger jar, c.1925.

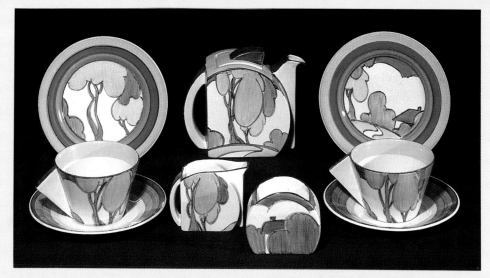

Clarice Cliff, Tea for Two service in hand-painted Fantasque pattern, 1931.

Bizarre ware were held in London and throughout Great Britain (even as far afield as Australia and New Zealand), and Cliff's plump, cloche-hatted figure became well-known, making special appearances and otherwise helping to publicize her designs. Harrods, Selfridges, Waring & Gillow and Lawley's were among the retail outlets stocking Bizarre dinner-and tea-sets, as well as the purely decorative, or novelty, items. The latter included face masks, or wall medallions as the makers called them, such as Flora, whose hair comprised a garland of flowers, and Chahar, a dark siren in an Egyptian headdress; the stylish and *moderne* Age of Jazz figures, block-china centrepieces painted with modish dancers and musicians; candle-holders in the shape of kneeling maidens, book-ends adorned with playful teddy bears and the 16-in-long Viking Boat flower-holder.

For a short time between 1932 and 1934, Cliff engaged several well-known artists to paint their original designs on Wilkinson's wares in a well-intentioned attempt to fuse art and industry. The concept was that of Thomas Acland Fennemore, art director of E. Brain & Co. of Foley China (which produced the designs in bone china, while Wilkinson's provided earthenware). Limited edition sets, executed by factory decorators from the artists' originals, were the result, with such names as John Armstrong, Vanessa Bell, Frank Brangwyn, Duncan Grant, Laura Knight, Paul Nash and Graham Sutherland participating in the project. The full range was presented at Harrods in 1934, in an exhibition called "Modern Art for the Table", but although the endeavour was termed a "brave venture" and "interesting and unusual", it failed to attract buyers and was soon abandoned.

Until her marriage to Colley Shorter in late 1940, Clarice Cliff had worked long, demanding hours with little rest. In 1941 the Bizarre shop had closed, the Newport factory was used as a depot by the Ministry of Supply and, except for a few decorated export pieces, only white wares were produced during the Second World War. When the conflict was over, interest in Bizarre had waned considerably, and lack of labour and high cost of materials more or less signalled the end of the line. Some ever-popular patterns, like Crocus, continued to be made into the 1950s, but in general the demand was for old-fashioned, conservative designs, some of which were marketed in North America. By the 1950s, Cliff's role at both Newport and Wilkinson's was more administrative than artistic, although she was still decorating manager. In 1965, she retired, the company having been sold to Messrs Midwinter soon after Shorter's death in late 1963. By the 1960s, with the resurgence of interest in art deco, Bizarre ware began to capture the fancy of collectors, and in 1972 a retrospective of Cliff's work took place at the Brighton Museum, to which she donated several of her pieces and contributed catalogue notes before her death later that year.

Through the 1970s and 1980s, the popularity of Clarice Cliff's pottery has spiralled ever upward in interest (and price), with numerous exhibitions, auction sales, articles and books devoted to her colourful output. Indeed, Clarice Cliff's achievement within a mere decade – the mass production and concomitant commercial success of bold, quirky, even somewhat revolutionary dinner-ware totally at odds with previous, conservative tastes – was quite remarkable, unprecedented and so far unequalled by any designer working in Great Britain.

C

COATES Nigel b.1949   British

Katharine Hamnett Shop, Caffe Bongo and Noah's Ark.

After training at the Architectural Association Coates taught at the school, where his delight in being provocative led to a furore. His students, who called themselves the NATO group (Narrative Architecture Today), offered up a series of anarchic drawings, models and collages to outside examiners. At first the entire group of students was failed, but the decision was eventually overruled.

Coates experimented with his ideas on designer decay at his flat which was featured in a number of magazines. The half stripped doors, unpainted plaster walls and chunks of broken marble caught the attention of developer Shi Yu Chen who offered Coates work in Japan.

Coates began his series of projects in Tokyo at the Metropole (1985) – part gentleman's club, part European café. Then came the Caffe Bongo (1986), which resembles an ancient Greek ruin destroyed by a plane-crash. The tall interior space is sliced through with a sweeping aeroplane-wing bar canopy and balcony supported on leaning iron lamp-posts, above which stand tarnished statues of classical heroes. The ceiling paintings, lamps and metal sculptures were produced by Coates' circle of friends – among them Tom Dixon, Zaza Wentworth Stanley and Adam Lowe.

In the same year Coates also designed the Bohemia Jazz Club in Tokyo, which recycled the aircraft-wing idea, but without the classical references.

Coates first achieved notoriety in Britain when he was invited by Katharine HAMNETT to design her clothes store in Sloane Street. Here he combined walls of illuminated fish tanks with a huge sofa in the shape of lips (borrowing from Salvador Dali's idea), an elabo-

Nigel Coates, Caffe Bongo, Tokyo, 1986.

rate baroque mirror and walls swathed with thick white swags of fabric.

In the same year he worked on the delightful Noah's Ark restaurant in Japan. This is a fantasy inside and out. Shaped like an ark, it has a sculpted stone-like exterior topped with a classical-style temple. Inside, the restaurant has furniture designed by Coates.

Coates' idiosyncratic use of materials and features has delighted critics and has prompted a new avant-garde style of shop and restaurant design.

COATES Wells 1895–1958   Canadian

Radios for EKCO, co-founder of ISOKON.

Wells Coates was a journalist, engineer, architect, interior designer and product designer. He studied engineering at the University of British Columbia and after the First World War came to London to research a PhD thesis on diesel engines.

After working briefly as a journalist, he turned to design and became a key member of the small group of designers and architects who were responsible for developing the ideas of the Modern Movement in Britain, including the Modern Architecture Research (MARS) Group and UNIT ONE.

Partly because of his background in engineering research, Coates was interested in exploring new technologies and materials. In 1931 he joined forces with Jack Pritchard of the Venesta Plywood Company to form a new company, ISOKON, which set out to design modern, functional buildings and furniture. Isokon's most famous project was the Lawn Road flats in Hampstead, London. The flats were completed in 1934, and became home to some of the leading lights in the Modern Movement including MOHOLY-NAGY and GROPIUS. Both the Lawn Road and other flats designed by Isokon, Palace Gate, London, and Embassy Court, Brighton, were innovative because they were "fully fitted" and because they used new materials such as concrete, steel and plywood.

Coates also designed a studio for the BBC in the modern style and shops for Cresta Silks, where he first worked with Pritchard.

In 1932 Coates designed a circular radio cabinet (AD65) in the new plastic material, Bakelite, for the Ekco Company. This was followed by several more products for Ekco, including a fire, television, alarm clock and other radios, the A22 (1946) and the Princess

Wells Coates, Embassy Court, Brighton, 1935.

handbag portable radio (1947). His products were known for their sculptural qualities and the successful exploitation of new materials. Coates went on to work on aircraft interiors (for De Havilland and BOAC), transport projects and planning.

COLOMBO Joe 1930–71   Italian

interior, furniture and lighting designer

Total furnishing unit.

Colombo studied painting at the Milan Academy of Fine Art and then architecture at the Polytechnic of Milan. He was one of the leaders of post-Second-World-War Italian design, making use of new materials and new technology in lighting. He designed one of the first one-piece injection moulded chairs. One of his plastic chairs, made for Kartell, has interchangeable legs. He also designed a complete kitchen on wheels containing cooker, refrigerator, drawers, cupboard, chopping block and a stove cover/serving tray. In the New Domestic Landscape exhibition held at the Museum of Modern Art in New York (1972), he was represented posthumously by his project of a "total furnishing unit".

    Colombo was interested in the notion of economy and scale, and of combining functions into single units; this was not his concern alone, but was part of a general post-war design fascination with prefabrication, unity and multi-purpose tools for living. It was a trend that interested designers more than consumers.

Joe Colombo, Birillo bar stool for Zanotta, 1972.

CONRAN Jasper b.1959   British

fashion designer

Fine tailoring, classic simplicity; luxurious fabrics.

Conran attended Parsons School of Art and Design in New York from 1975 to 1977 and briefly worked for Fiorucci before returning to London. He then designed a collection of womenswear for Henri Bendel, the New York department store, and briefly joined Wallis, a British retail chain, as a consultant.

    In 1978 he launched his first collection under his own name. This was made entirely in luxurious black cashmere with cream satin lining. At a time when many young British designers were generating a reputation for the eccentricity of their design, Conran's classical, understated styles stood out.

Jasper Conran.

Conran seeks to create enduring, wearable designs, which define the figure, for working women from the age of 25 years onwards, in addition to his tailored menswear. He is noted for his use of soft tweeds, cashmeres, silk, linen, leather and suede, which he designs into timeless modern classics. He frequently uses striped fabrics and makes much use of black. Conran has a professional approach to fashion as an industry and has helped to revive Britain's tradition of fine tailoring.

CONRAN Sir Terence b.1931   British

designer and retailer

Founder of Habitat stores.

Sir Terence Conran has done more to raise design awareness in Britain than any other individual through his work as a designer, retailer and philanthropist. After training as a textile designer (1949–50) he worked for the Rayon Centre, London, and then as an interior designer for Dennis Lennon (1951–2). During the later 1950s he built up his business as a freelance designer, founding the Conran Design Group in 1956 with John Stephenson. Conran's flair for creative retailing became apparent when, in May 1964, he opened the first Habitat store at 77 Fulham Road, London. Habitat sold Conran's modern furniture as well as French farmhouse kitchenware, pale-wood tables, ethnic rugs and Victoriana.

    The shop was an immediate success and Conran built up a chain of stores, starting in the home counties, then the rest of Britain, France and lastly America. Habitat stores also function under franchise in Japan, Iceland, Singapore and Martinique. Conran built on his extraordinary success with a series of expansionist moves in the 1980s, which included a merger with Mothercare in 1982 and the takeover of Heal's prestigious furniture firm in 1983. In 1986 the Storehouse Group was created as an umbrella organization, which, by 1990 on Conran's retirement as Chairman, owned 1,000 outlets selling affordable, well-designed goods.

    Conran has also promoted his belief in "good design" through the Conran Foundation, which funded the adventurous Boilerhouse Project at the Victoria & Albert Museum (1982–6) and the ambitious Design Museum at Butler's Wharf, London, opened in 1989. In the late 1980s Conran acquired the historic Michelin Building in London, from where the Conran empire has subsequently been run.

Jasper Conran, high waisted mini-dress, spring/summer 1988.

Sir Terence Conran.

C

COOPER Muriel b.1925   American

graphic designer and design researcher

Theory and practice of design; book design.

In 1986, the American Institute of Graphic Arts awarded its second Design Leadership Award to the three MIT graphics groups which Muriel Cooper had founded and led, thereby acknowledging her major contribution to design at MIT (the Massachusetts Institute of Technology). The first group was MIT Design Services, formerly Office of Publications; she was their first designer and Art Director (1952–58). The second was the Media Department of the MIT Press, which she created and directed (1966–74). The third group, the Visible Language Workshop, was co-founded by Cooper (by then Professor of Graphics) in 1976, and she has remained its Director ever since.

The Visible Language Workshop has been praised as her most important project to date. It was founded "to investigate the changes implicit in the electronic revolution in relation to the tradition, theory and practice of graphics, graphic arts and visual communication". Its earlier work dealt with the generation, display and manipulation of traditional graphic forms (i.e., words and images) on the computer screen. But in 1984, the Workshop – and Cooper – became a part of the MIT Media Laboratory. In that broader, multidisciplinary centre, it has extended its explorations into the realms of multimedia, interactivity and artificial intelligence.

Cooper is also a distinguished book designer, having designed and art-directed over 500 books throughout her career (many of which received awards), including the highly acclaimed Bauhaus book published by MIT Press in 1969.

COOPER Susie b.1902   British

ceramics painter and designer

Founder of Susie Cooper Pottery; designated Royal Designer for Industry; awarded OBE for industrial ceramics design.

A formidable presence in English ceramics for some six decades, Susie Cooper not only designed and decorated handsome dinner services and other pieces of refined earthenware and bone china which were reasonably priced and extremely popular, but she also headed her own company.

Susan Vera Cooper was born in Burslem, the

Susie Cooper, hand-painted ginger jar, c.1926.

Potteries district of Staffordshire, in 1902. She started at A. E. Gray & Co. Ltd. in 1922 as an assistant designer; soon she was creating her own designs.

She began painting freehand onto vases, plaques, etc. in 1923. The designs were mostly simple floral and geometric ones, with the occasional singular decorative piece, such as an earthenware ginger jar of about 1926 painted with three animal-decorated panels – an ibex, ram and deer – now in the Victoria & Albert Museum. Her plain but classic banded pieces proved successful for many years, with their various sized, concentric rings in greens, peaches and other warm hues, as well as bright enamelled shades of red, yellow, black and so on.

In 1929 Susie Cooper left Gray's Pottery. The Susie Cooper Pottery was set up in October 1929. At the British Industries Fair in 1932 the Pottery exhibited to great acclaim: among the pieces shown were her first elegant Kestrel shapes. By 1933 over 40 painters worked for Susie Cooper.

Susie Cooper's output was extensive and varied by this time, the Curlew shape having joined Kestrel, and such decorative items as candlesticks, lamps, wall masks, ashtrays and vases being offered alongside the popular tea and coffee services, tureens, pitchers and dinnerware. Band patterns were joined by loop and leaf designs, and by the Polka Dot, Scroll and other hand-painted motifs. In the early 1930s carved or incised designs appeared on solid-coloured, matt-glazed pieces, and by the mid-1930s transfer-printing and tube-lining were added to the repertory of decoration techniques, with Cooper creating for the former her own lithographs – the pastel-floral "Dresden Spray" arguably the most popular of all. New

C

shapes – Wren, Spiral and Falcon among them – appeared in the late 1930s.

During wartime the Susie Cooper Pottery reduced its production somewhat, and the birth of a son in 1943 brought increased family responsibilities for Cooper, who in 1940 had been designated a Royal Designer for Industry. The post-war years put a strain on the domestic market for Susie Cooper's wares. But new wares were displayed nationally, and by the 1950s a wealth of new nature-inspired patterns and shapes of Susie Cooper pottery appeared. For the first time the bone china comprising her wares also bore her name, since Cooper had acquired Jason China Co. of Longton in 1950, renaming it Susie Cooper China Ltd. Her contemporary designs were praised for their "clear, modern colours" and "clean lines". Bone china began to dominate Susie Cooper's output, so much so that by the early 1960s earthenware production had all but ceased.

In 1966 the Wedgwood Group took on Susie Cooper Ltd. as a partner, with Cooper keeping her position as the company's only designer until 1972, when she resigned as company director. In 1979 she was honoured with an OBE for her invaluable contributions to industrial ceramics design. She still designs for Wedgwood as a freelancer.

COPER Hans 1920–81   German

potter

Studio pottery and architectural work.

After training in textile engineering in Germany, Coper came to London in 1939 as a refugee and was imprisoned as an enemy alien. He then served with the Pioneer Corps, from which he was discharged in 1943. In 1946 he became an assistant to Lucie RIE and later became her colleague, friend and collaborator.

Some of his early work in the 1950s reflects the huge influence that Picasso was exerting through the Western art world, especially on the decorative arts. In some ways the naturalistic figurative sculpture that Coper was also producing at this time, such as a portrait head of Lucie Rie, is more sensitive and engaging.

In 1959 the Digswell Arts Trust opened in Hertfordshire, England, and Coper went there. He produced both studio pottery and fulfilled architectural commissions. His most famous architectural commission is the group of six man-sized candle-holders for Coventry Cathedral designed by Basil SPENCE.

Hans Coper, Form in stoneware clay, 1972.

Coper's work is generally sleek, organic and indebted to Brancusi and to Henry Moore. They are artefacts of their time, reflecting the fashionable decorative simplicity of the 1950s and 1960s.

In 1963 he returned to London; he started teaching and eventually became a part-time teacher at the Royal College of Art.

In the late 1960s and 1970s his pots were heavily influenced by his interest in Cycladic sculpture. From 1968 onwards he became widely exhibited and prices began to rise; by his death his pots had become regarded as financial investments.

COPIER Andries Dirk b.1901   Dutch

glass designer

Artistic director of the Royal Leerdam glassworks; one-off and limited-edition decorative pieces as well as mass-produced tableware.

Copier was born in Leerdam, in the Netherlands, and was long associated with the Vereenigde Glasfabriek Leerdam. After his studies and apprenticeship at Leerdam, he was appointed staff designer in 1923, and soon he was experimenting with novel methods and shapes, to the end of designing both individual pieces and mass-produced series. In 1927, after receiving a silver medal for mass-produced glass at the 1925 Paris Exposition, Copier was appointed artistic director of the Royal Leerdam glassworks.

Also in 1927, Copier unveiled the company's Unica series. Shown first in Stuttgart, it comprised a limited edition of individual items of glass sold for high prices to museums and affluent private collectors. Inspired by German design of the time, many of his subsequent designs took on less organic, more straightforward Functionalist and Modernist overtones.

In addition to Unica and Serica pieces, Copier also designed mass-produced useful ware – handsome, everyday glass such as tumblers, jugs, wine glasses and other stem pieces. From 1947 until about 1960, his Primula range – clear, pressed glass tableware of undecorated simplicity and stark functionalism – was likewise a success. In 1940 Copier was named director of the new Glass School at Leerdam, and he extended his creative talents, designing porcelain and textiles for other firms. In 1970 Copier left Leerdam. In recent years he has provided designs for one-off, experimental pieces to glassmakers in Murano, Italy.

Andries Dirk Copier, glass vessel with internal decoration for Royal Leerdam, c.1951.

C

CORAY Hans b.1907 — Swiss

Landi aluminium chair.

Hans Coray is essentially known for one thing – the Landi chair, made from aluminium which is forged and heat-treated. It is light, durable and modern. Designed in 1938, it appeared first in 1939 at the Swiss National exhibition, since when it has been in almost continuous production. It has surges of popularity whenever an engineering, technical or puritan fashion hits the design industry. In 1971 the Landi was quoted or referred to by the designer Rodney Kinsman (London, the OMK company) in his own chair, the Omstak.

Hans Coray, Landi aluminium chair, 1939; now made by Zanotta.

CORNING GLASS WORKS founded 1851 — American

Producer of the first light bulbs, Pyrex ovenware.

This famous American manufacturer of glass and glass wares produced the first glass bulbs for Thomas Edison's electric lamps. A high-quality, design-led company, Corning is particularly famous for its Pyrex glass ovenware, which it introduced in 1913. The design department was formed after the Second World War, when the Pyrex range was extended and redesigned in order to make the wares acceptable in both the kitchen and the dining room. Corning thus pioneered the "oven-to-table" concept.

In 1953 Corning perfected Pyrocream which, though glass, looks like bone china, but is more useful, being tolerant of wide extremes of temperature. Corning began using the material commercially in 1958 for a new generation of oven-to-table ware which, because it looks like superior ceramic, appeals to those consumers who find Pyrex somewhat too utilitarian for the dining room. Purists, however, see the clear glass forms of Pyrex as among the few genuinely modern additions to domestic tableware and a fine example of technology, function and functional aesthetics blending together.

As well as making items for mass production, Corning maintained an involvement in art glass. In 1918 it took over Frederick Carder's firm of Steuben Glass, which continued to operate as a separate art glass division. During the 1930s, under the direction of John Montieth Gates, the division embarked on a new policy of producing high-grade crystal forms engraved to designs supplied by leading artists of the day. These included Henri Matisse, Jean Cocteau and Eric Gill. This line proved highly successful and the exercise was repeated in the 1950s with designs being contributed by Graham Sutherland, John Piper and Lawrence Whistler.

The company's policy of "design as art and technology" has been enhanced by its marketing strategy, which includes its support of the world famous Corning Museum of Glass, in which both traditional and avant-garde wares are displayed.

COURREGES André b.1923 — French

Space Age Collection of spring 1964.

Courrèges trained as a civil engineer before changing career direction. He then studied fashion and textile design and became assistant to BALENCIAGA from 1949 to 1961, when he opened his own House.

Courrèges, like QUANT, lays claim to have pioneered the mini-skirt in 1962. He is, however, most famous for his revolutionary Space Age Collection, which he introduced in the spring of 1964.

During the post-war years great hopes were

pinned upon technological and scientific developments, which promised to transform lives for the better, and in the 1960s the space race provided a particular stimulus for design. Silver and white PVC (polyvinyl chloride) garments featured strongly in Courrèges' futuristic fashions. PVC had been developed during the war. Its synthetic, smooth and shiny surface had no clothing tradition and was a radical departure from conventional dress fabrics. Hailed as the fibre of the future, PVC was worked into exciting new forms, which had welded rather than sewn seams. Courrèges' Space Age Collection included silver PVC "moon girl" trousers, white catsuits, plastic goggles, astronaut hats and boldly monochrome-striped mini-dresses and skirts. His garments were cut in austere, angular shapes with black, white or brightly coloured trims. The flat-heeled, white kid or patent leather, mid-calf-length Courrèges boot has become a much-used iconographic symbol of the 1960s.

Courrèges' Space Age Collection was largely aimed at a young clientele, who could not afford his couture prices. As a result, he launched a ready-to-wear collection in 1965. Courrèges has continued to produce successful fashions, but has never again enjoyed the acclaim he enjoyed for his Space Age Collection.

Courrèges, cotton and machine-embroidered organza mini-dress, spring 1967.

CRANBROOK founded 1932 American

school of design and arts

Distinguished alumni include Harry Bertoia, Niels Diffrient, Florence Knoll, Jack Lenor Larsen and Fumihiko Maki.

The Cranbrook Academy of Art was founded in Bloomfield Hills, a suburb of Detroit, Michigan, by George Booth, a Canadian of British extraction who had roots in Cranbrook, England. The architect Eliel Saarinen was instrumental in determining the Academy's initial character. It was his intention to create not so much an art school as a community of working artists, designers and craftsmen, and it is this thinking that lies behind his overall design for the idyllic but isolated campus.

In addition to design, Cranbrook offers graduate courses in fine arts, photography, architecture, metalsmithing, ceramics and fibre-work. The design department's first principal was Charles EAMES, who held the post from its foundation in 1939 until his departure to set up his studio in California in 1941.

The department today covers industrial, graphic and interior design. The husband-and-wife team of Katherine and Michael McCoy have co-chaired the department since 1971 in addition to running their own commercial practices. Throughout the 1970s the department shared the social idealism that was then fashionable in many schools. Its legacy persists with a continuing commitment to local public design projects.

In the late 1970s, the Cranbrook Design Department began to find its own voice, first in graphic design and then in product design, as the formal experiments being conducted by Wolfgang WEINGART in Basel and the writings of Robert VENTURI signalled a more complex and ambiguous approach to design. The search for a new formal vocabulary was extended to vernacular sources, and trends in linguistic theory and literary criticism became important, leading to the movement of "product semantics". In recent years, it has come to be seen that theories from verbal communication do not offer a complete basis for a new design language, and the department has turned to other philosophical trends, notably that of phenomenology, in order to build a more complete theory of design.

Kathy McCoy and Robert Nakata at the Cranbrook Academy of Art, Heinz ketchup typography study, 1980s.

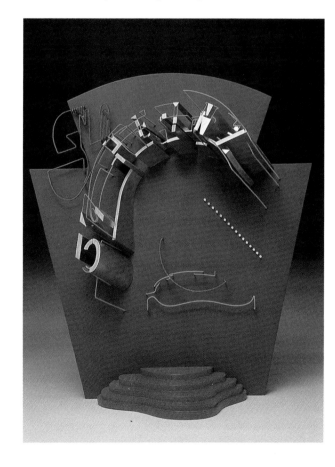

DAEHLIN Lisbet b.1922   Danish

`potter`

Work in tradition of Bernard Leach.

Daehlin was born in Denmark but today lives in Norway. She studied at the College of Art and Design, Copenhagen, followed by workshop practice in Paris and Copenhagen. She was influenced by Bernard LEACH but was never a slavish imitator. Her own style, though simple, is quite far-ranging – thus she has produced a glacial white glazed range of tableware and also highly decorated cups and saucers with gold rims. She is a good example of a potter who has avoided the narrowness of the Leach "tradition". She has not yet had the recognition she deserves.

Lisbet Daehlin, wheel-thrown stoneware cups, 1985.

DAY Lucienne b.1917   British

`textile and ceramic designer`

Textile design for Heal's, including award-winning Calyx design.

Lucienne Day (née Conradi) studied textiles at the Royal College of Art in London. She married the industrial designer Robin DAY in 1942 and became a full-time freelance textile designer in 1948. In 1951 she was commissioned by Heal's (then considered Britain's leading fabric retailer) to create a fabric design for her husband's exhibition at the Festival of Britain. Her famous Calyx design was the result. With its spindly black lines, sharp graphics and clear palette of ochre, rust and orange it was seen then, as it is today, to encapsulate the new spirit and aspirations of post-war textile design. Awarded a golden medal at the Milan Triennale in 1951 and first prize by the American Institute of Decorators in 1952 (the first time this award had been given to an overseas designer), it proved to

be a highly influential and much-copied design.

Day's work of this period was inspired by artists such as Klee, Miró and the inventor of the mobile, Alexander Calder. She transformed these influences into a series of elegant, finely wrought designs, such as Perpetua, Silver Birch and Linear. Day shared the prevalent ideals of creating good design at an affordable price. The screenprinted furnishing fabrics she created for Heal's over the next 20 years (1950–70) and her carpet designs for the Edinburgh Weavers are some of the finest examples of the marriage of this philosophy with quality production in Britain. Day has also worked as a colour consultant for John Lewis and Rosenthal, and successfully collaborated with her husband on the interior of BOAC aircraft.

In the late 1970s, in response to the recession and its effect upon the British textile industry, Lucienne Day turned her attention to the production of hand-crafted wall-hangings.

DAY Robin b.1915   British

`furniture and industrial designer`

Poly stacking chair.

Robin Day won first prize, with Clive Latimer, at the 1948 competition for low-cost furniture held at the Museum of Modern Art in New York. Their joint design was for tapered wooden and tubular-metal storage units. In 1949 he began his collaboration with Hille (one of Britain's leading contract furniture manufacturers, and one of the few which is design-orientated). For Hille, Day designed for materials such as moulded plastic, plywood and upholstered metal framework. Comfort and ease of manufacture were his chief aims.

Day was responsible for one of the most successful post-Second World War chairs for the contract (non-domestic) market. This was the ubiquitous Poly stacking chair, launched in 1963: it is a single plastic shell on a tubular steel frame. It uses a polypropylene invented in Italy in 1954, especially suitable for injection moulding and had the right mixture of lightness, durability and flexibility to make a single-shell seat practical. Commercially, Day's chair is an excellent all-rounder, and its general toughness and cheapness enable it to withstand use by schoolchildren and students. On top of its virtues of economy and durability, it is also comfortable.

Day has also designed aircraft interiors, electrical appliances, cutlery, carpets and exhibitions.

Robin Day, stackable Polypropylene chairs, designed in 1963.

DELAUNAY Sonia 1885–1979   Russian-French

textile, theatre and interior designer

Exploration of the use of colour in the fine and applied arts.

Born in the Ukraine, Sonia Delaunay (née Terk) studied painting in Karlsruhe, Germany, before moving to Paris in 1905. She married the painter Robert Delaunay in 1910. He was to provide the decisive influence on her life and work. With him she participated in the development of Orphism and his theories on Simultaneous Colour (a move away from the drab palette of Cubism), which held that vibrant colour was the principal means of expressing the dynamism and movement of contemporary experience.

In 1917, following the Russian Revolution, she was forced to commercialize her talent in order to support her husband and son. Her approach to design was novel in that she regarded it as an extension of her painting, and in later years she became a successful advocate for the fusion between fashion and art. She designed bold, geometric costumes for Diaghilev's productions *Cleopatra* and *Aida*, and opened La Casa Sonia in Madrid to sell her Simultaneous designs. In 1920 the Delaunays returned to Paris and became involved with the Dadaist movement. Sonia produced a series of dress poems and curtains, incorporating bright colours and pieces of text, and designed costumes for the controversial plays of the Dada artist Tristan Tzara. In 1923 she was commissioned to create 50 fabric designs for a silk manufacturer in Lyon. Her simple geometric patterns, which used the resonance of different colours to set up syncopated rhythms, were both innovatory and very popular. By 1925, when she set up the Boutique Simultanée with the *couturier* Jacques Heim, her decorative geometric designs had reached the height of fashion.

The 1930s depression forced a return to painting, and she and her husband became members of the group Abstract-Creation. After her husband's death in 1941 she continued to work as a painter and designer.

DESIGN LOGIC founded 1985   American

industrial design consultancy

Products for View-Master; design studies for Dictaphone, RCA Corporation, Bang and Olufsen.

David Gresham and Martin Thaler founded Design Logic after leaving the design department of the communications company ITT. Gresham had worked for IBM after graduating from CRANBROOK Academy of Art; Thaler had come via Siemens in Munich from the Royal College of Art in London.

The firm's manufactured designs suggest the designers' wish to break away from the constraints of the high-tech industry with which they had been associated. Design Logic restyled the ever popular 3-D Viewer and designed a number of new toys for the View-Master Ideal Group.

More influential, however, are Design Logic's experimental studies for a variety of top American clients. The first of these was a video camera, designed by Gresham while still at Cranbrook, for the RCA Corporation. It used African face-masks as depicted in Cubist art as the basis for a more sculptural form for a product that is held to the face. A semantic approach is also used to enrich the forms of a range of answering machines for Dictaphone. The studies sport allusions ranging from modern art to the American vernacular.

Design Logic has good connections with Denmark, where it has undertaken design studies for the RC Computer company and the home entertainment equipment manufacturer, Bang and Olufsen. Here, as in all its studies for technology products, Design Logic sees an object-oriented approach to design as a rejuvenating alternative to the stale and anonymous forms of BAUHAUS-descended modernism.

DESKEY Donald b.1894   American

industrial and interior designer

Radio City Music Hall, Rockefeller Center.

Deskey was educated at a variety of establishments: the University of California, Berkeley; Chicago Art Institute; California School of Fine Arts, San Francisco; and three schools in Paris: Ecole de Grande Chaumière, Académie Coalrossi, and Atelier Léger.

Like several of the pioneer design consultants in the USA, Deskey began in advertising and display design, but by 1930 he was also working on a variety of industrial and product design commissions including washing-machines, printing-presses and vending-machines. In 1930 he designed the interior for the Rockefeller apartment, which led to his being commissioned to design the interior of Radio City Music Hall in the Rockefeller Center, New York. Deskey's design is generally regarded as one of the masterpieces of American Deco.

Donald Deskey, Nicotine wallpaper for Radio City Music Hall, New York, 1932.

D

DIFFRIENT Niels b.1928   American

Helena and Jefferson chairs.

Diffrient studied at CRANBROOK Academy, Michigan; among his fellow-students were Florence KNOLL and Charles EAMES. Diffrient is an expert on ergonomics, and some designers consider his Helena chair to be definitive in its category. The Helena is an adjustable office chair in steel and leather, manufactured by Sunar Hauserman. Of this chair Diffrient said: "I thought I could do a simple chair with a rather vast ergonomic or human factors idea and make it quite good-looking. One of my first criteria was that Helena be a comfortable fit for a wide variety of people. It is a completely adjustable chair."

More recently, he has designed the Jefferson executive chair, which has as adjuncts to the main seat facilities for computer, telephone, fax and a small vase of flowers – a seat from which to run the world.

Diffrient is co-author, with Alvin R. Tilley, of *Humanscale 1-2-3* (1974), *Humanscale 4-5-6* and *Humanscale 7-8-9* (1981).

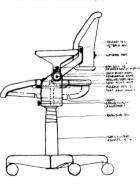

Niels Diffrient, Helena chair for Sunar Hauserman, 1984.

DIOR Christian 1905–57   see facing page

DOMINGUEZ Adolpho date of birth unknown   Spanish

Loose, elegant men's and women's clothing in silks, cottons and linens.

In the 1980s Spain emerged as a new centre of fashion, with international markets for its desirable clothing. One of Spain's leading fashion designers is Adolpho Dominguez.

After studying first languages, and then cinema and aesthetics, in Paris, he formed the Dominguez fashion label in 1974 with several members of his own family. The business is run from his home town in Orense, in the north-west of Spain.

Dominguez draws his ideas from the classic Greek and Japanese cultures. His simple and elegant clothes use silks, cotton and linens, or a mixture of all three. His menswear includes generously cut linen suits, hooded blousons and coats worn with shorts (spring/summer 1990). Dominguez womenswear regularly includes A-line, Empire-line and halter- or strap-necked dresses.

Adolpho Dominguez, high-waisted dress, spring/summer 1989.

DORN Marion 1899–1964   American

Cubist-influenced figurative designs for carpets.

Marion Dorn was a leading modernist designer in Britain during the interwar years. Her success coincided with the growth of awareness about modernism in Britain and the first influx of women working in textile design, which was then believed one of the few areas of design suitable for them to work in.

Born in San Francisco, Marion Dorn studied graphic design at Stanford University, California. She started to experiment with textiles before moving, first to Paris and then London, where she settled with her husband, the artist and graphic designer Edward McKnight KAUFFER, in 1923.

Dorn launched her career as a craftswoman, with a finger on the stylistic pulse, making exclusive, one-off batiks for interiors, such as her Matisse-inspired curtains. Batik was then at the height of fashion, and Dorn's fabrics were featured in *Vogue*.

During the 1930s Dorn turned to designing tufted carpets at a time when the austerity of modernist interior design gave carpets particular prominence in the decorative scheme of a room. It was in her carpet designs that the simplicity and originality of Dorn's work found its fullest expression. She soon became an acclaimed designer in this field. Her art-based designs, influenced by the work of Cubist painters in Paris, combined figurative and geometric elements and a sombre palette in a way that showed sensitivity to the requirements of the modernist interior. This awareness earned her the reputation of being an "architect of floors" and resulted in a string of commissions for distinguished hotels, ships and private domestic interiors, which included Oliver Hill's Midland Hotel in Morecambe Bay, the Savoy Hotel (1933–5), Claridge's (1932), the SS *Orion* and the *Queen Mary*.

In the early 1930s Dorn's eye for innovation led her to collaborate with Warner's Fabrics, one of the first companies to experiment with screen-printing in Britain. By the end of the decade Dorn was setting the pace with her classically inspired designs, had diversified once again into weaving and had formed her own retail company, Marion Dorn Ltd. Marion Dorn left Britain for New York with her husband in 1940; she continued to work as a designer until 1962, but despite a commission to design carpets for the diplomatic lounge at the White House, her work did not enjoy the acclaim it deserved. She died in Tangiers in 1964.

Dior, spotted evening dress, autumn/winter 1989-90.

DIOR Christian 1905–57 French

fashion designer

The New Look.

Dior abandoned his early training in political science to become a fashion designer. He taught himself to draw and successfully sold his images to couture houses and fashion magazines. He then trained formally at the Paris houses of Piguet and Lelong. In 1946, to boost his flagging textile sales, the textile manufacturer Marcel Boussac financed the foundation of the House of Dior. Dior's first collection was launched on February 12, 1947. No single show has ever created such an impact and outcry.

During the Second World War, women's clothes had been designed to use minimal quantities of fabric and time in the making, to preserve scarce national resources in Britain and America. The French fashion industry had virtually collapsed: many houses had closed during the German occupation and the others produced frivolous fashions for a small, favoured clientele. The general trend of wartime fashion was towards close-fitting, rather military-looking styles. Dior's first collection, called the Corolle line, was the antithesis of this. His dresses had narrow shoulders, exaggerated busts, tiny corseted waists that were emphasized by padding the hips, and full, ankle-length skirts. Many of these garments consumed as much as 50 yards of material. This collection was dubbed the New Look by the fashion press.

During the hostilities America and European countries had developed their own fashion industries which were, for the first time, stylistically independent of Parisian dictates. However, with this collection Dior instantly re-established Paris as the capital of fashion.

Christian Dior.

In many ways it seemed anachronistic to return women to such impractical, corseted styles, but the extravagance and romance of the New Look proved enticing after the long years of war. Mass-produced copies, often using less fabric, soon appeared in main-street shops everywhere.

Dior enjoyed only one decade as a leading *couturier*. He introduced the Princess line in 1951, the high-waisted H line in 1954, the A and Y lines in 1955 and finally the chemise dress in 1957, the year in which he died. Design at the House of Dior has since been directed by Yves SAINT LAURENT (1957–60), Marc Bohan (1960–89), and Gianfranco Ferré (1989–). Dior is still one of Paris's top couture houses.

Christian Dior, New Look suit, 1947 (below left).

Dior, tribute to the New Look, spring/summer 1987 (below).

DREYFUSS

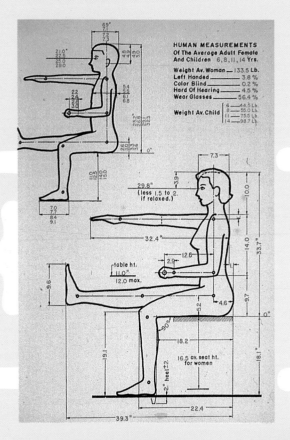

HUMAN MEASUREMENTS
Of The Average Adult Female
And Children 6, 8, 11, 14 Yrs.

Weight Av. Woman ____ 133.5 Lb.
Left Handed _____ 3.8 %
Color Blind _____ 0.2 %
Hard Of Hearing _____ 4.5 %
Wear Glasses _____ 56.4 %

Weight Av. Child

DREYFUSS Henry 1903–72   American

industrial designer

Telephone for Bell Corporation; ergonomics.

Henry Dreyfuss, whose family were theatrical costumiers, began work as a stage-set designer in 1921. He worked with another pioneer of American design, Norman BEL GEDDES, on Broadway. But, just as 1929 was the year Raymond LOEWY got *his* first product-styling commission, it was also the year Dreyfuss opened an industrial design office.

He was less interested in design as an end in itself than in the function of design in society. In his seminal book, *Designing For People* (1955), Dreyfuss wrote: "We bear in mind that the object being worked on is going to be ridden in, sat upon, looked at, talked into, activated, operated, or in some other way used by people individually or *en masse*. When the point of contact between the product and the people becomes a point of friction, then the industrial designer has failed. On the other hand, if people are made safer, more comfortable, more eager to purchase, more efficient – or just plain happier – by contact with the product, then the designer has succeeded."

Dreyfuss is credited with pioneering the application of ergonomic principles (human factors) to industrial design. With his colleagues, notably Alvin Tilley and Niels DIFFRIENT, he was responsible for the anthropometric diagrams which have become widely used in industrial design. In 1969 he published his series of technical charts under the general title *The Measure of Man*. Among these were two life-sized diagram figures of Joe and Josephine – an average man and an average woman. Each diagram plots in detail the measurements and the movements of the figure.

Henry Dreyfuss and colleagues, human measurements in guides published for designers.

Henry Dreyfuss, locomotive for the New York Central Railroad, 1934.

Dreyfuss was not the only pioneer of ergonomics. The subject had emerged in Scandinavia in the 1940s; it was pursued with some vigour in West Germany, and it had a number of its roots in the practical design of military combat aircraft cockpits – partly because the performance of the emergent jet fighters appeared to be outstripping the pilots' ability to fly them.

Dreyfuss himself worked on civilian aircraft. When Lockheed converted the C–69 military transport aircraft into the Constellation civil airliner and Eastern Airlines adopted it as the Super Constellation, stretching it to seat 95 passengers instead of the original 65, Dreyfuss was called in to design the interior and he did a great deal of work with the seating. He was also commissioned to design the interior of the Boeing 707s bought by Eastern Airlines. The original interior design and seating for the 707 was carried out for Boeing by one of Dreyfuss's rivals, Walter Dorwin TEAGUE.

Like his contemporaries, Dreyfuss began to achieve international recognition through exhibiting in the 1939–40 New York World's Fair, where he created an exhibit called "Democracity." But he had already established himself as a designer through his work for Bell Telephones. His 1933 telephone design – the Bell 300 – gave the telephone a form which stayed more or less intact until the 1980s, although Dreyfuss also did a succession of designs for Bell including the Bell Trimline (1965).

He designed military equipment, farm machinery (the John Deere 720 Tractor of 1956), vacuum cleaners for Hoover, televisions for RCA and the Pal razor with disposable blades for the American Safety Razor Company. He retired in 1969. He and his wife committed suicide together in 1972.

DUMBAR Gert b.1940   Dutch

graphic designer

Founder of Studio Dumbar design group.

After studying at the Royal College of Art in London, Gert Dumbar returned to the Netherlands in 1967 to set up a Graphic Design Department within the studio of Tel Design in The Hague. While there, he was responsible for the corporate identity for the Dutch Railways (Nederlandse Spoorwegen), a massive undertaking involving everything from timetables and signage on stations to the exterior graphics on rolling stock. The scheme received wide acclaim for its clear handling of information and vibrant use of colour (e.g. the popular yellow carriages), and gained the Netherlands worldwide attention for new developments in graphic design.

In 1977 he started his own design group, Studio Dumbar, known for handling complex information problems with a clear and rational approach – but adding a touch of humour, emotion, surprise or even fantasy. Producing everything from theatre posters to hospital signage, they continued their experimental, "humanizing" approach and became a central force in Dutch avant-garde graphics throughout the 1980s.

Both Gert Dumbar and his studio have also played an influential educational role. Dumbar has lectured throughout the world, and was engaged as Professor of Graphic Art and Design at the Royal College of Art in the mid-1980s.

Studio Dumbar, poster for the Holland Festival.

Gert Dumbar, poster for a De Stijl exhibition, 1982.

D

DUNAND Jean 1877–1945 — Swiss

Oriental-inspired lacquerwork in wide range of media including ceramics, jewellery, clothing, sculpture and furniture.

Born in Lancy, Switzerland, Dunand studied art in Geneva before moving to Paris, where he was apprenticed to the sculptor Jean Dampt. Until 1902 he worked as a sculptor, after which time he began to experiment with copper and other metals on a small scale. He finally made his name as a lacquer-worker, applying coloured resins to wood and metal surfaces and creating jewellery, vases, bookbindings, tables, chairs, panels, screens and mantelpieces of the utmost beauty and art deco elegance.

The vases Dunand single-handedly created were his most significant contributions to 20th-century design, not only embodying the opulence and beauty of art deco, but also proving an inspiration to designers in various media. Their shapes were traditional Oriental ones – mostly ovoid and spherical – but they were transformed into three-dimensional masterpieces by means of Dunand's application of coloured lacquer to them, often in bold zigzags, streaks or triangles of black, gold or red. He was also adept at encrusting tiny bits of crushed eggshell, or *coquille d'oeuf*, into the lacquer, another Eastern technique whose application he expanded by creating handsome patterns with the fragments. Some vases were Cubist inspired as well, sporting applied wings or ellipses, often off-balance. The jewellery Dunand designed – earrings, bracelets and brooches – was strongly geometric and highlighted in black, red and gold. In these pieces, as well as in larger works, he was also inspired by the exotic forms and patterns of Africa, which wove its spell over many art deco designers in a variety of media.

Dunand's cabinets, screens and panels were often adorned with figural and animal designs created by Dunand himself or after a noted artist, whereas the actual pieces may have been provided by RUHLMANN or another furniture-maker. An especially stunning black-lacquered cabinet in the 1925 Paris Exposition, where Dunand's talents were much in evidence, was designed by Ruhlmann and lacquered by Dunand.

Dunand also designed whole interiors, such as a smoking room in the *Ambassade Française* pavilion of the 1925 Paris fair, several rooms filled with lacquered furniture for the *couturière* Madeleine VIONNET, and a vast smoking room with lacquered furniture and wall panels depicting hunting and other masculine leisure activities for the *Normandie* ocean liner.

Dunand's impeccable craftsmanship as a metalsmith and lacquerer, combined with his own immense talents as a designer (and often those of other notable individuals as well), resulted in both two- and three-dimensional works of art that were to influence many later designers. Much of his *oeuvre* has come to embody the singular eloquence and elegance that marked the art deco period.

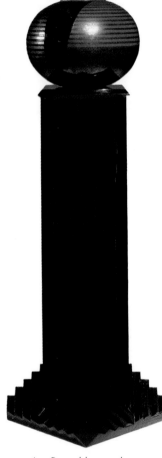

Jean Dunand, lacquered metal vase on a macassar ebony column-base by Clément Rousseau.

DWIGGINS William Addison 1880–1956 — American

High quality book design; Caledonia typeface.

Born in Ohio, William Addison Dwiggins studied lettering with Frederic W. GOUDY in Chicago, and then moved East. He spent 20 years working in advertising, experience which eventually yielded the classic text *Layout in Advertising*, published in 1928, then concentrated on publishing projects. His great love and talent for calligraphy and lettering are apparent in both his advertising and publishing work. He also founded a fictitious organization, The Society of Calligraphers, to promote excellence in book design and production, lettering and type designs. The Society's publication, *Extracts from an Investigation into the Physical Properties of Books as They Are at Present Published* (1919), was instrumental in the improvement of book design and printing during the 1920s.

Not surprisingly, Dwiggins is often credited with having changed the face of American book design. His 30-year association with the publishing company Alfred A. Knopf established their reputation for high-quality book design. He designed around 280 books for Knopf, and also produced designs for private presses and fine printers, particularly the Limited Editions Club. Of equal importance was his association with Mergenthaler Linotype, for whom he designed 18 typefaces. Only five of these were issued but among them was Caledonia (1939), which became the most widely used book typeface in America.

In addition to these professional achievements, Dwiggins also pursued "hobbies" which have received wide acclaim, most notably his marionette theatre. He carved, and helped to operate, the marionettes, devised the stage and its machinery, wrote the plays, and produced programmes and other ephemera, conducting the project with astounding attention to detail.

Harley Earl, Chevrolet Bel Air for General Motors, 1955.

EAMES Charles 1907–78   American

interior and furniture designer

Furniture using new moulding techniques.

Charles Eames is one of the major designers of the USA but his design work was frequently collaborative, often with his wife Ray (née Kaiser) who has had little credit for her work. New research is awaited which will balance the picture. Nevertheless, Charles Eames' achievements cannot be trivialized.

His career, like that of many designers, was rooted in teamwork; among his early collaborators were Florence KNOLL, Harry BERTOIA and Eero SAARINEN all of whom were at CRANBROOK Academy of Art in Michigan, where Eames taught for a while. Ray Eames, Charles Eames and Eero Saarinen collaborated on a moulded plywood chair with complex curves that won two prizes in the organic furniture competition run by the Museum of Modern Art, New York.

During the Second World War the Eames couple worked for the United States Navy, designing low weight equipment using moulded plywood techniques. After the war the interest in moulding continued, and in 1948 Charles and Ray Eames produced the first of the one-piece fibreglass shell chairs. This led on to wire-based furniture, a lounge chair and ottoman in laminated rosewood (1956), and a die-cast aluminium chair in 1958. The house that Charles and Ray Eames designed in Pacific Palisades, California, in 1949 was also of interest to designers. It was a steelframe building made with standard prefabricated parts.

EARL Harley 1893–1969   American

car designer

Numerous models for General Motors.

Harley Earl lived in Hollywood, where his family's firm, the Earl Automobile works, had built up a profitable business making customized cars for film stars.

General Motors realized more quickly than Ford that for the second generation of car buyers, appearances mattered a great deal. Earl joined General Motors in 1928. His contribution to the development of the US car industry was enormous. He devised the technique of using clay models to develop the shape of the bodywork – a practice that is now universal – although Raymond LOEWY claims to have been the first to use clay modelling as a tool in industrial design. Earl is also credited with introducing annual model modifications to General Motors to entice the car-buyers to change their cars yearly.

His approach to car design had a psychological element; he knew that cars were much more than just a means of transport, and he worked to make them desirable. Many of the features which characterize cars of the 1940s and 1950s, such as tail-fins, chromium plating and two-tone paint, were Earl's innovations.

Earl was inspired by air and space travel, and borrowed imagery from jets and rockets not only for his car designs, but also for domestic appliances, such as the carpet-sweepers he designed for Bissell. In 1937, he became head of General Motors' styling division and worked on a huge range of mass-produced cars. The 1948 Cadillac is famous for being the first car with tail-fins and was inspired by the Lockheed P-28 Lightning jet. Another jet, the Douglas F-4D Skyray, was the inspiration behind cars such as the 1958 Buick and the 1955 Chevrolet. Earl's flights of fancy reached their height in the 1950s with the experimental Firebirds, although, of the automobiles that went into production, the Cadillac Eldorado is considered the apotheosis of the long, low, ornate, phallic-centred style that suddenly went out of fashion in the early 1960s.

EBENDORF Robert b.1938   American

artist-jeweller

Jewellery in precious, semi-precious and non-precious materials.

Ebendorf is one of the USA's best-known jewellery-makers and designers. As with a number of studio craftsmen, his work is concerned as much with art as with design. Ebendorf's jewellery has changed over the years, keeping up with jewellery's leading edge. His early work included coffee-pots, tea-infusers and umbrella-handles, each item wrought in precious and semi-precious materials such as silver, ebony, moonstone and walnut. His work is eclectic; thus in 1965, for example, he produced a coffee-pot in silver with an ebony handle, and although it is distinctively American, it is also Scandinavian in appearance. By the late 1980s he was producing jewellery in non-precious materials, including paper and Formica laminate.

Sometimes Ebendorf mixes precious materials with the non-precious in abstract compositions which echo Dutch modern jewellery designs. Evidence of an Eastern influence is apparent in his bracelets, produced in 1987.

In the 1970s Ebendorf's work tended to be semi-figurative. The figurative brooches hinted at a narrative, and there are allusions both to Christianity and to pop imagery.

In the early 1980s he produced a series of "objects" which are compilations of paper, wood and photographs. In this series Ebendorf brought to jewellery some of the ideas found in the collage work of Robert Rauschenberg, the American artist.

Although Ebendorf is an eclectic, he brings his own voice and coherence to his work. However, a part of his significance in American jewellery rests in his demonstrations of the possibilities for jewellery in borrowing from other disciplines and cultures.

EDINBURGH TAPESTRY COMPANY — British

tapestry manufacturer

Translation into tapestry of works by artists.

The Edinburgh Tapestry Company, also known as the Dovecot Studios, has its roots in a company established in 1912 by the 4th Marquess of Bute. It was influenced by William Morris's workshops at Merton Abbey, near Wimbledon, London, and the first two master-craftsmen of the Dovecot Studios came from Merton Abbey. It is one of the world's few tapestry manufacturers (the most famous is probably the much older Gobelins works in France), and it specializes in working with world-famous artists and translating their paintings into tapestry. Pepsi-Cola commissioned from the Edinburgh Tapestry Company a suite of 11 tapestries, each one based on an illustration by the American painter Frank Stella.

The craftsmen and craftswomen involved are clearly not designers in the conventional sense, but they do work on equal terms with the artist, working towards one common goal – the tapestry. Tapestry is essentially a decorative art, and the artists with whom the company has worked tend to have a flair for the decorative, David Hockney being one of them. Perhaps the most taxing aspect of this work is colour-matching. The Edinburgh Company stocks yarns in about 1,500 hues. But at Edinburgh they believe in using a technique that is not unlike pointillism (the technique of laying dabs of different colour next to each other to create the desired hue). The Edinburgh weavers mix yarns, and with the combination of three or four variously coloured yarns loosely or tightly entwined together, subtle gradations and nuances are possible.

EKCO — British

wireless produced by E. K. Cole

Early mass-produced examples of British Modern Movement design.

Ekco was the brand name for wirelesses produced by the firm E. K. Cole Ltd. The company was founded by Eric Kirkham Cole (1901–65) in 1921 and was based in Southend, Essex, England. Ekco wirelesses are important because they are one of the few examples of British Modern Movement design to be mass-produced during the 1930s.

Ekco wireless in promotional photograph, 1934.

The firm began by manufacturing wooden cabinets which resembled conventional pieces of furniture. However, in 1930 the firm began using the new, thermo-setting plastic, Bakelite. At first, the designs changed little in response to the possibilities offered by the new material, with the Ekco 313 Radio of 1930 and J. K. White's M25 Radio Receiver of 1932, which attempted to imitate wood. Cole was dissatisfied with the results, and approached the Modern Movement architect Serge CHERMAYEFF to design a cabinet in Bakelite. The AC64 went into production in 1933, and projected a much more futuristic image, with its rounded corners, centrally-placed speaker and geometric grid. Judged as a success, E. K. Cole Ltd went on to commission other modern architects to design their radio cabinets, including Wells COATES. His model AD65 with its chrome grille, circular form and prominent dials broke all conventions, and set a precedent for all future radio design. Coates continued to work for the company, and in 1945 designed the concentric plastic and chrome A22 shown at the Britain Can Make It exhibition at the Victoria & Albert Museum in 1946.

ELECTROLUX founded 1901 — Swedish

electrical appliance manufacturers

Horizontal cylinder vacuum cleaner.

Founded in Stockholm under the name of AB Lux, Electrolux were the first electrical appliance manufacturers to perfect the horizontal cylinder vacuum cleaner. The Electrolux Model 111 was first produced in 1915, and galvanized the American market when it was introduced there in 1924. With its flexible hose and various attachments, the vacuum cleaner could be used to clean any surface at any height. American manufacturers, most notably Hoover, were forced to introduce similar accessories for their upright models.

In 1919 AB Lux was renamed Electrolux, reflecting the company's commitment to the design and manufacture of electrical products. From its earliest days, the company also recognized the importance of design and appropriate symbolism. Their Model 111 vacuum cleaner featured a pistol grip decorated with the rod of Aesculapius, symbolizing medicine and health, on the butt.

During the 1930s Electrolux followed the US lead by using consultant designers, including the Americans Raymond LOEWY and Carl Otto, and the Swede, Sixten SASON. Sason was also responsible for the

characteristic appearance of the Saab 96 and early Hasselblad cameras. He brought a clean, streamlined style to Electrolux products, notably their refrigerators and vacuum cleaners. The firm is now one of the foremost European makers of domestic appliances.

Rendering of an Electrolux vacuum cleaner by Sixten Sason, 1930s.

ELLIS Perry 1940–85 — American

fashion designer

Comfortable modern classics and sportswear.

Ellis took a business studies degree and an MA course in retailing in New York. From 1963 to 1967 he worked as a buyer for the Miller and Rhoads department store in Virginia, and in 1968 joined John Meyer of Norwich, New York, as design director. In 1974 he was appointed sportswear designer for Vera Companies, which was part of Manhattan Industries, and was given his own label in 1975. In 1980 he formed his own company, also a subsidiary of Manhattan Industries.

Feeling that a great deal of women's clothing was unnecessarily pretentious, Ellis sought to reduce fashion, designing carefree and amusing clothes which he showed on models with free, flowing hair and natural make-up. Ellis's heavy Aran and tweed hand-knits and relaxed, loosely tailored and often interchangeable garments secured him early success. His appreciation of humour in clothing was evident in his

E

Perry Ellis, classic womenswear topped off by a trilby, spring/summer 1984.

trompe l'oeil knitwear designs, which included black jumpers with flesh-coloured insets at the top to give an off-the-shoulder look. Much of his womenswear was generously cut on the lines of his classic menswear, in luxurious cashmeres, linens, silks, satins and tweeds, and generally made in neutral colours – whites, beiges, tans, greys and khaki.

Since the founder's death in 1985 the company has continued to prosper, keeping Ellis's philosophy of stylish and practical clothes alive.

ERSKINE Ralph b.1914   British

architect

Byker Wall, Newcastle upon Tyne.

After studying at London's Regent Street Polytechnic, Erskine moved to Sweden in 1939, where he undertook further studies at the Stockholm Art Academy. Much of Erskine's early work reflects the need to cater for the extremes of the Swedish climate. Examples include the Ski Hotel, Borgafjall (1948–50) and the housing estate, Kiruna (1961–2).

Ralph Erskine was one of the key pioneers of a new movement in Britain called Community Architecture, where architects work side by side with local people on building projects. His major achievement was the Byker Wall in Newcastle (1968-74).

The city council, aware of the failure of so many post-war municipal tower blocks, decided to try the unusual method of asking the intended residents what they wanted. Erskine was invited to set up and lead a team which would design and rebuild a slum close to the centre of Newcastle.

Erskine's first step was to set up a team office. Here he invited local people to describe the sort of homes they would like. After many meetings a design emerged which consisted of a long, snaking wall of flats, some small houses, children's play areas and the retention of local features such as the pub and church. The wall idea was conceived to act as an enclosure and also to keep out noise from a nearby motorway. It varied in height up to eight floors, was constructed of multicoloured bricks and was given a shed roof.

Despite the lengthy consultation period, construction costs were comparable with the more usual concrete towers. A strong sense of neighbourhood pride was created, vandalism and litter became rare, and such was its success and popularity that, shortly afterwards, it won a Best Kept Village award.

EYCK Aldo van b.1918   Dutch

architect

Ysbaanpad Orphanage, Arnhem Pavilion and Zwolle Housing.

Aldo van Eyck was a member of the Socialist Team Ten group of architects which included the British partnership of Peter and Alison SMITHSON, and, in common with others in the group, worked on a number of public housing projects.

Van Eyck became renowned for his concept of "labyrinthine clarity" – breaking down huge structures such as housing complexes into a series of small-scale units. Inspired by primitive cultures, he criticized many modern designers for ignoring the past and for being "pathologically addicted to change".

The Ysbaanpad Orphanage, Amsterdam (1958–60) is one of the most striking examples of how the study of primitive cultures inspired van Eyck. It was constructed, like a primitive village, as a cluster of small interconnecting square and rectangular units. The concrete and brick buildings, just one and two storeys high, are topped by small domes. The scale is intimate and the effect far from institutional.

Shortly after this van Eyck worked on the Arnhem Pavilion, built in rough-finished stone blocks and designed as a series of parallel walls set across the width of a circular frame. The walls incorporated semicircular alcoves and divided the space into a number of chambers (as in a labyrinth) in which sculptures were displayed.

Van Eyck's two major residential projects, the Zwolle Housing (1975–7, with Theo Bosch) and the Housing for Single-Parent Families (1976–80) were built in Amsterdam. Here, as at the orphanage, he was concerned with keeping the scale small and with creating a sense of place and community. However, the designs were quite unlike those of the orphanage.

Van Eyck's buildings were in direct contrast to the anonymous concrete tower blocks which had spread through Europe. The Zwolle Housing followed existing medieval street patterns and was based on traditional designs – narrow, three-storey, brick-built terraced homes with a Dutch gable. There were also balconies, outdoor sheds and small gardens.

The single-parent housing marked a new departure for the architect with its use of bold primary colours and large expanses of glass. Van Eyck intended the rainbow of colours to act as a contrast to the dreariness of the inner city.

F

Salvatore Ferragamo, cork-soled platform shoe with gold kid leather uppers, 1938.

FATHY Hassan b.1899   Egyptian

architect

Gourna New Town.

Hassan Fathy was responsible for reintroducing Egyptian peasant architecture at the new town of Gourna (1947–70). He was convinced that modern building styles and materials were inappropriate for the rural area near Luxor because they were expensive and difficult to transport, and were unsuited to the climate. Instead he envisaged recreating an ancient architecture using local materials and 5,000-year-old Nubian building techniques. The town's plan echoed that of old towns with tightly packed streets filled with flat-domed, whitewashed buildings. Fathy revived the craft of making sun-baked mud bricks and taught the residents to use these to build spheres and barrel vaults.

Fathy claimed that the peasant could build a more suitable home for himself than an architect. Defending that statement, he said: "Modernity does not necessarily mean liveliness, and change is not always for the better. Tradition is not necessarily old-fashioned and is not synonymous with stagnation."

FERRAGAMO Salvatore 1898–1960   Italian

shoe designer

Introduced "Wedgies" and the "invisible shoe".

Ferragamo was the eleventh child of 14 born to a family of landowners. Even as a small boy he felt he had a vocation as a shoemaker; after serving his apprenticeships, locally in Benito, then in Naples, he had his own workshop by the age of 14 with six employees. In 1923 he emigrated to the United States to see modern factory shoe production, but he was disappointed with the inferior quality of the mass-produced shoes and opened his own shop selling custom-made shoes. Ferragamo won a contract with the American Film Company making shoes for historical and costume dramas, and also began to attract the private custom of leading Hollywood stars, such as Mary Pickford, Pola Negri and Gloria Swanson. The shop then moved to Hollywood, and Ferragamo consolidated his links with the film industry, designing both for film productions and for the stars.

Ferragamo was noted for creating styles that were original and outrageous, and for the use of exotic materials such as the skins of python, lizard and ostrich. As well as being visually exciting, his shoes were comfortable, works of skilful engineering and technical expertise.

Ferragamo returned to Italy in 1927 where he continued to produce inventive and individual designs. In the early 1930s he invented the wedge shoe, using cork, which was particularly popular, especially with the American market. The difficulty of obtaining leather during the Second World War led him to turn increasingly to more commonly available materials, such as raffia, which he did much to popularize.

Ferragamo's fame continued to grow after the war, when his so called "invisible shoe" – a sandal with an upper made of transparent nylon – became the most celebrated shoe of its time and perfectly complemented DIOR's New Look garments. Although in his later years Ferragamo's designs became more conservative, famous clients such as the Duchess of Windsor and Audrey Hepburn still valued his products.

FERRIERI Anna Castelli b.1920   Italian

architect and industrial designer

4870 stackable chair and other designs for Kartell.

Ferrieri studied architecture at the Milan Polytechnic, from which she graduated in 1942. She practises as an architect and also designs modular furniture and kitchen and tableware, and, most recently, a solar-assisted town car.

As an industrial designer Ferrieri works closely with Kartell, an Italian company specializing in the manufacture of injection-moulded plastic artefacts, including chairs, tables and storage systems. She is expert in plastics technology and says she is one of the few industrial designers working in furniture in Italy.

One of her most influential designs is the Kartell 4870 stackable chair – it has two arms. These arms posed Ferrieri a major problem: how could they

F

Anna Castelli Ferrieri, polymer armchair designed for Kartell.

be made of a piece with the seat in the chair but with elegance and sufficient rigidity? The arms of any chair take a lot of stress: when people sit down or get up they use them to support themselves; moreover, people all move slightly differently, and not all stresses are predictable. Ferrieri's solution was to make the internal plane of the 4870's arm turn in space like a Möbius strip.

Ferrieri's influence lies in having brought to plastic furniture and plastic domestic artefacts solutions which neither disguise the material nor try to opt out by being "funky".

FIORUCCI Elio b.1935   Italian

fashion designer

"Total experience" retailing.

Elio Fiorucci trained as a shoemaker, and began his career by marketing three pairs of brightly coloured plastic galoshes in Milan. In the mid-1960s he was highly influenced by London street style. He opened his first clothes shop, designed by Ettore SOTTSASS, in 1967.

Fiorucci has always expressed a healthy contempt for couture, which he describes as "pathetic". Known as "The Titan of Flash Trash", he has developed a different fashion system based on recycling mass-produced popular culture. Strictly speaking, he is not a designer so much as an expert retailer, wholesaler and *assembleur*. His formula was to coordinate a network of designers, whom he commissioned to work on single items of clothing. They used intelligent detailing, pop

art and cartoon imagery to transform or embellish articles of junk clothing into a "total look" of sophisticated Milanese kitsch. Fiorucci was one of the first designers to develop the concept of "total experience" retailing, using a successful combination of strobe lighting, new-wave music and zany retail design.

By the mid-1970s the Fiorucci label was appearing on plastic folders, figure-hugging jeans, T-shirts, sweatshirts, socks and headbands. His look appealed across the board to chic teenagers and celebrities such as John Travolta, Jackie Onassis, Madonna and the Princess of Wales, to whom he sent a wedding present of a sweatshirt decorated with a sequinned crown. In 1974 the company was bought by the major trading company, Montedison, and Benetton took a 50-percent interest in 1981.

FLÖCKINGER Gerda b.1927   Austrian

jeweller

Innovative jewellery designs.

Flöckinger emigrated to Britain in 1938, and after the Second World War, having studied fine art, she took up design, jewellery-making and enamel work at the Central School of Arts and Crafts in London. She made a particularly important contribution to modern jewellery in the 1960s with her precious and semi-precious rings, necklaces, bracelets and brooches. These were organic in style, expressive, rather baroque and clearly a liberating influence on what was, hitherto, a moribund craft. Her role as a founder of *modern* British jewellery and as a contributor to the wider international movement was confirmed by her course on experimental jewellery, which she established during the 1960s at Hornsey College of Art, London.

Her work has continued to develop, and she has shown a consistency in her designs that is interesting when they are compared with the more volatile excursions into fashionable cul-de-sacs taken by some of her contemporaries. They are of renewed interest and influence to a new generation of collectors.

Gerda Flöckinger, silver and gold ring with diamonds and topaz, 1984.

FORD Henry 1863–1947   American

car manufacturer

Engineering genius and management innovator.

Henry Ford did not go from stage Zero to father and manufacturer of the Model T in one go; several of his car designs preceded the Model T, including the successful and innovative Model N. Moreover, while Henry Ford had a hand in everything and had a genius for engineering, the Model T, like other automobiles in the series, was a team effort. The Model T was an engineer's design; it was not a stylist's car. Its strengths were its relative cheapness, its durability and its ease of maintenance. The car itself was a breakthrough, involving the adoption of the world's first moving assembly line in 1913.

Ford rapidly became a major employer, and although he had adopted the fashion of scientific management, which in essence sought to make every man a unit in the overall "machine", he soon had problems with high labour turnover. He introduced a generous five dollar-a-day pay rate, bonus and profit-sharing schemes, thus becoming an innovator in management by bonus incentives. Again, these incentives were the result of team efforts; the design of profits, management of labour and the design of the product itself knitted together like a good gearing system. He also pursued a policy of employing and promoting black workers.

Ford became a public figure. In 1915 he sought to intervene in the First World War by sending a "Peace" ship to Europe. But when the USA entered the war he switched his factory to military needs. He constructed a naval dockyard to turn out Eagle ships for the US Navy on the same assembly line principles of his Model T.

Ford was forced into rethinking the need for new automobiles by rivalry from General Motors, and by the end of the 1920s Ford had to think of the automobile in terms of style as well as function. The Model A, which replaced the T in 1927, was not especially elegant, but it had all the latest technological developments. Ironically, outdated management attitudes and manufacturing difficulties caused the Model A to lose money for several months.

Henry Ford's son, Edsel had difficulties with his father, who outlived him, and never acquired total control of the company, but he is credited with two important and elegant streamlined automobiles: the Zephyr (1935) and the Lincoln Continental (1939). It was Henry Ford II, Edsel's son, who took over. Ford, today an immensely strong company, busy with the strategy of adding value to its products through good design and high quality manufacturing and finishes, went through some dramatic troughs and attained some peaks. One trough was a reputation in the 1950s for rust; one peak was in 1964, when the Mustang four-seater sports car was unveiled.

FORTUNY Mariano 1871–1949 Spanish

fashion designer

Aesthetic-style garments in unique pleated and printed fabrics (early 1900s to 1949), in particular the Delphos dress.

Born in Spain, Fortuny spent most of his life in Venice. He was a talented artist and saw himself primarily as a painter rather than a dressmaker. Fortuny's garments were timeless, hardly changing during his working life from the early 1900s until his death in 1949. Although he was one of the most inventive and creative designers working in the first half of the 20th century, his work rarely appeared in contemporary fashion magazines. Fortuny produced his own fabrics and styled and made his garments himself. He had originally studied mechanics and chemistry, and channelled his knowledge of these subjects into the making of unique fabrics. He discovered a secret method of printing and embossing fabric to convey the appearance of ancient silk brocades, and also created a technique of producing textiles with inherent woven pleats. Fortuny worked with silks, velvets and cottons and used vegetable dyes to achieve rich colours.

His garments included aesthetic-style Empire-line dresses, capes and coats. As with the Pre-Raphaelites and later the Parisian *couturier* POIRET, they were designed to be worn without corsets and to emphasize the natural female form. Fortuny's most famous garment is the Delphos dress, which he patented in 1909. The fabric of this pleated sheath dress was so fine that the hem had to be weighted with tiny beads. The Delphos dress retained its pleats when stored tied in a knot in a small box.

Model T Ford, 1908.

FOSTER

Norman Foster, Building B3, Stockley Park, Uxbridge, 1987–9.

FOSTER Norman b.1935   British

`architect`

Exponent of high tech; designer of the Hong Kong and Shanghai Bank.

With Richard ROGERS and James STIRLING, Foster makes up the triumvirate which gives current British architecture its international status. Whereas Stirling has come to design in a populist form of post-modern classicism, Foster and Rogers in their different ways are exemplars of British high tech.

Foster studied engineering at Manchester University and entered architecture after a period of national service. After graduating from Yale University he formed Team 4 with his late wife Wendy and Richard and Su Rogers, with whom they built the Reliance controls building in Swindon (1966). This adumbrated some of the design principles of high tech: exposed structure, an overtly technological image, internal flexibility and adaptability over the building's lifetime.

Foster Associates was formed in 1967. Early works of the practice are the passenger and distribution building for Fred Olsen in London's Docklands (1971), and the well-known Willis, Faber and Dumas office in Ipswich, Suffolk (1975). This building has an undulating glass curtain wall which follows the existing lines of the site. The building is reflective during the day (arguably allowing it to be absorbed by the local environment), but it is transparent at night when it is lit internally. The scheme probably owes something to the glass skyscrapers of the 1920s envisaged by MIES. But, given Foster's attachment to technological solutions, the design perhaps owes more to the technique which enabled it to be achieved. The

frameless glass panels are hung from the roof and make use of weatherproof joints.

In contrast to Richard Rogers, who tends to place all the services and structure on the outside of the building, the early Foster work tended to make use of a skin. This approach, however, changed with the Renault Distribution Centre in Swindon (1983), which makes use of gantries (painted in bright primary colours – another high-tech trait) from which the roof is suspended. But there is a difference between the two former partners, since Rogers' abiding concern with flexibility leads to a completely a-formal arrangement of structure and services, as in the Centre Pompidou in Paris, whereas Foster's designs are more composed. This is clearly seen in his designs for the Mediathèque arts centre in Nîmes, France, for which he won the competition in 1984.

Something of the same harmony can be seen in the Hong Kong and Shanghai Banking Corporation Headquarters in Hong Kong (1979–86), with its rational-looking exposed structure. The design attempts to reconsider the 20th-century tower and is layered and stepped, owing something to the ideas of the 1960s about "mega-structure". It also uses escalators to produce movement in the building (a feature first seen in the Wills, Faber and Dumas office) and to link areas together inside the building, so avoiding the isolation of floors in a traditional monolithic office block with lifts. Like the rest of Foster's work it is explicitly technological: for example, it uses huge "sun scoops" to reflect light into the open central areas. It also draws on technology from outside the traditional building industry – from aircraft and marine design – in an eclectic mixture of technology, romanticism and allusion to local practice described as "late modern".

Norman Foster.

F

Norman Foster, Modular
Office Furniture for Tecno,
designed in 1985 (left).

Norman Foster,
headquarters of Hong Kong
and Shanghai Banking
Corporation, Hong Kong,
1979–86 (right).

These mixed motives are reflected in the fact that, despite its use of advanced technology, it has been widely criticized for structural irrationality. Hanging the floors from the external frame is far more complex than simply supporting all the floors from underneath, with all the forces running straight to the ground. The bank is reputed to be the most expensive building ever built, and a large proportion was spent on the elements in the structure and the expensive finishes which were at least partly necessary to protect the externally exposed parts.

High tech has been largely a British phenomenon, reflecting the highly technical training which British architects receive, which makes them more inclined to evolve a one-off solution to a problem than to take standard manufacturers' parts. It has not been without its drawbacks, because it is often not strictly functional, and there is an added risk of failure in developing unique solutions for each building, as has been seen with Foster's Sainsbury Centre for the Visual Arts at the University of East Anglia (1978). However, the technological image of late modernism has been pursued elsewhere by other means.

As well as the Nîmes arts centre, Foster Associates are currently working on an office tower for Tokyo, a communications tower for Barcelona, and a new headquarters for ITN in London. They have also designed a new terminal building for Stansted Airport. These later works are taking Foster in the direction of a lighter, more refined and poetic use of highly technological solutions.

In a new departure, Foster Associates have also been the master planners for the King's Cross site in London – the largest inner-city redevelopment in Europe – as well as producing designs for the station.

F

FROGDESIGN founded 1969 — German
industrial design company

Designs in computer electronics and furniture.

Frogdesign, set up by Hartmut Esslinger, is today one of Germany's most renowned consultancies. Esslinger was born in 1945 and studied electrical engineering at the University of Stuttgart, and later at the Fachhochschule für Design in Gmund.

Frogdesign now has offices in Altensteig, West Germany, and Japan, and has worked for clients such as AEG, Louis Vuitton (luggage), Erco, Apple Computers and SONY. Its main areas of interest are consumer electronics and furniture. Among its more recent projects are the Apple 11GS (a personal computer with graphics and sound), the NeXT computer and a prototype 35mm SLR camera for Olympus. Its work is generally considered to be a more commercial and more lively version of German design than the cooler style of Dieter RAMS.

Frogdesign also invests in its own experimental design work. This includes products aimed to help the elderly, such as a television set with rotating screen, which the viewer can see from any position.

FRUTIGER Adrian b.1928 — Swiss
type designer and graphic designer

Designer of Univers and many other typefaces.

Adrian Frutiger's most visible piece of work has been the typeface Univers – a geometric sans serif which, when it first appeared in 1957, heralded a new era in typeface design. It brought with it an air of unlimited possibilities (sporting 21 variations of slant, weight and width), and a new consideration for the requirements of legibility and technology. Its large x-height enhanced readability in smaller sizes, and made capital letters look less obtrusive (important in a language such as German, which makes extensive use of "caps"). Optical corrections, for instance, in the thinning of letter-strokes, strokes where they meet or connect, ensured a more uniform and balanced appearance to the page. These, and other qualities, contributed to Univers' claim to versatility and universality.

Frutiger has in fact been responsible for the design of over 20 typefaces (not including adaptations of existing faces), as well as designing for different technologies. His adaptation of Univers for the IBM composer in the 1960s opened up a whole new level of

low-technology "typesetting", bridging the gap between typewriting and conventional typesetting. At the other end of the technology scale, he brought about vast improvements in the design of computer typefaces, particularly with his OCR-B typeface (Optical Character Recognition – Class B), which achieved international standardization in 1973.

Other familiar typefaces designed by Frutiger include Méridien (1955), Serifa (1967), Iridium (1975) – and Frutiger (1976), which was an adaptation of the sign alphabet he had designed for Charles de Gaulle airport. His book *Type, Sign and Symbol* (Zurich, 1980) discusses his work approach and methods, and provides interesting background information on selected typeface designs.

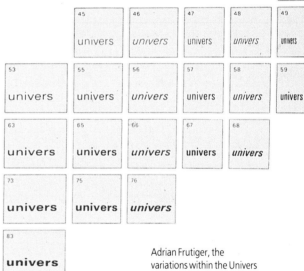

Adrian Frutiger, the variations within the Univers typeface family, 1957.

FUKUDA Shigeo b.1932 — Japanese
graphic designer and sculptor

Work in various media incorporating visual jokes and fantasy.

Shigeo Fukuda's designs are typified by the use of optical illusions, puzzles, "impossible objects", metamorphosis – a whole range of devices that transform ideas and fantasies into whimsical, playful visual jokes. He works in both two and three dimensions, and his compositions can be beautifully simple, or extremely complex. Either way they are, more often than not, lighthearted or humorous.

His graphic works encompass everything from postcards and posters to massive murals and floor mosaics. Particularly famous is the floor mosaic of Abraham Lincoln's face. The image can only be seen from a distance; close up it is merely a smattering of abstract shapes. His sculptural objects range from toy-like models and "coffee-cup phantasies" (where, for example, the handle appears inside the cup), to large wooden sculptures which reveal different images when viewed from different sides, all conveying the suggestion that reality is solely a matter of viewpoint: nothing is ever as it seems.

Fukuda combines the qualities of traditional Japanese craft, as shown, for example, in puzzles or paper-folding (origami), with Western imagery and meanings, thus spanning the worlds of avant-garde art and commercial design. He is as much at home with toys and puzzles as with sign systems. He has participated internationally in many important graphic arts exhibitions and biennales since 1966, and has won many awards and prizes. His work is included in museums around the world, such as the Museum of Modern Art in New York and the Poster Museum in Paris.

Buckminster Fuller, American Pavilion, Expo 67, Montreal, 1967.

FULLER Richard Buckminster 1895–1983   American

engineer and architect

Union Tank Car Repair Shop; American Pavilion at Expo 67.

Trained as an engineer, Fuller became fascinated with the idea of creating lightweight, easily constructed buildings from mass-produced parts. He hoped that by the development of technology to function at its most efficient the quality of life could be improved.

His greatest triumph was the design of the geodesic dome – a hemisphere created by a webbed frame of geometric parts arranged like a honeycomb – which has influenced many modern architects, particularly those, such as Norman FOSTER, Richard ROGERS and Nicholas Grimshaw, designing in the industrial high-tech style.

Fuller said: "It seems perfectly clear that when there is enough to go around man will not fight any more than he now fights for air. When man is successful in doing so much more with so much less he can take care of everybody at a higher standard."

In his early career he developed the Dymaxion House (1927). This was a circular aluminium and glass structure constructed around a central mast through which were threaded services such as plumbing and electricity. He designed the components to be mass-produced in the same way as car and aeroplane parts.

In 1946 he designed the Wichita House, Kansas. Weighing just 6,000 lb, the circular metal building was designed to collapse and fit into a steel cylinder, making it easy to transport. Neither of these houses went into production.

His first major building was the Union Tank Car Repair Shop, Baton Rouge, Louisiana (1958). This was built as a geodesic dome with spaces between the fine struts filled in with panels. When it was built it was the largest clear-span enclosure in the world.

In 1962 Fuller suggested that an even larger, clear dome could be constructed over central Manhattan to act as an environmental bubble inside which air conditions could be controlled.

His last major dome was built as the American Pavilion at the Expo 67 exhibition in 1967. It attracted enormous attention as one of the most popular structures at the show. The dome was left as a frame through which visitors could travel on the high-level monorail which circled the grounds.

GALLIANO John b.1961   British

Progressive tailoring, circular cutting and garments without fastenings.

Born in Gibraltar, Galliano worked for the London tailor Tommy Nutter while he was studying fashion at St Martin's School of Art. He graduated in 1983 with a collection called "Les Incroyables" based on the theme of the French Revolution. This was acclaimed by the press and fashion buyers and was displayed in the front window of a leading London fashion store, Browns in South Molton Street.

Galliano produced his first professional collection in October 1984. Entitled "Afghanistan Repudiates Western Ideals", this show combined traditional tailoring methods with Eastern fabrics and styling. The mismatched buttoning which was a feature of these garments was much copied. His 1985 collection "Fallen Angels" introduced high-waisted Empire-line dresses and transparent silk blouses. Since "Forgotten Innocents" in 1986 he has ceased to name his collections.

One of Galliano's trademarks is his use of circular cutting, which involves skilfully cutting the fabric in spirals. Another characteristic feature is his use of elastic panels on garments which have no zips or buttons. He has also made a feature of *devoré* velvets, which is a technique in which acid is used to burn away areas of fabric to reveal the backing only.

GAROUSTE Elisabeth b.1949   French

Work in association with Mattia Bonetti.

Garouste trained as a set and costume designer for the theatre and now works as an interior and furniture designer in association with the French-born designer Mattia Bonetti. Bonetti (b. 1953) is also a colour consultant, set designer and an actor.

Their first joint project was the decoration in Paris of a restaurant called *Le Privilège*, and this led to a series of furnishings with titles such as *Objets primitifs* and *Objets barbares*. In 1987 they decorated the salon of, and designed the furniture for, the *couturier* Christian LACROIX. Their work since then has included stage, interior and furniture design. Their style is graphic and linear, and the decorative influences of artists such as Miró and Matisse, as well as a suggestion of art nouveau, are present in their work.

GATE Simon 1883–1945   Swedish

Artistic director of Orrefors glassworks, Sweden; co-developer of Graal art glass.

A farmer's son, Gate was born in S. Fågelås, Skaraborg, Sweden. In the early years of the 20th century, he studied at the National College of Art, Craft and Design in Stockholm, and from around 1909 at the Royal Swedish Academy Art School, also in the capital.

In 1916 Gate began his long association with the Swedish glassmaking firm, Orrefors, where he worked as an artistic director and, along with Edvard Hald, Vicke Lindstrand, Knut Bergqvist and others, laid the firm foundation of the significant modern glass industry in Sweden. In his three decades working for Orrefors, Gate designed a wide variety of utilitarian and decorative glass – delicate goblets in soft hues (these and other functional wares were often made at Orrefors' Sandvik subsidiary); plain, heavy-walled vases and bowls; handsome exhibition pieces crisply engraved with art deco style neo-classical figures.

Around 1920 Gate, Hald and master glassblower Knut Bergqvist developed the complex Graal technique (the name, related to "Holy Grail", refers to its elusive qualities). Graal art glass was made by encasing a thick core of clear glass with a thin coloured layer, which was then cut away to create a design that was surrounded by the underlying clear "background". The vessel was heated once more to give it a smooth, more "liquid" appearance, after which step the entire piece was cased with yet another layer of clear glass before being blown into its final shape. These Graal pieces were often of multiple hues and featured internal decorations of flowers or human figures.

Gate won a Grand Prix at the 1925 Exposition des Arts Décoratifs et Industriels Modernes in Paris, and his designs are in the collections of major museums.

Simon Gate, Graal glass vase for Orrefors, 1918.

GAUDI I CORNET Antoni 1852–1926   Spanish

Casa Batlló, Casa Milà, Palau Güell, Park Güell, Expiatory Church of the Sagrada Familia.

Working in Barcelona at the time of a vigorous Catalan revival, Gaudí was obsessed with the idea of devising a truly Catalan style of architecture.

Gaudí began his working life as a Gothic Revivalist; this was a style used at the Casa Vicens

Antoni Gaudí, Expiatory Church of the Sagrada Familia, Barcelona, 1884-1926.

Gaudí's sense of the bizarre was not just restricted to the exterior, for inside no room had straight walls nor any right angles. In a similar vein he built the Casa Milà (1905–10), in the same street, known locally as La Pedrera – the quarry. The great, sculpted façade swirls and curves from street level to the top where curious twisted chimney-pots meet the skyline.

Gaudí's masterpiece is the Expiatory Church of the Sagrada Familia, on which he worked between 1883 and his death in 1926, when he was killed in a tramcar accident outside the church. Work on the church clearly charts the progress of Gaudí's career. Although construction began with a fairly restrained Gothic-style crypt and Gothic-style façade at street level, as one's eyes scale the building it becomes progressively more intricately decorated and outlandish, passing through an art nouveau phase to finish, at the four openwork cone-shaped towers.

GAULTIER Jean-Paul b.1952   French

fashion designer

Quirky, erotic fashions and exquisite tailoring.

Gaultier worked for CARDIN, Jacques Esterel and PATOU before setting up on his own in 1976. From the onset Gaultier was dubbed the "enfant terrible de Paris". He renounced the late 1970s vogue for natural fibres, featuring mock leather, fake fur, nylon, viscose, metal and rubber in his collections. Gaultier is greatly influenced by abstraction, surrealism, 1950s kitsch and London street style, especially punk. He has caught the headlines with his unusual juxtapositions, such as teaming bikers' leather jackets with ballet tutus. His high-tech collection included bracelets which were made from tins of cat food, and he has featured corsets, conical bras and velvet corset dresses.

Gaultier has abandoned modern Western society's obsession with the thin ideal, using models of varying ages, shapes and sizes. He has also promoted masculine glamour by reviving heels, lace and powdered faces and by using male models such as the English pop star Marilyn. In 1985 he introduced skirts for men and skirt/trousers which were made in conventional pinstripes or worsted, and encased one leg in trouser, the other in skirt.

While Gautier is notorious for his gimmicks, he is also held in extremely high esteem for the superb cut and fine tailoring of his garments.

(1883–5) in Barcelona. However, around the turn of the century he began to develop his own idiosyncratic and unmistakable designs which were to mark him out as an exponent of Spanish art nouveau and as a formative, though little imitated, Modernist much admired by many, including his fellow-countryman, the Surrealist Salvador Dali.

Under the patronage of textile magnate Count Güell he designed the Palau Güell in Barcelona (1885–9). Here he experimented with unusual, sculpted chimney-pots and with using tiled mosaic – two elements which were to occur frequently in his later work. For the same patron he worked between 1900 and 1911 on the Park Güell in the outskirts of Barcelona. Here he further explored the use of gaudy, glittering mosaic, the creation of odd beasts to decorate public areas and park benches, the formation of underground grottoes and an art nouveau interpretation of a Greek theatre.

Gaudí's Casa Batlló (1905–7) in Barcelona was one of the first projects where he allowed his imagination full rein. He was charged with the job of remodelling a block of flats, and produced a building which would not look out of place in Disneyland. Gaudí played with all sorts of maritime imagery, creating waves and fishbone shapes in the concrete window surrounds and bulging balconies.

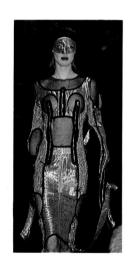

Jean-Paul Gaultier, cutaway dress with zip detail, autumn/winter 1989–90.

G

GEHRY Frank b.1929   Canadian

architect and designer

Mid-Atlantic Toyota Distributorship Offices, Loyola Law School, California Aerospace Museum, Rebecca's Restaurant; Vitra Museum.

Gehry was born Frank Goldberg in Canada. However, he has spent most of his working life in the USA and is frequently described as a Californian architect. He has become something of a folk hero in California because of his unusual designs, and his irreverent, exploded-then-reassembled punk style has spawned many imitators in the late 20th century.

After working on a number of private houses early in his career, Gehry has completed his major buildings since the late 1970s. His off-beat style began to emerge at the Mid-Atlantic Toyota Distributorship Offices, Santa Monica, California (1978). Here the interior of the plain cubic building is turned into a maze of small, cellular offices placed at odd angles to each other. The space is criss-crossed with walls, some painted pink and with holes punched through to form partitions, and some cut at an angle to climb from head height to the ceiling. Threaded and punched through the walls is a series of boxed ducts.

Following this, Gehry worked on the Loyola Law School at Los Angeles, California (1981–4) and the California Aerospace Museum, Los Angeles (1982–4).

By the mid-1980s Gehry's work had found favour with the Japanese, and his taste for the outrageous led him to design the Fishdance Restaurant in Kobe in the shape of an enormous, scaly, flapping fish. Gehry's obsession with fish has continued: he has made fish lamps and even proposes a fish skyscraper. When taunting the Post-Modernist designers for their love of classicism he once said: "If everyone is going to say that classicism is perfection then I'm going to say fish is perfection, so why not copy fish?"

In 1986 his punk style was used in the interiors of Rebecca's Restaurant, Venice, California. Here he used rough-cast walls and subdued lighting combined with rich oranges and greens, along with features such as a glass octopus and tin crocodile. The use of odd artefacts and distressed finishes has spawned numerous copies. His latest work includes the much-praised Vitra Design Museum, Weil am Rhein, Germany (1989).

In 1989 Gehry was awarded the top American architectural award, the Pritzker Prize, and won commissions to build the Disney Concert Hall in Los Angeles and the American Cultural Centre in Paris.

Frank Gehry, California Aerospace Museum, Los Angeles, 1982–4.

GEISMAR Thomas H.   See CHERMAYEFF AND GEISMAR

GERNREICH Rudi 1922–85   Austrian

fashion designer

Youth fashion and dance clothes.

In 1938 Gernreich fled the political and religious persecution in Vienna and, as a refugee, moved to California. There he studied at the Los Angeles City College and at the Los Angeles Art Center School. Gernreich initially became a dancer with the Lester Horton Modern Dance Troupe, for whom he worked as costume designer from 1942 to 1948. He then became a freelance fashion designer and in 1959 went into partnership with Walter Bass, a clothing manufacturer, to supply ready-to-wear clothes to a Los Angeles boutique, called Jax.

In 1964 he formed Rudi Gernreich Inc. and became a leading and innovative force in the field of sportswear and separates for the youth market, becoming renowned for his mini-skirts and knitted tubes and the use of psychedelic-coloured garments with hosiery. Throughout his career Gernreich campaigned to provide clothes which facilitated complete freedom. As early as 1954, when the fashion was for boned swimwear, he removed the inner structure from his swimsuits. His most publicized, but least worn, design was the topless swimsuit, which he introduced in 1964. This radical garment had a high waist, held up with thin straps, which ran between the bare breasts.

Gernreich gave up his business in about 1967 to resume fashion design on a freelance basis and pursue his greatest love, the design of dance clothes.

Sir Frederick Gibberd.

GIBBERD Frederick 1908–84   British

architect

Liverpool Cathedral.

In his early career Sir Frederick Gibberd became one of Britain's earliest exponents of the new, under coated, cubic-shaped modern style which emerged in the 1930s. During the post-Second-World-War building boom, Gibberd designed the plan and some of the principal buildings for the New Town of Harlow (from 1947), and then worked on administrative and terminal buildings at London's Heathrow Airport (1950–70). He is, however, best known for his designs for Liverpool's Roman Catholic Cathedral (1960–5).

Work began on the cathedral in 1960 when Gibberd's design was chosen to replace an earlier and much larger project envisaged by Sir Edwin LUTYENS.

Gibberd's cathedral, made of reinforced concrete and brickwork faced in Portland stone, provided a landmark in modern church design as one of the first in the UK to break with tradition – it was circular, given minimal decoration, simply furnished with plain, wooden bench pews and focused on a central altar. Above the circular base is a bell-tent-shaped roof. Above the roof rises a tall cylinder of stained glass which casts a rich blue light on the interior. On the very top is a band of slender metal spikes symbolizing the crown of thorns. The building's unusual shape has earned it the local nick-name of the "Mersey Funnel".

GILL Eric 1882–1940   British

sculptor, wood engraver, typeface designer

Gill Sans and Perpetua typefaces; sculptures for Broadcasting House, London.

Artist and craftsman Eric Gill referred to himself as a stone-carver but in fact his activities throughout the 1920s and 1930s were extraordinarily broad, encompassing sculpture, book illustration and design, wood engraving, type design and writing. Although his greatest output of work might in its nature be categorized as art, his widest area of influence has undoubtedly been in the world of design.

Gill studied at Chichester Art School and, at the turn of the century, was apprenticed to an architect. During this time he also attended lettering classes given by Edward Johnston. Both the experience and the man had a profound influence on Gill's work. He initially supported himself as a letter-cutter, and from

Eric Gill, chapter heading in *The Four Gospels*, 1931.

1904 was also commissioned by Count Harry Kessler to design and engrave lettering for the title-pages of books published by Insel Verlag in Leipzig. From 1907 he began to carve sculpture, and quickly gained high esteem; his large public commissions, such as the work for the BBC's Broadcasting House in London, completed in 1932, would eventually make him internationally known. In 1913 Gill joined the Roman Catholic Church, and from then on his art and his religious fervour were intertwined.

In the course of the 1920s Gill became a prolific book illustrator, and particularly versatile in the medium of wood engraving. He illustrated books for Count Kessler and the Cranach Press, and produced a wealth of work for Robert Gibbings' Golden Cockerel Press, including designs for *Troilus and Criseyde* (1927), *The Canterbury Tales* (1928-31) and *The Four Gospels* (1931). It was also during the 1920s that Stanley MORISON of the Monotype Corporation approached him to produce a typeface of "original design" to offset their repertoire of classic revivals. This led to Gill's designs for Gill Sans (1928), a sans serif typeface modelled on Edward Johnston's London Transport alphabet; Perpetua (1929); and a host of other typefaces such as Joanna, Bunyan and Pilgrim. Gill Sans and Perpetua remain two of the most popular faces of the century.

Gill's writing is also of interest. He produced a number of dogmatic (and sometimes cranky) essays on subjects as varied as sex, politics and typography. His classic book entitled *An Essay on Typography* (1931) is essential reading for any typographer or graphic designer.

Eric Gill.

GIUGIARO Giorgetto b.1938   Italian

industrial designer

Car design.

Giorgetto Giugiaro has had an enormous influence on car design throughout the world and has designed cars for most of the major European and Japanese manufacturers, including Audi, BMW, VOLKSWAGEN, Fiat, Alfa Romeo, Lotus, Lancia and Maserati.

Giugiaro worked at the Fiat Styling Centre in Turin from the age of 17, after studying at the Turin Academy of Fine Arts. He left after four years to work for the sports car manufacturer Nuccio BERTONE, and in 1965 he became head of design for another Turin manufacturer, Ghia.

In 1968 Giugiaro and Aldo Mantovani formed

G

their own consultancy, ItalDesign, to work on car styling. ItalDesign has since worked on models which range from dream cars to mass-market models such as the Fiat Panda and the VW Golf, Scirocco and Passat. Both the Fiat Panda and VW Golf created new styles in car design that have been much copied.

Giugiaro has also worked on a range of other products through his product design company Giugiaro Design (formed in 1981). These include watches for Seiko, sewing machines for Necchi, televisions for Sony and cameras for Nikon – most recently the Nikon F4, for professional photographers. A separate design company, Giugiaro SpA, is responsible for men's clothing and accessories.

Giugiaro is a versatile and meticulous designer who has proved that he can turn his hand to everything from cars and high technology products to pasta.

Giorgetto Giugiaro, Fiat Uno, 1983.

Hubert de Givenchy.

GIVENCHY Hubert de b.1927 French

fashion designer

1950s tailored suits and dramatic evening wear.

Givenchy studied at the Ecole des Beaux-Arts, briefly studied law, and then worked for the Paris couture houses of Fath, Piguet, Lelong and SCHIAPARELLI, before opening his own business in 1951. BALENCIAGA often claimed that Givenchy was his heir: they shared a love of the luxury of couture, and their collections were often reviewed together. Like Balenciaga's, Givenchy's workmanship was impeccable – he was a master tailor.

Givenchy's most famous client was the gamine young 1950s filmstar Audrey Hepburn, whom he dressed on and off the screen. The wardrobes he designed for her to wear in *Funny Face* (1956) and *Breakfast at Tiffany's* (1961) were copied by millions of women. Givenchy dressed Hepburn in loosely cut, waisted suits

with small neat collars and tiny hats, and in oversize jumpers and trousers, with flat ballet pumps and hoop earrings. He also built his reputation on his sack dresses, low-cut cocktail dresses with matching boleros, duster coats, and coloured gloves.

When Balenciaga retired in 1968, Givenchy recognized that the future of fashion lay in the ready-to-wear market and expanded into this area, designing leopard-printed trouser suits and denim skirts for his young customers. His early 1970s collections featured appliqué designs inspired by the paintings of Georges Braque and Joan Miró.

In 1978 Givenchy changed direction, abandoning the loosely cut garments which had become his trademark, and designing a range of closely fitting garments, many of which were decorated with rhinestones. Givenchy still heads a thriving fashion empire, which is particularly famous for evening wear in brightly coloured silks, satins, taffetas and organzas.

Audrey Hepburn dressed by Givenchy in the film *Breakfast at Tiffany's*, 1961.

GLASER Milton b.1929 American

graphic designer

Co-founder of Push Pin Studios.

To the Woodstock generation, the colourful posters of designer-illustrator Milton Glaser typify an era. His psychedelic "American Sixties style" was in fact a combination of diverse influences, ranging from Surrealism to Islamic painting – and this continuing interest in different subjects and techniques has kept his work fresh and constantly changing over the years.

A co-founder of PUSH PIN studios in New York in 1954, Glaser remained one of its main driving forces, along with Seymour Chwast, throughout the 1960s. During that time he produced images of immense popularity, such as "the Dylan poster", intended as an enclosure for one of Bob Dylan's albums. Flowers appeared often in his work, as a symbol of life and love; another familiar feature was his use of heavily decorated, novelty alphabets with names like "Baby Fat" and "Baby Teeth". Glaser's artful imagery appeared in a multitude of graphic forms – book jackets, posters, record covers, and more.

A celebration of his popularity came in 1973 with the publication of the large, glossy collection of works, *Milton Glaser: Graphic Design* (Overlook Press, New York, 1973). Glaser was the first graphic designer to be profiled in this manner – and so began the creation of coffee-table books on graphic design.

Milton Glaser.

Milton Glaser, design entitled *Geometric Landscape*, 1975.

Milton Glaser, logo for the New York State Department of Commerce.

The 1970s brought prestigious one-man shows (Museum of Modern Art in New York, the Pompidou Centre in Paris, etc.); it also saw his involvement with Push Pin dwindle. As time went on he branched out into new graphic areas such as corporate identities and interiors, and was responsible for one of the most popular motifs of modern times – "I♥NY" – which has been pirated and produced in innumerable variations.

GOLDEN William 1911–59   American

advertising and graphic designer

Corporate image for CBS.

When American corporations first became conscious of "corporate image" in the 1940s, Columbia Broadcasting System set the pace for others to follow. CBS's corporate approach was initiated by company head Frank Stanton, and throughout the 1940s and 1950s art director William Golden developed the corporate image in design and advertising. This included the design of the classic CBS "eye" symbol (dated 1950), and the art direction of countless advertisements, corporate and publicity material and exhibitions. Much of it was pioneering work and set high standards of design, while also providing a model of the co-operative relationship needed, and possible, between design and top management.

Golden, by all accounts, was a model in himself – of integrity, creative energy and professionalism. In

both articles and talks he argued for the designer's need to develop a sense of responsibility, that is, to communicate clearly and be understood, and to avoid the traps of designing for other designers. He was an advocate of honesty and clarity in design, and of the "thinking" designer. In 1972 he was elected to the New York Art Directors Club Hall of Fame. He was married to the graphic designer Cipe Pineles (later BURTIN).

GORDON Lady Duff 1863–1935   see LUCILE

GOUDY Frederic W. 1865–1947   American

type designer and typographer

Goudy Old Style, Kennerley, Italian Old Style.

Frederic W. Goudy was one of the most prolific type designers of this century. His typefaces, numbering well over 100, including italic versions, are highly distinctive in character and have become popular for use in display work and advertising design.

Goudy began his career as a freelance type designer around the turn of the century. As time went on he also became increasingly involved in the manufacture of his types. By maintaining control of every stage of production, he felt that he was able to retain the spirit in which the typefaces had been designed. He also marketed the founts himself.

Originally from Illinois, Goudy moved to Hingham, Massachusetts in 1904 and not long after moved on to New York. His first major typeface, Kennerley Old Style, was designed in 1911 and established his reputation both at home and abroad. Kennerley was followed in 1915 by one of Goudy's most successful types, Goudy Old Style, designed for American Type Founders (ATF). It had many variations including Goudy Open and Goudy Modern, both designed in 1918.

In 1920 Goudy was appointed adviser on type design to the Lanston Monotype Company and produced the typefaces Garamond and Italian Old Style, considered to be his best book face. Apart from this role, he also produced a wide variety of faces for private presses, such as Franciscan, for the Grabhorn Press, in 1932; a number of black letter and semi-black

Frederic Goudy, Copperplate Gothic typeface, American Typefounders, 1901.

ABCDEFGHIJKLMNOPQRS TUVWXYZ&?!

letter faces; and a variety of faces for specialist use, such as Saks (for the department store). His last major typeface was University of California Old Style, now known as Berkeley Old Style in a 1983 version issued by the International Typeface Corporation.

Books written by Goudy include *Typologia, studies in type design and type making* (University of California Press, Berkeley, 1940), and *A half-century of type design and typography, 1895–1945* (The Typophiles, New York, 1946).

GRANGE Kenneth b.1929 British

industrial designer

Electrical appliances (Kenwood), Venner parking meter, Parker pen.

Kenneth Grange is one of Britain's best-known product designers. He studied art at Willesden School of Arts and Crafts, and developed his skills as a technical illustrator while on national service.

His first jobs were as an assistant in architecture and design offices in London. He set up his own consultancy in 1958 and worked on a variety of products including a food-mixer for Kenwood, the Parker 25 pen, the Kodak Instamatic camera and the Milward Courier razor. The Milward razor won the Duke of Edinburgh Prize for Elegant Design in 1963.

Grange has also designed lighting, office machinery and furniture systems and he was responsible for the styling of the British Rail Intercity 125 trains. The flying-wedge shape of the 125 has its critics, but its modern style made it wholly appropriate for British Rail's slogan of the time – "This is the age of the train". Recent projects include novel-style watering-cans for Geeco and an automatic kettle for Kenwood. Since 1982, Grange has also been a consultant to Wilkinson Sword.

In 1972 Grange and his fellow-designers Theo Crosby, Colin Forbes and Mervyn Kurlansky formed PENTAGRAM, the multidisciplinary design group that is renowned throughout the world.

Grange has had an enormous influence abroad, particularly in Japan, where he has worked for 20 years. Fifty per cent of his work is now for Japanese clients. He has designed sewing-machines for Maruzen, toiletry bottles for Shiseido and a range of bathroom fittings for the tile manufacturer Inax.

In 1969 Grange was made a Royal Designer for Industry and in 1984 he was awarded the CBE.

GRAPUS founded 1970 French

graphic design collective

Left-wing cultural and political posters.

Paris-based design collective Grapus was founded by Pierre Bernard, Gérard Paris-Clavel and François Miene in the wake of the student rebellion of 1968, and much of its spirit and philosophy derives from those events. All its members belong to the French Communist Party (PCF). Although the size of the group increased in the 1980s to 20 people, operating in three separate collectives, two of the three founders, Pierre Bernard and Gérard Paris-Clavel, still remain as "creative leaders". Members of Grapus have also over the years achieved widespread fame as delightful and bizarre pranksters of the graphics world – funny, unpredictable, and known to broadcast themselves as being "completely mad".

At first they rejected commercial advertising and worked only for the Left, producing cultural and political posters for theatre groups, progressive town councils, the PCF, the CGT (communist trade union), educational causes and social institutions. Their party connections have relaxed in recent years, and they have broadened their range of projects – for example, they were responsible for the corporate identity of the Parc de la Villette, the new park of science and culture in Paris. But they remain communists and idealists, dedicated to developing a socially responsible form of graphic design in France.

Grapus are also without a doubt the premier poster artists of France. Full of colour and excitement, their images range from the naïve and childlike to the hot and risqué – and often bear a dynamism that threatens to explode off the page. Their impact on recent generations of students has been considerable.

Grapus, poster for an exhibition of work by Grapus, 1985.

GRAVES Michael b.1934 — American

architect

Snyderman House, Portland Public Service Building, Humana Building.

As a young architect Michael Graves was inspired by the early-20th-century undecorated, white cubic buildings of LE CORBUSIER and Josef HOFFMANN. However, later in his career, Graves changed style dramatically to become a pioneer of post-modernism.

During the late 1960s Graves was a member of a group called the New York Five, which also included architects Peter Eisenmann, Richard MEIER, Charles Gwathmey and John Hejduk. This group of young designers admired the classic early modern white, flat-roofed buildings such as Josef Hoffmann's Palais Stoclet, considering the 1920s to be the golden age of modern architecture. In common with the other members of the New York Five, Graves designed a number of private houses. Among his earliest commissions was the Hanselmann House, Fort Wayne, Indiana (1967). By the early 1970s Graves showed signs of breaking away from the 1920s revivalism of the New York Five and developing his own style when he built the complex and colourful Snyderman House, Fort Wayne (1972).

The use of colour appeared again in his designs for the Fargo-Moorhead Cultural Center (1977–8) – an odd folly featuring a decorated bridge which he envisaged would link the states of North Dakota and Minnesota. Graves borrowed from a number of sources – the visionary drawings of the 18th-century French architect Claude-Nicolas Ledoux, Roman classical architecture and the bold, geometric shapes and colours of art deco design.

All these sources were again combined for the Portland Public Service Building, Oregon (1979–82). This bold and playful building provoked a public outcry shortly after it was opened for being insensitive to the surrounding buildings. However, Graves remained undeterred and went on to design the even more outrageous Humana Building, Louisville, Kentucky (1982–5). This observes the early-20th-century skyscraper formula of having a base, shaft and decorated crown. The building stands on a tall, rectangular colonnaded base in the style of an ancient Greek temple, and then rises through 12 floors of a pale pink square shaft.

The top, on the north face, has a huge bowed section protruding above an expanse of glass almost the entire building's width. The remaining three sides also feature enormous, column-flanked blue and green glass panels with small temples at their centre.

Graves has earned a place as one of the early Post-Modernists. He is ranked alongside Philip JOHNSON. Both Johnson and Graves have influenced the style of many new shopping and office developments in America and Europe.

GRAY Eileen 1878–1976 — Irish

architect and designer

Lacquer screens, geometric rugs, tubular furniture.

Eileen Gray was recognized as a pioneer of modern design in the 1920s and 1930s; her achievements were then ignored for decades until the last few years of her life. She studied at the Slade School of Fine Art, London, and then in Paris. Her studies in lacquerwork and in weaving and rugmaking resulted in a series of lacquer bowls and plates, and a range of modern, geometrically patterned abstract rugs.

In 1913 Gray began exhibiting alongside designers such as Jacques-Emile RUHLMANN and Robert Mallet-Stevens, and in the early 1920s there was a considerable interest in her lacquer screens. She began experimenting with tubular furniture, which usually had geometric upholstered cushions in either leather or canvas; these designs were at least contemporary with, if not precursors of, similar combinations of upholstery and tube steel that characterize the designs of other designers of the period.

From 1927 Gray began designing buildings, especially houses, and although these are in the style of the prevailing Modern Movement, her interiors did break new ground in terms of how space was divided, and walls and ceilings used. For example, she was adept at using screens as room dividers, at using shelving and storage units as both furniture and as architecture, and for her use of blinds and shutters.

She possessed a great sensitivity towards nuances in surfaces, juxtaposing ceramic tiles with metal and metal with rugs.

GRAY Milner b.1899 — British

industrial designer

Society of Industrial Artists and Designers.

Milner Gray was a pioneering designer, whose efforts helped to establish design as a profession in

Michael Graves, INFO TK.

Michael Graves, Humana Building, Louisville, Kentucky, 1982–5.

Eileen Gray, multi-functional lacquered cabinet, 1923.

Britain. Born in London, he trained as a painter before working in the first Camouflage Unit (1917–19). In 1922, he set up Bassett-Gray, a consultancy made up of artists and writers which was reorganized in 1935 as the Industrial Design Partnership. During the Second World War, as head of the Exhibitions Unit of the Ministry of Information, he worked on such campaigns as Dig for Victory.

Building on his wartime experience, in 1945 Gray established the Design Research Unit (DRU) with Misha BLACK. This was the first British design consultancy to be based on the American model, with a large team of multi-skilled designers able to take on any commission. Gray was responsible for the overall design of the "Britain Can Make It" exhibition, and was jointly responsible for the signs on the South Bank site of the Festival of Britain in 1951. During the postwar years his numerous achievements include improving the London taxi-cab by introducing an indicator on the roof, corporate identity for Courage, the brewers, and Austin Reed. More recently, he designed the emblem for Queen Elizabeth II's Silver Jubilee.

April Greiman.

GREIMAN April b.1948   American

graphic designer

Experimental graphics, particularly using the Apple Macintosh computer.

April Greiman completed her graduate studies under the instruction of typographic rebel Wolfgang WEINGART at the Kunstgewerbeschule, Basle in 1970–1, when his innovative approach to the teaching of typography was still creating shockwaves. Following her return to America she moved to the West Coast.

She was a leading figure in the New Wave graphics movement of the late 1970s and early 1980s and her name became synonymous with a new breed of West Coast design. Borrowing a love of structure and order from her Swiss experience (the influence is still clearly discernible), she added to it her own sense of colour, texture, and sometimes frenzied collage, creating a buzzing visual poetry that many admired but few could copy.

As the 1980s sped on, she became immersed in working with new technology and video-graphics, and is particularly known for her experimental work using the Macintosh computer (a brilliant example of which is the poster fold-out for *Design Quarterly* No. 133

in 1986). Now an international name, she is widely acknowledged as having provided an invigorating influence on contemporary American graphics.

April Greiman, promotional design for the China Club restaurant, Los Angeles, 1988.

GRES Madame Alix b.1910   French

fashion designer

Sculptural, neo-classical, draped white evening dresses of the 1930s.

Madame Grès' early ambitions to become a sculptor were thwarted by poverty and parental disapproval. Instead she channelled her creativity into making *toiles* for couture houses before serving a formal apprenticeship at the Paris house of Premet. In 1933, with a Miss Barton, she formed the house of Alix Barton; when her partner left a year later, it became known simply as Alix, the name she used until she adopted the name Grès in 1940.

Grès' love of sculpture was clearly reflected in her garments, which became famous for the ingenuity of their intricate pleating, draping and classical styles. Her timeless garments, shown without any distracting accessories, were largely made in wool jersey for daytime wear and in silk jersey for the evening. Grès loved Far Eastern textiles and some of her collections were embroidered. Her trademark, however, was her sustained use of white, which she believed represented clarity and peace. Her garments were formed directly onto the model or customer, pinned and then removed carefully for sewing.

Grès was at the forefront of the vogue for neo-

Madame Grès, sculptural pleated evening dress and rouleau belt in fine white jersey, 1955.

classicism in the 1930s. She presented her fashions as sculpture, showing them on motionless models so that the cut and drape could be fully appreciated. Her garments were immortalized by leading photographers of the day, who posed her models in the setting of classical columns and ruins. Her approach to design has remained unchanged to this day.

GRESLEY Herbert Nigel 1876–1941   British
designer of railway locomotives

Pacifics and Mallard locomotives.

Ambitious, authoritarian and questioning, Nigel Gresley served a five-year apprenticeship with the famous Victorian railway engineer Francis Webb. Upon graduation and after working as a draughtsman he became carriage and wagon superintendent of the Great Northern Railway. He made his mark in this job by introducing new articulated carriages; he also introduced heating into carriages. Later he designed modified versions of existing steam locomotives before, in 1912, introducing his own first design.

Gresley became famous, however, for a class of locomotives called The Pacifics, the first of which appeared in 1922. They were fast and innovative. The Pacifics had corridor tenders, which meant that a relief crew could travel in the first carriage of the train and exchange places with the crew in the locomotive, thus enabling non-stop rail services. Speed was a passion with Gresley; so too was the appearance of speed, and he developed a class of express locomotive called the A4 class which was streamlined, but not in the ponderous American style.

Gresley was knighted in 1936. He was recognized as a brilliant engineer, but his engines did have mechanical and structural faults which became more apparent during the Second World War.

Nigel Gresley, Mallard locomotive, 1938.

GRIGNANI Franco b.1908   Italian
graphic designer, painter and photographer

Design for printers Alfieri and Lacroix; "optical-visual experiments".

Franco Grignani was born and educated in Pavia and studied architecture in Turin. From 1932 he worked as an independent designer in Milan and made a significant contribution to the fields of graphic design, photography and painting, both in his commercial work and in a massive number (tens of thousands) of private, visual "experiments".

His professional projects included art direction for a number of magazines, such as *Bellezza d'Italia*, from 1948 to 1960, but his most famous graphic design work was done for the Milan printers Alfieri and Lacroix. Working on their publicity material from 1952 onwards, he created some of the most avant-garde typography of the following three decades, often in combination with unusual photographic effects. His experimental approach and visual flair were obviously influenced by his other well-known range of activities – his "optical-visual experiments".

From 1950 he conducted in his own studio rigorous investigations of the world of optics and visual phenomena. Using "technical knowledge and scientific methods" he explored such themes as visual dynamics, illusions and distortions. Indeed, one of his greatest achievements was the development of photo-mechanical techniques used for the distortion of shapes and letterforms (an effect which was put to use in much of his work). His experiments yielded photographs, typographic works, paintings and constructions which have been published and exhibited widely. His graphic design work is still admired today as the best in Italian avant-garde graphic design.

GROPIUS Walter 1883–1969   German
architect

Founder and first director of the Bauhaus.

Walter Gropius has become known as one of the fathers of modern architecture. His early factory and housing designs and his work as founding director of the German BAUHAUS School inspired several generations of 20th-century architects.

Gropius, the son of the architect Walther Gropius, studied in Berlin and Munich. He then went on to work in the studio of Peter BEHRENS.

Walter Gropius, student ateliers at the Bauhaus school, Dessau, 1926.

In 1910 he set up his own practice and worked with Adolf Meyer on two seminal projects. The first was the Fagus shoe-last factory at Alfeld (1911). This borrowed from some of Behrens' early designs for simple rectangular blocks constructed using large areas of glass walling, but Gropius achieved an even lighter-looking structure.

The second major project was the Werkbund Pavilion for the Cologne Exhibition of 1914. Again with Meyer, Gropius designed a model factory intended to house examples of German industrial design.

During the First World War Gropius fought as a cavalry officer; he saw action at the Somme, was badly injured and was awarded two Iron Crosses. The war affected him deeply; his pre-war belief in the benefits of the machine age and mass production was shaken when he saw how deadly machines could be. The change in thinking manifested itself when, in 1919, at the age of 36, he became director of the merged Academy of Fine Arts and School of Arts and Crafts in Weimar. The school became known as the Bauhaus.

During the early years the school was heavily crafts-based. One of its major projects was the construction of the Sommerfeld House (1921–2). Designed by Gropius for a timber merchant, this house was constructed entirely in timber.

At this time Gropius displayed his ability to design in a variety of styles and worked on an entirely different commission – the Monument to the March Dead, Weimar (1921), an abstract sculpture resembling a crashed plane. He also drew up plans for the Chicago Tribune Building (1922).

Within two years of the Sommerfeld House the emphasis on design at the Bauhaus changed and moved towards a more abstract, modern style. Gropius overcame his immediate post-war dislike of machinery and in 1923 published a new paper on Bauhaus philosophy: "The Bauhaus believes the machine to be our modern medium of design and seeks to come to terms with it."

The Bauhaus began to attract criticism from local people for being decadent and for encouraging subversive anti-social behaviour in its students. Such was the strength of this protest that Gropius decided to move the school and was offered land by the sympathetic mayor of Dessau. Here Gropius designed the new art school – a complex of rectangular buildings built with concrete, glass and steel – which stood as the symbol of the new thinking.

Gropius resigned his Bauhaus directorship in 1928. He was succeeded by Hannes MEYER. The rise of Hitler's regime led Gropius to move first to Britain, where he worked briefly with Maxwell Fry, and then to America, where he lectured at Harvard. However his design work – such as the Temple of Oheb Shalom, Baltimore, Maryland (1957) and squashed octagonal skyscraper Pan-Am Building in New York (1958) – lacked the clarity displayed in his early career.

GUGELOT Hans 1920–65   Dutch-Swiss
architect and industrial designer

Slide magazine for Kodak; electrical appliances for Braun.

Hans Gugelot was a key figure in German post-war reconstruction. Born in Indonesia, he studied in Zurich at the Federal Technical College.

He was a versatile designer whose products and furniture have influenced a generation of designers. He was known for a functional "building-block" approach to design and for avoiding decorative detail, whether in furniture, such as the M125 storage unit for Bofinger (1956), or the electrical products he designed for BRAUN. The Carousel S projector and round slide magazine Gugelot designed for Kodak in 1962 was considered a classic of design.

In 1954 Gugelot met Edwin Braun and worked as a consultant to Braun over the next 10 years. The Braun Sixtant shaver (1962) set a new international standard in shaver design. Gugelot and his former pupil, Dieter RAMS, created a style for Braun which was reductionist and expressed the spirit of mathematical order. Gugelot also had an enormous influence as head of product design at the Hochschule für Gestaltung in ULM (1955–65).

Hans Gugelot and Dieter Rams, Phonosuper record player, 1956.

HADID Zaha b.1950 — Iraqi-born

Projects in Deconstructionist idiom.

Hadid was born in Baghdad. She graduated in mathematics from the American University in Beirut in 1971 and then studied at the Architectural Association in London (1972–7).

On graduating she joined Rem Koolhaas and Elia Zenghelis to form OMA, and worked with them on a project for the Dutch Houses of Parliament extension (1971). Subsequently she has taught at the AA, where she has pursued research in Suprematism and the Russian Constructivist architect Malevich. She has continued to work independently on projects, notably the Peak, Hong Kong (1983), an exclusive club, and the Kurfürstendamm Office Building, Berlin (1986).

Although her work to date has been confined to unbuilt projects, Hadid has achieved considerable international recognition and two projects are now being built: Tomigaya in Tokyo (1987) and a fire station for Vitra in Basle, Switzerland (1989). The Tokyo project uses a characteristic splintering treatment of both space and form, and the Vitra project arranges the functions of a fire station in a series of planes.

Hadid identifies herself with the "Second Modernism", which emerged during the 1980s, in opposition to what is seen as the reactionary tendencies of post-modernism. Her work is vaguely futuristic, utopian and avant-garde, and like the *first* Modernism it is concerned with space and form as the primary means of architectural expression. However, her architecture is fundamentally abstract and sculptural rather than functional. She has no interest in technology *per se*, and her projects have been described as "unbuildable".

Hadid has been associated with Deconstructionist architecture, especially since the MOMA exhibition (1988) of the same name, but she stresses the intuitive nature of her work as opposed to an architecture of ideas.

HALD Edvard 1883–1980 — Swedish

Long-standing association with Orrefors glassworks and with Rörstrand and Karlskrona potteries, Sweden.

Edvard Hald, the Stockholm-born son of an engineer, studied painting in Copenhagen and afterwards in Paris with Henri Matisse. In 1917 he became associated with the glassmaker Orrefors and the Rörstrand pottery. He worked on a freelance basis for the latter until 1924, at which time he began work as a designer and art director for Karlskrona, another ceramic tableware manufacturer. His association with Orrefors was a long and fruitful one, extending from 1917 to the late 1970s (he was its managing director from 1933 to 1944, after which time he was a freelance designer/consultant).

Hald is less well known for his ceramics designs than for those in glass, but like his lovely engraved-glass objects, his earthenware decorations, such as Rörstrand's 1919 Halda range, were examples of what one critic called the "Swedish grace" of the time.

Hald's reputation and his deserved place in the pantheon of significant figures in modern glass were achieved through his half-century association with the Orrefors firm. Like those of Simon GATE, who joined the company a year earlier, in 1916, Hald's designing talents ran the gamut from simple, elegant mould-blown carafes and tumblers with gentle fluting and ribbing, to complicated or highly decorative pieces.

Edvard Hald, engraved glass vase for Orrefors, 1919.

HAMNETT Katharine b.1948 see page 112

HARTNELL Norman 1901–79 — British

Society dressmaker, appointed dressmaker to the Queen in 1940; also designed uniforms for the armed forces.

After working for a brief period with LUCILE, Hartnell opened his own premises in 1923, and emerged as one of the few successful and acknowledged British fashion

HAMNETT

Katharine Hamnett, shiny gold mini-dress.

HAMNETT Katharine b.1948   British

fashion designer

Simple functional garments promoting peace and ecological issues.

Hamnett was taught fashion at St Martin's School of Art, briefly formed her own company, called Tutta-bankem, and then designed on a freelance basis in Rome, New York, Paris and Hong Kong. She formed Katharine Hamnett Ltd in 1979 and has achieved great success with the design of her largely utilitarian, comfortable, body-conscious garments. Many of her clothes have been widely copied, especially her ragged jeans, crumpled silks and sloganned T-shirts.

Hamnett brought peace and ecological issues to the forefront of fashion in 1983, with her Choose Life collection. In 1984 she was much publicized for wearing one of her T-shirts, emblazoned with "58 PERCENT DON'T WANT PERSHING", to meet Prime Minister Margaret Thatcher at 10, Downing Street. Other slogan T-shirts have included "STOP ACID RAIN NOW", "STOP KILLING WHALES" and "EDUCATION NOT MISSILES". Hamnett has also funded a Friends of the Earth project to research into the environmental effects of clothing production. Her jeans are washed with pumicestone instead of bleach; she uses fake fur and makes much use of silk, which is the least environmentally damaging of all fabrics.

Her garments are primarily aimed at a young market, and many collections have been rebellious and sexy, featuring skin-tight Lycra dresses with under-wired bras, revealing swimwear and tiny mini-skirts. The bulk of her garments are, however, essentially functional and wearable. Her shops have been designed by leading architects, including Norman FOSTER

and Branson Coates Architecture, and have included metal furniture by Ron ARAD. In the spring of 1989, exasperated with British clothing manufacturers, Hamnett moved her clothing production to Italy and now shows in Paris.

Katharine Hamnett.

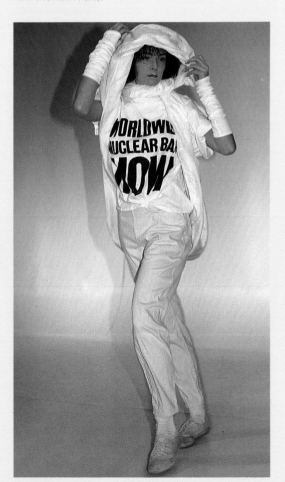

Katharine Hamnett, T-shirt, autumn/winter 1984–5.

Norman Hartnell.

designers of the years between the two World Wars – a period dominated by Parisian designs. He became famous for his luxurious satin, sequinned and embroidered evening gowns and ballgowns, as well as for his wedding dresses. From the mid- to late-1930s he received much publicity for his full, hooped and corseted crinoline dresses, which created a great impact when worn by Queen Elizabeth (now the Queen Mother), and which were copied by other designers. In 1940 he was appointed dressmaker to the Queen.

In 1941 Hartnell designed collections for the American market to gain Britain much-needed revenue. From 1947 to 1956 he was chairman of the Incorporated Society of London Fashion Designers, the group which originated the utility clothing scheme.

In 1947 Hartnell designed Princess Elizabeth's wedding dress, and in 1953 he received his greatest commission: to provide the gowns for her Coronation.

But Hartnell did not confine his talents to the design of one-off couture garments: in the 1950s he designed for Berkertex, a manufacturer of ready-to-wear women's clothing, and by the late 1950s he had added ready-to-wear garments to his own label.

HAVINDEN Ashley 1903–73　　　　　British
graphic designer, textile designer and painter

Work for Crawford advertising agency.

The name of Ashley Havinden (he signed his work "Ashley") is largely associated with the W. S. Crawford advertising agency. He started his career there, as trainee and designer from 1922 to 1929, and from 1929

onwards acted as their Director of Art and Design.

His early campaign for Chrysler, carried out in 1925, introduced dramatic, new Continental influences to British graphics – the use of bold, sans serif type; an emphasis on structure in layout; and other elements extracted from the BAUHAUS and Constructivists. It was ground-breaking work, and one of the most successful campaigns of the time. The typeface he designed for Chrysler was produced by Monotype as "Ashley-Crawford".

The 1930s brought a more relaxed mood to his work, as shown by his classic illustrated posters for the Milk Marketing Board (mid-1930s), with their use of rough brushwork and chalkboard lettering; his postwar work employed a wide variety of approaches, encompassing both machine-age hardness and relaxed decorative forms. His client list was extensive and also included work for Simpson's of Piccadilly (he was responsible for their entire graphic house style and advertising), posters for Eno's Fruit Salts, and designs for Pretty Polly Stockings (the logo is still in use).

Throughout his career Ashley Havinden continued to work and exhibit as a painter, and was also a renowned designer of rugs and textiles for leading firms such as Duncan Miller Interior Design, Campbell Fabrics and the Wilton Carpet Factory. His own publications included the book *Advertising and the Artist* (London, 1956), and he was the subject of many books and periodicals of the time.

HEARTFIELD John 1891–1968　　　　　German
graphic designer and stage designer

Political photomontage.

John Heartfield pioneered the use of photomontage for social protest and political propaganda, as well as developing it into a major art form. The photomontages he produced, particularly during the 1920s and 1930s, have had an extraordinary influence on succeeding generations in art, design and photography.

He was born Helmut Herzfelde in Berlin, and studied art at the Kunstgewerbeschule in Munich. Returning to Berlin in 1916 he worked for a film company, while also co-operating on films with his close friend, artist George Grosz, and experimenting with the new technique of photomontage. (It was also in 1916 that he anglicized his name to John Heartfield, in protest against the anti-British climate in Germany at the time.) In 1918 he was a founding member of the

H

Berlin Dada group, dedicated to the radical Communist movement, and was also associated with the Malik Verlag, a left-wing publishing house headed by his brother Wieland Herzfelde. With his brother and George Grosz, Heartfield published the avant-garde periodical *Neue Jugend* (New Youth).

In the early 1920s, he worked in stage design as artistic director for Max Reinhardt. But as the political situation in Germany deteriorated, Heartfield's art became more politically aggressive. From 1924 to 1933, he concentrated on producing photomontages, mainly for Malik Verlag and the Communist magazine *AIZ/ Arbeiter Illustrierte Zeitung* (Workers' Illustrated Paper), retitled *Volks Illustrierte* in 1936. Not surprisingly, in 1933 both Heartfield and the magazine *AIZ* were pressured out of Germany, but they continued to work together in Prague. During the heated years of the 1930s, Heartfield produced some of his most memorable works, among them: "Goering, the Executioner of the Third Reich" (showing Goering holding an axe in front of the burning Reichstag, 1933); and "Adolf, the superman: swallows gold and spouts junk" (Hitler with gold coins rattling down his throat, 1932).

Heartfield was finally forced to take refuge in England in 1938, and remained there until 1950, producing book jackets for Penguin books, and photomontages for *Picture Post* magazine and others. On moving to Leipzig he continued to work as a graphic and stage designer, notably for Bertolt Brecht's Berliner Ensemble in East Berlin, until 1961, and was subsequently Professor at the Academy of Art in East Berlin until his death in 1968.

HENNINGSEN Poul 1894–1967   Danish

lighting designer

PH lamp.

Poul Henningsen was a pioneering proponent of the Modern Movement in Denmark, where he was a leading designer of lighting. With furniture designer Kaare KLINT he edited the architectural periodical, *Kritisk Revy* during the late 1920s. Inspired by the Deutscher Werkbund, Klint and Henningsen introduced the notion of design standards and attempted to bring together art and industry through the magazine. Henningsen in particular deplored the élitism of fine art and urged painters to leave their ivory towers and enter the factory.

Henningsen worked as an industrial designer, contributing to the success and influence of Scandinavian design during the later 20th century. His PH lamp is a classic piece of modern design; created in 1925 it remains in production today, manufactured by the Copenhagen firm of Louis P. Poulson.

HENRION F.H.K. 1914–90   British

graphic and industrial designer

Pioneer of corporate identity programmes.

Frederick Henri Kay Henrion (known as F.H.K. Henrion) was born in Nuremberg, and trained in Paris in textile design and the graphic arts. He moved to England in 1936, and during the Second World War worked for the UK Ministry of Information and the US Office of War Information, designing posters, publications and exhibitions. After the war he acted as art director for various publications, for Max Parrish and others, and designed the Agriculture and Country pavilions for the Festival of Britain in 1951. By this time he had established his own studio, which became Henrion Design Associates in 1959, Henrion Design International in 1971, and Henrion, Ludlow and Schmidt in 1981.

John Heartfield, political photomontage, 1927.

F. H. K. Henrion, Keep Britain
Tidy leaflet, c.1960.

Over the years he demonstrated remarkable versatility, encompassing posters, packaging, illustrations, magazine design, symbols, advertising and publicity campaigns, as well as sign systems, exhibitions and pavilions, office interiors and product design. But more than that, he also pioneered the concept of corporate identity in Europe. Beginning with the Bowater Paper Corporation in 1949, his studio produced corporate identity programmes for many distinguished companies and government agencies including Blue Circle Cement, KLM Royal Dutch Airlines and the British Post Office.

Throughout the 1970s and 1980s Henrion remained active – teaching, advising on national education boards, serving on judging panels, and lecturing all over the world. He also published a number of highly informative design books: *Design Co-ordination and Corporate Image*, with Alan Parkin (London, 1969); *Top Graphic Design* (Zurich, 1983); and *AGI Annals* (Zurich, 1989). He held presidencies in a number of professional organizations, notably ICOGRADA (International Council of Graphic Design Associations) and the AGI (Alliance Graphique Internationale).

F. H. K. Henrion, logo for
KLM Dutch airlines, c.1964.

HERMAN Sam b.1936   American

studio glass artist

A primary figure in the international modern glass movement.

The artist-teacher Samuel J. Herman was born in Mexico, where he lived until the age of 10. Thereafter he moved to, and was educated in, the United States. He was a student of the sculptor Leo Steppern at the University of Wisconsin at Madison, but soon after beginning that course his primary – and what turned out to be lifelong – pursuit became the creation of hot-blown glass in a studio environment. Herman's

passion for that fluid medium was fuelled by Harvey Littleton, founder (with Dominick Labino) of the contemporary studio glass movement in America.

In 1966 Herman travelled to Great Britain, where, first, he was a Fulbright Fellow at the Edinburgh College of Art and then, a year later, received a Research Fellowship at the Royal College of Art in London. From 1969 to 1974 he was an influential, even charismatic, teacher at the RCA, and he became tutor in charge of glass in the Department of Ceramics and Glass.

Some of Britain's foremost glassmakers in contemporary glass studied with Herman, including Dillon Clarke, Annette Meech and Pauline Solven. His free-flowing, unorthodox, wholly original style yielded colourful, thick-walled, freeblown glass vessel-sculptures, with both externally applied and internally included decoration. Besides thriving in a creative academic milieu, Herman (with Graham Hughes, then chairman of the British Crafts Centre) helped set up a co-operative in 1969 – The Glasshouse, in London's Covent Garden.

The years 1974 to 1980 largely found the somewhat peripatetic Herman, whose works were now being exhibited widely, on the other side of the world, but in just as influential a position, introducing the contemporary glass movement to Australia, where he helped found the Jam Factory, a glass workshop in Adelaide. Also in the 1970s, Herman collaborated with Louis Leloup, Val-Saint-Lambert's chief designer, to create glass objects for that established but forward-looking Belgian firm.

HOFFMANN Josef 1870–1956   Austrian

architect

Palais Stoclet; founder of Wiener Werkstätte.

Hoffmann lived in the Austrian capital at a time when the city was one of the foremost cultural centres of Europe and trained at the Vienna Academy of Fine Arts under the leading architect Otto Wagner. He was a great admirer of the English ideals of architecture working together with craftsmanship, as expounded in the writings of John Ruskin and William Morris.

At the end of the 19th century Hoffmann taught at the applied art school attached to the Austrian Museum for Art and Industry, and in 1900 he designed a suburb of Vienna, where he built four villas between 1901 and 1905. He was also a founder mem-

H

Josef Hoffmann, Palais Stoclet, Brussels, 1905–11.

ber of the Vienna Secession. In 1903, Hoffmann became one of the founders of the Wiener Werkstätte, created as a craft studio for the design, production and marketing of high-quality domestic objects.

In 1905 he was invited to design the Palais Stoclet, a luxurious three-storey mansion in Brussels, for a wealthy Belgian financier who had lived in Vienna. It was to be a suburban palace of the arts where the Stoclets could show off their treasures. Hoffmann had clear ideas about his building design style. He was also undoubtedly inspired by Mackintosh's entry into the 1901 competition to design the House of an Art Lover.

The smooth-faced, cubic-shaped, asymmetrical Stoclet building was given minimal decoration. The interior, which included a two-storey, galleried great hall, was at once simple and elegant with its polished marbles, mosaics, onyx, glass, gold, teak and leather, and murals by Gustav Klimt. Hoffmann took his duties seriously, and designed all the furniture, china, glass and cutlery, which was then made at the Werkstätte.

Hoffmann went on to work for the German Government, promoting Austrian arts and crafts, when Austria was incorporated into the Third Reich in 1938.

HOFMANN Armin b.1920   Swiss

graphic designer

Poster design; author of *Graphic Design Manual*.

Armin Hofmann has produced a broad range of work throughout his career as a graphic designer, and became particularly known for his posters – most of them for social and cultural organizations, and characterized by the disciplined Swiss approach.

His influence on graphic design education has been profound. He began teaching at the Basle School of Arts and Crafts in 1947 – the beginning of an association that lasted for decades and achieved international renown for both school and master. Visits abroad to America, most notably Yale University, in the 1950s, and the National Institute of Design in Ahmedabad, India, in the 1960s, ensured the spread of his teaching approach.

His book *Graphic Design Manual: Principles and Practice* (Arthur Niggli AG, 1965) represented a distinct attempt to get to grips with fast-changing developments in technology and communications by "going back to basics". It offered a course of instruction in graphic design, promoting a methodical approach to problem-solving and placing great emphasis on the manipulation of rudimentary elements such as the dot and the line. The book became a Bible for practising "Swiss design" and the approach, more often abused than not, became the basis for a rigid style of formula design that was propagated well into the 1970s throughout the graphic design world.

HOLLEIN Hans. b.1934   Austrian

architect

Retti Candle Shop, Schullin Jewellery Shop, Austrian Travel Bureau.

Hans Hollein is noted for his unusual and frequently bizarre interior designs. Among his early work was the Retti Candle Shop, Vienna (1965). In the 1970s Hollein worked on the Schullin Jewellery Shop, Vienna (1974). Hollein's love of using materials in an unusual way was demonstrated on the façade, where the grid of black marble blocks was dramatically broken; in the fissure were crammed strata in shiny metal and protruding metal tubes. The strata idea was continued in the sculpted door.

During the 10 years from 1972, Hollein worked on one of his few large projects in the Mönchengladbach Museum, which he designed as a series of small, intimate top-lit spaces. One of his most bizarre projects was the Austrian Travel Bureau, Vienna (1976–8). This open-plan space featured chessboard flooring, palm trees with brass trunks and metal fronds, crumbling classical columns containing smooth steel pillars, a part pyramid emerging from a wall, and a theatre ticket-desk draped with a metal curtain swag.

Hollein's ability to juxtapose styles and materials is also demonstrated at the Museum of Glass and Ceramics, Tehran (1977), based on an old Qajar man-

Armin Hofmann, exhibition poster.

sion. He restored much of the original interior, such as the ornate plaster ceilings and carved wooden doors, and then placed his large modern display cabinets in the central areas. His glass-walled Haas House in Vienna has aroused considerable controversy owing to its proximity to St Stephen's Cathedral.

HOLSCHER Knud b.1930   Danish

architect and designer

Designs in the Danish modernist tradition.

Holscher graduated from the Architectural School at the Royal Academy of Fine Arts, Copenhagen, in 1957.

He worked independently, winning several competitions for schools and houses, and also taught. From 1959 to 1964 he was attached to the practice of the distinguished architect and designer Arne JACOBSEN, who had pioneered the modernist style in Denmark, while retaining a Danish identity in his work.

Like Jacobsen, Holscher is a comprehensive designer and he has produced many designs for furniture and architectural fittings, as well as acting as consultant to a number of firms.

Since 1968 he has been a partner and then majority shareholder in the firm of Krohn & Hartvig Rasmussen, as well as being professor of architecture at the architectural school in Copenhagen (1968–88).

The firm has won a wide variety of commissions, both in Denmark and overseas, in an idiom of flexible modernism which is responsive to the site and local traditions. Their design for the National Museum in Bahrain was completed in 1989 and is a successful attempt to get away from Arab kitsch by fusing an Arabic feeling for geometry with modern abstraction.

HONDA founded 1948   Japanese

motorcycle manufacturing company

Honda 50 motorcycle.

The Honda Motorcycle Company is an outstanding example of the post-war economic boom in Japan. It takes its name from Soichiro Honda, who started the business using surplus army engines to motorize ordinary bicycles.

Ten years after the company's foundation, Honda launched the famous Honda 50, also known as the Super Cub. It was destined to become the world's most popular motorcycle. In the immediate post-war

years people needed a cheap and economical means of transport, and the small engine Honda fitted the bill. Although the bike never enjoyed the youth cult status bestowed on rival machines, it allowed Honda to establish an international profile.

In 1964 Honda diversified into car production, which now accounts for the majority of its turnover, but it is for stylish and reliable motorcycles that the company remains famous.

Honda Gold Wing motorcycle, 1989.

HOOD Raymond 1881–1934   American

architect

Chicago Tribune building, American Radiator building, Daily News building.

Raymond Hood was one of the great and influential pioneers of early-20th-century skyscraper design. However, his architectural career was almost doomed before it began when he was given zero for drawing at his entry examination to the Paris Ecole des Beaux Arts. After taking a crash course, he applied again for a place at the school and was accepted.

After his stay in Paris, he returned to America and achieved instant notoriety when he won the Chicago Tribune Building competition of 1922. Staged at a time when there was great commercial rivalry between the cities of New York and Chicago, the contest was held to find a design which would give Chicago "the world's most beautiful building". Hood's submission, completed with John Mead Howells (1868–1959), was selected from among 260 entries. The ornate skyscraper (1922–5) with its tall shaft and stepped, spiky, carved-stone crown, drew its inspiration from earlier Gothic buildings.

The success of the building led to a commission

Raymond Hood, Chicago Tribune Tower, Chicago, 1922–5.

for the art deco-style American Radiator Building (1924) in New York. While the Tribune and American Radiator buildings demonstrated Hood's love of whimsy, he resisted adhering to one consistent style. His last major design was for the Daily News Building (1929–30) in New York. The smooth-sided skyscraper was distinguished by alternating vertical lines of undecorated stone and glass, which accentuated the building's height and impressive appearance.

HOPKINS Michael b.1932 — British
architect

Glass house, Hampstead, Lord's Cricket Ground Stand, Schlumberger Research Centre.

Michael Hopkins.

Michael Hopkins began his training at the small Bournemouth School of Architecture, but left the course before it was completed, to work for Frederick GIBBERD in London.

He returned to college aged 23 and completed his training at the Architectural Association. After college he worked for Norman FOSTER and designed his own house in Hampstead, London (1978). The family home has been featured in countless magazines and helped found Hopkins' career. In complete contrast to the surrounding town houses, it was constructed as a delicate, elegant glass box with no partitions thicker than a venetian blind.

Hopkins' fascination with the industrial high-tech style of building led to a commission for the Schlumberger Research Centre, Cambridge (1985–6). This long glass rectangle is topped by a tent-like, glass-fibre canopy held taut over the structure with tension wires fixed to an exterior skeleton of metal posts. It resembles a huge marquee which, when illuminated inside, glows at night.

Following this in 1987, Hopkins redeployed the tented-roof idea over the Lord's Cricket Ground Stand, heaped with praise by the Prince of Wales, where the seating is given shelter under the elegant canopy.

HORDEN Richard b.1944 — British
architect

Designed the Yacht House, high-tech Modernist.

Horden trained at the Architectural Association (1964–9) and worked for the Farrell Grimshaw partnership (1971–2) and Foster Associates (1974 –84). He set up his own practice, Richard Horden Associates, in 1985.

Horden was involved with a number of Foster's most significant high-tech projects including the Hong Kong and Shanghai Bank (1979–86). His work has continued the idiom of uncompromising modernism and self-conscious utilization of the lastest technologies, often from outside the traditional building industry. The notably Yacht House in the New Forest, England, which is a largely "self-build" project, is based on lightweight yacht technology. In its modular planning and its celebration of detail it is clearly inspired by MIES VAN DER ROHE. However, it is more technological in its construction and imagery. There have been several commissions for other private houses utilizing this technology and a commission from America for a mobile exhibition centre. Horden is currently working on a dramatic office building in London, which will feature a multistorey glazed atrium. Horden sums up the design as "calm, light, and straightforward with the beauty in the details"

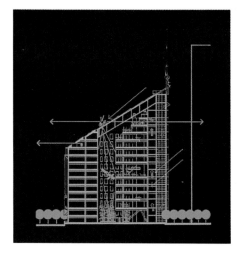

Richard Horden Associates, new Atrium Building, Stag Place, London. Winning competition entry, 1987.

HORNBY Frank 1863–1936 — British
toy designer

Meccano; Dinky toys; Hornby model trains.

Frank Hornby's early years were spent as a struggling amateur inventor, supported by working in a Liverpool office. The father of two small boys, he had always been fascinated by model-making, and his talents eventually found an outlet. It was when he was faced with the problem of constructing a model crane that the idea of using adaptable parts, which could be used for the construction of other models, first struck Hornby. He painstakingly cut out perforated strips of copper in varying lengths to form the crane. The dimensions, size of hole and distance between them remained unchanged throughout production.

The original idea was patented in 1901 under the name "Mechanics Made Easy" and replaced by the more familiar Meccano in 1907. The tin boxes, containing nickel-plated strips, brass wheels and nuts and bolts, proved immensely popular and a broader range of parts were introduced, including an electric motor. Basic changes were made by Hornby during the 1920s, including the painting of strips in red and green instead of nickel-plating from 1926. During the 1920s Hornby introduced model trains, and the No. 2 special series of semiscale locomotives came into the shops in 1929, and the forerunners of Dinky toys in 1933.

HORTA Victor 1861–1947 — Belgian

architect

Created original vocabulary of art nouveau ornament and became a leading figure of the continental art nouveau movement.

Horta studied at the Ghent Academy (1876) and the Académie des Beaux-Arts in Brussels. The simplicity of his first work, three small houses in the Rue des Douzes Chambres, Ghent (1886), owes something to the neo-classicism of his first employer, Balat.

Horta came to complete maturity in the Hôtel Tassel, Brussels (1892–3), one of the key architectural works in the art nouveau movement. Its use of interconnected spaces broke with traditional planning and opened the way for the planning by volumes of the modernists. It was also the first private house to make extensive use of iron as a structural material and for decorative elements in the curved linear style which is so characteristic of art nouveau. The "Horta Line" or whiplash line was derived from the study of natural forms and was a manifestation of the aesthetic impulse of the movement to turn to nature and traditional crafts.

Horta's Hôtel Solvay (1895–1900) represents art nouveau in its final development, an extraordinary *mélange* of styles and forms in the increasingly reactionary and bourgeois mode that the movement had come to assume.

After a stay in America (1916–19) Horta's architecture assumed an austere classical direction which represented a return to his early simplicity. The Palais des Beaux-Arts in Brussels (1922–28) is his principal work of this period and was designed in concrete.

In 1912 Horta was appointed a professor at the Académie des Beaux-Arts in Brussels, and became the school's head (1927–31).

HULANICKI Barbara b.1936 — British

fashion designer

Teenage fashions (1963–75).

Born in Palestine, of Polish parents, Hulanicki arrived in England in 1948. After studying at Brighton Art College for two years, she worked as a freelance graphic designer for leading fashion magazines, including *Vogue*. In 1961 she married Stephen Fitz-Simon and two years later the couple started their own mail-order, teenage fashion business.

Their first garments were advertised in popular newspapers. Encouraged by the phenomenal response, they opened their first boutique, called Biba, in London in 1964. Biba sold mini smock-dresses with matching kerchiefs, mix 'n' match fashions, rubberized macs, floppy hats, and dyed and lengthened rugby shirts which were worn as mini-dresses. Hulanicki cut the armholes of her garments extremely high and the sleeves skin-tight to make her customers' bodies look longer and thinner. Many of her garments were decorated with printed op art and geometric designs. Hulanicki became most famous, however, for her palette of muted purples, dull reds, sepias, pinks, blues and greys.

Clothes from Biba were within the price range of working teenagers, although Biba's customers included the wealthy and famous as well. Biba went from strength to strength and in 1965 Hulanicki and Fitz-Simon moved to larger premises. Customers continued to queue outside the shop and scrambled to buy the merchandise within moments of its going on display.

In September 1969 Biba moved to yet another site, this time an enormous department store in London's Kensington High Street. This shop sold men's, women's and children's clothing (right down to purple nappies), household goods and food. Its enticing and exotic interior attracted thousands of visitors, but Hulanicki and Fitz-Simon had overstretched themselves. Biba closed in 1975.

Barbara Hulanicki in the Rainbow Room of Biba, London, *c.*1973.

IBM founded 1924 American

computer multinational

Pioneer of design and design management under Thomas J. Watson, Jr.

IBM came to realize the value of design in the mid-1950s under Thomas J. Watson Jr., the son of the company's founder and then chief executive.

Watson was responsible for retaining Eliot NOYES as a consultant on all aspects of the company's presentation. Noyes was responsible for hiring Paul RAND for the design of the IBM logotype and Charles EAMES to make company presentations. The best architects of the day, among them MIES VAN DER ROHE, BREUER and Eero SAARINEN, were employed to design company buildings around the world. The trend has continued to the present, and a number of IBM buildings in Britain were designed by Foster Associates.

Watson continued to extol the merits of design leadership and coined the much-repeated maxim: "Good design is good business." Without doubt, IBM's example has done much to change corporate America's attitude to design.

As IBM grew, it was obliged to sacrifice the personal nature of its design patronage. First under Walter Kraus, and since 1989 under Tom Hardy, the company has maintained its Design Program within the Corporate Communications department in Stamford, Connecticut. Hardy, an industrial designer with IBM since 1970, has four staff, responsible respectively for industrial design, interface graphics, packaging and other graphics, and strategic design.

After Eliot Noyes' death, the Milan-based German industrial designer Richard SAPPER became IBM's corporate industrial design consultant in 1980. More recently, IBM appointed Edward Tufte, author of *The Visual Display of Quantitative Information* as a consultant on interface graphics.

IBM Selectric typewriter, designed by Eliot Noyes, 1961.

ISOKON founded 1931 British

architecture and design company

Penguin "donkey" display stand; Breuer's plywood Long Chair.

The Isokon Furniture Company was set up as an experiment in Modern Movement architecture and design. During the inter-war years Britain did not develop a sustained modernist movement to compare with its counterparts abroad, but there were some exceptions, of which Isokon was one of the most notable.

The company was founded by a trio, dedicated to the principles of modernism, which included Jack

Isokon, bentwood dining table, designed by Marcel Breuer, 1936.

Pritchard, his wife Molly and the architect Wells COATES. Nor was Isokon their only venture: Pritchard also commissioned Wells Coates to design a white concrete block of flats in Lawn Road, Hampstead, London. Completed in 1934, these flats became a centre for avant-garde intellectual and artistic life in London, and in the late 1930s a haven for BAUHAUS refugees fleeing Nazi Germany. The list of residents at Lawn Road reads like a roll call of the International Style, and included Walter GROPIUS, Marcel BREUER and László MOHOLY-NAGY. Inevitably Jack Pritchard recruited these designers into his Isokon project, and the resulting furniture remains one of British modernism's most interesting ventures.

Isokon furniture was largely made in plywood, a material much admired by the modernists for its ability to bend into dramatic sculptural shapes. Pritchard had also worked for the famous plywood company Venesta, and was in a position to exploit his experience and contacts. By the end of the 1930s Isokon was marketing a pioneer range of plywood furniture. The best known examples were the Penguin donkey, a bookstand designed for the distinctive range of paperback books, and the Long Chair in bent plywood designed by Marcel Breuer.

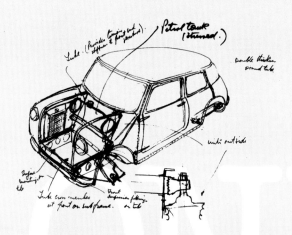

Alec Issigonis, an early drawing for the Mini.

ISSIGONIS Alec 1906–88   British

industrial designer

Morris Minor and Mini.

Alec Issigonis was born in Turkey in 1906 and moved to Britain in 1921. He trained as an engineer at Battersea Technical College and worked for four years in a London design office before joining Rootes Motors, initially as a draughtsman and eventually becoming chief engineer. In 1936 Issigonis joined Morris Motors, where he worked on the design of the Morris Minor. Launched in 1946, the Morris Minor was a revolutionary car in its day, and remained in production for over 20 years. It was also relatively successful in the USA where at one time it was selling at a rate of 15,000 a year. There were elements of US cars of the late 1940s in its styling.

But it was the Mini Minor, launched in 1959, which really earned Issigonis his place in the history of the car industry. After the Suez oil crisis of 1956 the need to reduce fuel consumption was a major preoccupation of the car industry, and the Mini was designed specifically to be economical to run.

The Mini proved to be an enormously successful car, not only because of its engineering achievements but also the great popular appeal of its novel body shape – 5,000,000 models came off the production line. It could achieve 50 miles to the gallon and speeds of 70 miles per hour, and it was also easy to park and manoeuvre; it had front-wheel drive and a fully independent suspension system. Issigonis had developed a rubber suspension system for his "Lightweight Special" hillclimber car, which he designed with George Dawson and elements of which were adapted for the Mini production line.

Alec Issigonis, Mini for Austin Rover, 1964 winner at Monte Carlo.

Issigonis maximized the interior space of the Mini by placing the engine sideways. In all, the Mini demonstrated Issigonis' practical and common sense approach to design. He had the practical abilities of an engineer but the vision of a designer, as his drawings for the Mini show.

In 1961, Issigonis became chief engineer and technical director of the British Motor Corporation. When he retired at the age of 65, Issigonis was engineering director of what had by then become Austin Rover.

Issigonis also worked on numerous other cars, including the Austin Seven, the Morris 1100 and various versions of the Mini (Mini estate, Mini van, Mini Moke). He was knighted in 1969 and received numerous other honours including the CBE in 1964, the Leverhulme Medal in 1966 and Fellowship of the Royal Society in 1967.

Alec Issigonis with the first production Mini and a 1965 model.

J

JACKSON Betty b.1949 — British

fashion designer

Stylish, imaginative fashions since 1981.

From 1968 to 1971 Betty Jackson studied fashion and textiles at Birmingham College of Art. She worked as a freelance fashion illustrator from 1971 to 1973, helped to launch the Wendy Dagworthy label (1973–5) and for the following six years was chief designer at the Radley Cooper Quorum Group, designing top quality womenswear for Quorum and a younger, cheaper range for Cooper.

Betty Jackson Ltd was formed in 1981 and from the start attracted a large international clientele. Loose shapes and bold prints – including deckchair stripes, vivid patterns and figurative designs – have become her signature, combined with body-hugging stretch-fabric garments. Jackson always works with soft, malleable fabrics and is particularly renowned for her printed textiles, many of which have been influenced by the paintings of Chagall, Matisse and Magritte. She has often used just one print, in different colourways, to determine the character of her collections, employing leading designers such as Timney and Fowler, who are particularly famous for their monochrome graphic designs, and Brian Bolger of the Cloth.

In 1986 she launched Betty Jackson for Men, which employed the same relaxed approach that is found in her women's clothing. In 1987 she signed an agreement with Vogue patterns to widen the market for her designs, and in 1988 introduced Betty Jackson accessories. Jackson's collections are always wearable, display humour and cull inspiration from many sources. Her fashions appeal to a broad age-group and her influence on contemporary fashion is far reaching.

JACOBSEN Arne 1902–71 — Danish

architect

Munkegård School, Gentofte; SAS Hotel, Copenhagen; Kuwait Central Bank.

At a time when Denmark had abandoned the heavy, ornate architecture of the 19th century, Arne Jacobsen emerged as one of his country's first modernists and became a pioneer of the refined new style known as International Modern. While he had a great respect for the classical designs of the ancient Greeks and Romans, Jacobsen was interested in devising a new interpreta-

tion of those styles more suited to the 20th century. He was greatly influenced by the Swedish architect Gunnar ASPLUND.

Jacobsen began working at a time when the influence of the Modern Movement was spreading rapidly across America, Europe and Scandinavia. The new plain, cubic, flat-roofed, asymmetrical buildings with their large windows designed by pioneers such as Frank Lloyd WRIGHT, Josef HOFFMANN and Walter GROPIUS had caused considerable excitement in the design profession when they first appeared in the early part of the 20th century. However, by the late 1930s Jacobsen felt that many designs being produced were bland and nondescript. While continuing to combine classical theories with modern style, he also crossbred it with traditional Danish building and design techniques.

He built a number of elegant and simple town halls in the suburbs of Copenhagen at Aarhus (1938–42), designed with Erik Møller, Søllerud (1939–42) and Rodovre (1955–6), but among his major triumphs was the Munkegård School at Gentofte (1952–6). Here he designed the perfect environment for children, where the scale was kept small and intimate.

Later, as his international reputation grew, he worked on larger structures such as the SAS Hotel in Copenhagen (1958). The simple, tall glass tower standing on a podium displayed the influence of MIES VAN DER ROHE. Then towards the end of his career, he designed and built the Kuwait Central Bank in Kuwait which, at the time, was the world's most costly building, with its gold-leaf dome and vaults built to withstand nuclear attack.

Jacobsen's design skills extended from buildings to a whole range of goods including furniture, bathroom tiles, cutlery, carpets and light fittings.

Betty Jackson, printed trouser suit, spring/summer 1985.

Arne Jacobsen, Munkegård School, Gentofte, Denmark, 1952–6.

JAMES Charles 1906–78 — British

fashion designer

Luxurious and sculptural garments.

Charles James worked as a fashion designer from the late 1920s until his retirement in 1957. He trained first as a milliner, and the use of millinery ribbons on his fashions was to become one of his trademarks. James worked in Paris and London before settling in New York in 1940. He dressed high society and leading Hollywood stars, and boasted that his garments were among the most highly priced in the world. James became one of the first American-based *couturiers* to receive international recognition.

James was particularly famous for his sculptural, formed garments. He worked like an engineer, using wire and padding, to form dresses that could stand independently of their wearer. He had a detailed knowledge of historical dress, and was particularly passionate about the full and corseted styles of the 1860s, translating the essence of this period into his *décolleté* evening gowns. These were ruched, puffed and swagged and made in luxurious satins and silks. James cut many of his garments on the cross and even created dresses from spirals of fabric.

In 1938 James created a white satin jacket which was heavily padded, in channels, with eiderdown. It has often been credited as the forerunner of the US Air Force quilted jackets worn during the Second World War, and of today's skiwear.

JENSEN Georg 1866–1935 — Danish

silversmith

Craftsman in silver of enduring fame.

One of the most successful and influential individuals in 20th-century Scandinavian decorative arts and international silver, Georg Jensen – and the talented group of designers in his employ – produced fine silver jewellery and objects, first in the organic art nouveau and more traditional neo-classical veins, later in more modern modes.

As a boy, Jensen was drawn to sculpture, but he was at first apprenticed to a goldsmith. At the age of 18, Jensen was accepted at the Royal Academy of Art, where he studied sculpture. In 1892 Jensen graduated from the Academy, by which time he had already exhibited his sculpture to some acclaim. But work as a sculptor did not come about, so Jensen turned to pottery-making with Joachim Petersen.

Jensen and Petersen displayed some of their ceramics at the 1900 Exposition Universelle in Paris, where they earned an Honourable Mention and healthy sales, and Jensen was also given a considerable grant by the Danish Academy which allowed him to travel for two years abroad, to study art in Paris, Rome, Florence and other places. Upon his return to Copenhagen Jensen determined to devote his artistic career to designing and producing handsome as well as useful objects, *à la* William Morris and Henri van de Velde, two European designers whose output and philosophy he deeply admired. Out of economic necessity, he continued producing ceramics with Petersen for some time, but their success was limited, so Jensen was prompted to take on additional work in the discipline in which he had originally trained, namely as a goldsmith.

He worked for the silversmith Mogens Ballin, an exponent of the curvilinear, organic art nouveau style that had reached its apex at the 1900 Paris fair, and around 1904 Jensen was able to set up his own silver workshop, so successful and well-known had he become working for Ballin. Late that same year he exhibited pieces under his own name at Copenhagen's Museum of Decorative Art.

For the first few years, Jensen's output was chiefly jewellery: silver brooches, rings, necklaces, bracelets, earrings, hat-pins and hair-combs decorated with fruit, bird, floral and leaf motifs, occasionally fish and even a shimmering dragonfly, and embellished with coral, moonstone, amber, lapis lazuli, carnelian, agate and other stones, mostly cut in cabochon and drop shapes. Although his motifs related to the nature-inspired art nouveau repertory, in their thickness and richness his pieces resembled no one else's work and comprised their own distinctive "Jensen style".

In 1905 Jensen's success led him to set up larger premises. He began producing hollow-ware in large numbers and also commenced his collaboration with Johan Rohde, the multi-talented architect/artist who had shown Jensen's sculpture at the 1897 Free Exhibition. Two years later Rohde was designing silver on a regular basis for Jensen, and their rich collaboration was to last until 1935.

By 1909 Jensen silver was becoming famous beyond Denmark, with a shop in Berlin devoted to selling Jensen silver opening on the Kurfürstendamm that year. In 1912 Jensen established an expanded workshop and, with the introduction of sophisticated

Georg Jensen, silver and coral ring, 1904.

Georg Jensen.

machine production, the output of Jensen silver greatly increased, with assorted vessels, beverage sets and cutlery patterns being produced in huge numbers. With the changing times, decorative styles changed as well, and Jensen, though not discontinuing production of his popular, mostly organic patterns, embellished with characteristic clusters of silver beading, also created pieces in contemporary styles.

In 1919 Jensen relinquished his position as chairman of the company (he had never much cared for the business side of his operation), though he remained its artistic director.

Jensen actually left the company for a time in 1925 to try and work on his own in Paris, but his limited finances forced him to return to Copenhagen to work in 1926. The subsequent years, leading up to his death in 1935, were spent mostly working on his own and having little contact with the company. Still, Georg Jensen silver was to grow ever more famous. When he died at the age of 69, obituaries the world over honoured the man and his talents. The *New York Herald Tribune* called him "the greatest craftsman in silver of the last 300 years".

JENSEN Jakob b.1926   Danish

industrial designer

Audio equipment (for Bang & Olufsen).

Jakob Jensen trained as an industrial designer in Copenhagen and worked for seven years as chief designer for Count Sigvard Bernadotte; he then spent two years in the USA, where he taught at the University of Illinois. He returned to Copenhagen in 1961 to form a design consultancy.

Jensen's minimalist designs were for many years regarded as the ultimate in elegant audio styling (although in recent years Danish design has lost favour and Bang & Olufsen products have perhaps become over-refined in style). He was also responsible for technical advances such as the tangential pickup arm system, a method of playing records which has now become standard. This system first appeared in 1972 on the Beogram 4000 record-player.

The Beolit 600 radio introduced in 1960, with its more simplified controls, was an ergonomic advance on previous transistor radios. Since then, Jensen has designed a succession of audio equipment for Bang & Olufsen. More recent products include the Beosystem 5500 – a four-unit music system controlled through an infra-red control panel – and the Beocenter 9000 music system and compact-disc player with touch-sensitive illuminated controls.

Jensen has received numerous design prizes for his work, which is included in the collection at the Museum of Modern Art in New York.

JIRICNA Eva b.1938   Czech

architect

Exponent of an elegant high tech: has specialized in retail work.

Eva Jiricna qualified as an architect/engineer at the University of Prague in 1963 and gained a postgraduate MA from the Academy of Fine Arts the same year. She arrived in the UK in 1968 and worked for a year with the GLC Schools Division before becoming an associate with the Lois de Soissons Partnership, working principally on the planning design and construction programmes of Brighton Marina.

Jiricna set up her own practice in 1979 with David Hodges. In 1980 she met Joseph Ettedgui, the fashion retailer who then was beginning his colonization of London's most fashionable shopping areas. There has been a strong association which helped to create the matt black style which was fashionable in 1980s London. The Joseph style became synonymous with her elegant interiors, in which high-tech features are softened by a slight romanticism and soft muted colour. Her designs for his shops and restaurants culminated in the Joseph flagship store in the Fulham Road (1988). With Richard ROGERS her practice collaborated on the interiors of the Lloyds building, and commissions followed from Harrods for their Way In department where she collaborated with fellow-Czech Jan Kaplicky.

In 1987 the practice became Eva Jiricna Architects, and the scope of their work has broadened to include product design and numerous commissions.

Eva Jiricna.

JOHNSON Clarence b.1910   American

aircraft designer

P-80, U2 and SR-71 Blackbird aircraft.

Clarence Johnson, chief designer to the Lockheed Aircraft Corporation from 1952, is best known for the P-38 (1941), a hugely successful pursuit fighter aircraft, the P-80, the USA's first jet fighter (1943), and the U2

Clarence "Kelly" Johnson, Lockheed P-38 Lightning, 1941.

spy plane of 1952 onwards, and from 1958 the SR-71 Blackbird reconnaissance aircraft, which was, until the appearance of the Stealth bomber, built by Northrop (1988), the most advanced aircraft in the world. He is also credited with the Hercules transport aircraft – the C-130 – which is now one of the workhorses of the Western world.

Most of Johnson's career has been spent with the Lockheed Corporation and he became Senior Vice-President of the company in 1969.

JOHNSON Philip b.1906   American

`architect`

Seagram Building (with Mies van der Rohe); the Glass House; New York State Theater; AT&T.

Philip Johnson, born in Cleveland, Ohio, the son of a lawyer, studied classics at Harvard and enjoyed a successful career as a critic before training as an architect in his mid-30s. His early interest in architecture led him to write a book entitled *The International Style* in 1932 with his mentor Henry-Russell Hitchcock. This influential publication was the first to examine the rise of the early 20th-century modern design.

In 1941 he returned to Harvard to study architecture under Gropius. In 1947 Johnson wrote a book on MIES VAN DER ROHE's work which was published by the Museum of Modern Art, where Johnson was director of Architecture and Design.

Mies wielded a powerful influence, most clearly demonstrated in Johnson's designs for his Glass House at New Canaan, Connecticut (1949). It was built shortly after Mies began work on his

Farnsworth House (1945–50) at Illinois. Johnson's own house bears a remarkable resemblance to the Mies design – based on the same simple, rectangular box shape. Johnson acknowledged a large number of inspirational sources from Mies and LE CORBUSIER to Theo van Doesburg and Claude Ledoux.

The Glass House, set in beautifully landscaped grounds, attracted considerable attention from critics and the public alike. The only privacy afforded by the design was by drawing the curtains or by entering the off-centre, circular brick "ablution tower".

The homage to Mies led to an offer of work, and in the mid-1950s Johnson worked with his hero on the towering 39-storey Seagram Building in New York (1954–58), in bronze and smoked brown glass. Following this, Johnson experimented in different styles and designed a number of museums and art galleries using abstract interpretations of classical architecture. His most notable is the Amon Carter Museum of Western Art at Fort Worth, Texas (1961).

Johnson's admiration for monumental buildings – which even extended to the massive structures built in Germany during the rule of the Third Reich – was expressed in his design for the New York State Theater (1964), a part of the Lincoln Center complex.

The AT&T skyscraper in New York (1978–84) has undoubtedly been Johnson's most influential building. It has also earned him the title of the father of post-modernism.

Philip Johnson and John Burgee with Henry Simmons, street level and exterior views of the AT&T building, New York, 1978–84.

JONES

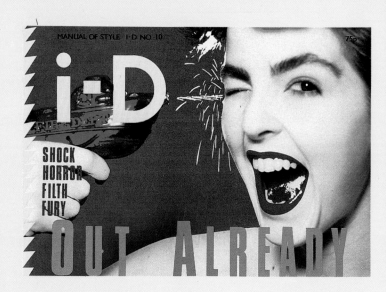

JONES Terry b.1945   British

graphic designer and magazine art director

Publisher of *i-D* magazine, mouthpiece of the Punk movement.

Instant Design, the name of Terry Jones's present company, describes the creatively-chaotic graphic style he initiated in the early 1980s, which centred on random clutter produced by "instant" or low-tech methods: photocopier distortions, handwriting, type-writer, stencils, Letraset – and just about anything else at hand. Derived from the low-budget graphics of Punk, it was anti-grid, anti-layout, and full of energy, speed and recklessness. Its main vehicle, *i-D* magazine (the brainchild of Jones), became one of the most important British style magazines of the 1980s, and consequently "instant design" made a significant impact on the progressive graphics of that decade. Meanwhile Terry Jones himself emerged as one of Britain's most innovative editorial designers.

Terry Jones studied graphic design in Bristol, England, in the early 1960s. After working in a London design studio and on *Good Housekeeping* magazine, he became art director of *Vanity Fair* (1970–1) and then art director of British *Vogue* (1972–7). While he was at *Vogue* handling high fashion, the Punk movement was on the rise – and Jones crossed over into new and exciting territory in 1977 when he designed and edited the highly illustrated *Not Another Punk Book* (Aurum Books, 1978), now considered a classic product of the Punk era. It was, as far as graphic products go, an extraordinary hybrid. It owed much to the graphic innovations of Punk; an IBM golfball was used for the text, Dymo tape for headlines, printer's red tape to stick photos to the page, typewriter and handwriting

for captions and quotes, frenzied collages made from news cuttings and snapshots (all these telltale signs were soon to grace the pages of *i-D*). But it also benefited from the artistic eye and the style-conscious flair of a highly experienced fashion-magazine art director. *Not Another Punk Book* contains a journalistic record of Punk, as well as a fashion parade of its bizarre street fashions and accessories – and Jones's fascina-tion for the wearers is clear throughout. Acting as a photo-call for a subculture, it provides an absorbing portrait of those times.

The book was also a turning-point for Terry Jones. Unable to convince his colleagues at *Vogue* that British style was taking off in strange and exciting new directions, he left the magazine and engaged in a flurry of freelance work (designs for the record indus-try, publishers, etc.), the art direction of *Sportswear Europe* magazine (Düsseldorf), and the role of consul-tant to German *Vogue* (Munich) and *Donna* (Milan) – all the while intending to put together a new maga-zine on emerging British street style. In 1980, on the strength of his own money and friends, Terry Jones launched *i-D* magazine, and from then on played the multiple roles of publisher, editor and art director.

i-D started out as a fashion "fanzine": it prowled the streets of London documenting a new form of fashion – "street style". It also introduced a new graphic language, based on spontaneity, speed and a low budget; sporting typewriter text, tickertape headlines, little colour, and pages simply stapled together. It was intended to feel "instant" and hand-made – able to exploit the occasional "happy accident" or technical error, and defiant in its refusal to make use of graphic conventions such as grids. Photographs played a journalistic role, like snapshots or news-shots

Terry Jones, front cover of *i–D* magazine (issue no. 10), c.1980.

Terry Jones, inside spread from an early *i–D* magazine.

in a documentary study. They recorded teenagers and students who bought their clothes from low-budget sources – charity shops, bargain basements, markets, secondhand shops – and combined them to create their own distinctive style or fashion (all with the air of rebellion heavily encouraged by Punk). *i-D*'s editorial approach was minimal, early issues carried very basic information on fashion and music (cabarets, clubs, gigs, etc.)

i-D soon earned the title of "style magazine" and, as time went on, acquired a substantial following and expanded into colour and more sophisticated production techniques. Its "instant" visual style was seen to be highly successful in reaching the youth market, and was copied by other institutions wanting to cultivate their image with young people – such as banks, building societies and fashion retailers – in the mid 1980s.

By its fifth birthday (1985), *i-D* had become an A4 glossy magazine and was also receiving financial backing from *Time Out* magazine's publisher Tony Elliot, with whom Jones set up a publishing partnership. In addition to his role at *i-D*, Jones also undertook a phenomenal amount of design and advertising work, including ad campaigns for Swatch (UK), Lorenzini (Italy), St Moritz (Switzerland), Fiorucci (Italy), Brylcreem (UK) and Mr Joe (Italy). In the area of video and TV, he produced titles for the weekly events programme *01 for London* (Thames TV, 1987–8 and 1988–9 series); logo, titles and art direction for the youth news programme *Reportage* (BBC); new identity graphics for Superchannel/satellite TV; and many other projects. In 1986/87 a major retrospective exhibition of his work, entitled "Instant Design: 1966–1986", was staged in Tokyo, Italy and London.

Most recently he was appointed European Art Director for *Esprit*; and was responsible for the book *Decade of Ideas* (published with Penguin Books) – a catalogue/overview of the 1980s, which (with heavy reference to *i-D* magazine) offers a suitably frenzied look at an exciting period in terms of youth culture, design and fashion. Moving into the 1990s, neither Terry Jones nor his energetic creation *i-D* show any signs of slowing down.

Terry Jones, inside spread, featuring Vivienne Westwood and Johnny Rotten, from *Not Another Punk Book*, 1978.

J

JONES Stephen b.1957   British

milliner

Unconventional, inventive hats since 1979.

Jones studied at High Wycombe and St Martin's Schools of Art. While he was still a student he worked at Lachasse Couture, where he learned to make hats. In 1979, having left college, he went to Paris to sell his unconventional millinery designs, but was unsuccessful and returned to London, where he met the pop-star and style leader Steve Strange, who promoted his hats. Jones's reputation grew, which enabled him to open his own shop in 1980. He has since established himself with his exquisitely made, witty, often outrageous, fantasy and cheeky headwear, which he designs primarily for the fashionable club scene. His humorous French-fries hat (1984) and colander hat (1985) played with the Surrealist love of displaced and everyday objects. Jones also progressively restyles traditional millinery such as stetsons and top-hats, and remodels his famous pork-pie hats each winter.

His much-acclaimed millinery is now in great demand. His diverse talents are sought by a wide spectrum of international fashion designers – he has designed for Jean MUIR, Zandra RHODES, BODY MAP, GAULTIER (his trilby hats for Gaultier received much attention), MUGLER (for whom he designed balaclavas) and for the Comme des Garçons' Bird's Nest collection of 1985. In addition to his much publicized daring designs, Jones is also noted for the stylish hats he creates for his more conventional clientele, which includes the Princess of Wales. He also designs raffia wigs and hairpieces.

Stephen Jones hat, 1983.

JONES Terry b.1945   see page 126

JOURDAN Charles founded 1921   French-based

shoe design company

Brightly coloured suedes and leathers.

Charles Jourdan founded his shoe company in 1921 at Romans, in the Drôme region of France. After the Second World War the owner's three sons joined and expanded the business: Charles Jr supervised the manufacture, René undertook the administration and Roland designed. It was Roland's progressive and imaginative designs which put the company at the forefront of shoe design during the 1950s and 1960s.

Until the 1950s, fashion and shoe design operated in virtual isolation. With the expansion of ready-to-wear business, fashion designers increasingly commissioned shoe designers to create complementary styles for their clothing. During this period Jourdan secured orders from leading fashion houses including DIOR (from 1959) and CARDIN. Between 1971 and 1981 Robert Clergerie trained with and designed for Jourdan and the company became famous for his progressive styles, which greatly simplified shoe design. During the late 1960s and early 1970s their advertisements featured avant-garde images by the Surrealist photographer Charles Bourdin. Also during this period, the company was bought by the retailing giant Genesco and expanded into accessories, including jewellery, watches, swimwear, ties, belts and luggage.

Jourdan has initiated new production techniques and employed leading designers, photographers and retail designers, including the Italian architect Janet Manasce. All these factors have contributed to public awareness of shoe design.

JUNGER Hermann b.1928   German

jeweller

Bauhaus-influenced jewellery.

Junger studied at the Staatliche Zeichenakademie, Hanau, and is currently Professor of Goldsmithing at the Akademie der Bildenden Künste, Munich. Junger's importance to modern jewellery is considerable.

Junger's work begins with his watercolours and line drawings, which have considerable merit in their own right. The drawings are for discovering ideas and capturing a spontaneity which would be difficult to attain if all the exploratory work was done through making the jewellery itself. His development owes little to other jewellers, but a great deal to a German painter called Julius Bissier, whose fluid, almost Oriental compositions conveyed an emotional and mental attitude which Junger wanted in his own work.

Expressiveness in Junger's work derives from two aspects of BAUHAUS designs – an inclination to keep design to essentials, while at the same time incorporating a freer and sometimes more playful ingredient. Paul Klee is a covert mentor. Junger works in gold and other precious materials, employing shapes that are quasi-ritualistic and echo the decorative devices of pre-Christian and pre-classical civilizations.

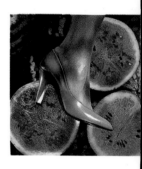

Charles Jourdan, court shoe advertisement, 1990.

KÅGE Wilhelm 1889–1960 Swedish

ceramic designer

Art director of AB Gustavsberg ceramics factory, Sweden; diverse and eclectic designs for household wares and studio pieces.

One of the greatest influences on 20th-century Swedish ceramics, Wilhelm Kåge first trained as a painter, studying at the Valand Art school in Gothenburg, then under Carl Wilhelmsson in Stockholm (1908–09) and Johan Rohde at the Artists' Studio School in Copenhagen (1911–12). His long association with ceramics began in 1917, when AB Gustavsberg, the Swedish ceramics factory, took him on as a designer; in time he became its art director, retiring to devote himself to painting in 1949.

Kåge was introduced to Gustavsberg by the Swedish Association of Arts and Crafts, which at the time was strongly campaigning for the design of beautiful objects in everyday life; to this end, they desired to place artists in industry. Kåge and Gustavsberg served each other well for three decades, and Kåge's designs for elegant, painterly art vases as well as practical, handsome dinnerware laid a firm foundation and set high standards for modern Swedish ceramics. He introduced such innovations as heat-treated dinner services (the Pyro and Marina lines of the 1930s) and stackable china (the 1933 Praktika earthenware. One of his aims was to produce good-looking, good-quality, low priced tablewares for the working classes. An example of these was the 1920 Liljeblå (Blue Lily) range, also known as the Workers' Service.

Much more successful and popular were the luxuriant art-glass pieces, including the Argenta vases, bowls, boxes and platters (made from 1930 up to the 1950s), their dark green-glazed grounds featuring stylish silver-inlaid designs. Lively art deco motifs appeared on many of Kåge's mass-produced 1920s and 1930s designs, not just the opulent Argenta pieces.

When subtle, organic designs began to have public appeal once more, Kåge brought out his Mjuka Formernas (Soft Forms) in the early 1940s, which in turn looked forward to the free-flowing, curvilinear shapes that were to epitomize classic Scandinavian design in the 1950s.

Added to Kåge's diversity and productivity was a sense of wit, as evidenced by his Surrea series of the early 1940s, with its whimsical references to Cubism and other art movements (one stoneware bowl juts out from a tall architectonic extension, and the whole white-glazed construction bears an uncanny resemblance to a WC). Beginning with the Stockholm Exhibition in 1917, Kåge's designs received great acclaim at numerous international shows; among his laurels was a Grand Prix at the 1925 Paris Exposition des Arts Décoratifs et Industriels Modernes (whence art deco received its name).

Wilhelm Kåge, stoneware Farsta vase for Gustavsberg, 1953.

KAHN Louis 1901–74 Estonian-American

architect

Yale Art Gallery; Richards Medical Laboratories; Salk Institute; Kimbell Museum (all USA); Dacca Parliament Buildings.

Louis Kahn was one of America's foremost designers of monumental buildings. Born in Estonia, but resident in the USA from 1905, he was trained in the Beaux-Arts system in Philadelphia.

One of Kahn's major preoccupations when approaching a design was to try to identify the essence of the proposed building – something he called "form". He believed building was a spiritual act, and that once the essence of the proposed structure was understood, then its design would naturally follow.

Kahn was essentially a Brutalist – one of the school of architects who designed in a chunky, rough-hewn style and who liked to use materials, particularly concrete, in a raw, unpainted state to demonstrate clearly how the building was made. Among Kahn's early work is the Yale University Art Gallery (1950–4). Here there is reference to the designs of MIES VAN DER ROHE with the construction of simple glass and steel façades, but Kahn adds his own distinguishing mark, breaking up the formality of the sheer frontage by creating a pattern with rectangular windows.

Following this, Kahn worked on two research laboratories, which allowed him to explore further his ideas about form and the creation of order. The Richards Medical Laboratories building at the University of Pennsylvania (1957–62) is divided into working spaces and service areas – what he described, respectively, as the served and the servant. Kahn decided to annexe all services, such as the flues and stairs, into enormous brick towers. Working areas were built as a number of connecting square cells. In common with most of his major designs, these laboratories were based on the simple forms of squares, rectangles, circles and triangles and had clearly defined routes for circulation.

The second set of laboratories was for the Salk Institute at La Jolla, California (1959–65). The architect took his inspiration for the planned layout from ancient monasteries, and initially devised the institute as a group of three clusters – for working, meeting and living. Only one section was built – that for working in. Two parallel, flat-roofed five-storey blocks ran either side of a water garden. To ensure large, uninterrupted working spaces he placed all the electrical and plumbing services on separate and easily accessible floors between the laboratories. Running along the edge of the buildings closest to the water garden were the scientists' study blocks which were angled to give views out across the Pacific Ocean.

One of Kahn's most startling designs was for the Dacca Parliament Buildings, Bangladesh (1963). Aptly described by the architect as a citadel, the enormous central meeting chamber is encircled by a series of small spaces and a mosque to one side facing Mecca.

While Kahn had to wait until late in his life to achieve recognition, he has proved to be highly influential in the post-war years. He taught at Yale between 1947 and 1957, then went on to teach at the University of Pennsylvania. Among his many pupils were Charles Moore and Robert VENTURI.

Louis Kahn, Salk Institute, California, 1959-65.

KAMALI Norma b.1945 American

fashion designer

Popularized dance and exercise clothing for day and evening wear from 1979.

Kamali studied fashion illustration at the Fashion Institute of Technology in New York, and graduated in 1964. Three years later she opened a boutique with her husband, for which she designed a diverse range of clothing including jewel encrusted T-shirts, glamorous

evening wear and more conservative tailored suits, alongside imported fashions from Barbara HULANIKI's Biba and the Carnaby Street boutiques in London.

Following her divorce, she opened another boutique in 1978 called OMO (On My Own) and became famous for innovative swimwear, brightly coloured suedes, nylon-fibre-filled padded "duvet" coats and draped sculptural evening wear. Kamali was also noted for her use of unusual fabrics such as parachute nylon. She used antique lace to make dramatic, body-hugging evening dresses, and made garments from exquisitely embroidered tablecloths which she imported from China. During this period Kamali also started to incorporate the design of sportswear into her ranges.

From 1979 Kamali's name became synonymous with sportswear: more than any other designer she was responsible for bringing sweatshirting out of the sports and dance arena and into the forefront of fashion. She initially worked with fleece-backed grey sweatshirting, then introduced the bright colours for which she was famous, fashioning it into gathered ra-ra mini-skirts, bandeau tops, puff shorts, jumpsuits and leotards. Kamali also made this versatile and comfortable fabric into glamorous evening wear.

More recent collections have continued to exploit the wearability of jersey, and have included elegant stretch jersey dresses which wrap, tie and mould around the figure.

Norma Kamali, loose shoulder-padded trouser suits, autumn/winter 1984-5.

KARAN Donna b.1948 American

fashion designer

Smart, loosely tailored business and leisure clothing.

Donna Karan made her name with her comfortable, multi-purpose clothing. She designs for the successful modern woman who combines an active career with motherhood. Karan studied at Parsons School of Design in New York, and then designed for Anne Klein, until she formed her own label in 1984.

Karan introduced the body-suit (a close-fitting top that buttons between the legs) which prevents creasing and achieves a strong line from the shoulders to the hips. Jersey sarong dresses also feature regularly in her collections. Her colours are predominantly black, white, navy and beige, and her garments are elegant, softly tailored and, above all, versatile and comfortable.

Donna Karan, black evening dress, autumn/winter 1985–6.

KAUFFER Edward McKnight 1890–1954   American

painter, poster artist and textile designer

Commercial graphics and London Underground posters.

American artist Edward McKnight Kauffer became one of the most distinguished poster designers of his time. Influenced by European artistic developments such as Cubism, as well as the English art and literary scene, he succeeded in thrusting the painter's art into the world of commercial graphics.

Born Edward Kauffer, he adopted the name McKnight in honour of Professor Joseph E. McKnight, the man who financed his visit to Paris to study painting in 1913. By 1915 he had started to produce work for Frank Pick, publicity manager for London Underground Railways, and one of his major clients over the next 25 years. Under the influence of Vorticism (the British movement that drew on both Cubist and Futurist ideas), Kauffer created one of his best-known designs. "Flight", showing a flock of geometric birds, was originally produced as a woodcut in 1916, then reproduced in *Colour* magazine in 1917, then used as a poster for the new Labour newspaper, the *Daily Herald*, in 1919, and eventually led to the flying-bird symbol of Imperial Airways.

Throughout the 1920s and 1930s, Kauffer produced posters for the great design patrons of the period: London Underground Railways, of course, as well as Crawfords, Shell, Cresta Silks and the Great Western Railway. He also produced book designs, book illustrations (for Francis Meynell's Nonesuch Press), rugs and interiors, and later theatre designs. But at the height of his career, war was imminent and he was forced to return to the United States, settling in New York with his wife, the textile designer Marion DORN. Although he continued to work in New York, his English success was not repeated.

Edward McKnight Kauffer, poster entitled *Power* for London Transport, 1930.

KAWAKUBO Rei b.1942   Japanese

fashion designer

Loosely structured, dark or neutral-coloured garments, often based on Japanese ceremonial wear or workwear; post-Hiroshima collection (1982).

Rei Kawakubo studied literature at Keio University in Tokyo; she worked for the textile company Asahi Kasei and as a freelance journalist before forming Comme des Garçons, the company over which she now presides and for which she designs, in 1969.

Her clothing was first shown in Paris in 1981, not at a conventional show, but on coat-hangers at the Chiltern Hotel. Her dramatic collection and unusual vehicle of display generated much publicity, and the following year the Chambre Syndicale permitted Comme des Garçons to show officially in Paris.

Kawakubo has created a distinctive fusion of traditional Japanese work and ceremonial clothing with modern European styling and sizing. Many of her collections are based upon Japanese farming clothes – loose three-quarter-length trousers, T-shaped tops, smocks, rice-paddy slippers – and the kimono. Her garments are creased, torn, slashed, draped and wrapped. They are often asymmetrical, with unexpected, misplaced lapels, buttons and arms, creating a look of contrived disarray. Always loosely cut, Kawakubo's clothing has often been described as feminist, because it conceals the wearer's shape. Indeed, Kawakubo states that her clothing is designed for modern women – "Women who do not need to assure their happiness by looking sexy to men, by emphasizing their figures, but who attract them with their minds". (N. Coleridge, *The Fashion Conspiracy*.)

Comme des Garçons moves into colour, spring/summer 1989.

K

Kenzo, multi-coloured ethnic fashion, autumn/ winter 1985–6.

KENZO (Kenzo Takada) b.1940   Japanese

fashion designer

Ethnic-inspired fashions, dramatic shapes, multi-patterned and richly textured textiles.

Kenzo studied art in Japan before moving in 1964 to Paris, where he worked as a freelance designer and for the Bureau de Style. In 1970 he opened his own shop, called Jungle Jap.

Kenzo was at the forefront of the vogue for ethnic-inspired fashions from the late 1960s until the emergence of punk in about 1976. During these years much of Europe was experiencing high inflation and rising unemployment, and there was growing dissatisfaction with the 1960s emphasis on the ephemeral. In reaction, this period witnessed a craft revival in design and a growing interest in health foods, ecology and world peace. In dress this mood was expressed in the use of peasant styles culled from non-industrialized countries, and of chunky ethnic jewellery. Kenzo introduced pouch bags, leg-warmers, loose drawstring trousers which were often tied at the ankle, quilted jackets, tabards, and kimono sleeves added to Western-style garments. His collections of spring 1975 and spring 1976 were greatly influenced by tribal African and American Indian cultures respectively. His garments were, and still are, characterized by their use of strong and rich colours, dramatic shapes and layered textures, while his unconventional, multi-patterned printed textiles, incorporating unusual design combinations such as cabbage roses, tartans and stripes, have been much copied.

KEPES György b.1906   Hungarian-American

graphic and exhibition designer and painter

Teacher at New Bauhaus School, Chicago; author of *Language of Vision*.

György Kepes was born in Hungary, and studied painting in Budapest in the 1920s. In 1930 the artist/ designer László MOHOLY-NAGY (also Hungarian) invited Kepes to join his office in Berlin. There Kepes experimented with photography and worked in graphic and exhibition design, while coming into contact with some of the leading avant-garde artists of Europe and Russia. In 1936 Kepes went with Moholy-Nagy to work in London, and in 1937 once again accepted his invitation to work in the New Bauhaus School (later the Institute of Design) in Chicago. Kepes was placed in charge of the Light and Colour Department. During this period he also produced advertising designs for the Container Corporation (1938–44) and started work on his influential book *Language of Vision*, which was based on his classes at the New Bauhaus/School of Design and published in 1944. It played an important role in spreading Bauhaus educational methods.

He left the School of Design in 1943 and carried on teaching in various institutions until after the war. He was then invited to the Massachusetts Institute of Technology (MIT) to be Professor of Visual Design, and there he stayed until he retired in 1974.

Throughout his career Kepes remained committed to the social role of art and design, as well as promoting the value of group work and interdisciplinary projects, encouraging links between design and architecture, and between the arts and sciences. Kepes also produced innovative work in graphics, using photography and photograms, and explored the creative use of light and technology in his exhibitions and environmental work.

KIESLER Frederick 1890–1965   Austrian

designer and architect

Multifunctional furniture.

Kiesler studied at the Academy of Design and Technology in Vienna. In 1923 he joined the De Stijl group. He later went to New York, where he settled, and became director of stage design at the Juillard School of Music in New York (1934–47) and Director of the Laboratory for Design Correlation of the School of Architecture at Columbia University (1936–42).

Kiesler is, perhaps, most famous among industrial designers for his unorthodox furniture. In 1942 for Peggy Guggenheim's New York Art of This Century gallery, he designed solid furniture that was multifunctional – a chair could be a table or a storage container according to which way up it was placed. His exhibition installations set unframed paintings and photographs on armatures that projected into space – it was a series of attempts to escape the wall and give every work of art its own space. It was a fight to elevate paintings above the status of wallpaper.

Later on in the 1940s he worked with Surrealists. In his ideas for housing Kiesler pursued the idea of organic rather than geometric form – his house designs swell up like round loaves of bread. He was especially interested in "one space units". By doing away with rooms he thought you could achieve maximum flexibility. Kiesler was ruled by two ideas: individuality and communality. He respected the individual but yearned for art and architecture to transcend the particular and unite us all by creating environments that we would all feel at one with. It is a potent theme in 20th century art and architecture.

KING David b.1943   British
graphic designer and archivist

Archive of visual material from USSR history.

Over the past 20 years David King has built up a visual archive relating to the history and politics of Russia and the Soviet Union in the 20th century. As a practising graphic designer, he was also responsible for some of the most powerful political graphics to appear in Britain in the late 1970s.

Born in London, King was art editor of *The Sunday Times Magazine* from 1965 to 1975. Thereafter he ran a highly productive freelance practice, undertaking work for Penguin Books, *City Limits* weekly magazine (designing at least three dozen covers), the Arts Council, the Museum of Modern Art in Oxford, and others. King's designs for MOMA exhibition catalogues – notably on the RODCHENKO (1979) and Mayakovsky (1982) exhibitions – broke new ground. Additionally, throughout this freelance period he produced a large quantity of non-commercial graphic work (posters, pamphlets, handbills, etc.) for political causes of the Left.

It was also during the 1970s that King began making trips to the USSR, building his archive of "visual politics" in earnest. It contains 200,000 photos (from the turn of the century to Khrushchev), and an astounding collection of books, posters, pamphlets, and magazines, harbouring everything from revolutionary handbills to a complete run of the monthly magazine *USSR in Construction* (with individual issues designed by artists such as Rodchenko, LISSITZKY, etc.). In addition to managing and maintaining the archive, King has pulled material from it to publish a number of highly successful books on Soviet subjects, including *Stalin*, a six-volume photo-history of Stalin's rule (Fabbri, 1980), and *Trotsky: A Photographic Biography* (Blackwells, 1986). He is currently working on the first Russian language edition of the Trotsky book, due to be published in Moscow; it is the first photographic book on Trotsky ever to be published in the USSR.

David King.

David King, poster for the British anti-apartheid movement.

KING Jessie M. 1875–1949   British
illustrator and designer

Book illustrations and covers in Glasgow School style; also Cymric designs in silver for Liberty, fabric and wallpaper designs.

Jessie M. King was one of the most successful and significant British designers and illustrators of the early 20th century. Jessie Marion King was born in Bearsden, near Glasgow, and enrolled at the Glasgow School of Art in 1892, after a year at Queen Margaret College studying anatomy.

In 1899 she was appointed a tutor in book decoration at the Glasgow School of Art, by which time she had already received several awards. While teaching art in Glasgow, she exhibited and travelled extensively, at the same time designing and illustrating books for Scottish, English and Continental publishers. She won a gold medal for book design at the 1902 Turin Exhibition of Modern Decorative Art, for *L' Evangile de l' Enfance,* executed by Maclehose of Glasgow in gold-tooled white vellum. Her first solo exhibition was in 1905, and around this time she also provided designs to Liberty of London for fabrics and Cymric silver jewellery.

She moved with her husband, furniture designer E.A. Taylor, to Paris in 1909, where they both exhibited and taught, and where they set up the Atelier Shealing in 1911. In 1915 they returned to Scotland. The Taylors provided murals for schools in Lanarkshire in the late 1920s, and in 1932 Jessie helped to design the Paul Jones Tea Rooms in Kirkcudbright, where her gaily decorated pottery, which she enthu-

K

Jessie M. King, silver and enamel belt buckle, 1906.

siastically hand-painted until her death in 1949, was offered for sale to tourists.

Without doubt, King's book illustrations and covers brought her her greatest and most-deserved fame. Her vast repertoire of minutely detailed, fairy-land motifs – castles, sprites, flowers, birds, hearts, long-tressed maidens – was in part influenced by Aubrey Beardsley, the Pre-Raphaelites and fellow Glas-wegians Charles Rennie MACKINTOSH, his wife Margaret Macdonald and her sister Frances Macdonald, but it came to be identified largely with King herself.

By 1910, she had begun to adopt a brighter, bolder palette and more conventionalized style, large-ly because of Léon Bakst's drawings of the Ballets Russes, but her subject matter on the whole remained unaltered. She provided book illustrations and/or covers for the writings of numerous well-known authors (over 100 projects in all) – among them Wilde, Tennyson, Spenser, Zola, Omar Khayyám, Scott, Shelley, Keats, Morris, Coleridge and Kipling – and she even wrote and illustrated two books of her own. From 1901 she designed covers for mass-produced paperback books by Gowans & Gray.

Her fabric, textile and wallpaper designs, for Liberty and others, in the main used motifs from her early Glasgow School flower and bird repertory. Her later, brightly hued printed and batik fabrics, influ-enced by the Ballets Russes, were used by Liberty for dresses. King's Cymric designs for Liberty – next to Archibald KNOX she was Liberty's best-known designer in silver – were likewise in the Glasgow School manner, such as her silver and enamel hairbrushes of around 1906. She also designed larger objects.

Although she worked largely in the 20th cen-tury, the varied works of Jessie King reflected a romanticized vision of the past. None the less, her continued success in the face of art deco, modernism and functionalism – to which her style gave subtle nods now and then, as in her use of bolder colours and lessening of busy details – is notable and remarkable.

KING & MIRANDA founded 1978 Italian
industrial design consultancy

Lighting (for Flos and Arteluce), typeface (for Olivetti).

Perry King (b. 1938) and Santiago Miranda (b. 1947) have worked together from their office in Milan since 1977. Perry King, a Londoner, studied at Birmingham

College of Art; in 1965 he moved to Italy to work for OLIVETTI as a consultant, collaborating with Ettore SOTTSASS on equipment and furniture design. One of the best-known products of their work together is the Valentine typewriter, an attempt to bring fun and colour into the grey world of the office.

King and Miranda have designed light fittings, typefaces, interiors and furniture. Their experimental work with quartz-halogen light sources, which led to such products as the Triana and Palio lamps for ARTELU-CE, has secured their position as leading lighting desig-ners. Their approach to design, whether of lights or furniture (which includes the Cable and Airmail sys-tems for Marcatre) is questioning and analytical. They have called this approach "interactive design", which King describes as giving designs value and meaning. He has said that design "isn't simply reconciling functional necessities and formal requirements into a harmonious whole but is instead a process which tries to include communication between man and his artefacts" (*ID*, January/February 1989).

KLEIN Calvin b.1942 American
fashion designer

Understated, tailored sportswear.

Klein graduated from the Fashion Institute of Technol-ogy in 1962. He then worked for various clothing manufacturers before setting up in business, with his childhood friend and business manager Barry Schwartz, in 1968. They now own one of the largest fashion empires in the world.

By the mid-1970s Klein had gained a good reputation for his fine, understated tailoring and elegant sportswear collections, as well as for his casual separates made in the finest linens, silks and cashmere. His name is also associated with the introduction of "designer jeans", which have retained their popularity for over 10 years, and during the late 1980s alone generated sales of around $150 million a year. Klein produces garments for men, women and children, including underwear; in 1983 he launched a range of women's underwear which was boldly designed along the lines of menswear. Thigh-high bikini briefs had thick, labelled, elasticated waistbands, and boxer shorts came complete with fly. These designs have been widely copied. He also produces his own cos-metics. Klein has successfully marketed both himself and his affluent life-style to promote his fashions.

Calvin Klein, tailored womenswear, spring/ summer 1988.

K

KLINT Kaare 1888–1954 Danish

furniture designer

Safri chair.

Klint trained as a painter, but worked as an architect (in his father's office) until he opened his own practice in 1920. He became a professor of architecture in 1944. However he is most famous for his furniture designs and was director of the School of Cabinet Making at the Copenhagen Academy of Arts. His ideas were rooted in a respect for English 18th-century cabinet making and, in particular, for the English country vernacular furniture which is simple and quite plain. But to this simplicity Klint added his own craft-based aesthetic – a fondness for unvarnished wood and plain textiles. He designed a number of light shades and was particularly fond of working with scored paper and, as they became available, PVCs. He was also influenced by contemporary design and architectural ideology – he called his furniture "tools for living" and he liked to stress that function dictated his forms. Klint is regarded as a father of modern Danish design; his own son Esben Klint (1915–69) was also a well-known designer.

KNOLL Florence b.1917 American

interior, textile and furniture designer

Quality office systems furnishings.

Florence Schust, as she was born, studied architecture at the Kingswood School, Michigan, under the tutelage of Eliel and Eero SAARINEN, and with the same tutors at CRANBROOK Academy of Art, Michigan. Later she studied at the Architectural Association, London, and the Illinois Institute of Technology, Chicago, under Ludwig MIES VAN DER ROHE. She worked with Walter GROPIUS and Marcel BREUER and then joined Hans Knoll in 1943 to set up an interior design and planning service.

Married in 1946, they formed Knoll Associates (today known as Knoll International), and made the company an influential design-led business. Her earlier contacts and friendships with the leading designers of the former BAUHAUS enabled Florence Knoll to start manufacturing some of the classic designs such as Mies van der Rohe's Barcelona chair.

It was Knoll Associates that produced Eero Saarinen's classic Womb chair, and then, in 1952, the famous wire basket chair by the designer/sculptor Harry BERTOIA (1952).

Florence Knoll, as well as being a protagonist of good design into production, did a great deal of designing herself for the contracts and office market. These designs, especially for executive office furnishings, fitted exactly the ambitions of corporate America for quality style tempered by quietness.

Knoll International has continued to be a leader in quality office systems furnishings and has also commissioned designers and architects for limited ranges of more avant-garde work. From 1982 to 1985 the architect Robert VENTURI designed a range of chairs, including a luxurious sofa in the postmodern style.

KNOX Archibald 1864–1933 British

designer of metalwork and carpets

Promoter of the Celtic Revival; Cymric silver and Tudric pewter wares for Liberty & Co.

Born in Cronkbourne on the Isle of Man, the son of a marine engineer, Knox studied at the Douglas School of Art from 1878 to 1884, then taught there until 1888. In 1897 Knox moved to London, first teaching at the Redhill School of Art, in 1898 designing textiles for the Silver Studio (which he also used as an agency for his designs for some years), and then, in 1899, becoming allied with the Art School of Kingston-upon-Thames as a Design Master and with Arthur Lasenby Liberty's retail emporium as a designer. His decade-long association with Liberty resulted in hundreds of designs in various media, though his silver and pewter jewellery and objects notably Cymric silver and Tudric pewter wares are most notable.

Almost single-handedly Knox was responsible for the Celtic Revival spurred by Liberty, and his distinctive Celtic *entrelac* (interlace) motif appeared on jewellery, boxes, frames, vases, etc. Knox had become enamoured of Celtic design while still a student; its lovely motifs nicely complemented the curvilinear art nouveau and *Jugendstil* movements fashionable on the Continent at the same time.

Knox also provided Liberty with designs for Donegal carpets (produced about 1902), pottery and textiles. He spent the years 1900–4 back on the Isle of Man, sending some of his finest Celtic patterns to Liberty in London during those four years. After his return to London in 1904, Knox continued to design for Liberty and to teach in Kingston (also teaching evening classes at the Wimbledon Art School, 1906–7). He

Archibald Knox, silver and enamel covered cup for Liberty, c.1900.

K

resigned from Kingston in 1911 – his teaching style had been criticized by the South Kensington Examiners – and stopped working for Liberty a year later, with his design style markedly falling out of fashion. A group of his art students, interestingly enough, protested against his more or less forced resignation, "seceding" from the Kingston Art School and establishing the Knox Guild of Craft and Design, which, remarkably, lasted until 1939. Knox went to the United States in 1912, where he found some work designing carpets for Bromley & Co. of Philadelphia, and also lecturing at the Pennsylvania School of Industrial Art, but apparently his search for lasting work was not very successful in either Pennsylvania or New York, so he returned to the Isle of Man in 1913, where he spent most of the rest of his life painting and teaching. He also designed a memorial stone upon Arthur Lasenby Liberty's death in 1917, as well as other gravestones adorned with Celtic crosses and script on the Isle of Man.

Knox's approach and attitude to industrial design made him one of the earliest exponents of, and participants in, high-quality commercial mass production. His methods were decidedly modern (or at least proto-modern), although the almost too pretty and precious end results of his design concepts appear – especially to post-modern viewers at the end of the century – far from that, and even impossibly at odds with a progressive approach.

Archibald Knox, silver and mother-of-pearl clock for Liberty, c.1900.

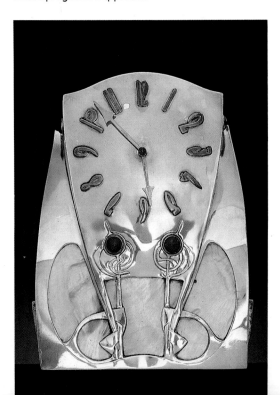

KOMENDA Erwin   1904–66 German

`car designer`

Styling of original Volkswagen (1933–9) and Porsche 356 (1949).

Erwin Komenda was a designer with Daimler Benz, to whom he was responsible for car body development; he joined Ferdinand PORSCHE's design bureau in Stuttgart in 1934, and began work on the styling of the people's car – the Volkswagen. The car itself was designed by Porsche. The streamlined style of the car derives from Komenda's experiments in the wind tunnel of the ZEPPELIN works at Friedrichshafen, and later at a wind tunnel in Stuttgart operated by the Swiss Wunibald Kamm (1893–1966). Kamm's work on aerodynamics laid down the principles of scientific streamlining in automobile design. Like Komenda, he had worked for Daimler Benz.

Komenda's styling for the Porsche 356, styling which set the pattern for the subsequent Porsche range, owes much to Kamm's theories. One stylistic convention that runs from the Volkswagen "Beetle" through to the Porsche 911 is the way the car's body slips away rapidly at the rear.

Erwin Komenda, Type 356 Porsche, 1948.

KOPPEL Henning   1918–81 Danish

`ceramics, glass, metal and plastics designer`

Silver designs for Georg Jensen, combining beauty with functionality.

Like several other significant figures in Scandinavian design, the Dane Henning Koppel worked in several media. He studied sculpture at the Royal Danish Academy of Fine Arts in Copenhagen (1936–7) before spending some time (1938–9) in Paris at the Académie Ranson (founded in 1908 by the Nabis painter Paul Ranson). He stayed away from his homeland during the occupation, working from 1940 to 1945 in Stockholm, where he designed for both Svenski Tenn and Orrefors (he also designed glass for the latter in the early 1970s).

Henning Koppel, steel
cutlery for Georg Jensen,
1977.

When he returned to Denmark in 1945, he began his long association with the pre-eminent maker of silver, Georg JENSEN, for whom he designed jewellery, hollow-ware and flatware until his death. His stunning designs for Jensen silver were the main source of his fame, as well as the reason he was awarded gold medals at the Milan Triennale in 1951, 1954 and 1957, and the prestigious Lunning Prize in 1953. Koppel applied his talents to porcelain as well, however, creating dinner-ware for Bing & Grøndahl (1961–81), and he also provided some designs for lighting and clocks in 1967 to Louis Poulsen.

Koppel's designs in metal were among the finest examples of the applied-arts style of the 1950s known as Danish Modern. His elongated, silver-teardrop shape of a covered fish dish by Jensen (1954), is arguably his most renowned design. Intensely per-sonal and expressionistic, Koppel's style was em-inently sculptural and organic, possessing a rhythmic allure that loudly bespoke modern times.

KOSTA GLASBRUK founded 1742   Swedish
glass factory

Design innovations from the early 20th century.

Kosta Glasbruk is of special interest to designers because in the early 20th century it became more design-orientated, producing wares that are charac-teristic of the Scandinavian flair for modern style, together with some of their craft aesthetic. One of the first designers to make an impact in the company was the Swedish ceramics designer Gunnar Wennerberg; he was inspired by the works of Emile Gallé, and designed overlay glass. This consists of a core covered with one or more layers of glass in different colours, which is then cut, and etched so that each layer contributes to the overall surface.

In the inter-war period Kosta Glasbruk pro-duced several innovative designs, including the blown glass work of Elis Bergh; typically this work is organic and rather pumpkin-like in form, but it is also at home with modernist upholstered furniture.

Since the Second World War the company has continued to be important in glass design. Among designers to have worked for it are Anne Warff and Goran Warff who, in the early 1970s, developed a range of flashed glass bowls. Here, transparent layers of colour are "peeled back" through an etching process to expose layers of colour beneath.

KRIER Leon b.1946   Luxembourg
architect

Influential anti-modern polemicist.

Leon Krier was born in Luxembourg, the younger brother of Rob KRIER. In his youth he was an enthusiastic modernist, but at Stuttgart University, where he began his architectural training, this changed to antipathy. As he says, he fell "in love with the Italian Cities".

In 1968 he came to London as an associate of James STIRLING, a book about whom he has edited. In 1974 he set up his own practice and came to atten-tion through his romantic drawings of a stripped-down vernacular classicism, and his writings, which advocated a return to the traditional pre-industrial European city.

Krier criticizes what he sees as the modern movement's concern with industrial technique over artistic and human values and the obsession with zoning, which he considers undemocratic social en-gineering. He believes that a sense of community cannot arise unless people live within 10 minutes of their work.

Krier's opinions about planning have had a considerable impact on architectural circles and in Britain he has been taken up by the Prince of Wales, whose plan for a model town on his estates at Poundbury are a concrete realization of Krier's ideas. He has also been a consultant to a similar project in the United States, where he also designed a house – his first building for about 20 years. Krier is not prepared to compromise on his view of architecture as a fine art. But his actual projects have been criti-cized for a lack of scale. He has also done his case no good by his defence of the Nazi architect Albert Speer. Krier dislikes the modern world, but his design pre-scriptions may, ironically, be social engineering too.

KRIER Rob b.1938   Luxembourg
architect

Has developed a return to traditional concepts of urban and public space.

Rob Krier was born in Luxembourg and is the older brother of Leon KRIER. He worked in the offices of O.M. Ungers (1965–6) and Frei OTTO (1967–70). Since 1975 he has been a professor of architecture in Vienna.

Both Kriers have reacted against the ideology of modernism. Rob, however, has been described as

K

the more pragmatic of the two, as he has accepted modern building methods to create the traditional urban spaces they both desire. Rob Krier's simplified form of modern, rational classicism belongs to what the critic Charles Jencks terms "new Tuscanism".

Like his brother Leon, Rob is an influential author and has published *Architectural Composition* (1983) and *On Architecture* (1982). But he has also had more opportunities to build than Leon, notably in Berlin under the auspices of the IBA project for the "Critical Reconstruction" of the Südliche Friedrichstadt area of the city. Krier was responsible for planning of the Rauchstrasse site and its gateway building which introduces a figural sculpture in a monumental manner. He was also responsible for the reconstruction of the Feilner House by the 19th-century architect Schinkel, realizing his aims of a link between the historical city and contemporary development.

KUNZLI Otto b.1950   German

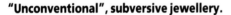

`jeweller`

"Unconventional", subversive jewellery.

Kunzli first studied metalwork in Zurich, and then jewellery under Hermann JUNGER in Munich. Although Kunzli can be described as an anti-establishment jeweller, his work is better conceived and crafted than that description might suggest. Its cleverness rests in its ability to subvert conventional decorative jewellery while remaining attractive in itself.

He has produced a series of large but wearable ornaments in foam block and wallpaper; he has also made a wearable but not very practical brooch in the form of a brick wall (made from foam block and wallpaper) and has frequently played games using mock gold bars and coins.

Kunzli came to wider attention in the late 1970s, making play with geometric shapes; the block, cube and stick. His "jewellery" was intended as a reflection on jewellery and the conventions within which it works. In producing his unconventional objects, Kunzli is not saying that they are, in fact, perfectly reasonable and obvious things to wear. The point is that they deliberately break rules in order to reveal how binding conventions, especially in dress and ornament, really are. Kunzli's work is, to an extent, ideological: he loathes the power and status that so much ordinary jewellery parades through its use of precious materials.

Otto Kunzli wearing his foam and wallpaper brooch 1984.

Otto Kunzli, The Big American Neckpiece, stainless steel, 1986.

KURAMATA Shiro b.1934   Japanese

`interior and furniture designer`

Interior designs for Issey Miyake shops.

Kuramata trained in architecture and, later, cabinetmaking. He has executed many interiors for the shops of the internationally known clothes designer Issey MIYAKE. In the field of furniture, perhaps his best-known pieces are his glass chair (1976) and his homage to Hoffmann, Begin the Beguine (1985).

Kuramata is alert to the possibilities of optical distortion and pattern. Many of his interior designs make great use of expanded lattice metal, and the moiré effects are enchantingly like being dazzled by light playing on bright moving water. A particular case is the Boutique Issey Miyake Men, Seibu Department Store (1987); the walls and ceiling are steel expanding mesh with a fired black melamine finish, while the racks and shelves are of the same material.

There is no designer quite like Kuramata, because although he uses industrial materials, he manages to suppress their more brutalist connotations.

Kuramata's portfolio of work is wide. In 1970 he devised furniture in irregular forms; there is a particularly famous chest of drawers of his (in wood) which stands like a gently curling letter S. In 1972 he devised some large lamps that are beautiful in conception and actuality: he took milk-white plastic sheets of 2-3 mm in thickness and 2-3 m square and heated them in an electric kiln to 120-30° Centigrade, removed the sheets while soft and hung them over poles and allowed them to harden. The weight of the plastic causes it to fall in natural curves while soft. The lighting elements are then put into the resultant plastic shapes.

Shiro Kuramata, Apple Honey chair, 1985.

Shiro Kuramata, Boutique Issey Miyake Men, Shibuya Seibu department store, 1987.

L

LACROIX Christian b.1951 — French
fashion designer

Glitzy evening wear and sports styles in luxurious materials since 1987.

The house of Lacroix was opened in the summer of 1987, financed by Bernard Arnault, whose company Agache also owns DIOR.

Lacroix studied European art and the history of dress. He then joined Hermès in Paris and revitalized design at the house of PATOU before working under his own name. He was first associated with the puffball skirt, which was derived from the more outrageous mini-crini introduced by Vivienne WESTWOOD. Lacroix combines the finest detailing and fabrics with practical styling, designing boiler suits in rich satins and deep velvets, and parka-style coats in taffeta with mink-trimmed hoods. He has a strong and adventurous sense of colour, mixes patterns and blends ethnic designs with classic European wools and tweeds. Many of his collections have derived inspiration from India, where some of his ready-to-wear garments are made.

The couture clients of Lacroix, like those of most houses in the late 1980s and 1990, are few, numbering around 100, of whom Paloma Picasso is among the most famous. In dressing this privileged élite, Lacroix has done much to revitalize the trades of the craftspeople – the beaders, embroiderers, lace-, braid- and tasselmakers – who traditionally supported the Paris couture houses. He has also commissioned Paris's leading *coiffeur*, Monsieur Alexandre, to make chignons and pompadour beehives for his shows. The silk painter Sylvie Skinazi designs many of the vibrant textiles for which the house of Lacroix is famous. Lacroix's summer 1989 collection also featured more modest materials – raffia, hemp, straw and linen – and was influenced by the designs of the British artist-craftspeople who worked at Roger Fry's OMEGA WORKSHOP (1913–19).

LAGERFELD Karl b.1938 — German
fashion designer

Furs, flamboyant evening wear as well as understated designs.

Lagerfeld has enjoyed a long, varied and hugely successful career in fashion. At the age of 14 he left Germany to study the arts in Paris. His talent for design was recognized early: in 1955 he won the first prize in a coat design competition, sponsored by the International Wool Secretariat. As a result, Lagerfeld was employed by the Parisian *couturier* BALMAIN, who put his winning design into production. He remained with Balmain until 1958, then moved to PATOU until 1964 when, briefly disillusioned with the world of fashion, he went to study art history in Italy. He returned just one year later and designed fashion on a freelance basis for Chloë and Krizia and footwear for Charles JOURDAN. From 1967 he also created fur designs for the Rome-based company Fendi. Lagerfeld has continued to work with real fur, in spite of the trend against this. He produces unconventional fur garments, such as beaver trousers and mink T-shirts, and also dyes fur in vibrant colours.

In 1983 Lagerfeld was appointed design director at the house of CHANEL. His immensely popular designs revived and updated the 1920s Chanel look. Since 1984 he has worked under his own name. Lagerfeld has earned a high reputation for his superbly made, flamboyant evening-wear designs.

Karl Lagerfeld, womenswear, spring/summer 1985.

LALIQUE René 1860–1945 — see page 140

LAND Edwin b.1909 — American
industrial designer

Polaroid instant film processing.

Dr Edwin H. Land was a Harvard-trained physicist, inventor and businessman. In 1937, he set up the Polaroid Company to develop optical products such as sunglasses and photographic polarizing screens.

In 1947 he invented the Polaroid-Land instant print processing camera. The story goes that he was inspired by his small daughter's impatience at having to wait for a film to be processed before she could see the pictures he had taken of her.

Land demonstrated his revolutionary new process to the Optical Society of America in 1947 and the following year he launched the Polaroid-Land camera, Model 95.

Land's idea was to create a camera that would make photography as simple as possible for the user. Model 95 took one minute to yield a print. It was an immediate success. Within eight years Polaroid had sold a million cameras. Land went on to develop the colour instant processing camera – the Polaroid-Land SX70 (launched in 1972).

LALIQUE

René Lalique, selection of perfume bottles with carafe at rear left and atomizer at front left, 1930s.

LALIQUE René 1860–1945   French

Outstanding craftsman in glass and creator of family firm Cristal Lalique.

René Lalique was born in 1860 in Ay, a small town in the province of Champagne. The family moved to Paris and Lalique was apprenticed to the well-known Paris goldsmith, Louis Aucoc, and later was enrolled in some courses at the Ecole des Arts Décoratifs.

After about two years of study in London, Lalique returned to Paris to study sculpture under Justin Lequien at the Ecole Bernard Palissy. By 1881 he was wholly devoted to goldsmithing, designing at first for other jewellers on a freelance basis, then in 1886 officially starting up his own fully staffed workshop.

By the turn of the century, Lalique's revolutionary, beautifully crafted, deeply nature-inspired jewellery – rings, bracelets, brooches, necklaces, hair-combs, even purse frames and pocket watches – were all the rage for France's élite, and his list of clients was a Who's Who of *fin-de-siècle* Paris, with the actress Sarah Bernhardt and the oil magnate Calouste Gulbenkian his premier customers (Lisbon's Gulbenkian Museum has the finest single collection of Lalique jewellery). Like no one before him, Lalique combined precious metals and gems with semi-precious stones, ivory, rock crystal, even with glass and enamel, to create wearable objects of the most exquisite beauty. His inspiration came from a variety of sources – from the Orient, from classical literature, from Symbolist verse, directly from nature and especially from a rich imagination. He also produced larger metal objects, such as a full-length bronze mirror, its sinuous silhouette-frame the body of two serpents; a sublime chalice of ivory, enamel and

René Lalique, Peacock Head car mascot, c.1928.

gold, and a silver and glass centrepiece of about 1902 in the form of a pond and four nymphs.

Although Lalique's splendid jewels were produced well into the first decade of the 20th century, he had already in the 1890s begun to work with the medium of glass, which he incorporated in bits and pieces into his jewellery and which he shaped into lovely vases and bowls using the *cire perdue*, or lost-wax, technique.

By 1902 Lalique's experiments with glass had blossomed and he also expanded the retail end of his business considerably, opening a shop in the fashionable Place Vendôme in 1905. Near Lalique's Paris shop was the newly opened establishment of the *parfumeur* François Coty, with whom Lalique was soon collaborating on the design and manufacture of glass scent bottles. Heretofore scents had been offered in plain pharmaceutical bottles and then transferred to fancy containers in *madame*'s collection; Coty's and Lalique's novel concept was to present scents in specially designed bottles. Over the years Lalique was to produce fragrance bottles and other items – and often their cardboard packaging as well – for Coty, Roger et Gallet, Molinard, Houbigant, Worth and numerous other *parfumeurs*.

The 1920s witnessed perhaps Lalique's finest hour, in terms of the sheer quantity of pieces he produced, their variety and the acclaim he received worldwide. Lalique was now creating, in addition to one-off *cire perdue* vessels, mass-produced table lamps and chandeliers, picture frames, inkwells, paperweights, automobile mascots, clock cases, jewellery (all-glass pendants and rings, for instance), statuettes and a huge variety of table-ware. From his early clear-glass *demi-cristal* objects, he proceeded to produce lovely opalescent wares, dark-coloured glass, cased pieces (two coloured layers of glass sandwiching a white layer) and colourless glass lightly tinted with an enamel *patine*, in blue, sepia and other tones. He even produced large-scale architectural glass, such as a door for the Paris flat of the great fashion designer (and modern art and art deco collector) Jacques Doucet.

Throughout much of the 1930s, Lalique remained head of his now huge firm. After Lalique's death in 1945 his son, Marc, took over as chief designer of the firm. New techniques were introduced by the younger Lalique, outdated methods and out-of-fashion lines were eliminated, and many of Marc Lalique's own 1950s and 1960s designs – some of them not unlike elegant Scandinavian glass of the period – proved relative market successes. In 1956, Marc's daughter Marie-Claude joined the firm, and she succeeded her father as Cristal Lalique's principal designer upon his death in 1977.

René Lalique, Gui and Volubilis bowls, c.1924.

LARCHER Dorothy 1884–1952   See BARRON AND LARCHER

LARSEN Jack Lenor b.1927   American

textile designer, craftsman and artist

Designs for Lever House, Park Avenue, New York, and for Cassina; innovations in fabric structure and power-loom weaving techniques.

Jack Lenor Larsen has been a dominant figure in American textile design for nearly 40 years and his writings and exhibitions have established him as a world authority on American fibre art. One of his major contributions to textile design is his transformation of archaic craft techniques by means of new technology to create commercially viable designs for the modern interior furnishings market.

Born in Seattle, Larsen was trained at CRANBROOK Academy and opened his own design studio in New York in 1952. A strong advocate of the craftsman-designer, he modelled his practice on the great craft workshops of the 19th century – Morris, Fortuny, Tiffany – while looking to pre-Columbian and Sassanid textiles for decorative and technical inspiration. From the beginning of his career he started exploring methods of transferring the vivacity and irregularities of hand-woven samples to machine-woven products. His earliest successful collections, such as the Andean (1956), the African (1963) and the Irish (1969), were all inspired by textiles from other cultures. He is known to be an obsessive collector of fabrics, and is interested in exploring the expressive content in ethnic textiles. He has travelled extensively and has worked on a number of overseas projects, including consultancy work for the United States Department of State on grass-weaving projects in Taiwan and Vietnam.

In his search to give textiles a voice, Larsen went on to become a champion of the fibre art movement in America and collaborated with Mildred Constantine on *Beyond Craft, the Art Fabric* and *The Art Fabric Mainstream*, which have become classic works on the subject.

Despite his interest in craft, Larsen remains a designer of his time, and he has used his extensive knowledge of synthetic fibres and power-loom weaving techniques to transform these influences into a sophisticated modernism. He has frequently collaborated with architects. His first major commission, to create the draperies for the Park Avenue Lever House,

L

New York. (designed by Skidmore, Owens and Merrill – SOM), has been recognized as the first clear articulation of the American Modern Movement. More recently, his textile designs for CASSINA in the early 1980s confirmed his position as a leading contemporary designer.

Throughout his career Larsen has adapted his orientation as a designer to meet the prevailing mood of the time. He is currently interested in exploring the potential of textiles for the artificial environment and protecting standards of quality in industry.

LASDUN Denys b.1914   British

architect

Bethnal Green Cluster Flats, Royal College of Physicians, National Theatre (all London).

Sir Denys Lasdun has become best known for his design of the National Theatre on London's South Bank (1965–76). During the heated architectural debate of the 1980s the building came under heavy attack and was not only criticized by the Prince of Wales, but also nominated on a number of occasions, including an *Observer* readers' poll of June 1989, as Britain's Worst Building.

The theatre was designed in the Brutalist style – typified by the use of large expanses of rough finished grey concrete which were left unpainted and raw-looking. While the exterior is harsh, the space inside is made congenial by being divided into a series of foyers, bars, restaurants and exhibition spaces. Again the rough concrete is left exposed, but the effect is softened by a carpeted floor and subtle lighting.

In his early 20s Lasdun worked for Wells COATES and then (1938–48) joined the Russian Berthold LUBETKIN as a partner in the group named Tecton, renowned for its high-quality, modern-style block of flats at Highpoint, London. While Lubetkin was a great influence on Lasdun, the young British architect was also an admirer of modernists LE CORBUSIER and Frank Lloyd WRIGHT, together with the 17th-century British architect Nicholas Hawksmoor.

After leaving Tecton, Lasdun designed a "cluster" block of municipal high-rise flats in Bethnal Green (1954). Lasdun moved away from designing public housing in the 1960s and was commissioned to design the Royal College of Physicians in Regent's Park (1961–4). Placed beside the fine early-19th century classical-style terraces of John Nash, the building demanded a design which would be appropriate in such a sensitive

Sir Denys Lasdun.

Sir Denys Lasdun, National Theatre, London, 1965–76.

setting. Despite the fact that Lasdun's building was designed in an uncompromisingly modern style, its graceful shape and plan make it an acceptable neighbour.

During the 1960s Britain saw the building of a number of universities, and Lasdun was commissioned to design the new University of East Anglia (1963–8). In common with the others, the campus was placed in a rural setting.

While most of the buildings were rectangular blocks finished in precast concrete, Lasdum devised a series of highly unusual students' residences, in the shape of stepped, triangular ziggurats.

His recent buildings include the Institute of Education and Advanced Legal Studies in London (1973–8). This long, low "groundscraper" slab is fronted by a row of narrow, concrete columns interrupted by chunky square columns. It is topped by four horizontal bands of dark glass and solid panels – the highest floor is stepped back from the fascia.

In 1977 Lasdun was presented with the coveted architectural award of the Royal Gold Medal.

LAUREN Ralph b.1939   American

fashion designer

Garments recalling the American prairie style and British country clothing in their design and fabrics.

Ralph Lauren was born Ralph Lipschitz in New York. After a period in which he both undertook business studies at night school and worked for Brooks Brothers and Allied Stores, he joined Beau Brummel Neckwear in 1967. There he created the Polo range of neckties and later a full range of "Ivy League Style" menswear.

Lauren formed his own label in 1972. His designs have changed little since this date. Lauren makes a virtue of their traditional American styling and fabrics, which are fused with an aristocratic British country look. His garments for men, women and children are characterized by their comfortable, restrained and assured elegance. They are designed to look worn in and to improve with age. He makes much use of denims, white cottons, flannels, tweed hacking jackets and Fair Isle knitwear, as well as traditional quilting and embroidered sampler designs.

In 1973 he designed the men's clothing for *The Great Gatsby*, set in the 1920s, and in 1978 the women's clothing for *Annie Hall*.

Ralph Lauren, velvet trousers and floral brocade coat, autumn/winter 1985–6.

LEACH Bernard 1887–1979 — British

studio potter

Highly influential pottery employing Oriental, especially Japanese, methods and principles.

Britain's foremost early studio potter, Bernard Howell Leach was in large part responsible for Western acceptance of the dual role of the potter as artist and craftsman, a long-established Oriental concept Leach absorbed from his own abundant contact with the East. Born to British parents in Hong Kong, Leach was brought up in Tokyo and in 1897 went to England, where he studied engraving with Frank Brangwyn, as well as pursuing painting and etching. He returned to the Orient in 1909, teaching design and engraving and also studying pottery – mostly stoneware and *raku* techniques – under Ogata Kenzan VI, a master in a long line of Japanese potters founded by Ogata Shinsei, called Kenzan (1663–1743). He travelled to both China (specifically Peking, in 1916–18) and Korea, and in 1920, after helping Kenzan VI build a new stoneware kiln near Tokyo, he settled in England, where he set up his own pottery in St Ives, Cornwall.

Several notable Japanese potters worked with Leach at St Ives over the years, foremost among them Shoji Hamada (who eventually returned to his native country, where he helped found the Japanese Folk Craft Movement and became Japan's premier art potter of the *Mingei*, or folk, ceramics school), and among his Western students were Michael CARDEW, Katherine Pleydell-Bouverie, Keith MURRAY, and Leach's own wife Janet and his son (and later partner), David. In 1933, Leach set up another pottery, in Shinner's Bridge, South Devon, also for a time teaching at nearby Dartington Hall. Besides using teaching to relate Eastern philosophies and methods to other potters, the highly influential and prolific Leach was the author of several significant books, including *A Potter's Outlook* (1928), *A Potter's Book* (1940) and *Kenzan and His Tradition* (1966). He worked at his art until well into his 80s, stopped only by worsening eyesight.

Not only did Leach adhere to simple yet lofty philosophies of the East (such as the Zen discipline of repetition) and adopt many Eastern pottery methods, notable among these *raku*, but he also looked at and incorporated into his repertoire techniques from Western tradition, especially the methods and decoration of medieval and English 17th-century pottery, notably slipware. He preferred uneven surface textures to perfectly smooth ones, and his extensive, expert range of decorative methods encompasses stencilling, incising, relief stamping, hand brushwork and modelling (the latter for knobs and the like), and abstract "splashing". Although his methods were anathema to those employed in industrial design and mass production, many of his simple and subtle shapes, glazes and motifs somewhat ironically proved a source of inspiration to makers of commercial pottery.

Bernard Leach, Leaping Fish vase, 1960s.

LE CORBUSIER 1887–1965 — see page 144

LENICA Jan b.1928 — Polish/French

poster, animated film and stage designer

Experiments in animated film since the late 1950s.

Jan Lenica initially studied music in Poznan, then architecture in Warsaw (1947–52); he also drew satirical cartoons, particularly for the Polish weekly *Szpilki*. But by 1950 he had given himself over to poster art, concentrating on posters for film and theatre. He was Teaching Assistant to Henryk TOMASZEWSKI at the Warsaw Academy of Art from 1954 to 1956.

With his broad graphic experience and musical training, he was soon drawn into creating experimental films. The first were done using a collage/stop-motion technique, in partnership with Walerian Borowczyk; their film *Once upon a Time* won several international awards in 1957/58. His pioneering animated films drew many of their ingredients from the graphics world. Elements such as engraved images, old postcards and type were all combined in movement, and accompanied by musical effects or sounds such as shrieking, buzzing and grating. The result was a new kind of animated montage, or "graphics in motion" – particularly appropriate to the themes conveyed in his films, such as "society and the individual" concepts of power, loss of identity, technology fantasies and fears, and so on.

Lenica emigrated to France in 1963, and has continued to live in Paris ever since. His films have won many awards and include: *Monsieur Tête* in 1959, *Labyrinth* in 1962, *Rhinoceros* in 1963, *A* in 1964, *Adam II* in 1969, and *Ubu* in 1977 (*Adam II* was his first full-length work, 80 minutes long; it was written, designed and animated by Lenica). During the 1970s Lenica became active in stage design, particularly for playhouses in West Germany.

Jan Lenica, Polish Surrealists poster, 1970.

LE CORBUSIER

Le Corbusier, General Assembly Building at Chandigarh, 1953–61.

LE CORBUSIER 1887–1965   French-Swiss

Immensely influential in 20th-century architecture, design, town planning and theory.

Le Corbusier was born Charles Edouard Jeanneret in the Swiss watchmaking town of La Chaux-de-Fonds. The intensity of his character and a duality which runs through his creative life can, perhaps, be attributed to his Calvinist background. Certainly, there must have been another early and basic conflict between the rational gridded industrial town and his training in his late teens as a designer/engraver in the last phase of the Arts and Crafts movement. His teacher L'Eplattenier taught that ornament should derive from the immediate natural environment. Le Corbusier's first work, the Villa Fallet (1905), embodies these ideas.

From 1907, however, his horizons were widened by contact with the most important 20th-century architectural pioneers and developments. From the meeting with the architect Tony Garnier in 1908 stems his concern with large-scale utopian town planning. A short spell at Peter BEHRENS' office in Berlin in 1910 was to open his eyes to modern production engineering – the technology of ships, aircraft and automobiles – and result in his early optimism about the workings of industrial civilization. With Auguste PERRET in 1908 he realized that steel-reinforced concrete was the material of the future.

Over the next few years he travelled widely in Europe, mostly on foot, sketching and absorbing elements which would eventually form his new visual vocabulary. In parallel with this new visual awakening he also developed his technical ideas, and with a friend, the engineer Max du Bois, he developed two

Le Corbusier, bentwood and cane chair made by Thonet Bros.

technical aesthetic ideas which were to inform the first phase of his architecture up to 1935. One was the "Dom-Ino" unit of construction (1914), a modular house intended to be built with unskilled labour. It consisted of concrete planes supported between steel pillars, so doing away with load-bearing walls, and gave complete freedom of plan. The other was the "Villes Pilotis", a city projected to be elevated on piles. These ideas reverberate in his work and in 20th-century architecture.

Le Corbusier eventually settled in Paris in 1917, where he developed the aesthetics of "Purism". This formed the basis of Le Corbusier's book *Toward a New Architecture* (1925), and was to be the major theoretical and polemical text underlying modernism. Le Corbusier argued that in art and architecture there is a distinction between "primary" sensations, which everyone experiences simply by virtue of being human, and "secondary" sensations which depend on belonging to a particular culture.

The theory enabled Le Corbusier to make a decisive break with the past. Architecture in the future should be appraised by reference to objective human needs rather than culturally conditioned "secondary sensations". It also followed that modernism was universal and relevant to all societies.

From now every stylistic reference was removed, and in conjunction with his new technical thinking Le Corbusier started on the reduction of building to pure form. As is well known, it also led to the reconsideration of the house as, by analogy, "a machine for living in". Also, in the same way that internal living areas would be grouped according to functions, metropolitan areas could be adapted to the requirements of modern life.

Le Corbusier, Villa Savoye,
Poissy sur Seine, 1929–31.

A number of works and projects worked the principles out in practice. The Maison Citrohan (1920) developed the Dom-Ino and Ville Pilotis concepts to produce a standardized dwelling. This basic cell or *immeuble-villa* was used in his Pessac housing estate (1926), and also developed as a solution for high-density urban living in the form of terraced duplexes in the cellular perimeter blocks of the plans for the Ville Contemporaine (1922), and would be used again, stacked up for his high-rise designs.

Le Corbusier was interested in urban forms. His concern to break with the conventional past in favour of a rational solution led to a number of city projects. The final ideal vision was the Ville Radieuse, a city of towers elevated above a continuous park, which was to be a pervasive theme of modernism. A similar plan, the plan Voisin, was evolved for Paris, which would have entailed huge demolition. This image of authoritarian utopianism is perhaps Le Corbusier's most controversial legacy.

After 1925 Le Corbusier returned to the villa in the Maison Cook (1926), demonstrating "Les 5 points d'une architecture nouvelle" published in 1926: (1) the pilotis elevated the mass off the ground; (2) a free plan was achieved through the separation of load-bearing columns and walls, subdividing space; (3) the free façade was a corollary to the free plan in the vertical plane; (4) long horizontal sliding windows; (5) the roof garden, restoring the area of ground covered by the house. The most famous houses of this period are the Villa Stein (1927) and the Villa Savoye (1929).

After this time commissions from wealthy patrons dried up and Le Corbusier spent his time on town-planning projects and projects for large buildings, notably for the League of Nations Building in Geneva (1927). These large projects mark a shift in Le Corbusier's thinking, as they seemed to demand a more "artistic" traditional approach to composition. At the same time as he was abandoning the Purist aesthetic of his earlier work, he was losing faith in the machine age and industrial civilization.

After the war Le Corbusier made use of crude *in situ* concrete casting in contrast to his earlier machine aesthetic. The Maisons Jaoul (1954–6) shows his switch from machine prefabrication to widely adopted "brutalist" methods of construction, and was highly influential in developing a taste for rough unfinished surfaces. The post war work is also far more expressive, poetic and less rationalistic, and he creates a new vocabulary of forms, often drawn from natural or human forms.

The Unité d'Habitation (1947–52) brings his domestic architecture to a final monumental form, where the parts are related to the whole by the modular system of proportion based on the human figure. The pilotis on which it stands, relating back to the Ville Pilotis scheme, also seem to reflect Le Corbusier's more sensual nature and are said to resemble a female thigh. The architecture is also more organic in the way it relates to the landscape as well as drawing on natural forms. The poetic tendency was particularly marked in the sculptural shape of Notre-Dame du Haut, Ronchamp (1950–4), but Le Corbusier also created a more formal classical language, though without explicit classical reference, in the sculptural forms which are a feature of the Supreme Court, Chandigarh (1950–6). Although the concerns of the pre- and post-war work are different, they are united by Le Corbusier's interest in forms which are not based merely on cultural precedents.

L

LESAGE AND CIE founded 1922   French

embroiderers and embellishers

Embroidery and embellishments for Paris *couturiers.*

Since the death of the main competitor, Rebe, in the late 1960s François Lesage has manned the leading French company of *parurières* (embroiderers and embellishers) to supply the Parisian *couturiers.*

An anachronism from pre-revolutionary France, the *parurières'* work acts as a guarantee of exclusivity that adds considerable value to a piece of couture. The ultimate in power dressing, it is an important element of the couture system. The company was bought by Albert Lesage in 1922 from Michonet, who created elaborate embroideries for the first independent *couturier,* the Englishman Charles Frederic Worth. His first major client was Madeleine VIONNET. By radically simplifying his designs, loosening the tension of his embroidery with the aid of a logarithmic table, he met the technical requirements of the bias cut.

It was his collaboration with the Italian *couturière* Elsa SCHIAPARELLI that brought Lesage international repute. Her use of *trompe l'oeil* and decorative fantasy, inspired by the Surrealists and her close friend, the French artist Jean Cocteau, was the perfect complement to his craft.

During the 1960s François Lesage, having inherited his father's business at the end of the war, earned his reputation as the "King of Glitter" by capturing the graphic mood of the moment with dresses that were totally encrusted with plastic beetles' wings, transparent beads and rhinestones. François also looked to contemporary artists for inspiration; this resulted in such oddities as his delicate interpretations of Jackson Pollock's work in tangled drakes' feathers, coral and pearls on tangerine silk for GIVENCHY (1969).

During the late 1980s the boom in the international art market and the return of female power dressing found its expression in Lesage's sequinned copies of Van Gogh's painting *The Irises* for Yves SAINT LAURENT, and his copy of the decoration of a Ming vase for the bodice of a CHANEL dress.

LISSITZKY El 1890–1941   see page 148

LOEWY Raymond 1883–1986   see page 150

LOOS Adolf 1870–1933   Czech

architect

Steiner House, Chicago Tribune competition, author of "Ornament and Crime".

Born the son of a stonemason and educated in Dresden, Adolf Loos became one of the greatest influences on International style architecture. His private houses are often considered his most important buildings.

One of his most important essays "Ornament and Crime" appeared in 1908. In this he declared that ornament and decadent culture were inextricably linked. Two years later he published another essay "Architektur" which again criticised decorative features. He wrote "Only a very small part of architecture belongs to art, the tomb and the monument. Everything else, everything that serves a purpose, should be excluded from the realms of art".

In his Steiner House (1910) in Vienna, the strict symmetry, cubic form and severe exterior were enriched by interiors incorporating glorious stones and woods. In 1923 he produced one of his most startling designs for the Chicago Tribune competition. This has remained a powerful symbol of Modernist architecture. In the mid 1920s he ceased designing for the working classes to design for the bourgeoisie.

LUBALIN Herb 1919–81   American

typographer and typeface designer

Founder of International Typeface Corporation.

Herb Lubalin first achieved international acclaim in the graphic and typographic worlds during the 1950s. His hallmark in design was an emotive and often flowery use of typefaces, especially favouring the curves and swashes of hand-drawn lettering, in contrast to the mechanical austerity of the Swiss–German style. He used his type and letterforms in such a way as to enhance the meaning of the message to be conveyed.

During the 1960s when hot-metal type and its traditions were giving way to photo- and film-setting, Lubalin was able to see the creative possibilities that lay in store for a freer approach to typographic layout, as well as for new typefaces. In 1970, with Aaron Burns and Edward Rondthaler, Lubalin established the International Typeface Corporation or ITC, a licensing house which did much to aid typeface designers (by paying typeface royalties) and even more to make a broader

Adolf Loos, Chicago Tribune competition entry, 1922.

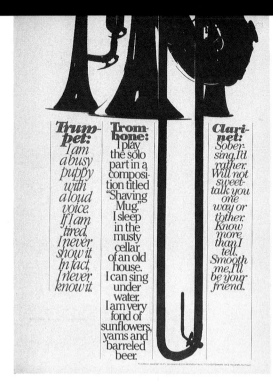

Herb Lubalin, page from
U&lc magazine, 1978.

Trum-pet: I am a busy puppy with a loud voice. If I am tired, I never show it. In fact, I never know it.

Trom-bone: I play the solo part in a composition titled "Shaving Mug." I sleep in the musty cellar of an old house. I can sing under water. I am very fond of sunflowers, yams and barreled beer.

Clari-net: Sober, sing, I'd rather. Will not sweet-talk you one way or t'other. Know more than I tell. Smooth me, I'll be your friend.

range of fonts available to typesetting manufacturers. The result was an explosion of new typeface designs. Lubalin himself was responsible for a number of typefaces, among them Lubalin Graph and the popular Avant Garde family of typefaces.

ITC also published a lively journal to show off its new typefaces, named *U&lc* (Upper and lowercase). It played a major role in popularizing not only ITC typefaces, but the whole new world of photosetting.

LUBETKIN Berthold 1901–90   Russian

architect

Highpoint I and II; London Zoo Penguin Pool.

Berthold Lubetkin left Russia to study in Paris at the Atelier Perret and then came to England in 1932.

In 1932 he founded the group of architects called Tecton with Denys LASDUN, Anthony Chitty, Lindsay Drake, Val Harding and Michael Dugdale. Among the first commissions was one to build a block of flats on a hilltop in Highgate, London.

Highpoint I (1933–5) was built on a cross-shaped plan, eight floors high. In the modern style of LE CORBUSIER and post-Revolution Soviet collective housing, it was flat-roofed, built in concrete with long horizontal windows and balconies, and painted white.

Despite the protests of locals, the nearby High-point II was built in 1938. In a less crisp style, and rectangular in shape, Highpoint II was built on similar lines using concrete and glass. This second, seven-storey block contained maisonettes and had the added

luxury of a swimming pool and squash courts.

Between 1934 and 1938 Tecton worked on buildings at London Zoo, the most beautiful and innovative of which was the Penguin Pool. This great concrete crater – like an abstract stage set – was prophetic of the free moulded concrete used in the 1950s and included a structurally brilliant use of reinforced concrete to create two interwoven spiral ramps suspended over the shallow water.

Lubetkin became disenchanted with archi-tecture later in his career and gave up design in favour of farming.

LUCILE 1863–1935   British

fashion designer

Luxurious teagowns and picture dresses.

Born Lucy Sutherland, Lucile was the sister of the famous romantic novelist Elinor Glyn. Following her divorce in 1890, Lucile began dressmaking for her friends. Her garments were soon much in demand and she opened her own house in 1891. Lucile was the first English *couturière* to gain an international reputation. By 1911 she had branches in London, Paris, New York and Chicago.

High fashion during the early 20th century was luxurious and extravagant. Rich women were required to possess a tremendous variety of clothing for every occasion: a weekend away involved as many as 16 complete changes of clothing. Lucile was one of the leading British designers who provided this elaborate and expensive wardrobe.

She was most famous for her picture dresses, tea- and ballgowns, which were made of the finest chiffons and silks trimmed with the most costly hand-made laces, beads, sequins and rich embroidery. These were predominantly made in the subtle sweet-pea colours which were fashionable during the late 19th and early 20th centuries. Bertha collars, layered puff skirts, batiste undersleeves and the use of silk roses were all Lucile trademarks. She was the first designer to popularize coloured underwear and was also respon-sible for making fashion shows into exciting events, using tall models (couture garments had, in the main, been shown on wax or sawdust dummies until this date).

Lucile continued to design clothing through-out the 1920s but grew disillusioned with the more utilitarian styles which were coming into vogue.

LISSITZKY

El Lissitzky, propaganda poster *Beat the Whites with the Red Wedge*, 1919.

LISSITZKY El 1890–1941   Russian

graphic designer and typographer

Pioneer of modern graphic design, typography.

El Lissitzky produced a huge body of graphic and typographic work, photographic experiments and paintings that proved to be influential in spreading the principles of Russian Constructivism and Suprematism throughout Europe in the 1920s. He also acted as a crucial connecting figure, or link, between the different art movements of the time – through his contact (through meetings and visits) and collaborations with leading personalities of the Modern Movement; his involvement in various important art publications; and the extraordinary energy he applied to spreading the word of Constructivism in the course of writing articles, talking, travelling, and lecturing all over Europe. His influence has been equally far-reaching over the decades, and he remains a favourite subject of study for graphic designers today.

Born in Polschinok in the province of Smolensk, he left Russia in 1909, aged 19, to study engineering and architecture in Darmstadt. He returned in 1914 after war broke out, and worked in Moscow as an architectural assistant from then on. From 1917 to 1919 he designed a series of experimental Yiddish picture-books and, being a fervent supporter of the Revolution, also designed a Soviet flag in 1918 that was used in procession in Red Square.

In 1919 the painter Marc Chagall, at that time principal of Vitebsk art school, appointed Lissitzky professor of architecture. While at Vitebsk, Lissitzky was strongly influenced by the Suprematist painter Kasimir Malevich. He helped to organize the publication of Malevich's *New System of Art*, a manifesto of Suprematism, while beginning to design posters and book covers. He also started working on experimental designs called "PROUNS" (an acronym from the Russian for "Project for the Affirmation of the New") which combined Suprematist and Constructivist elements, and were intended to be a union between painting and architecture (he later designed a PROUN room in Berlin in 1923, and another in Hanover in 1927). Also in Vitebsk he designed the renowned abstract Soviet propaganda poster *Beat the Whites with the Red Wedge* in 1919, and the next year designed the Suprematist story *Of Two Squares*: an abstract children's book, also intended for the enjoyment of adults. It was published in Berlin two years later, as well as in a Dutch version in the journal *De Stijl*.

In 1921 Lissitzky began to teach architecture at the New Vkhutemas art school in Moscow (now sometimes referred to as the Russian Bauhaus) where the Constructivist movement was beginning to gather strength; his colleagues included Vladimir Tatlin, the founder of the movement. By the end of 1921 Lissitzky had taken up residence in Berlin, the rising intellectual centre of Europe. He participated in the Constructivist Exhibition held there in 1922, an event of crucial importance as it was the first time that Constructivist art and artists were exhibited as a major movement outside of Russia; the exhibition had a tremendous impact on the prevailing art and design scene. Berlin was honoured at that time with the presence of a number of Russian artists and intellectuals – Ehrenburg, Pasternak, Mayakovsky, and Gabo among them. Lissitzky and writer Ilya Ehrenburg collaborated on the Constructivist magazine *Veshch/Gegenstand/Objet* (a trilingual product, and devoted to "the new objectivity"). Also that year Lissitzky participated in the

El Lissitzky, double-page spread design for Mayakovsky's *For the Voice*, 1923.

Constructivist-Dadaist congress in Weimar: an historic meeting of the major movements. He wrote articles, lectured, made visits to the BAUHAUS, and had meetings with Theo van Doesburg, László MOHOLY-NAGY and Kurt Schwitters.

This was also the beginning of a period of tremendous graphic activity for Lissitzky, for from 1922 to 1924 he took advantage of Berlin's sophisticated printing facilities and produced a large quantity of superb typographic work. (From this point on Lissitzky, along with Moholy-Nagy and Herbert BAYER at the Bauhaus, would develop the concept of Constructivist typography or, as it would become known, the New Typography.) Lissitzky designed covers for the American magazine *Broom*, as well as producing covers and illustrations for a variety of other publications. In 1923 he designed and illustrated Mayakovsky's book of poems *For Reading Out Loud*, now considered to be a landmark in 20th century typography and book design.

By the end of 1923 he was taken ill (and eventually diagnosed as having pulmonary tuberculosis) and in 1924 entered a sanatorium in Switzerland. There, while he was ill, his output of work was still phenomenal. He worked on the design and editing of a special issue of the Dadaist journal *Merz* (in collaboration with Kurt Schwitters, who produced the journal), and contributed to the Dutch journal *De Stijl* and to Mart STAM's periodical *ABC*. To earn money, he designed abstract posters and publicity material for Pelikan ink. He produced a series of photographic experiments, and collaborated with Hans Arp on *The Isms of Art*, in which he gave a summary of the aims of Cubism, Futurism, Constructivism, and other modernisms. Beset with financial difficulties, illness and news of his sister's suicide, in 1925 he returned to

Moscow, where he again became a professor (this time, professor of interior decoration and furniture) at the Vkhutemas.

Lissitzky visited Germany briefly in 1926 to design an exhibition room as part of the International Art Exhibition in Dresden, and also on that trip proposed to a German widow, who joined him in Moscow to be married in 1927. Now moving heavily in the direction of exhibition design, he designed the 1927 Union Polygraphic Exhibition in Moscow and, on the strength of its success, was appointed to design the Soviet pavilion at the International Press Exhibition in Cologne in 1928. He also completed a number of other important Soviet exhibitions staged in Germany over the next two years.

Lissitzky's contribution to modern typography was recognized by Jan TSCHICHOLD in his book *Die Neue Typographie*, published in 1928. During the 1930s Lissitzky devoted himself mainly to teaching, but his work became increasingly disrupted as his health worsened over the years.

El Lissitzky, *Merz* programme cover, 1923.

LOEWY

Raymond Loewy, Lucky
Strike cigarette pack, 1940.

Raymond Loewy, Gestetner
Duplicator, redesigned in
1929.

LOEWY Raymond 1883–1986   American

industrial designer

Lucky Strike cigarette pack; Coldspot refrigerator; Gestetner Ream Duplicator.

Raymond Loewy, perhaps the father of the American design profession, has attracted admiration and envy in equal measure.

Ostentatious, high-living, friend of the famous, he was a gifted entrepreneur who had his first business, in France, when he was 17, manufacturing a model aeroplane he had designed. French-born but, like his father, in love with new technology and the USA, he made his career as an industrial designer in the USA.

Although he had studied electrical engineering in Paris, his design career began in New York where he dressed windows for Macy's, and then did fashion illustrations for Condé Nast. He secured his first product design commission in 1929 for the Gestetner duplicating company, who required a modern restyling of the Gestetner Ream Duplicator 66. Using a clay model (he claimed to be the first designer to use clay as a prototyping material), Loewy repackaged the machine in a neat sheath, as well as making some improvements to its internal workings.

Another, much cited, early Loewy success is his design for the Coldspot refrigerator marketed by Sears Roebuck. Following Loewy's redesign of the refrigerator, sales went from 65,000 to 275,000 a year in five years (1935–40). Loewy's restyling, which transformed a box on four legs into a rounder, more agreeable form, was an important ingredient in this sales success.

Loewy's success is largely due to the fact that he knew industrial design was basically about advertising and selling (not moralistic ideologies about truth to materials and honest functions). Even his showmanship helped to consolidate the link between design-as-style and design-as-advertising, though Loewy himself insisted, in spite of most evidence to the contrary, that he was more than a stylist.

Loewy was a tenacious businessman. He was not a theorist, and expressed himself epigramatically in a manner that flattered other businesspeople. For example: "I believe in natural talent; if you don't have it, do something else." He could encapsulate the core of an industrial designer's work in a few words, as when he described the parasitical factors which designers had to fight off, namely "noise, vibration, water or air resistance and villainous smells".

Loewy's imagination was excited by transport and by speed: his most expressive designs were the S-1 locomotive for the Pennsylvania Railroad Company (1937), a succession of Greyhound buses for the Greyhound Corporation and the Studebaker Starlight Coupé. Loewy's work for the NASA Saturn-Apollo Skylab spacecraft between 1967 and 1973 took industrial design into an area where there were genuinely new functional problems to be solved. But even here styling was important because, unlike most state-of-the-art industrial design in the defence industries, the space projects were very public – they were a part of the Cold War propaganda on behalf of "USA Inc". Loewy was in his element.

He did not, of course, design everything himself. One of his abilities was finding good staff and leading them. His signature would be on every drawing, his film-star face upfront in every interview, and behind him his staff were working.

Raymond Loewy, locomotive for the Pennsylvania Railroad, c.1934.

He established an office in London in 1937, and after the Second World War Loewy's success and his professionalism were an inspiration and a model for nascent British design consultancies.

In 1951 he wrote his autobiography, *Never Leave Well Enough Alone*, and in 1979 he published a pictorial survey of his work: *Industrial Design*. Both books are distinguished by his anecdoctal, buddy-to-buddy salesman approach to design and designing. He loved telling and retelling the story of how he got the job to redesign the Lucky Strike cigarette pack: "The President of American Tobacco visited my office in 1940, 'I'm from American Tobacco. Someone told me that you could design a better pack, and I don't believe it.' 'Then why are you here?' I asked. He looked at me for a moment, grinned, and we were friends".

The Lucky Strike design has long been held out as another of design's mileposts, but for a sceptical review of Loewy's claims for this design readers should refer to Adrian Forty's book *Objects of Desire* (Thames & Hudson, 1986). Loewy was a Goliath in the story of 20th-century design for capitalism; as such, he attracts a queue of Davids with sharp analytical slingshot in their pouches.

LUTYENS Edwin 1869–1944   British

architect

Lindisfarne Castle; Castle Drogo; Gledstone Hall; Whitehall Cenotaph; Viceroy's House, New Delhi.

Sir Edwin Lutyens worked in a traditional English style, and while he admired the classical buildings of ancient Greece and Rome, he preferred to use distilled versions of the designs which had been "so well digested that there is nothing but essence left".

Among his early commissions were large houses such as the bijou fortress of Lindisfarne Castle (1903), and the magnificent Castle Drogo in Devon (1910–30). In the first decade of the century Lutyens helped to plan and design the Central Square for London's Hampstead Garden Suburb.

His reputation was at its peak before the First World War; however, shortly afterwards he was commissioned to design the Cenotaph in Whitehall, London (1920). He also designed the Memorial to the Missing of the Somme at Thiepval, France (1927–32).

His largest and most important commission was for the Viceroy's House, New Delhi (1912–31). Placed at the end of a three-mile avenue, the stately building, covering an area equal to that occupied by the palace of Versailles, was a hybrid of classical and Mogul design and also borrowed from state buildings at Washington, DC. Constructed in pink and cream Dholpur sandstone, the building had a floor plan which resembled the letter H, with a deep, long crossbar.

One of Lutyens' last, and potentially greatest, commissions failed to reach completion – that for the new Roman Catholic Liverpool Cathedral (1930–9). It was designed to be twice the size of St Peter's in Rome. Work began on the crypt in 1930, but was halted at the outbreak of war. Because of its high cost the scheme was never realized.

Edwin Lutyens, Viceroy's House, New Delhi, 1923–31.

M

M&CO founded 1979 — American
multi disciplinary design group

Humorous and stylish designs such as the 10:1:4 watch.

M&Co. is a New York-based design consultancy founded by Hungarian-born Tibor Kalman. Over the course of the 1980s it has become one of the most popular design studios in America, and is known for a unique sense of humour and sophisticated wit, applied to the work of clients both large and small in the form of jokes, puns and satire.

Although its main area of concentration is graphic design, product design has become an increasingly important part of the group's repertoire. Its projects include record covers and publicity for the rock group Talking Heads; the title sequence and publicity material for David Byrne's film *True Stories* (1986); and all manner of graphic material for clients ranging from trendy local restaurants, to real-estate developers and large corporations. M&Co.'s product work includes the design of the delightful 10:1:4 watch (a watch missing all numbers except 10, 1 and 4), which is now housed in the permanent design collection of the Museum of Modern Art in New York.

The group's most memorable satires emerge, not through client work, but through teasing comments and articles on the design profession and its sacred cows. A good example appeared in an article in a parody issue of *Print* magazine (late 1980s), in which M&Co. lampooned the world of corporate identity graphics, and indeed the whole profession, by creating fictitious solutions to a hypothetical commission to re-design the national identity programme for Canada.

MACKINTOSH Charles Rennie 1868–1928 — Scottish
architect, designer and painter

Glasgow School of Art; Cranston tea-rooms.

Mackintosh was one of the earliest British designers to use the art nouveau style – the sinuous, linear decorative style that drew much of its imagery from stylizing the human figure and plant forms. Active as a designer and architect in the 1890s and early 1900s, Mackintosh was operating in a period which was dominated by revivalism. In England there was an interest in the Gothic and the medieval, but in Scotland there was a loathing for Gothic, and the favoured style was classicism. Mackintosh contributed to a newer

Charles Rennie Mackintosh, Glasgow School of Art, 1898–1907.

architecture by designing buildings that were classical in appearance but somehow starker and bolder.

His most important and singular design is the one he executed for the Glasgow School of Art (built between 1898 and 1907), a radical building, but not altogether surprising, since in Glasgow at that time there was a tradition of building stark, plain tenement housing blocks.

A number of his furniture and interior design schemes were designed in collaboration with Margaret Macdonald, whom Mackintosh married in 1900. The Mackintoshes' style of interior design, an interpretation of art nouveau, was developed through a variety of commissions, among them the four tea-rooms designed and built during the years 1897–1912 for Miss Cranston. Early publicity in the magazine *The Studio* brought him to the attention of European designers, especially those connected with the Viennese Secessionists, such as Josef HOFFMANN and Joseph Maria Olbrich.

Perhaps Mackintosh's *tour de force* is the library he designed as an extension for the Glasgow School of Art (1907–9). In the interior of the library the wood beam and post structure is reminiscent of Japanese structures of similar design.

Apart from the Glasgow School of Art, he designed several domestic buildings, including country houses such as Windy Hill at Kilmalcolm (1899–1901) and Hill House, Helensburgh (1902–3).

He designed furniture for 30 years, including the now very familiar ladderback chairs. Between 1898 and 1904 he had his furniture painted an ivory-white colour in an attempt to kill off the traditional connotations of wood. Mackintosh withdrew from architecture in 1919 and ceased all designing in 1920.

MAGISTRETTI Vico b.1920   Italian

furniture designer

Selene chair; Maralunga sofa; Villabianca chairs.

Magistretti graduated in architecture from Milan University in 1945, and went to work in his father's practice. He began designing furniture in the 1960s, and since then he has worked with a number of manufacturers, including KNOLL International and CASSINA. Some of his work is in the permanent design collection of the Museum of Modern Art, New York.

Among Magistretti's notable designs are the Selene all-plastic chair, manufactured by Artemide in 1968, the Maralunga sofa (Cassina, 1973) and the Villabianca chairs (Cassina, 1985). He won the Compasso d'Oro in 1967 and 1979, the gold medal at the 9th Milan Triennale, and the first prize of the International Jury at the Cologne Furniture Fair in 1982. Some of his work (the 1986 Cardigan sofa, for example) has been criticized as dull. Others see it as simply quiet, a measured attempt to serve the domestic landscape rather than bawling egocentrically in it.

Magistretti's early classics, such as the Modello 115 chair (Cassina 1964), recall Italian vernacular 19th-century design. Modello 115 has a red-painted wooden frame and rush seating. It is an example of the way post-war Italian design, in spite of its reputation for radicalism, tends usually to stress a continuity with tradition rather than a rupture with the past.

Vico Magistretti, Veranda folding/extendable chair for Cassina, 1983.

MAGNUSSEN Erik 1884–1961   Danish

silversmith, jewellery and metalwork designer

Silver jewellery and objects in art nouveau and modernist styles.

Erik Magnussen was a versatile and highly talented silversmith and metalwork designer who worked both in Europe and America, and much of whose output, from curvilinear art nouveau jewellery in the early 1900s, to boldly *moderne* coffee services in the late 1920s, was widely praised and much imitated. Born in Denmark in 1884, he studied sculpture with Stephan Sindig and chasing with the silversmith Viggo Hansen. From 1907 to 1909 he was in Berlin, studying at the Kunstgewerbeschule and working as a chaser for Otto Rohloff. He returned to his native country in 1909, opening his own silver workshop. From 1901 he exhibited his silver jewellery and objects widely (in Copenhagen, Paris, Berlin and Rio de Janeiro), and in the 1920s he went to America, working as a silver designer for Gorham in Providence, Rhode Island, from 1925 to 1929 and for the German firm August Dingeldein and Son for some time afterwards (they had a retail outlet in Manhattan). Magnussen opened a workshop in Chicago in 1932, worked in Los Angeles (1932–8) and designed for the International Silver Company in Meriden, Connecticut, about 1938–9. He returned to Denmark in 1939, and reopened his workshop there.

Along with Georg JENSEN, Magnussen was a premier Danish figure creating silver art nouveau jewellery. His style varied from Gallic-inspired, rather conventional art nouveau, to a more kinetic, even jaggedly electric mode, for instance, a chased-silver belt-mirror whose central motif spells out the date "1901" in rather ghoulish type.

His 1920s and 1930s American output, which comprised less wearable silver than decorative "useful ware" such as tea and coffee services, tazzas, bowls and the like, drew its inspiration from a variety of sources, both traditional and modern. A covered cup in sterling silver and ivory for Gorham (1926), gently hammered and containing typical Danish beads and scrolls, was elegant and neo-classical, while a tea service for Dingeldein (1930) – a teapot, creamer, sugar-bowl and tray of sterling silver with jade accents, made in Hanau – was altogether bolder in its smoothness and angularity.

Arguably his best-known creation was the 1927 silver coffee service for Gorham, ambitiously called The Lights and Shadows of Manhattan. More Cubist

M

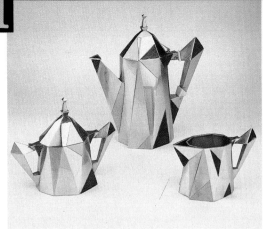

than urban-architectonic, the strongly geometric components comprised panels of burnished, gilded and oxidized silver facets, these occupying multiple planes in a dramatic configuration. Except for a trapezoid shaped tray that accompanied the service, and a matching salad set, no other such exuberant works made up Magnussen's oeuvre. When Magnussen returned to Denmark in 1939, he continued producing silver, although it gradually grew more conservative.

MAINBOCHER 1891–1976 — American

fashion designer

Understated classical simplicity and the introduction of the strapless boned evening dress in 1934.

Mainbocher (born Main Rousseau Bocher) studied at the University of Chicago, Chicago Academy of Fine Arts and the Arts Students League in New York. Between 1911 and 1917 he studied and worked in Munich, Paris and London, then served with the American hospital unit in France and remained in Paris after the First World War. There he became a fashion illustrator for *Harper's Bazaar* in 1922, was promoted to fashion editor in 1923 and then moved to become editor-in-chief-of French *Vogue* until 1929. In 1930 he opened his own couture house and became the first American to establish a successful fashion business in Paris.

Throughout the 1930s Mainbocher was noted for the understated, classical simplicity of his day and evening wear, and in 1934 he was the first *couturier* to design boned, strapless evening dresses, which were much copied towards the end of the decade. In 1937 he dressed Mrs Wallis Simpson for her much-publicized marriage to the Duke of Windsor. His last Paris collection, in 1940, featured wasp waists, which anticipated DIOR's New Look in 1947.

In 1940 he returned to New York and opened a business there. During the Second World War he designed the uniforms for the Marine Women's Corps, the American Red Cross and the Girl Scouts. After the war he returned to his 1930s philosophy of designing elegant and refined styles for the wealthy. As the fashion trade became increasingly youth-orientated in the 1960s, Mainbocher's luxurious and exclusive garments became less desirable. He was a purist and refused to sell his designs to wholesalers and copyists or license his name.

MAKEPEACE John b.1939 — British

furniture designer

Founder of School for Craftsmen in Wood.

Makepeace is a furniture designer and maker and entrepreneur. In 1977 he established the Parnham Trust and School for Craftsmen in Wood at Parnham House, Dorset. In 1989 he established a further project, training students in product design and development to use wood thinnings, hitherto regarded by some countries as a waste product. Makepeace's project is triple-pronged – aesthetic, environmental and entrepreneurial. The marriage between craft ideals and new business is symbolized by the project's building – a new structure made from wood and designed by the engineer architect Frei Otto.

Makepeace said in 1981: "The work of craftspeople is conceptually accessible and interesting to a substantial part of the population – especially where the products fulfil a useful purpose. It seems to me important that this factor should be nurtured, whereas the more pretentious commentary associated with the 'arts' is likely to make the crafts remote, even irrelevant."

John Makepeace.

John Makepeace, writing table and chair made in his workshops at Parnham House, 1986.

MAKOVECZ Imre b.1935 — Hungarian

Creator of an alternative "organic architecture".

Makovecz was born in Budapest and qualified from the Technical University in 1959. He worked in various state offices on the typical projects of Communist Hungary – notably social housing and a collectivist supermarket in Sarospatak (1969–70), which is a typical piece of Eastern Bloc brutalism.

However, between 1975 and 1977 he built a mortuary chapel at Farkasret, near Budapest, which was the beginning of his search for an organic architecture. The structure is anthropomorphic, and resembles a rib-cage, with wooden ribs whose geometries alter from one end to the other. Other details were designed by his collaborator Gabor Mezei.

In 1977 Makovecz was appointed as the architect to the forestry company Bilis, and subsequently his organic architecture has developed over a huge number of projects, largely outside the state system, typically in the many community halls for outlying districts. The technology is alternative in its intentions and draws on traditional craft skills.

His designs are also highly expressive and charged with metaphor. The community hall at Bak (1985–8) takes its form from the outspread wings of an eagle, and Forest Community centre at Visegrad is an earth mound full of allusion to traditional structures and natural forms. A favourite motif is the incorporation of whole trees as pillars, for example the Zalaszentlaszlo community hall.

Makovecz's work has proved difficult to interpret for many Western critics and he has been charged with a "wilful individualism", which misses the political and philosophical significance of his work – and its commitment. As well as the more obvious influences of Jung, Rudolf Steiner and Frank Lloyd WRIGHT, Makovecz has been influenced by the holism of the Hungarian thinker Bela Havmas.

MARI Enzo b.1932 — Italian

Delfina and Sof Sof chairs.

Mari was one of the first designer/commentators to compare the process and the results of design to linguistic analysis and language. He refused to create a designed environment for the major Italian design exhibition in 1972 held at the Museum of Modern Art (The New Domestic Landscape) and contributed instead an "anti design statement". This asserted "the only correct undertaking for 'artists' is that of language research – that is, critical examination of the communications systems now in use". However, Mari added that research was not an end in itself because the point of it was to produce work that met the needs of society, including "meaning".

Mari takes a classical view of design insofar as he appears to believe that there are certain proportions and volumes, for example, that are "right" for the human psyche and sensibility. Mari has initiated research into the psychology of perception of colour, form and space. In 1970 he published a treatise on function and aesthetics in design (*Funzione della ricerca estetica*, 1970).

His work as a designer spans children's toys, graphic design, household utensils and furniture. He works for companies such as Driade and Gabbianelli and possibly his most famous designs to date are the Sof Sof (1972) and Delfina (1979) chairs, both produced by Driade. The Sof Sof is particularly prized by other designers; it is made up from nine grey lacquered tubular iron rings that are welded together; the seat and the back are two cushions of grey leather.

MARINOT Maurice 1882–1960 — French

Innovative designs in glass, stressing the inherent qualities of the medium.

Born in Troyes, Marinot was a somewhat rebellious student at the Ecole des Beaux-Arts in Paris. His nonconformity continued throughout his career, which he began as a painter, a member of the renegade Fauve group, known for its exuberant, colourful canvases.

He showed his paintings regularly at the Paris salons until 1913, when he also exhibited at the Armory Show in New York, but by that time his primary interest lay in glass. This interest had been sparked by a 1911 visit to the Bar-sur-Seine glassworks of his friends, the brothers Eugène and Gabriel Viard.

At first he provided designs for the gaffers, decorating the resultant blown vessels with colourful flowers, figures and abstract designs, but in time he himself was producing pure, undecorated vases, jars and flasks, bringing the glass to life by fire and

Maurice Marinot, bottle and stopper with flecked inclusions, 1923.

"eternalizing its beauty", as he thought of it. The vessels Marinot was creating and exhibiting to great acclaim by the 1920s were thick-walled and simply shaped, enabling the viewer to concentrate on the inherent properties of the medium itself, its transparency and brilliance, and not to be distracted by applied colour or other decoration. By emphasizing the actual physical qualities of glass, by seeming to trap its fluidity in three dimensions, Marinot produced pieces that elevated the medium to new artistic, aesthetic heights.

Marinot was in effect setting the stage several decades in advance for the glassmakers of the Studio Craft Movement of the 1960s. What heretofore had been considered physical flaws, ingredients to be got rid of or disguised – bubbles, internal fractures, chemical inclusions necessary to produce colours and the like – he turned into primary decorative elements. He also submerged pieces in acid baths, creating deeply etched designs with bark-like or other coarse but not unattractive textures. The simple but strong forms and rich, luminous palette of Marinot's one-off pieces were harmonious with the art deco taste of the 1920s, and his output captivated public and critics alike.

When the Viard Fils factory closed down in 1937, Marinot ended his career as a glass artist and returned to painting, the medium with which he had begun his professional life.

MARTINAZZI Bruno b.1923 — Italian

jeweller and sculptor

Combination of figurative and abstract themes.

Martinazzi studied first as an industrial chemist, but later trained at the State School of Art, Florence.

Modern avant-garde jewellery has sought since the Second World War to be classified as both art and design. Practitioners have tended to follow one of two routes: overtly figurative and organic or highly abstract. Martinazzi has used a limited range of images – usually parts of the human body – to create metaphors for various humanitarian ideas, and has sought to combine the figurative and the abstract approaches to jewellery. Thus he has produced rings and brooches on the themes of energy, time and measurement as well as love and sex. All his work is finely crafted and sensuous, and although his reputation dipped in the 1970s and early 1980s, the cycle of fashion is again in his favour.

Bruno Martinazzi.

Bruno Martinazzi, "gold finger" ring, cast in gold, 1990.

MARX Enid b.1902 — British

textile and industrial designer

Designs for London Underground train seats; London Transport posters; stamp designs.

Enid Marx has been one of the most significant designers of pattern during the 20th century although full credit for her work was denied for a long period because of her early connections with the Arts and Crafts movement and her own championing of the design qualities of folk art.

She trained in painting, ceramics and textiles at the Central School of Art and Design and did postgraduate work as a painter at the Royal College of Art. She joined the handcrafted-textile workshop of BARRON AND LARCHER in 1925, and then established her own studio in 1926. She is famous for her textile designs for London Transport, her designs for postage stamps for the Post Office, and for her many designs for books and book jackets. She was made a Royal Designer for Industry in 1944, partly in recognition of her contribution as a textile designer in the wartime Utility Scheme for domestic furnishings established under Gordon Russell in 1943. During the 1960s she became an art-school teacher and lecturer, and has since continued to work as a designer of prints and an artist of wood and lino cuts.

Her year's apprenticeship with Barron and Larcher was gruelling: "I was virtually their washing machine". Barron and Larcher's rigorous and austere craft, based on the revival of virtually obsolete techniques, such as the use of the labour-intensive vegetable and mineral dyes, had a formative effect on her own production philosophy. Her early work as a designer is characterized by small pattern repeats, block-

Enid Marx, self portrait, c.1925.

Enid Marx, design for the covers of London underground train seats, 1937.

printed by hand, and executed in a limited range of colours. This ability to work within relatively narrow colour ranges without recourse to elaborate industrial printing techniques gave her the grounding that made her utility designs such a success. The core of the utility design scheme was economy, modesty and restriction. Her success with the Utility Scheme lay in the early training at wringing a lot from a little.

Early classics of her work from the 1930s include covers and pattern papers for Chatto & Windus, such as her design for their edition of Marcel Proust's *Remembrance of Things Past.*

One of the characteristics of the English public is their love for textiles as a surface finishing as opposed to harder, more industrial surfaces. This is especially noticeable in public transport. Thus, while it would be more practical for London Transport to adopt hard surfaces for its underground railway carriages, the passengers prefer fabrics, and always have done. In 1937 Enid Marx became more widely known when she successfully designed a range of moquette fabrics for London Transport that were durable and did not show too much dirt, but which were also modern and appropriate to electric transport. This brief was difficult to fulfil because the makers of the textiles refused to give all the technical information she needed. Frank Pick, commercial manager of London Transport, had to intervene.

Her London Transport work and her Utility Scheme designs became important reference points for a new generation of designers who graduated in the 1950s for, contrary to popular mythology, modernism, especially in the United Kingdom and the United States, did not mean the death of decoration. In the 1950s Marx expanded her repertoire to include

plastic laminates and synthetic fabrics. She says: "Designing for synthetic textiles, for example, is far more difficult than designing for natural ones; with synthetics it is necessary to discover, or introduce, qualities to validate them in their own right; they have for too long been used purely imitatively."

A scholar and collector of traditional British folk art, she brought out the first book on the subject in collaboration with her historian friend, Margaret Lambert, in 1939 (it was called *When Victoria Began to Reign*). This interest inspired much of her later work as an illustrator of children's books for Chatto & Windus.

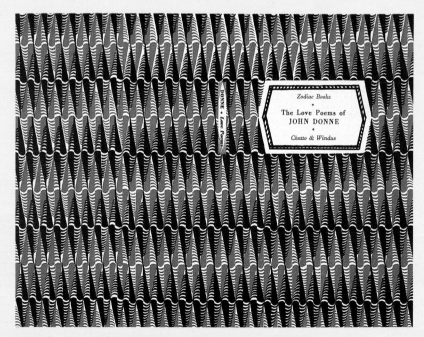

Enid Marx, book jacket cover for Zodiac Books, published by Chatto & Windus.

M

MATHSSON Bruno b.1907   Swedish

Use of natural materials in modern designs.

Like fellow Swede, Alvar AALTO, Mathsson experimented with laminated woods, bending them into complex curves. He developed a range of lightweight, simply formed chairs with cloth or leather webbing forming the seats and backs. His family owned a furniture factory at Varnamo, and it was here that much of his work was manufactured before the Second World War.

Mathsson came to international attention during the 1930s because people were ready for a modern style in natural materials – he used beechwood. He also researched into the ergonomics of seating, seeking to find anatomical as well as aesthetic criteria for his designs. In the 1960s he adapted his work and his ideas to suit production in cloth and tubular steel.

He also has an established reputation in Sweden as an architect, based on his advocacy of the glass curtain wall system following his return from a visit to the United States in 1946.

MAURER Ingo b.1932   German

lighting designer

Ya Ya Ho and Tijuca systems.

Ingo Maurer is one of the most innovative of contemporary lighting designers. Born in Germany, Maurer trained and worked as a graphic designer before turning to lighting design. He set up his own lighting design consultancy in Germany in 1966 after living in the USA for several years.

Maurer's work has been much admired for the way in which he harnesses the latest lighting technology in artistic, novel and sometimes playful lamps and lighting systems. It has been described, along with the work of Italian lighting designers the CASTIGLIONI brothers, as "trans high-tech" – a style which arose in the mid-1980s out of a disillusionment with the high-tech of the 1970s and is characterized by an almost casual approach to lighting technology.

This is seen in works like Ya Ya Ho (1984), an installation of pendant lights in a variety of material including plastic, glass, metal and ceramic, employing state-of-the-art low-voltage light sources. Ya Ya Ho was considered to be one of the most original lighting designs for years.

Maurer always stresses the teamwork involved in his lighting projects, not least the contribution made by electronics experts. More recently Maurer has started a series of designs intended for task lights as well as domestic use. The first of these, Tijuca, has miniature low-voltage light sources on the end of metal arms which are mounted on cables. The lamps can be moved freely and the light is turned on and off just by touching the metal arm.

McCARDELL Claire 1905–58   see page 160

MEDIA LAB founded 1979   American

design research group

Interdisciplinary research in new media.

Founded by computer graphics expert Nicholas Negroponte and Jerome Wiesner, president emeritus of MIT and science adviser to President Kennedy, the Media Laboratory grew out of MIT's Architecture Machine Group and other research activities in 1979. In 1985, it moved to a purpose designed building by I.M. PEI on the MIT campus in Cambridge.

Supported by sponsorship from publishing companies, television networks, and consumer electronics and computer manufacturers in the United States and Japan, the Media Lab embraces studies under the following titles: Spatial Imaging; Television of Tomorrow; School of the Future; Electronic Publishing; Computer Graphics and Animation; Music and Cognition; Movies of the Future; Speech Research; Advanced Human Interface; Visible Language Workshop; Interactive Cinema; and Vision and Modelling.

Despite its formidable depth of expertise in many areas, it is for the breadth of its interests that the Media Lab is unique. Many projects benefit from the cross-fertilization of ideas as researchers in varied disciplines come together to solve problems in contemporary and future media technology.

If one theme can be said to drive such a diversity of study, it is the thought that the gulf of understanding between the developers of a technology and its users that has widened during the 20th century can be bridged. Negroponte believes that many Media Lab projects can renew the Victorian spirit when the inventors of a technology were also the people who put it to creative use.

MEIER Richard b.1934 American

Smith House; Douglas House; The Atheneum; High Museum of Art.

Meier has been described as the ultimate American villa architect. Inspired by the simple, white cubic designs of LE CORBUSIER and Josef HOFFMANN, Meier has produced a number of sparkling white buildings.

During the late 1960s Meier was a member of a group called the New York Five, which also included architects Peter Eisenmann, Michael GRAVES, Charles Gwathmey and John Hejduk. The group were great admirers of the classic early modern buildings, such as Josef Hoffmann's Palais Stoclet. They considered the 1920s to be the golden age of modern architecture.

Among Meier's most successful villas was the Smith House, Darien, Connecticut (1965–7). The design played with convention, and Meier eschewed putting a grand frontage on the house in favour of making it an understated plain, white wall with small, asymmetrically placed windows. He saved the excitement for the back where the three-storey, flat-roofed house was given a delicate white frame and enormous windows, some two floors high, which overlooked the garden and local wooded landscape.

The horizontal slabs of the floors were dramatically juxtaposed by a towering, off-centre chimney and squat, rounded stair tower which protruded from the otherwise flat façade.

Another of his successful private commissions was the Douglas House, Harbor Springs, Michigan (1971–3). The house was constructed on a steep wooded hillside overlooking Lake Michigan and resembled the front of a mighty white liner which had somehow come crashing through a forest; its nautical design incorporated a white prow, balustraded decks, outdoor, metal staircases and even two tall silver flues. The flat façade was constructed almost entirely of glass set in a delicate frame. To add to the 1920s feel, the interior was filled with furniture of the period designed by Le Corbusier and Ludwig MIES VAN DER ROHE.

Shortly after this Meier worked on the Bronx Development Center, New York (1970–6). Meier's fascination with cubic shapes and large plain surfaces has not always been employed successfully. The designs for this centre for mentally retarded and physically disabled children appear unsympathetic and institutional.

However, Meier once again regained his digni-

Richard Meier, The Atheneum, New Harmony, Indiana, 1975–9.

fied style with The Atheneum, New Harmony, Indiana (1975–9). The white exhibition and reception centre is composed as a cluster of geometrical shapes. The building is dramatic and complex in its incorporation of so many shapes, but is given unity with a white finish.

Meier's skill at creating light and inviting structures and in pulling together a variety of fragmented geometric blocks was displayed once again at the High Museum of Art, Atlanta (1979–83). The white painted interior displays the influence of Frank Lloyd WRIGHT's Guggenheim Museum with its spiralling walkways from which lead the galleries.

Meier's work in reviving and developing the modern styles of the 1920s has influenced many young architects, not least in Japan, where the grids of white panelling and clusters of cubic shapes can be seen in the work of architects such as Fumihiko Maki and Kisho Kurokawa.

MELLOR David b.1930 British

Designing and manufacturing cutlery.

David Mellor is a designer, manufacturer and retailer, with kitchenware shops in London and Manchester. He is a silversmith by training and studied in his home town of Sheffield and later at the Royal College of Art, London (1950–4).

Some of his earliest work was for the Sheffield company Walker and Hall. It included the silver-plate cutlery service Pride (1954) which won an award from Britain's Design Council, the first of eight Design Council awards made to Mellor. In 1962 Mellor became a Royal Designer for Industry and in 1981 was awarded an OBE.

In 1963 Mellor designed Embassy, a contemporary-style silver service for British embassies. This

David Mellor, cutlery.

▶ page 162

McCARDELL

Claire McCardell, full-circle skirt and knitted circlet shoulder wrap, 1947.

McCARDELL Claire 1905–58   American

fashion designer

Mass-produced sports-style clothing (1929–58).

Throughout her career, Claire McCardell produced exciting new designs within the constraints of mass production – a sphere in which America excelled. McCardell emerged on the American fashion scene during the late 1920s, a period when designers and manufacturers alike largely conformed to the stylistic dictates of the influential Paris couture houses. The department stores were the major American outlets of high fashion, and they promoted their allegiance to the capital of fashion by buying in some Parisian models and copying others. Some stores even went to the extent of sewing forged French couture house labels into their American garments. The one exception to this was the huge and distinguished department store, Lord and Taylor, which promoted American designers from 1932 and was instrumental in bringing McCardell's progressive clothing to the attention of American women.

McCardell studied for two years at Hood College in Frederick, USA, before transferring in 1927 to Parsons School of Design in New York and then on to their Paris branch. Here, she was taught the design tradition of French couture, which she instinctively felt was too constrained and expensive, although she greatly admired the work of VIONNET. She moved back to New York in the late 1920s and briefly worked as a sketcher for a dress shop. In 1929 she joined the clothing manufacturer Robert Turk and in 1931 moved, with him, to another firm, Townley Frocks. Turk died soon after and McCardell took over his job as chief designer. One of her most popular designs, introduced in 1938, became known as the "monastic dress", and was widely copied. She also became known for her full, peasant-style dirndl skirts, which were introduced following a trip to Austria. McCardell briefly left Townley in 1939, but returned two years later to design for the company under her own name.

McCardell reached her peak during the years of the Second World War. American suppliers, cut off from Paris following the German occupation, were forced to rely upon their native design talent. McCardell's work blossomed at this time, in spite of the constraints on fabric and man-hours in the making of clothing, which were imposed to preserve resources and redirect labour to wartime production. She created unstructured casual, but elegant, sports-style clothing for active wartime women, which have influenced designers of sportswear ever since.

Her garments were made from utilitarian fabrics – cotton, denim, mattress ticking, gingham, jersey and seersucker. Her mass-produced styles were designed primarily to be functional and multi-purpose. Indeed, they could be seen as the fore-runners of the mix 'n' match styles of the 1960s. In 1941 McCardell's separates were featured in *Vogue*. Six interchangeable pieces – three blouses, trousers and two skirts – cost $100. The understated garments that she designed to be worn with flat heels were the antithesis of the high-heeled, padded-shouldered and shaped garments generally associated with this period. McCardell did not embellish her womenswear with decorative detailing; instead she economically made a feature of their construction. She emphasized the brass hooks and eyes which appeared on many of her garments, including swimwear, rather than concealing them in the traditional manner. Another of her trademarks was her use

M

Claire McCardell, grey jersey halter-neck swimming costume, 1945.

of rows of double seams, which had originally been used only as reinforcement for durable work clothes. These added strength to her wartime designs and were featured in contrasting, coloured thread. She also made much use of metal rivets and shoestring ties (also known as bias cords), which she used to provide adjustable waists in her garments and for the ties of her popular halterneck designs. Her shirt-waist, wrap-around and bare-backed summer dresses produced during this period have all become classics.

In 1944 McCardell persuaded the shoe manu-facturer Capezio to make sturdier-soled ballet pumps for outdoor wear. These were the only form of footwear which were not rationed and immediately sold well, continuing to be worn throughout the 1950s. McCardell covered them with fabrics that matched her clothing. She also exerted a tremendous influence upon the design of swimwear, during a period when glamorous boned and shaped costumes were the prevailing fashion. McCardell's bathing suits followed the natural lines of the body and were made in soft black, beige or grey cotton and wool jersey. The fashionable swimwear of the late 1980s and 1990 bears a striking resemblance to McCardell's designs of almost half a century earlier.

In the post-war years McCardell continued to produce relaxed and stylish sports clothing, having established America's lead in this area. In the late 1940s she added evening sheath dresses to her repertoire. These were clearly based upon FORTUNY's Delphos dress, but instead of using luxurious silks in rich colours she fashioned them in dark and neutral cotton jersey and designed broad cross-over straps which formed the bodice.

McCardell's only apparent failure was her in-troduction during the war of dancers' leotards, with legs, made in wool jersey. Although not popular at the time, this style of dressing has enjoyed a great vogue since the 1970s. McCardell's influential career was cut short by her early death in 1958.

Claire McCardell, denim dress, 1942.

M

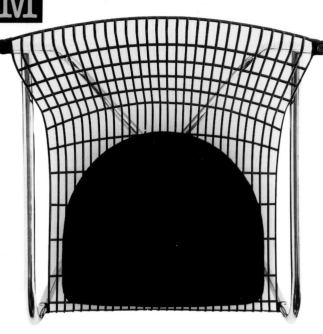

David Mellor, Abacus 700 outdoor seating system, designed for Abacus Municipal, 1973.

David Mellor.

sonal hi-fi sets that both European and Japanese companies began producing in the 1980s. For Memphis concentrated on making objects that were highly decorated and frequently eccentric in their form. Memphis was anti-rational. A number of its decorative ideas, however, were taken from cheap, mass-produced wares produced in the 1950s in the USA for working-class consumers. It was kitsch made respectable by being shown in an intellectual salon.

Memphis was playing an old-fashioned "arts and crafts" game, but doing so under a veneer of sophistication. For if there was a manifesto to the work, it was the claim that Memphis was interested in the debate about how people took pleasure in what they do, what they make, and what they choose to have around them. Certainly the brightly coloured rugs of Nathalie du PASQUIER, the eccentric, playful ceramics of Matteo THUN and the transparent bag radios of Daniel WEIL (all of them associates of Memphis) looked as if they were fun to make as well as to have and argue about. Moreover, most Memphis ware was handbuilt. It was an Italian version of the British pre-First World War OMEGA workshops.

was followed in 1965 by another commission from the Ministry of Public Buildings and Works, this time for use in Government institutions – a stainless-steel service which Mellor called Thrift. After years of concentrating on stainless steel, in 1988 Mellor designed Savoy, a range of silver-plate cutlery with nylon handles that is based on a traditional Georgian design.

Mellor set up his first factory to produce cutlery in 1974. In 1988 he moved production to a purpose built factory in Derbyshire.

Mellor's cutlery is included in collections at the Victoria & Albert Museum, London, and the Museum of Modern Art, New York.

MEMPHIS founded 1981   Italian

design studio

Radical anti-rational design.

Memphis, founded by Ettore SOTTSASS and others in Milan, grew out of STUDIO ALCHYMIA, another Italian design studio which, similarly, was a loose association of like-minded designers rather than a commercial company. Memphis did, however, have support from the lighting company Artemide, and during its lifetime (1981–5) it generated glassware, ceramics, furniture and lighting. Among the designers associated with Sottsass were Andrea Branzi, Michele de Lucchi and George SOWDEN.

Branzi said that Memphis demonstrated that the avant-garde in design could work with mainstream design and that mainstream manufacturers were influenced by Memphis. To an extent this claim is justified by the brightly-coloured, 1950s-styled radios and per-

Memphis, Oberoi armchair by George Sowden with printed cotton fabric by Nathalie du Pasquier, 1981.

MENDINI Alessandro b.1931   Italian

polemicist, editor, designer

One of Italy's leading design theoreticians.

Mendini was co-founder of STUDIO ALCHYMIA (with Alessandro and Adriana Guerriero) in 1976. Before that he was editor of *Casabella* (1970–6), and in 1976 he took over from Gio PONTI as the editor of the highly influential magazine *Domus*.

One of the "movements" he generated in the 1970s was "Banal Design", which was centred around a rediscovery of decoration, especially the mass-produced decoration used by industry in textiles, plastic laminates and wallpapers – complex, brightly coloured, often garishly abstract and, hitherto, despised by progressive designers.

Mendini's Banal Design thesis stated that design was all about *surface*. This seems obvious until one is reminded that for several decades those designers who thought of themselves as part of the Modern Movement had long been used to thinking that design was about getting the structure right. If the structure was right, then the general appearance would be right as well.

Mass-produced decorative design has tended to borrow from any source or culture which manufacturers have thought would make money. Mendini, in his own "banal" designs, played an ironic game with this notion of borrowing. He produced a number of designs which were garishly decorated and had titles such as Proust's New Armchair (1978). He also created, with colleagues from Studio Alchymia, room sets on the same theme of Banal Design.

Another of Mendini's interests has been the alteration of existing objects. Thus a carpet-cleaner, a coffee-making machine, a shoe, for example, would have a number of brightly coloured plastic circles or arrows added to it to emphasize its profile or draw attention to its volume.

MEYER Hannes 1889–1954   Swiss

architect

Bauhaus head of architecture, then director.

The Swiss architect Hannes Meyer achieved notoriety as the controversial professor of architecture at the BAUHAUS school in Germany, and then its director. He was a Marxist and a believer in the idea that it was the architect's responsibility to improve society by designing buildings that improved the lives of ordinary people. As a young man he travelled to Britain to study the English garden city and co-operative movements.

In 1926 Meyer teamed up with a fellow ABC Group member, the architect Hans Wittwer, to design an entry for the League of Nations Building competition. The proposal was for a cluster of irregularly shaped elements. Meyer was determined that the building design should put function before aesthetics, and proudly stated, "Our building symbolizes nothing." He considered a traditional-style building to

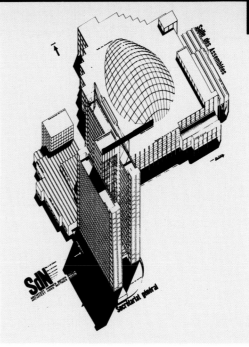

Hannes Meyer with Hans Wittwer, design for the League of Nations Building, 1926.

be inappropriate to the work of the League of Nations, and suggested that the requirements should include "hygienic workrooms" and "open glazed rooms for public negotiation of honest men".

In 1927 Meyer was invited by Walter GROPIUS to become head of architecture at the Bauhaus. Meyer and his architecture department – which he pointedly renamed the "building department" – helped Gropius with his experimental housing project at Torten in Dessau (1926–8). The ideas of building using concrete slab walls and mass-produced components were tried and tested here. Some of the flat-roofed, cubic houses took just three days to construct.

In 1928 Gropius resigned as Bauhaus director, and in a controversial move handed over his job to Meyer, who had been a lecturer for just one year. Meyer's promotion resulted in the resignations of László MOHOLY-NAGY, Marcel BREUER and Herbert BAYER.

Meyer was highly critical of the work at the Bauhaus. Under his guidance the Bauhaus steered a course away from producing finely crafted one-off items towards producing designs for mass production, using inexpensive materials.

The school thrived under his directorship – its income doubled, and the numbers of students rose from 160 to 197 – however, Meyer's strong political views gave fuel to right-wing and anti-Communist opponents wanting to close it. Eventually, in 1930, pressure against Meyer was so great that he was forced to resign. He formed a collective with Communist students, who also left the Bauhaus, and worked in the Soviet Union for six years before returning to Switzerland.

MIES VAN DER ROHE

Mies van der Rohe, interior
of Lake Shore Drive
apartment, Chicago,
1950–1.

Ludwig Mies van der Rohe.

MIES VAN DER ROHE Ludwig 1886–1969 German

`architect`

**One of the most important architects of the
20th century, an "idealist" and a "minimalist".**

Born in Aachen in Germany, Mies had no formal
architectural training; he absorbed his meticulous
sense of craftsmanship from his father, who was a
master mason. His draughtsmanship came from a
period he spent with a local builder as a stucco
designer. But in 1905 he went to Berlin and worked
for a minor architect, and was apprenticed to a
furniture designer, Bruno Paul, before joining Peter
BEHRENS in 1908. Unlike his important contemporaries
WRIGHT and LE CORBUSIER, Mies was not schooled in the
arts and crafts tradition, and in working for Behrens,
who was producing a corporate style for AEG, he
would be influenced by the prototype industrial
designer of the 20th century.

   Both men were influenced by the great 19th-
century Prussian architect Karl Friedrich Schinkel,
who made use of industrial techniques as well as
building in the traditional monumental style. After
leaving Behrens in 1911, Mies visited the Netherlands, where he came into contact with the other
important early influence – the work in brick, and the
thinking of Hendrick Berlage, which stemmed from
19th-century "moralistic" theory about honesty in
the expression of materials and revealed structure.

   Mies' career was interrupted by the First
World War. In 1919 he started to direct the architectural section of the Novembergruppe, a group
named after the month of the republican revolution
and dedicated to the revitalization of the arts in
Germany, through which he was influenced by the

expressionistic ideas about glass of Bruno Taut.

   Mies' glass skyscraper projects of 1919 and
1921 sought to produce dramatic effects through its
reflective quality. The glass tower has been a re-
curring theme in 20th century architecture, but
shortly afterwards, in 1922, Mies produced a building
project in the first edition of the magazine *G* which
was more functional, consisting of concrete "trays"
cantilevered from a central structure with ribbon
glazing, similar to Wright's 1904 Larkin building.

   There are very few completed works of
the late 1920s. He designed a monument to Karl
Liebknecht and Rosa Luxemburg and two houses:
The Wolf House (1928) and the Lange House (1926).
All these works are of brick, and show a variety of
influences, from the Berlage brick tradition and
Schinkelesque solidity and attention to detail to the
De Stijl arrangement of the masses. But by this time
he had fully assimilated the International Modern
style, as can be seen in his apartments designed for
the Wiessenhofsiedlung in Stuttgart (1927).

   The period reached a climax with a master-
work which brought together the different strands
in his work: the German State Pavilion at the
Barcelona exhibition of 1929. Although a temporary
structure, it has been one of the most influential
buildings in history. A horizontal slab is supported on
a grid of + shaped columns, and the space is arranged by non-structural vertical slabs. This building also displayed his famous Barcelona chair, one of
the classics of 20th-century design which Mies produced at this time.

   In 1930 Mies succeeded Hannes MEYER as the
head of the BAUHAUS, but he was forced to close it in
1933 and left for America in 1937.

M

Mies van der Rohe,
Commonwealth Promenade
Apartments, Lake Shore
Drive, Chicago, 1950–1.

Mies' first American work, The Campus and building at Illinois Institute of Technology (IIT), on which he began work in 1939, show the formal problems that were to characterize his later American phase: the relationship of the industrial, geometrically conceived metal structure to built form. Already before going to America he had, in the Reichsbank scheme (1933), been moving away from the De Stijl-influenced asymmetry back towards a more classical symmetry and formalism. He was also struggling with the relation of the column to the wall. In the Reichsbank it is placed behind the wall which becomes a skin, but in his first project at IIT the columns and frame are incorporated as part of the wall, beginning that refinement of structure, infill and fenestration which culminated in the Miesian curtain wall.

Idealization going hand in hand with use of industrial forms can be seen in the Farnsworth House (1946–50), a development of the two horizontal planes of the German Pavilion, but this time supported around the perimeter by exposed girders. Because of Mies' formalism and idealism he repeated basic building types over and over, and this idea reached its conclusion in the monumental treatment of Crown Hall, IIT (1952–6).

Another form which was duplicated in this way was the curtain wall over the steel-framed block. This reached its greatest refinement in the classic Seagram Building (1958).

Mies said "less is more", but he can be criticized for what he left out of architecture. His buildings have an undoubted beauty, which arises from his commitment to a narrow range of formal "universal" problems.

Mies van der Rohe, the
Seagram Building, New
York, 1958.

M

MINAGAWA Makiko (date of birth unknown)   Japanese

textile designer

Woven textiles drawing on Japan's rural craft tradition and sophisticated manufacturing base.

Makiko Minagawa has been the leading researcher and designer of woven textiles at the Issey MIYAKE Studio since 1971. Like many Japanese designers of her generation, her designs are firmly rooted in Japanese cultural traditions.

Minagawa's palette is predominantly neutral, but her feeling for surface qualities and texture is acute, being one of the first textile designers to stress the importance of tactile design for fashion fabrics. She has used the most up-to-date synthetic textile technology to recapture the slightly uneven texture of hand-woven materials.

MISSONI founded 1953   Italian

knitwear designers and manufacturers

Experimentation with new yarns and textures; co-ordinated knitted clothing.

During their 37 years of collaboration the Missonis have played a leading role in Italian knitwear design. The rich combinations of pattern, brilliant colour and texture that distinguish their work exemplify the qualities that have made Italy the international centre for beautiful, well-designed knitted clothing for the top end of the market.

Ottavio ("Tai") Missoni was born in Ragusa, Yugoslavia in 1921. A successful athlete before and after the Second World War (he was the Italian 400-metre champion in 1939 and a finalist in the 1948 Olympics), he began his career as a manufacturer of knitted tracksuits. In 1953 he married Rosita Jelmini (b. 1931), and together they established a small workshop and factory for the production of knitted ready-to-wear garments at Gallarate outside Milan.

Despite the scale of their fashion empire today (including men's and women's clothing, fragrances, bed-linen and home furnishings) the Missonis are keen to stress their involvement with the manufacturing process. They describe themselves as a family of artisans (their daughter and two sons have become closely involved with the business since the 1980s) rather than fashion designers. They see the research and development of new fabrics and their experimentation with production techniques as the most important aspects

of their work. Since 1953 they have concentrated their creative talent on refining and developing machine-knitting techniques, evolving a number of new yarns, stitches and patterns such as their patchwork knitwear (1961) or their technical masterpiece, the flame stitch (1962). During the 1970s they reached the high point of their popularity, introducing transparent fishnet, striped net, chenille, the zigzag stitch and tartan and herringbone patterns.

After an early association with Emanuelle Khanh and Biki of Milan in the mid-1950s, the Missonis launched their own label in the late 1960s. In 1969 Diana Vreeland, then editor of *Vogue*, introduced them to the United States, where the classic look of their multicoloured knitted separates soon achieved cult status. In the early 1970s they developed the marketing concept of co-ordinated clothing (or mix-'n'-match) which suited their knitwear beautifully and resulted in their becoming the leading fashion force in Italy. It was their decision in 1979 to start showing in Milan that established the city as the Italian capital of fashion design.

MIYAKE Issey b.1935   Japanese

fashion designer

Dramatic but also wearable and enduring designs in natural and synthetic fibres.

Miyake graduated in graphic design at Tokyo's Tama University in 1964. He then moved to Paris to study fashion, as a domestic industry did not then exist. He trained with Laroche and GIVENCHY in Paris and with Geoffrey BEENE in New York. On his return to Tokyo in 1970 he founded the Miyake Design Studio and one year later he established Issey Miyake International Inc. In 1971 he presented his first fashion collection in New York, and in 1973 in Paris, where he has continued to hold biannual fashion shows. Miyake was the first clothing designer working in the West truly to exploit his Eastern heritage.

Early in his career Miyake shunned the fleeting styles of high fashion and sought to create more enduring designs. He chose *sashiko*, a light quilted cotton worn by Japanese peasants, as an alternative to the ubiquitous denim, and looked to the timelessness of the kimono and Japanese smock for much of his inspiration. Many of his garments are made from natural fibres – from linens, silks, cotton, leather, furs, bamboo and *aburi-gami* (an oil-soaked handmade

Issey Miyake, sculptural outfit, spring/summer 1989.

M

Issey Miyake, womenswear,
autumn/winter 1987–8.

paper). These are woven in traditional Japanese ikat designs and printed with wood-blocks. In striking contrast, he also works with shiny silicone in primary colours which he forms into moulded bustiers, and polyester jersey coated with polyurethane, which he has made into dramatic, inflatable trousers (1985). Inner comfort is central to, and unites, his work.

He has not confined his talents to the fashion world, but has also designed jackets with detachable, zipped sleeves for Sony's 50,000-strong Japanese workforce. Miyake's is the largest fashion empire in Japan.

MOGGRIDGE founded 1969   International
product design consultancy

Compass computer; Archimedes computer; Dancall cordless telephone.

Moggridge Associates was founded by Bill Moggridge, a British industrial designer (b.1943). One of the first products Moggridge designed was a fan heater for Hoover in 1972. Until the mid-1970s the company specialized in industrial design, designing telephones and business machines for such clients as ITT.

In 1978, a separate model-making division, which eventually became known as IDM, was set up by Dick Grant, who is now managing director. IDM is used both by external clients and as a facility for in-house design projects. It has long been involved in architectural model-making, as well as more recently meeting the demands for models for use in TV commercials, films and videos.

Moggridge himself moved to California in 1979 to set up ID Two, now in San Francisco. The purpose of the move was to provide a design service to the computer companies in Silicon Valley. One of the first products it worked on was the Compass computer for Grid Systems. It became a classic piece of industrial

Moggridge, Dancall 5000
cordless telephone, 1986.

design, winning an Excellence Award from the Industrial Designers' Society of America.

While ID Two developed its client list in the US, Moggridge Associates, under the leadership of industrial designers John Stoddard and Hedda Beese, continued to work nationally and internationally, in association with its US arm, for some projects such as the design of in-car radios for Ford. Moggridge Associates' successes include the Archimedes computer for Acorn, designed by John Stoddard, which won the British Microcomputer of the Year award in 1987, and the Dancall cordless telephone, again designed by Stoddard.

Stoddard is now managing director of Moggridge Associates, London, while Hedda Beese has since 1987 been managing director of Design Drei in Hanover. Beese is well known for designing the highly successful BP Solar Lantern, a light source for use particularly in remote locations. The lantern has won awards in Germany and the USA.

MOHOLY-NAGY László 1895–1946   Hungarian
graphic designer and photographer

Experiments with light; teacher at the Bauhaus in Germany and founder of the New Bauhaus school in Chicago.

Born in southern Hungary, László Moholy-Nagy studied law at the University of Budapest. He then decided to work full-time as an artist and in 1920 moved to the avant-garde centre of Berlin. By 1922 he had begun to pursue his interest in transparent materials and the visual qualities of light, which led to numerous experiments, including his famous piece of kinetic design/sculpture the "light modulator".

In 1923 Walter GROPIUS asked him to join the faculty of the BAUHAUS in Weimar, where he was put in charge of the metal workshop and given joint responsibility for the preliminary course (with Josef Albers). Moholy-Nagy and Gropius worked closely together, and co-edited 14 of the Bauhaus books. Moholy-Nagy designed the books, as well as other Bauhaus material, and it was in this capacity that he developed his skills as a graphic designer. His light experiments had also by this time drawn him into photography and film. When the Bauhaus moved to Dessau in 1925, Moholy-Nagy went with it and continued to teach there until 1928. At this point he presented the foundation course in book form, pub-

Moggridge, Nile Light, 1986.

M

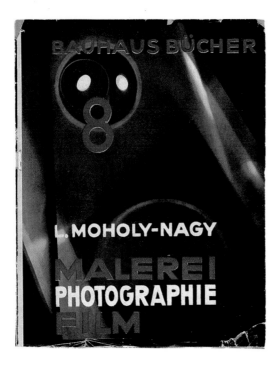

László Moholy-Nagy, cover design for the Bauhaus book *Painting, Photography, Film*, 1925.

lished as *Von Material zu Architektur* in German (Munich, 1929) and in English as *The New Vision* (New York, 1932).

On leaving the Bauhaus, Moholy-Nagy opened an office in Berlin designing sets for opera and theatre, as well as graphics, photography and film (assisted by fellow-Hungarian György KEPES); then in 1934 moved on to work in Amsterdam, and later London.

In 1937 he was invited by the Association of Arts and Industries in America to organize a new design school in Chicago. There he created "The New Bauhaus; American School of Design", based on the Bauhaus educational model. It closed after a year due to loss of finance but reappeared as an independent school and in 1944 became the Institute of Design, which Moholy-Nagy directed until his death in 1946. His book *Vision in Motion* (which concentrated on the work of the Institute) appeared posthumously in 1947.

MOLINO Carlo 1905–73   Italian

architect and furniture designer

Idiosyncratic furniture and the Ippica, Turin.

Molino was devoted to motor-racing, skiing and aeronautics and was for a time a stunt flyer. The forms of racing cars and aircraft were strongly reflected in his building and furniture designs. He was also very open in his interest in erotica, and his designs for women's clothing border on the lascivious, while much of his

furniture has an organic style that is overtly sexual.

He patented a number of engineering designs. His patents for universal joints show his rooted interest in aircraft engineering. His architectural masterpiece was the Ippica in Turin, a riding school and club built in 1937. Unfortunately the Turin authorities, who owned the land, demolished the building in 1960. What remains of this idiosyncratic designer are furniture items, drawings and photographs.

MONTANA Claude b.1949   French

fashion designer

Leather garments; ready-to-wear.

Montana's fashion career came about almost by accident – he came to London in the early 1970s "to escape studying", with no idea of what he wanted to do and without a work permit. He raised money by selling his handmade, rhinestone-studded, papier mâché jewellery, and through chance acquaintance his work came to be featured in *Vogue*. His success was such that he was able to remain a further year in London, and on his return to Paris he became a freelance designer for the leather company MacDouglas, whose owner's wife wanted the company to produce more extravagant designs. From this beginning, Montana became highly influential in the sphere of ready-to-wear fashions both in France and abroad, designing for the Italian labels Complice and Cadette and the Spanish knitwear manufacturers Ferrer y Sentis.

In particular, Montana is noted for his work using leather, employing skill and daring in its cut, texture and colouring. His clothes use strong colours, particularly black, red and grey, and are often masculine in inspiration – with large silhouettes, big-shouldered, reminiscent often of uniforms. Perhaps his greatest talent lies in his ability to transform masculine lines into a powerfully feminine look.

Claude Montana, shoulder-padded coats and leather trousers, autumn/winter 1986–7.

MORISON Stanley 1889–1967   British

typographic designer and print historian

Design of Times New Roman typeface.

Acknowledged as one of the leading typographic designers of this century, Stanley Morison was drawn to the subject through his own passionate interest. His early experience involved working for a succession of publishers and printing houses, including Francis

Jasper Morrison, Wingnut chair, hardboard, 1985.

Meynell's Pelican Press, and the Cloister Press. In 1922, with Oliver Simon, he launched the scholarly typographic journal *The Fleuron* (1922–30), and began his career as a freelance consultant. He was very soon appointed typographical adviser to the Monotype Corporation, and over the next 10 years became one of England's greatest type impresarios.

Morison joined Monotype at a crucial point of technological change – when the hand-setting of type was being replaced by hot-metal type-casting machines (notably Monotype's). In his advisory role, Morison was able to bring about the revival of the best classical faces, notably Garamond (1922) and Bembo (1929), and, in his search for new types, was also responsible for introducing Eric GILL, the sculptor and engraver, to Monotype. He commissioned the designs for Gill Sans (1928) and Perpetua (1929) by Eric Gill, as well as commissioning the typeface Albertus, designed by Berthold Wolpe (1938), and others. In the late 1920s (and at the height of his power) Morison became typographic consultant to *The Times*, an appointment which eventually led to the redesign of the entire newspaper and, furthermore, to Morison's own design for its typeface, Times New Roman (1932), perhaps the world's most widely used roman typeface.

Morison was also highly influential in his role as typographical adviser to the Cambridge University Press, from 1925 to 1944. His extensive writing on the history of typography, printing and other related subjects, amounted to more than 170 publications, the best known including *First Principles of Typography* (London, 1936, Cambridge, 1950) and his contributions to *The Fleuron*.

MORRISON Jasper b.1959   British

furniture designer

Furniture for European companies.

Morrison, who studied design at Kingston Polytechnic and the Royal College of Art, London, has become Britain's most influential young furniture designer, with a rapidly growing reputation in Europe. He owes a debt to the vocabulary of modernism and its materials – bent tubular steel, plywood and aluminium.

A recent design (1989) is a plywood chair, designed for a project in Berlin and to be produced by Vitra. This simple, light chair is inventive in that the cross-brace beneath the seat is concave, the surface of the seat is a thin sheet of ply which "gives" when it is

sat upon and takes the form provided by the cross-brace. The back of the chair is given life and interest by the shallow S-curve of the leg/back supports and a concave back rest. The West German company FSB has commissioned a range of door handles from Morrison, and his European reputation is being built through commissions and exhibitions carried out for Documenta in Kassel (1987), Berlin (1989) and at the Milan Furniture Fair (1989).

Disavowing the artiness of post-modern design, Morrison insists that there can be no design without production.

MOSCHINO Franco b.1954   Italian

fashion designer

Daring and provocative fashion.

Born in Milan, Moschino studied at the Accademia delle Belle Arti. His first jobs were varied: he worked in publicity, the theatre and as a computer programmer. In 1970 he started to draw for magazines, illustrate fashion collections and design publicity campaigns for fashion houses, most notably for VERSACE, with whom he worked for two years. During this period he also began to design clothing for other companies, including Cadette and Matti. The first Moschino line was shown in 1983 and immediately provoked great interest and generated much controversy.

From the outset Moschino has mocked Milan's tradition of luxurious evening wear and fine tailoring and satirized "good taste" in clothing. He does, however, admire the eccentric and outrageous aspect of London fashion and has culled several British fashion graduates to join his small team. He proclaims that fashion is a drug, behind which many people hide –

Moschino, teddy bear hat, autumn/winter 1988–9.

M

that it is for stupid people – and he seeks to subvert the fashion game with wit, satire and a celebration of bad taste. Even his most extreme designs, such as the skirt covered with dolls and the evening dress made entirely from brassières sell well.

Thierry Mugler, futurist quilted womenswear, autumn/winter 1984–5.

MUGLER Thierry b.1946   French

fashion designer

Modernistic and futuristic clothing.

While in his teens Mugler became interested in fashion, designing and making his own clothes. When he joined the ballet company L'Opéra de Rhin as a dancer he complained that no one wore colour, and he gave up ballet for a career in design, launching what became his personal campaign against sartorial drabness. From window-dressing in Paris, he moved to London for two years in 1968. He served brief apprenticeships, but felt constrained and preferred to work alone. In 1971 he presented his first collection in Paris under the name Café de Paris, and by 1973 was designing under his own name. Five years later he was firmly established, particularly in the ready-to-wear market, having gained a reputation for forward-looking design.

Mugler eschews references to the past and looks firmly and uncompromisingly to the future for design inspiration, saying that among past designers he has respect only for GRÈS. However, as well as his aggressive Space Age designs, Mugler also updates and exaggerates images of 1940s and 1950s glamour. His collections can range from avant-garde coats – such as that in his 1982 collection composed of large blocks of colour – to vampish suits and evening wear which pay satirical homage to glamorous femininity.

Jean Muir.

MUIR Jean b.1933   British

fashion designer

Tailored and fluid matt jersey womenswear.

Jean Muir gained her early experience in the fashion trade working in the London store Liberty from 1950 to 1956 and then at Jaeger from 1956 to 1961, when she started to produce her own fashion range. Her designs were marketed under the Jane and Jane label, which became part of the Susan Small organization and was later taken over by Courtaulds. In 1966 she opened her own house.

Muir is greatly respected for her classical, understated, elegant and comfortable womenswear. She has never been influenced by passing trends or novelty and has retained a puritanical approach to her work. Her timeless collections do not rely upon the constant change inherent to fashion, but rather develop and evolve. Muir has never attempted to reshape the body: instead, her clothes enhance its natural proportions. Her signature is her use of matt jersey, which she meticulously tailors, rather than drapes. She also makes much use of soft wools, crêpe and suedes.

Muir regards her trade as a craft, rather than an art, and frequently extols the virtues of solid technical training. She is one of Britain's most distinguished fashion designers.

MÜLLER-BROCKMANN Josef b.1914   Swiss

graphic and exhibition designer

Spokesman of the Swiss design movement; posters, corporate graphics and exhibition design.

Josef Müller-Brockmann was one of the leading exponents of the Swiss design movement throughout the three decades during which it was at its greatest strength. A keen advocate of the Grid as an ordering system and, more broadly, a mental attitude, he preached the logic of a systematic approach to design. The work of Müller-Brockmann represents Swiss graphics at its best.

Having studied and trained in Zurich, he established his studio there in 1936, producing a broad range of graphic design, as well as exhibition and stage design. In the late 1950s he produced his highly acclaimed series of posters for the Zurich Tonhalle concerts, using colour and strict geometric forms to express symbolically the dynamic forces and emotion inherent in the music. As the series developed into the 1960s, musical rhythms, structures and tone were depicted in pure typography. His road safety and anti-noise posters from the 1950s, employing photographic imagery, were equally famous: the first using a contrast in scale to create an illusion of perspective, and both examples of his use of the angle as a dynamic compositional force. He continued as one of the leading practitioners of Swiss graphics throughout the 1960s and 1970s, known for such high-profile endeavours as his role

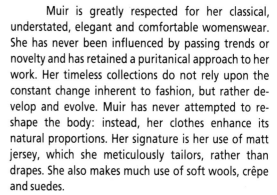

Jean Muir, fluid jersey dress, spring/summer 1986.

Josef Müller-Brockmann, road safety poster *(Protect the Child),* 1955.

of design consultant to IBM Europe (from 1966), working with Paul RAND, and the corporate identity of the SBB/Swiss Federal Railways (late 1970s).

Müller-Brockmann also made a substantial contribution in the way of design publications. In 1958 he was co-founder (and, until 1965, co-editor) of the progressive international periodical *Neue Grafik* (New Graphic Design). He is the author of a number of highly respected design books, including *The Graphic Artist and his Design Problems* (1961), *A History of Visual Communication* (1971) and *A History of the Poster* (with his wife Shizuko Müller-Yoshikawa, 1971).

MURRAY Keith 1892–1981   New Zealand-British

architect and ceramic, glass and silver designer

Leading industrial designer of 1930s Britain; simple but bold functionalist wares.

Keith Day Pearce Murray was born in Auckland, but moved to Britain with his parents in 1906-7. He served in the Air Force during 1915–18, then attended the Architectural Association school in London. Unable to

find architectural work upon completion of his course, he turned his abiding interest in old glass into a career. Impressed by Scandinavian, Viennese and Czechoslovakian glass, he duly determined to bring new life to the modern English glass industry, updating and streamlining it, bringing back plainer surfaces and subtle, shallow cutting.

For a short time he was employed by James Powell & Sons' Whitefriars glassworks, but it was not until he signed a three-month-per-year contract in 1932 with Stevens & Williams of Brierley Hill, Stourbridge, studying production methods and working as a designer for Hubert S. Williams-Thomas, that he was able to make his ideas a reality. The glassware which was soon in production was extensively publicized and proved a great success.

Besides plain, undecorated tableware, Murray designed somewhat more ambitious vessels, such as a clear-glass decanter (1933), its flared body highlighted with black-enamelled bands and its stopper of black glass, and a jaunty purple-tinted toilet set (about 1935), the stoppers and knobs of its assorted flared bottles, cylindrical jars and curved boxes in the form of tall glass fingers. He designed some rather traditional pieces as well, including a 1937 loving cup commemorating the coronation of George VI.

While continuing to design glass for Stevens & Williams, Murray struck a similar design agreement in 1933 with Josiah Wedgwood & Sons of Etruria, which produced his handsome lathe-turned (and occasionally hand-thrown) vases, mugs, bowls, whole coffee-sets, and so on, of earthenware and basalt, covered in what became his characteristic Moonstone (a creamy matt white), Matt Green and Matt Straw glazes, developed in 1933–5 by Wedgwood chemists. The pieces were bold, simple and sometimes quite architectonic. From 1934 Murray also designed some objects in metal for English silversmiths Mappin & Webb, including a graceful covered cup in silver and ivory and a *moderne* electroplate cocktail shaker.

Without doubt, the diversity, innovation and unrelenting modernism of his oeuvre made Murray one of the leading British designers of his time. Despite the accolades heaped upon his applied arts, however, Murray opened an architectural practice with C.S. White in 1936, their first commission being the new Wedgwood factory in Barlaston (1938–40). After the war he produced some ceramic designs for Wedgwood, but soon after returned full-time to architecture, in the practice of Murray, Ward and Partners.

Keith Murray, matt-glazed earthenware vase for Wedgwood, *c.*1935.

NEURATH Otto and Marie Austrian and German

graphic designers and design researchers

Created and developed the Isotype visual information system.

In the years following the First World War, Austria struggled with inflation, food shortages, housing and health problems. Otto Neurath (1882–1945), a social scientist in modern terms, became the Director of the Gesellschafts- und Wirtschaftsmuseum (Social and Economic Museum), Vienna, in 1925. It was there, in the pervading climate of social reform, that he created Isotype, a graphic system for presenting statistical information, using pictorial symbols. ("Isotype" stands for International System of Typographic Picture Education.) Within the museum he established the Isotype team, which included Marie Reidemeister (1898–1986). With the intention of educating the general public in social issues, the team produced Isotype charts on problems such as health and housing, for both publication and display in the museum. Marie took on a central role in the team as the "transformer", responsible for translating the collected statistical data into visual terms.

World events caused the team to move to the Netherlands in 1934, then to England in 1940. Otto and Marie married in 1941, and in 1942 they started the Isotype Institute, which Marie continued to direct on Otto's death in 1945. She extended the application to new areas – such as educational books for the young – until the Institute's closure in 1972.

Isotype and its design achievements hold important lessons for today's designers. For example, the concept of the "transformer" continues to be studied by designers dealing with today's complex information systems. And the Neuraths must be seen as pioneers of the concept of learning through pictures.

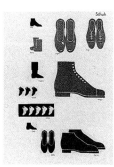 

Otto Neurath, sheets from the Symbol Dictionary of the Isotype Movement,

NIZZOLI Marcello 1887–1969 Italian

architect and industrial designer

Typewriters for Olivetti.

Between the two World Wars there was a passion for angular design and angular graphics among the avant-garde which found few followers among the wider public. But after the Second World War an organic design style dominated, just as an organic aesthetic dominated in fine art – most exceptionally in the sculptures of Henry Moore, but also generally in Italy with sculptor-designers such as Anton Fruhauf (son of Marino Marini), Mario Pinton and the sculptors Gio and Arnaldo Pomodoro. Marcello Nizzoli was a master of organic modelling, and his preferences for rounded, shell-shaped forms won him acclaim with the public for whom he designed as well as from fellow designers. So, just as American designers Charles and Ray EAMES were the doyens of organic furniture, Nizzoli's success rests in his having adopted the aesthetic in the more demanding area of product design.

Nizzoli's first public appearance was in 1914 when he showed two paintings in the *Nuove Tendenze* exhibition. He studied painting and architecture at the School of Fine Arts, Parma. He began his design career in 1918 in Milan, where he established his own studio and worked for the next 20 years in exhibition, fabric and graphic design. His influence in these fields in Italy was seminal and he was responsible for the design of early post-war Milan Triennales.

In 1938 Nizzoli began working for OLIVETTI, initially as a graphic designer in the advertising department. An important influence on Nizzoli's work at this time was the Rationalist designer Eduardo Persico, who was also the editor of the magazine *Casa bella*.

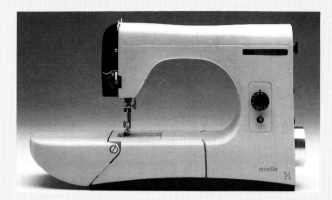

Marcello Nizzoli, Lexicon 80 typewriter for Olivetti, 1948.

Marcello Nizzoli, Mirella sewing machine designed for Necchi, c.1956.

Rationalist thinking was also a driving force behind the development of the Olivetti company. The factory and community buildings at Ivrea were designed by Rationalist architects.

Adriano Olivetti, son of the company's founder, adapted his father's principle that the typewriters they manufactured should be serious and elegant into a general strategy for design which applied to every aspect of the company's work and production. But rationalism, as an architectural style of geometric angularity, was rejected implicitly and automatically by Nizzoli for Olivetti's own products. Nizzoli retained the Rationalists' preference for cleanliness in design, but dropped the harshness.

Nizzoli's first product design for Olivetti was an adding machine, in collaboration with engineers Natale Capellaro and Giuseppe Beccio, but it was his typewriter designs that attracted public and professional attention: the Lexicon typewriter (1948), the Suma adding machine (1949) and the Lettera 22 typewriter (1950) are important examples. He also executed other, freelance commissions, including sewing machines for Mirella and Necchi, a kitchen mixer for Necchi and lighters for Ronson. In 1963 he designed a combine harvester for Laverda.

Nizzoli maintained a substantial second career in architecture: his architectural work included two shops for the Parker Pen company (1934) and housing for Olivetti workers (1953–6), and a church – the Church of Canton Vesco (1959). He was responsible for the design of the headquarters of Olivetti, Palazzo Olivetti, in Milan (1954–5).

Nizzoli styled for elegance, comfort and modernity. His sculptural forms, which combine elements of the old Futurist styling-for-speed influences, were both comforting and flattering. But as various critics have pointed out, his concern was with the precision of mouldings as well – he paid as much attention to the cut marks as to the graphics. Again context is important: the standards for plastic mould-injected and extrusion work in Italy has been high, and much higher than was demanded in a comparable period in, for example, Britain.

A description of Nizzoli's design for the Mirella sewing machine (*Design Since 1945*, Philadelphia Museum of Art, 1984) states: "Sleek, elegant, stylish, the Mirella revolutionized the domestic sewing machine in Italy and enhanced the self image of the housewife, suggesting as it did creativity and individuality in home sewing." The Mirella represented a high point in Nizzoli's personal style in which the form he gave to an object, albeit dependent upon function, materials and methods of production, might still allow what he referred to as the "freedom of fantasy".

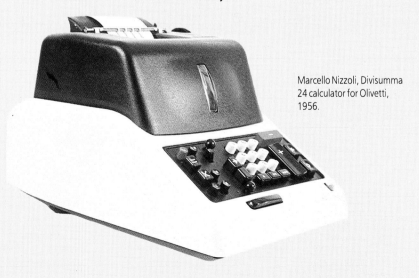

Marcello Nizzoli, Divisumma 24 calculator for Olivetti, 1956.

N

NICHOLS Maria Longworth 1849–1932 · American

ceramics painter and potter

Influential art potter; founder of Rookwood Pottery, Cincinnati, Ohio.

Though many know the name of the pottery she founded in Cincinnati, Ohio, in 1880 better than her own, Maria Longworth Nichols (later Storer) and her Rookwood Pottery deserve equal notice, the one for her enterprise, largesse and talents, the other for its outstanding art-pottery output, lasting until 1941. The extensive Rookwood output was renowned for its high-quality craftsmanship, its striking and often unusual, even unique, glazes, its masterful painting and its vast repertory of images, especially its blossoms and landscapes.

Maria married Col. George Ward Nichols in 1868, started painting on china around 1873 and then making as well as decorating pottery in 1879. The next year, she set up her own pottery in a disused schoolhouse on her father's extensive property, naming it Rookwood after her family's estate. Nichols also started up a school to train nascent decorators; the Rookwood employees were initially women decorators, with one man doing the throwing and firing. In 1883, when William Watts Taylor was hired as manager, the enterprise began to take shape and thrive.

Nichols herself was deeply influenced by Japanese ceramics design and imitated many of the Oriental masters' subjects. Talented employees such as Laura A. Fry, Clara Newton, Matthew A. Daly, Kitaro Shirayamadani, Artus Van Briggle and Albert R. Valentien were instrumental to Rookwood's success, for their painting skills and/or technical advances. Fry, for instance, developed a technique whereby coloured slips were sprayed onto still-wet clay with a mister, producing a ground which was easier to paint on.

Col. Nichols died in 1885, his widow married the lawyer Bellamy Storer the next year, and increasingly Maria Storer spent more time with her new husband and family and less at Rookwood. But her connection with the firm was never totally severed, even though Taylor had been made company president, a position he held from 1890 to 1913 (Mrs Storer transferred Rookwood's ownership to him as well): she proceeded with various experiments at the pottery, such as developing new glazes.

Maria Longworth Nichols' Rookwood Pottery, earthenware vase decorated by H. E. Wilcox, 1900.

NIZZOLI Marcello 1887–1969 see page 172

NOYES Eliot 1910–77 · American

industrial designer and architect

Design consultant to IBM and other major corporations; Model A Electric typewriter.

Eliot Noyes was one of the first designers to work as a consultant to large corporations, advising on everything from products to the company logo.

Noyes studied architecture at Harvard where, through meeting Marcel BREUER and Walter GROPIUS, he became exposed to European design developments, particularly the BAUHAUS. In 1940 he became the director of the new department of industrial design at the Museum of Modern Art, New York, where he organized an exhibition called "Organic Design in Home Furnishings", which stimulated the production of new designs in furniture, lighting and fabric.

In 1945 Noyes joined the consultancy run by Norman BEL GEDDES. Here he first came into contact with IBM, for whom he designed the Model A Electric typewriter. It went into production in 1947, and in the same year he set up his own consultancy. In 1956 he embarked upon a massive corporate identity programme for IBM which extended to new buildings, a new logo (by Paul RAND) and new products which Noyes himself designed, including the Executive and Selectric typewriters (1959 and 1961), the Golfball 72 typewriter (1961) and the 1440 Data Processing System.

After successfully revolutionizing IBM, Noyes was retained as a consultant design director by other major corporations, including Mobil Oil, Westinghouse and Pan American World Airways. His design for the Mobil Filling Station in 1964 was adopted by Mobil as a model for its filling stations throughout the world.

Eliot Noyes, Selectric typewriter, designed for IBM in 1961.

NURMESNIEMI Antti b.1927 · Finnish

industrial designer

Finel coffee-pot; design for Helsinki Metro.

Nurmesniemi studied interior design at the Institute of Industrial Arts in Helsinki, graduating in 1950. He has designed interiors for a wide range of buildings, and furniture for Artek, Lifjaama and Merivaara. He is an early example of the wide ranging industrial designer – his Finel coffee-pot of 1958 has become ubiquitous in Finland; his glassware, wallpaper and textiles are successful; and he has also done transport design for the Helsinki Metro.

Antti Nurmesniemi, lacquered wood chairs, 1986.

OGLE DESIGN founded 1954 British

Leyland truck design; Leyland London bus.

Ogle Associates was founded by designer David Ogle. It was initially a multi disciplinary practice, designing everything from products to packaging, but went on to specialize in transportation and product design.

After the death in a car accident of David Ogle in 1962, Czechoslovakian-born designer Tom Karen took over as managing director. Under his leadership the consultancy continued working for clients such as Bush (the TR130 Radio became a best-seller). They also built up new clients among whom were Philips, Raleigh, Reliant and Electrolux.

Ogle's first project for Reliant was the design of the Scimitar coupé, which went into production in 1965. Ogle also worked on the Scimitar GTE, the first sporting estate car, which was launched in 1968.

In the 1970s, Ogle began working on the design of dummies for vehicle crash-testing and rescue training. The consultancy has become well-known for its ergonomics (human factors) department, set up in 1983 and operating as a distinct consultancy service. In addition, the successful application of ergonomics into its many engineering and design projects has characterized much of Ogle's work. The consultancy has won several Design Council awards for products including the Britax car seat for disabled children, a knitting machine for Camber and the Leyland Roadtrain truck cab.

Ogle has been retained as a consultant to Leyland for many years, and in 1984 the consultancy embarked upon a major design and human factors project for Leyland on the new generation of London buses. The Leyland T45, launched in 1980, broke with traditional cab designs and was deliberately rounded to make it more appealing than its more aggressive rivals. It was voted European Truck of the Year.

While better known for its transport projects, Ogle has also designed a wide variety of products, including children's toys.

OLDFIELD Bruce b.1950 British

Luxurious couture evening wear.

The rags-to-riches story of Bruce Oldfield has been well documented: brought up in a children's home, he is now one of London's leading fashion designers.

Oldfield's fashion education was gained from Ravensbourne and St Martin's art colleges. He left in 1973 to start freelance work in London and held his first show in 1975. Until the early 1980s Oldfield's business went through a period of growth and retrenchment. Between 1982 and 1984 he concentrated on custom-made clothes, and it is for these that he has received international acclaim.

Bold and glamorous wide shoulders are a feature of his designs, along with a vivid use of colour, intricate pleating, the use of superb silks, organza and jersey and the simple sensuousness of the shapes. It is perhaps in his ability to flatter the female figure that the key to his success is to be found.

In 1984 Oldfield opened a shop in London's Beauchamp Place which offers off-the-peg garments as well as a made-to-measure service. Since the late 1980s Oldfield has arranged a number of licensing agreements to promote his business further and to help finance his shows. Companies for which he has designed under licence include the American Simplicity Style pattern range, Charnos hosiery, Murray Allan and Hilditch & Key.

Bruce Oldfield, evening dress for Diana, Princess of Wales.

O

OLIVETTI founded 1908   Italian

Mass-production of first Italian typewriter and first electronic typewriter.

The firm of Olivetti has produced a distinguished collection of well-designed goods since its foundation in 1908, having hired every well-known Italian designer during its history. Returning from a trip to America, Camillo Olivetti (1868–1943), the Italian engineer, designed and mass-produced the first Italian typewriter. From the outset Olivetti was convinced of the need for attractive as well as functional equipment.

Adriano Olivetti (1901–60) succeeded his father as president of the company in 1938. He too had an engineering background, and was convinced that design should play an important role for the company. He first galvanized Olivetti's advertising with the introduction of Modern Movement graphics, using BAUHAUS-trained Alexander Schawinsky to redesign the publicity material. In order to revolutionize the look of Olivetti's products, Adriano employed the Italian designer Marcello NIZZOLI (1887–1969) as a consultant. His much-imitated Lettera 22 portable typewriter of 1950 was highly sculptural and elegant. In 1958 Ettore SOTTSASS was hired as the consultant for the new electronics department.

Following Adriano's death the firm went into decline, to be revitalized in 1978 by a new chairman, Carlo De Benedetti (b. 1934), with a forward-looking programme in the electronic field, manufacturing the first electronic typewriter. Olivetti still pursues a programme of innovative styling, using only consultant designers, and enjoys a large share of the electronic typewriter and computer market.

Olivetti, two views of the ET Personal 55 typewriter.

Olivetti, Miram 100 multi-frequency analog telephone, designed by George Sowden and Simon Morgan.

OMEGA WORKSHOPS founded 1913   British

Influential work drawing together the fine and applied arts.

The Omega Workshops were founded by the eminent art critic and British champion of the Post-Impressionist movement, Roger Fry. Modelled on the Wiener Werkstätte and the playful experimentation of Paul POIRET's Studio Martine, Fry sought to end the binding historicism that plagued the British decorative arts. By commissioning impoverished contemporary artists to transfer the direct line and vivid palette of Post-Impressionism to the minor arts, Fry aimed to create a lucrative, new decorative idiom.

The studios at Fitzroy Square soon attracted many of the leading artists of the time including Paul Nash, Wyndham Lewis, David Bomberg, Nina Hamnett and the graphic designer Edward McKnight KAUFFER, though the disorganization of the workshops and Fry's unfortunate policy of non-attribution soon drove them away. Omega was the Bloomsbury set at play. It had neither the social enquiry, nor the attention to skill, nor the rigorous studio practice of William Morris or his successors. Despite his charm, Fry had difficulty in finding buyers. Fry's hit-or-miss approach led, naturally, to variable results: Omega furniture was accused of being rickety, and some of the painted pottery amateurish. Some of the more successful pieces were Fry's own work, such as his pottery which achieved success through its simplicity, and his Cubist textile design Amenophis.

Two other artists who thrived at the Omega and created some of the better carpets, textile designs and screens were Duncan Grant and Vanessa Bell. However, in 1916 they moved to a farmhouse, near Firle in Sussex, leaving Omega to limp towards closure in 1920. Through their painting and experiments at Charleston, which they gradually transformed into a total decorative environment, Bell and Grant did develop their own eclectic, decorative idiom, which found its public expression in a series of textile prints they created for Allan Walton in the 1930s (including Grant's famous design Daphne and Apollo), and Vanessa's book covers for the Hogarth Press.

Opinion remains strongly divided over the achievement of Fry, Grant and Bell and is all the more forcefully expressed because of the enduring influence of their rough painterly patterns on British textile designers.

OPSVIK Peter b.1939   Norwegian

Balans variable seat.

Opsvik graduated in design in 1964. He worked as an industrial designer for the Tandberg Radio company (1965–70), and has been a freelance designer since 1972. Perhaps his most famous design is the Balans variable seat (1980).

Peter Opsvik, Balans variable seat, 1980.

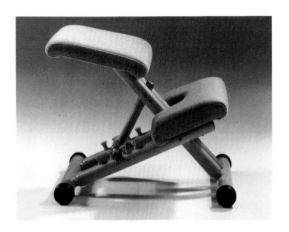

OTTO Frei b.1925   German

architect and engineer

Innovative lightweight structures, notably the roofs of the Munich Olympic complex (1972).

Otto is a highly original pioneer in the field of lightweight construction who has been responsible for a revolution in the technical possibilities of architecture. Coming from a family of sculptors, he showed an early interest in construction. He joined the German air force in 1943, and it was as a POW in charge of building and repair crews that he became concerned with "minimal construction".

He completed his architectural training at the Technische Universität, Berlin (1948–52), and spent a year in the United States, where work on suspended roofs was to influence his doctoral thesis.

Otto's ideas developed in the direction of prestressed tensile structures, and in 1954 he became involved with the Stromeyer Company of tentmakers. Otto's first fabric membrane structures appeared at the Federal Garden Exhibition at Kassel in 1955; this was followed by a large number of projects, including designs for retractable roofs for swimming pools and open-air events.

Otto turned from tents to network structures, which resemble tents in that a flexible membrane is stabilized by tensile forces and the compression forces are concentrated in masts. This technique resulted in the German pavilion, Montreal Exhibition (1967), and the dramatic parabolic roofs of the Munich Olympic complex (1972).

In 1957 Otto founded the Development Centre for Lightweight Construction in Berlin: in 1964 this was incorporated into Stuttgart University's Department of Engineering, where Otto was an honorary professor.

OXENAAR Robert b.1929   Dutch

graphic designer

Design of Dutch banknotes and stamps; Head of the Art and Design branch of the Dutch postal services (PTT).

Robert Oxenaar has been a crucial figure in the developing strength of the Dutch graphic design community, as well as having revolutionized the design of government publicity material and documents such as the girocheque, passports, stamps and, most notably, banknotes.

He began creating designs for Dutch banknotes in 1965 and since then they have been praised as the most modern and inventive in the world. They contain moments of startling beauty, as in the 50-guilder note, glowing yellow with sunflowers, and bear progressive social devices (raised marks to allow the visually handicapped to identify note values were used here for the first time). Lastly, and most famously, they sport intricate anti-counterfeit devices, elaborately displayed in the 250-guilder note where Oxenaar has incorporated rabbits, birds, and other oddities as watermarks and registration devices, thereby humanizing the most impersonal of government papers.

In 1976 he became Head of the Art and Design branch of the Dutch postal services (known as the PTT), operating as general "aesthetic" adviser responsible for the use of art in PTT buildings. This meant commissioning works of art for both inside and outside the buildings, as well as furniture sign systems and publicity material. In this surprisingly broad capacity, Oxenaar was instrumental in launching a new generation of Dutch designers in the 1970s (including such notables as Gert DUMBAR), and he continued to provide opportunities and encouragement to young artists, designers and studios throughout the 1980s.

PALEY Albert b.1944   American

Decorative but functional metalwork combining old and new methods.

Paley trained as a blacksmith and has become one of the world's leading designers and makers of architectural metalwork. His output includes furniture, gates, railings and staircases. He works with architects and space planners and is the head of craftsmen whom he employs at his workshops in Rochester, New York.

His work is decorative but sculptural in its scale; it owes much both to art nouveau forms and to the simpler harmony of curves found in Romanesque architecture. All his work functions very well – gates open properly and latches work. Paley puts function first: "What gets made has to work as it is supposed to do." He uses traditional blacksmithing techniques and modern hydraulic presses. Apart from the undoubted aesthetic and utilitarian successes of his work, Paley has managed to synthesize what many craft-based designers have failed to do – the practice of handwork and heavy industrial manufacture.

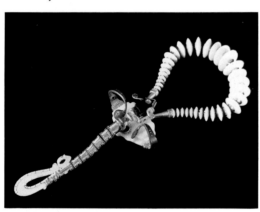

Albert Paley, fabricated silver and gold pendant with silver, gold and pearls, 1972–3.

PANTON Verner b.1926   Danish

furniture, textile and lighting designer

Chair designs, Pop furniture.

Verner Panton is best known for his brightly coloured, Pop furniture of the 1960s. He initially trained as an architect at the Royal Danish Academy of Fine Arts in Copenhagen before working with Arne JACOBSEN, from 1950–2. Panton then established his own practice in 1955, creating the Cardboard House in 1957 and the Plastic House in 1960. It was also in 1960 that he developed the world's first one-piece, cantilevered, plastic chair created from a single glass-fibre shell, well ahead of the Americans and Italians, who were experimenting in a similar field. The sculptural chair reflects the Scandinavian regard for soft, organic forms and technical excellence. In 1965 Panton designed the S-Chair, again a one-piece construction but this time in plywood. Panton also designed textiles for Mira X, lighting for Louis P. Poulsen, the Copenhagen – based firm, and the exhibition "Visiona 2" for Bayer.

However, he is best known for his chair designs and more recently he has experimented with postmodern forms. At the Scandinavian Furniture Fair of 1982 he showed a beech plywood, one-piece chair cut with a jig-saw to create a cloud shape which was then painted salmon pink. Panton now lives in Switzerland where he continues to experiment with chair and lighting design.

PAPANEK Victor b.1925   Austrian-American

product designer, writer

Design for the Real World (book).

Victor Papanek was born in Vienna and lived briefly in the UK during the Second World War before emigrating to the United States, where he became a naturalized citizen in 1946. His education was varied and extensive. He took a diploma in industrial design and architecture in 1948 and went on to study under Frank Lloyd WRIGHT.

Papanek also travelled extensively, living with and learning from indigenous cultures. His critical reappraisal of design in the United States earned him popularity with the ecology movement of the late 1970s. His book *Design for the Real World* was published in 1969 and appeared in 20 foreign editions. It was written out of his personal belief that the real needs of people were not being met by designers in the United States, where the prevailing ideologies of design were "planned obsolescence" and "conspicuous consumption", both of which amounted to wasting resources. He has explored the themes of the true purposes and consequences of design in further books, although *Design for the Real World* remains the best-known.

Papanek, who for many years has been professor of design at the University of Kansas, has said that design has a "social and moral" purpose, which means that it must meet the needs of the sub groups in society and the developing countries while at the same time using resources wisely. While better known for his writing and teaching than for the products he has designed, Papanek has nevertheless been able to put his principles into practice with great success. In 1981 he designed the Batta-Koya low-cost tape cassette for the governments of Tanzania and Nigeria; this is designed to be manufactured locally and used as a "talking teacher" to give information on health.

He has also designed a solar-powered refrigerator for Tanzania, a wheelchair for Sweden and an alcohol-powered cross-country vehicle for Brazil. More recently, he has been involved in developing biological packaging for a Japanese client, in which a growing plant forms a completely biodegradable packaging around a product.

PASQUIER Nathalie du b.1957   French

textile designer and painter

Textiles for Memphis Studio.

Nathalie du Pasquier is a self-taught artist who lives and works in Milan. She is currently working as a painter, but in 1981 began a series of brilliantly coloured rugs for the MEMPHIS Studio. She subsequently produced furnishing and clothing textiles, including designs for shows in collaboration with George SOWDEN.

As with many Memphis associates, her ideas for decoration are drawn from many sources, but her work was much less dependent than was that of her male colleagues upon the abstract designs gleaned from American laminates of the 1950s (designs which themselves were drawn from the paintings of Jackson Pollock and his followers). Third-world textiles, seen on travels in India and Africa, inspired her loosely geometric designs. However in 1989 she began to concentrate more upon her career as a painter, and her work has expanded to include figuration.

PATOU Jean 1880–1936   French

fashion designer

Garçonne Look and Cubist-inspired clothes.

Patou entered the fashion trade in 1907, working for an uncle who was a furrier. Between 1910 and 1912 he opened several dressmaking establishments but did not sell under his own name until 1919. Largely overshadowed by the publicity generated by CHANEL, the talent of Patou has often been overlooked – although he was equally responsible for creating the Garçonne Look in 1925.

One of Patou's most famous customers was the French tennis champion Suzanne Lenglen, whom he dressed both on and off court. This lean and active young woman epitomized the 1920s "new woman". She created a furore in 1921 when she wore Patou's knee-length pleated skirt, which revealed much of her legs when she ran. The headband she wore while playing tennis was widely copied by women throughout the 1920s for day and evening wear.

Patou was early in recognizing the kudos associated with a top designer's name and was possibly the first to use monogrammed garments in 1922. He was also famous for incorporating the style of contemporary painting to embellish his fashions. His jumpers and bathing costumes, emblazoned with bright Cubist images, have been much copied to the present day.

Patou was both creator and destroyer of the Garçonne Look. In 1929 he unexpectedly lengthened his dresses, returned the waist to its natural position and emphasized the bust, paving the way for the more fluid fashions of the 1930s.

The house of Patou has remained open under the direction of various top designers including Marc Bohan, Karl LAGERFELD and Christian LACROIX.

Jean Patou, tennis outfit as worn by French player Suzanne Lenglen, 1920s.

PEI Ieoh Ming b.1917   Chinese-American

architect

Dallas City Hall; John Hancock Tower (USA); Bank of China (Hong Kong); Louvre Pyramid.

At the age of 18, Ieoh Ming Pei left his home in China for the United States, where he studied at the University of Philadelphia. He became a naturalized American in 1954.

Pei frequently works on a large scale and in the late 1980s received acclaim for two very different buildings – the towering Bank of China in Hong Kong and the delicate, glass Pyramid in the courtyard of the Louvre in Paris.

One of Pei's first major projects was the Dallas City Hall, Texas (1966–78). Resembling a stretched, upturned pyramid which has been wedged into the ground, the structure was built in concrete with bands of dark glass windows. The building bears a passing

I. M. Pei, glass Pyramid, The Louvre, Paris, 1988.

resemblance to LE CORBUSIER's Chandigarh Court of Justice, India (1956), and its overall effect is heavy and the steep incline rather threatening.

In a different, and altogether more elegant, style is the John Hancock Tower, Boston, Massachusetts (1973–7), designed with Henry Cobb. The 60 floors of offices, on a rhomboid plan, are encased in a slender, shimmering, smooth mirror-glazed sleeve. The two short sides are given added interest with triangular incisions which run the entire height.

Pei returned to a more lumpen style in two large projects which followed the Hancock Tower. The first was the National Gallery of Art East Building in Washington, DC (1978). This long, low, smooth-faced slab has a wide, deep-set entrance resting under a long concrete lintel.

One year later came the John F. Kennedy Library, Boston, Massachusetts, a large squat, window-less drum shouldering a tall triangular block from which protrudes a steel-framed smoked-glass tower.

Pei has proved that his work is most successful when completed in glass – a fact demonstrated with the towering Bank of China in Hong Kong (1984–8). Starting with a classical-style base complete with columns and constructed, according to the bank's wishes, in granite, it climbs up through a series of fractured, triangular kinks and folds, looking like a dented space frame. The glass exterior is broken into triangular elements by exposed metal trusses.

Pei's greatest triumph is his Pyramid in the Cour Napoléon, the Louvre, Paris (1989). The simple and delicate metal-framed glass structure, along with the two scaled-down pyramid skylights which flank it, was commissioned as part of President Mitterrand's Grands Travaux – a series of bold new buildings constructed to celebrate the French Bicentenary of 1989.

The Pyramid has been criticized for standing in complete contrast to its surroundings, but because of its lightness and transparency it avoids competing with the gallery building. The Pyramid is, as it suggests, the tip of an iceberg, for below is a vast subterranean hall through which visitors pass from the Metro and an underground avenue of shops to the Louvre or Tuileries Gardens.

PENTAGRAM founded 1972 British

international design partnership

Architectural and interior design, product design, graphics.

The partnership of Fletcher Forbes Gill (Alan Fletcher, Colin Forbes and Bob Gill) was one of London's leading graphic design groups of the early 1960s – influenced by the New York scene, and expert in the art of the visual pun. With the departure of illustrator Bob Gill and the arrival of architect Theo Crosby, Crosby Fletcher Forbes emerged, with a slightly more serious tone. Success continued and in 1972, with the added talents of Mervyn Kurlansky and Kenneth GRANGE, the group transformed into Pentagram, a large inter-disciplinary design partnership devoted to offering clients "a comprehensive and integrated design service covering everything from architecture and environ-mental design to products, packaging and graphics". It was one of the first generation "mega-groups" in Britain, starting out with five partners (hence the name) and approximately 25 staff. Today it is a success-ful empire of 14 partners, split between offices in London, New York and San Francisco.

Their projects include such design classics as the 1960s bus advertisement for Pirelli slippers; John McConnell's house style and image for the fashion store Biba; corporate identity programmes for Lucas Industries and British Petroleum (BP); Alan Fletcher's fluorescent-coloured typographic calendar for Olivetti; Kenneth Grange's design for the Intercity 125 train (in service in Britain since 1976); and John

ff

faber and faber

Pentagram, logo for Faber and Faber publishing company, designed by John McConnell, 1981.

Pentagram, London bus ad. for Pirelli slippers, designed by Fletcher Forbes Gill, c.1963.

McConnell's logo and graphics for the British publishing company Faber and Faber – one of the design delights of the 1980s.

PERRET Auguste 1874–1954   French

Rue Franklin flats; Notre-Dame du Raincy.

Auguste Perret led the way for many other architects to follow in his pioneering use of reinforced concrete, one of the key materials used in modern building.

While he was influenced by the French classical tradition of urban design, characterized by framed and panelled façades, Perret became fascinated by the possibilities of building in a new way. In the place of traditional wood and stone construction he experimented with reinforced concrete.

Concrete reinforced with steel mesh and rods had been developed by François Coignet in the 1850s. Initially it was used for the construction of industrial buildings, but Perret was among the first to experiment with its use in multi-storey buildings such as his six-floor block of flats at 25 rue Franklin (1903-4), where the concrete frame was faced with decorative ceramic tiles. Perret's technical skills in handling this new material were passed on to LE CORBUSIER when he worked in Perret's Paris office from 1908 to 1909.

Perret used the concrete again at the Théâtre des Champs Elysées (1911-4) which was based on a design by Henri VAN DE VELDE. Once again the framework was covered, this time in marble.

Perret's most important building was the war memorial church, Notre-Dame du Raincy (1922–33), north-east of Paris. Here he took the radical step of leaving the concrete in its natural exposed state. The building was designed in a simplified Gothic style, with large tracery windows and slender tapering ribbed columns supporting the plain tunnel-vaulted ceiling. Minimal use of ornamentation and the delicate concrete construction gave a light and elegant look.

PERRIAND Charlotte b.1903   French

Collaborated with Le Corbusier.

Charlotte Perriand's work with the architect LE CORBUSIER was an equal partnership which had started after he had seen her work as a student of interior design in 1927. Their collaboration lasted until 1937. All the famous furniture attributed to Le Corbusier for these years was the result of a joint design process.

The temporary tyranny of aesthetic fashion is well revealed by her in an interview she gave to Charlotte Ellis (*Architectural Review*, November 1984) in which she explained her radicalism during the years of modernism: "Naturally, I made myself a necklace of ball-bearings, a cocktail bar in sheet aluminium with chairs of chrome tube, an extendable table with a rubber top – everything except that produced by the furniture trade. I was not interested in timber. . . I promoted metal. . . its potential for perfect triangulated jointing, the escape it offered from complicated joinery and fussiness. . . I contrasted it with timber, which perishes, expands, contracts, dries out."

But later she became less dogmatic. "I learnt there are no unusable materials. . . I saw shepherds make small seats from odd bits of wood, anything that came to hand. I asked myself, what's wrong with that? It is appropiate to their environment, the ecology. . . and it meets their needs. The value was obvious."

PESCE Gaetano b.1939   Italian

Pratt chairs; polemical architecture often based on the human body.

Pesce, who studied at the University of Venice, is a Northern Italian "artist-architect" who builds only a little but proposes a great deal. His biographer, France Vanlaethem, says that Pesce's "art architecture" is the product of the three pillars of 20th-century avantgardism – abstractionism, Expressionism and Surrealism. However, in essence, all Pesce's work begins and ends with the body, sometimes quite literally. The erotic and the visceral underline Pesce's aesthetic.

In his project for a Church of Isolation (1974–7), in New York, it was planned that the congregation would enter through the eyes and nose of the human figure. In a proposal for redeveloping Les Halles in Paris the scheme was for a vast rambling set of apartment blocks full of references to the images that make up 20th-century culture. It is an exciting but baffling proposal of organized decay.

One of Pesce's realized projects is for an apartment in Paris. The main double-storey-high room is divided across one-third of its area by a dramatic balcony/sleeping area from which one looks into the

Gaetano Pesce, cast-metal and steel rod chair for the Vitra Collection, 1987.

P

Gaetano Pesce, Feltri quilted armchairs, 1988.

Michael Peters.

space of the main room. Populated with Pesce's organic furniture and decorated with angular, edgy objects and detailing, the riotous assembly is kept in order by the classical geometry of the building itself. It is like looking into a jumbled-up jigsaw box.

PETERS Michael b.1941 — British

graphic designer

Packaging design.

The 1980s in Britain were characterized by an alleged economic revival, a new-found passion among Britons for business, for adventurous capitalism and design. Design was marketed by a new generation of design entrepreneurs, of whom Michael Peters is one example, as a key ingredient to business success.

Peters, like other design entrepreneurs in Britain, such as Rodney Fitch and Wally Olins, is famous for making design a business in its own right. In achieving this, and in Peters' and Fitch's case, getting their design companies floated on the Stock Market and taken seriously in the financial press, they achieved for design in Europe what Raymond LOEWY had achieved in the USA in the period 1930 to 1970. This achievement rests less on the quality of individual design projects, although some are very good, but more in raising the overall status of the designer: industry and business now comes to design groups such as that run by Michael Peters for advice, for improvements to their overall corporate image, for ideas on more effective planning of their design-to-production process and, of course, for individual projects in packaging.

Some claim that the approach to packaging design to emerge from Michael Peters' studio in the 1980s put vigour into a moribund design discipline and helped British retailing companies to revitalize their sales. The irony is that design groups such as Peters' found themselves designing products for foreign manufacturers while devising labels for British shops or identity logos for ailing nationalized industries such as British Rail Freight. Peters himself points with pride to packaging work done for Winsor and Newton Inks, Elsenham Jams and Penhaligon's perfumery. His product design section also designed a casing for a new British radio, although all the components came from the East.

Peters projects himself, his company and design in general as a force for good, citing his own environmental concerns, his participation in a retraining and design for manufacturing scheme to assist the unemployed, and the establishment of a foundation to support the applied arts. However, in 1990 Michael Peters Associates went into liquidation.

Michael Peters, Penhaligon's toiletries.

PIETILÄ Reima b.1923 — Finnish

architect

Expressionist, "mythological" architecture.

Pietilä graduated from the Institute of Technology in Helsinki. He worked in the master planning department of Helsinki (1953–4) and in private practice. In 1957 he started his own practice and since 1960 has been in joint partnership with his wife Raili (b.1926) who also graduated from the Helsinki institute.

Their first project was the Kaleva Church, Tampere, Finland (1966), which is built up from a series of concave concrete profiles, almost like inside-out columns, and owes something to Alvar AALTO. In their next work, the Dipoli Student and Cultural Centre at Helsinki University of Technology (1964–6), the Pietiläs evolved a more overtly organic and Expressionist language. The building echoes the natural shapes of its surroundings both in the sculptural forms of the elevations and in the freely conceived plan. It owes much to the expressionism of Scharoun and Taut and marks Pietilä's development outside the more functionalist tradition of Finnish design.

They next designed the Suvikumpto Housing area in Tapiola Garden City, Finland (1967–72), but then had no major commissions until they won the competition for various cultural buildings for Harventa

New Town, Tampere, Finland. The main library (1983–6) shows a fresh concern for various natural and archaeological metaphors and illusions. Their international reputation was sealed by the Sief Palace area buildings in Kuwait (1978–82), exemplifying Pietilä's principle of "cultural regionalism" – the building becoming part of its surroundings.

Pietilä has received numerous awards and distinctions and held a number of fellowships and academic positions. In Finland his recognition has led to the commission for the official residence of the state president. Its abstract concrete construction creates a mythology of the natural forces at work in the Finnish landscape – glaciation and the subsequent land upheaval. Construction began in 1990.

PINTORI Giovanni b.1912   Italian
graphic and exhibition designer

Long-term association with Olivetti and head of its publicity department in Milan in the 1950s and 60s.

Giovanni Pintori started designing for OLIVETTI in 1936 and became Head of Publicity in 1950. In this role, throughout the 1950s, he was responsible for the distinctive Olivetti graphic style – a style heavily influenced by developments in contemporary art, and which changed according to the latest art innovations.

Pintori created posters and all manner of print material, advertising campaigns and exhibitions for Olivetti. His most famous image is probably the highly unusual design of the word "Olivetti", with all of the letters superimposed and decreasing in size; the letters gradually pile up within each other, starting with a huge "O" and ending with a tiny "i". It is a design of great flair and confidence, for the word "Olivetti" is actually quite difficult to read, but what it loses in legibility, it gains 10 times over in memorability.

Other examples of his work include a poster advertising the Elettrosumma 22 calculating machine, showing a mountain of coloured cubes that seem to be multiplying of their own accord, as well as the renowned poster of the mid-1950s depicting a heavy shower of coloured numerals against a black background, with the word "Olivetti" appearing in white within the shower. Both posters exemplify the striking visual language, comprising abstract shapes, numerals and letterforms, which Pintori devised from the functions of business machines.

Pintori remained at Olivetti until 1967. On departing, he continued to work as a freelance designer from his own studio in Milan.

POIRET Paul 1879–1944   see page 184

PONTI Giovanni "Gio" 1891–1979   Italian
architect and designer

Ceramics, furniture (particularly chairs), interior, lighting and metalwork designs.

Italy's premier 20th-century designer, Gio Ponti created furniture, metalwork and ceramics, among other objects, and was also an esteemed architect/teacher and prolific writer/editor – a true Renaissance man for modern times. He was born in Milan, where he studied architecture after service in the First World War. From 1923 through the 1930s, he worked for the long-established Società Ceramica Richard-Ginori in Doccia, which he virtually rescued from impending financial failure by means of his highly original and unusual designs – part Italian neo-classical, part Mannerist, part *moderne* (heavily influenced by the Wiener Werkstätte designers Josef HOFFMANN and Kolo Moser). Most of the goblets, bowls, plates and vases Richard-Ginori produced were traditionally shaped, for instance urns on plinths, but Ponti's bold and colourful painted motifs, from suggestive reclining female nudes to visionary architectural images, took them out of the category of ordinary porcelain and earthenware vessels and into a new aesthetic realm. In the mid-1920s Ponti also provided elegant silver and cutlery designs to the French silversmith Christofle (for whose president, Tony Bouilhet, he designed a house).

The late 1920s witnessed Ponti's initial ventures into both publishing and exhibition organizing. In 1928 he founded the monthly Italian journal *Domus*, devoted to art, architecture and design. Except for a six-month hiatus, he was editor of this influential publication until his death (he also directed *Stile* in the 1940s). In 1925 he headed the second Monza Biennale, the significant international fair devoted to modern design, and he was instrumental in moving the fair to Milan in 1933, whence it became the Milan Triennale. He was a professor of architecture at the Milan Politecnico from 1936 and an active, committed architect throughout much of his long working life (he helped found the Italian Movement for Rational Architecture

Gio Ponti, Pontina chair made by Zanotta.

P

in 1927). His best-known buildings are the International Modern-style Faculty of Mathematics at Rome University (1934), the two office towers of the Montecatini Company in Milan (1936 and 1951) and the elegant, 34-storey Pirelli Building, also in Milan (1955–8). The concrete core of the skyscraper was the work of Pier Luigi Nervi.

Ponti's chair designs are among his most famous creations, and although his 1950s pieces are most familiar, he was designing furniture as early as the 1920s. In fact, the 1937 Lotus armchair for Figli di Amadeo CASSINA (for whom he began designing in the 1930s), with its curving, sculptured form and spiky legs, foresaw some of his post-war designs, such as the slim, elegant, rush-seated chair classic La Superleggera of 1955 (made by Cassina from 1957), which was strongly indebted to traditional chair design, specifically the fisherman's chairs made in Chiavari, Italy. He also designed somewhat quirky and/or highly distinctive furniture in the 1940s and 1950s for Altamira (such as a spiky-legged desk in 1953), Arflex, Giordano Chiesa, the Nordiska Kompanient of Stockholm and Singer. The Domus side chair of 1950, like the Superleggera, showed neo classical roots, and the refined Chiavari chair of 1951 was successfully mass-produced. The Letizia chair was a surprisingly comfortable, leather-seated folding model with brass feet, and the 1953 Distex chair (for Cassina) was an angular yet plush armchair that bespoke "modern Italian design", even the coming Space Age.

Another Ponti creation was an eminently practical institutional design: the dashboard-like headboard that accompanies many hotel beds. But perhaps the most classic Ponti "furniture" designs were created for Ideal Standard in Italy in 1953: his porcelain bathroom fittings, first shown at the Milan Triennale in 1954, where they earned Ponti the gold medal.

After the Second World War, Ponti also designed other objects for both home and industry, among them the famous, indeed even iconic, La Pavoni chrome-plated espresso-coffee machine (1949), a fixture in so many 1950s European coffee houses; cutlery for the German firm Krupps of Essen (1951); ovoid lighting fixtures for Arredoluce (1957), enamels for Paolo di Poli, printed textiles, mosaics, even ships' interiors and stage sets for Milan's La Scala opera house. In 1957 he published a manifesto, *Amate l'Architettura*, one of nine books and over 300 articles written during an extraordinarily productive, far-ranging and influential career.

Gio Ponti, Pirelli Building, Milan, 1955–8.

POIRET Paul 1879–1944   French

fashion designer

Empire-line dresses, Oriental fashions and the hobble skirt; the first designer to launch his own perfume, the founder of an influential school of decorative art and a great influence on fashion illustration.

Poiret worked as an umbrella-maker's assistant, and then trained in fashion at the Paris houses of Doucet and Worth. He opened his own couture house in 1904 and greatly influenced the world of fashion for the next 10 years.

Poiret was a great self-publicist. He boasted that he had freed women from the constraints of body-shaping corsets, which had dominated fashion for the last 100 years. In fact, he continued to compress his customers' figures with new and softer, but lengthier, elasticated girdles which were needed to create the long, lean line that he favoured. Poiret designed high-waisted, narrow-skirted dresses which revived the Empire line of the early 19th century. His garments hung from the shoulders and were greatly influenced by classical Greek sculpture. This influence was most noticeable in his sheath dresses, which were made from one length of fabric and fell from the shoulder to the ankle in straight folds.

In 1909 Poiret created a vogue for Oriental-style fashions and it is for these that he is best known. Their emergence coincided with Diaghilev's first Ballets Russes performances in Paris, which also created a passion for Oriental fashions and interiors, and stunned Western audiences. The Ballets Russes introduced a riot of bold and rich jade greens, purples, crimsons, oranges, midnight blues and blacks into the

Paul Poiret, evening ensemble called Sorbet, 1912 (right).

Paul Poiret, Salome evening dress, illustrated by Simon A. Puget for the *Gazette du Bon Ton*, 1914 (centre right).

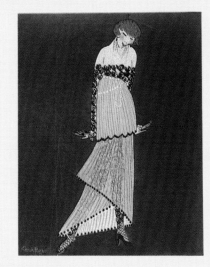

Paul Poiret, two pantaloon dresses illustrated by George Lepape for the album *Les Choses de Paul Poiret*, 1911.

world of fashion, replacing the popularity of pastels.

Poiret always claimed that he was the precursor of this trend. He revived Byzantine and Renaissance designs and dressed his daring customers in harem pantaloons and huge tasselled and jewelled belts, and wrapped their heads with plumed turbans. Many of his bold black-and-white, woodblock-printed textiles were designed by Raoul Dufy, later a leading Fauve painter. Poiret set him up in his own studio and commissioned many of his designs.

Poiret's lampshade tunics were introduced in 1912. These had wired hems, which were often covered with fur, and stood out from the hips in an independent, circular form. They were worn over lean, ankle-length dresses. His garments were sometimes split to the knee to reveal flat-heeled boots and brightly coloured stockings (traditionally these had been black).

In 1911 Poiret launched his own range of perfumes, toiletries and cosmetics, called Rosine after one of his daughters. He was the first *couturier* to diversify into this area.

In 1910 Poiret introduced the hobble skirt. This resulted in a great outcry from women who resented having their movement so restricted. Few women adopted it in its most extreme form, but instead wore long, narrow skirts with a more generous circumference.

Poiret sought to present his fashions in an exciting and new manner, and in doing so greatly influenced future fashion drawing. In 1908 he commissioned Paul Iribe, a leading decorative artist, to illustrate in ink an album of his fashions called *Les Robes de Paul Poiret*. Delighted with the result, in 1911 he commissioned Georges Lepape to illustrate his Oriental fashions, calling the album *Les Choses de Paul Poiret*.

In 1911 he founded a school of decorative arts called the Ecole Martine. Poiret disapproved of the rigid, artistic discipline imposed upon students which, he believed, drained them of their intuitive creativity. He wanted students with no preconceived artistic ideas, and thus scoured the working-class suburbs of Paris to find creative 12- year-olds who had no formal art training. Their spontaneous and charmingly naive images were then used as the basis of wallpaper designs, painted murals, carpets, rugs and embroideries, all of which they were taught to execute themselves. The Ecole Martine also sold furniture, designed by Pierre Fauconnet. The work produced at this school was exhibited in many of Paris's leading art galleries, was immensely profitable and greatly influenced much art deco design. The school was closed with the onset of the First World War.

Poiret continued to design women's clothing in the post-war years, but never again enjoyed his earlier successes; by the 1920s, his rich and exotic designs seemed anachronistic.

P

Ferdinand Porsche.

Production line of VW
Beetles.

PORSCHE Ferdinand (Ferry) b.1909 — German

`car designer`

Establishing Porsche as a leading name in sports cars and high-performance road vehicles.

It is unfair but convenient to single out just one of the Ferdinand Porsches; in fact there have been three men of that name in the Porsche family. The first, Professor Dr Ferdinand Porsche (1875-1951), was the brilliant and innovative engineer who worked for Austro-Daimler, Daimler-Benz and Steyr before founding his own Porsche automotive design company in 1931. His son Ferdinand (Ferry) Porsche (b.1909), who took over the running of Porsche after the Second World War, made the company name synonymous with high-performance road cars. And finally there is Ferry Porsche's son, another Ferdinand, nicknamed "Butzi". Butzi became the company's chief stylist and was responsible for the classic 911.

The collaboration of Dr Ferdinand and Ferry Porsche precipitated two landmarks in automotive history: the Auto-Union P-Wagen and the Volkswagen. The Auto-Union was a complete break from traditional racing-car design of the period, and was almost 30 years ahead of its time. But the arrival of the Volkswagen is of greater significance. It is claimed that Adolf Hitler created the design brief for the VW Beetle when, on the occasion of the Berlin Automobile Show in 1934, he called for "a car priced low enough to be bought by anyone with enough funds to purchase a motorcycle. Few parts to go wrong. Low repair costs... a *Volkswagen*".

Ferdinand "Butzi" Porsche set up his own

consultancy, Porsche Design, based in Zell am See, Austria, in 1972. The consultancy designs under its own label and works to commissions from Poltrona Frau (Italy), Artemide (Italy) and Inter Profil (West Germany), creating luxury crafted objects that combine technology and human skill for precise and sculptured results.

POWELL AND MOYA founded 1946 — British

`architectural practice`

Skylon for Festival of Britain.

Arnold Joseph Philip Powell (b. 1921) and John Hidalgo Moya (b. 1926) studied at the Architectural Association, London. Sir Frederick GIBBERD was principal, and on graduating in 1944 they worked as his assistants.

They founded their partnership in 1946 after winning a competition for the Pimlico housing scheme, London, for the redevelopment of 33 acres next to the Thames. In 1951 they designed the "Vertical Feature", or Skylon, for the Festival of Britain, an attempt to symbolize progress in post-war Britain.

The practice has been extremely successful as part of the post-war architectural establishment and has designed a wide range of buildings, often associated with public provision and the welfare state, such as schools and hospitals: Chichester Festival Theatre (1961); Mayfield School, Putney, London (1956); Princess Margaret Hospital, Swindon (1961–72).

The practice never developed in the direction of post-war brutalism but worked flexibly to provide distinct designs with more of the character of a modernist vernacular. They designed several buildings in Oxford and Cambridge in a modernist idiom: Cripps Building, St John's College, Cambridge (1967); Blue Boar Quad, Christ Church, Oxford (1968). In 1974 they received the RIBA Gold Medal.

PRICE Anthony b.1945 — British

`fashion designer`

Glamorous evening wear; designer for the Rolling Stones, and Bryan Ferry and Roxy Music.

Price studied fashion at the Royal College of Art, London, where he graduated in menswear. His first job was as a designer for Stirling Cooper, where he designed denim workwear, fashions for Miss Selfridge and the clothes for the Rolling Stones "Gimme Shelter"

Anthony Price.

P

Anthony Price, off-the-shoulder, short evening dress with fringe trim.

tour in 1967. He also worked part-time for the film, theatrical and television costumiers Bermans and Nathans, where he learned the techniques of theatrical dress construction, evident in many of his designs.

He subsequently designed the wardrobes, stage-sets and record covers for Bryan Ferry and Roxy Music, and was at the forefront of the 1970s glam-rock style. Price led the trend for heavily shoulder-padded, tapered men's suits and was the first to design the ubiquitous cap-sleeved T-shirt of the early 1970s. From 1974 he owned a King's Road boutique, which acted as a testing ground for his new ideas, and designed for the Plaza label.

Price has designed under his own name since 1979, and has continued to design for rock and media personalities. He has built a reputation for his sensual and luxurious evening wear, which often shows the influence of Hollywood glamour. Many of his garments are made with built-in corsets to achieve the structured and curvaceous shapes. Price places great emphasis on quality, and the technical cut of his garments is greatly admired.

PRICE Kenneth b.1935   American

potter

"Environmental" works in pottery.

Price studied at Chouinard Art Institute, the University of Southern California, and Otis Art Institute (all in Los Angeles), and New York State College of Ceramics, Alfred. Price has constructed a number of pottery "environmental" works. One of these, called *Happy's Curios: Town Unit 1*, was a "walkin work", a pottery store that was a celebration of decorated ceramic wares. In an interview with the writer Joan Simpson, Price described this work, which engaged him for five years, as his Vietnam: "I was wiped out in every way when I finished. I did what we did in Vietnam at the end – I called it a victory and got the hell out."

For many people Price's cups are among the most beautiful ceramic pots to have come out of the contemporary ceramics movement in the United States. He says: "With them the functional side can be metaphorical. . . the cup as a motif. . . I've used the cup form in various ways for over 20 years." Price frequently uses very sharp colours; some are glazes, but he has no compunction in using acrylic or automobile paint. The quasi-traditionalists of the Anglo-Oriental post-LEACH school are shocked.

PROUVE Jean 1901–83   French

engineer and designer

Industrial techniques in building.

Although he received some education in engineering, Prouvé was principally trained as a metalworker. He was the son of Victor Prouvé, one of the leading figures in the art nouveau movement, centred on Nancy.

Prouvé *fils* established his own works in Nancy in 1923; in 1931 this was reorganized for the production of prefabricated building products. Prouvé believed that problems of form could only be tackled by coming to terms with the industrialization of production. He had a close working relationship with various architects including LE CORBUSIER, helping to develop the new building tradition where construction was based on industrial design and production. The Roland Garros flying club, Buc (1937), designed in collaboration with architects Beaudouin and Lods, has been described as the first totally industrialized building. It utilized a curtain-wall system which was also seen on the Maison du Peuple, Clichy (1937–9).

After the Second World War he was involved in mass production, especially of houses based on the total prefabrication of building components, which nevertheless managed to retain a high degree of individuality. His firm prospered, but in 1954 he moved from Nancy to Paris, where he worked as an independent designer and consultant.

Prouvé's name is particularly linked with the use of lightweight sheet metal, often ridged for strength and rigidity. This theme has been exhaustively explored by high-tech architects. But in Prouvé's own work the aesthetic impact owes as much to the architectural concern with proportion and space, seen in his refreshment room at Evian (1957), for example, as to the extreme refinement of industrial detailing.

Jean Prouvé, Exhibition Village, St Michel sur Orge, 1966–8.

P

PUIFORCAT Jean 1897–1945 French

silversmith

Innovatory designs in silver and silver-gilt.

Born in Paris into a family of silversmiths, the young Puiforcat served in the First World War (he was decorated with the *Croix de Guerre*) before serving an apprenticeship in his father's atelier; at the same time he studied sculpture with Louis Lejeune.

He exhibited his first pieces, a pair of tea-sets, at the 1921 salon of the Société des Artistes Décorateurs: one of them was decorated with fruits and foliage in the popular, prevailing style of Georg JENSEN, the other was of similar shape but unadorned. His subsequent works were to follow in the innovative footsteps of the latter tea-set, and would comprise a unique oeuvre of, among other objects, covered bowls, vases, chalices, tureens, boxes, centrepieces, even cutlery and lamps whose simple, rational forms were strong artistic statements, enhanced by the play of light, not by, in Puiforcat's own words, "contortions in imitation of natural vegetation". This is not to say that he did not add elements to his silver and silver-gilt creations to heighten their appearance: many works contained subtle accents of semi-precious stones, or handles of ivory or rare woods, although as time passed he favoured neutral highlights of rock crystal or glass to coloured ones.

Despite the fact that his masterpieces were created in somewhat solitary, esoteric conditions, Puiforcat was an active, highly visible member of artistic society in Paris. He participated regularly in the salons; exhibited at, was on juries of, and reported on the 1925 Exposition, and successfully showed and sold his works throughout Europe, as well as in North and South America and in Japan. He was a founding member of the Union des Artistes Modernes in 1930.

Jean Puiforcat, silver and ivory tea service, *c*.1930.

PUSH PIN STUDIOS founded 1954 American

graphic design studio

Decorative illustration and graphic design.

Push Pin Studios in New York was founded in 1954 by Milton GLASER, Seymour Chwast and Edward Sorel, and grew to become one of the most revolutionary forces in American graphic design. Push Pin departed from the pervading formality of the Swiss/German influence of the 1950s. It instead offered a form of decorative illustration that absorbed influences from a colourful stew of past and present sources. These were applied with wit and vitality, and the result was that graphics – and particularly posters – became an important popular art form throughout the 1960s, appreciated by the American public as never before. At the same time, they broke new ground on the professional front: they pulled graphic design out of the realms of commercial art and advertising, and gained it appreciation as a serious art form – for in 1970 they became the first American graphic design studio to exhibit at the Louvre in Paris (an honour usually reserved for fine art).

Glaser's connection with Push Pin lessened over the years, but Seymour Chwast remained a central figure. A master of eclecticism and the use of nostalgic forms, his extraordinary contribution to the Push Pin past is evident in the book *Seymour Chwast: The Left-Handed Designer*, published in 1985. In addition to designs and illustrations applied to a vast number of products, he has illustrated more than a dozen children's books, was founder-publisher of Push Pin Press (1976–81) and publisher/editor of the Push Pin Graphic magazine (1974–81). In 1985 he became director of the Push Pin Group Inc.

Seymour Chwast of Push Pin Studios.

Push Pin Studios, Vietnam War protest poster by Seymour Chwast, 1967.

PYE David b.1914 British

craftsman in wood

Author of *The Nature and Art of Workmanship*.

Pye trained at the Architectural Association in London; he has been an architect and furniture designer and remains a practising craftsman in wood. He is the author of a number of books, including the seminal *The Nature and Art of Workmanship* – perhaps the best English-language text on the nature of craftsmanship written during this century. He is an exceptionally fine craftsman, working in a narrow field – he produces small carved bowls and exquisite lidded boxes.

QUANT Mary b.1934   British

1960s teenage fashion.

During the 1950s the wages of British teenagers rose dramatically and unemployment stood at just 1 per cent. Young people generally lived at home, and had few financial commitments. This group had, for the first time, relatively large disposable incomes, a large proportion of which they were prepared to spend on fashionable clothing. By the early 1960s London had established itself as the international centre of ready-to-wear youth fashions. Deliberately flouting wartime emphasis on quality and durability, fashion styles changed constantly. Garments were designed to be enjoyed for a short period only, and this trend reached a peak in 1967 with the brief vogue for disposable paper clothing. The leading designers of the day were art-school trained, and widely proclaimed that they only made garments that they wanted to wear themselves. Mary Quant emerged as one of the first and most successful designers of teenage fashion.

Trained as a milliner's apprentice and at Goldsmiths' College of Art in London, Quant is generally credited with opening the first boutique, called Bazaar, in the King's Road in 1955. Bazaar was financed by Alexander Plunket Greene (whom she had met at Goldsmiths', and married in 1957), and their business partner Archie MacNair. Bazaar was unique because it sold high fashion, ready-to-wear clothing which was aimed specifically at teenagers. Bazaar filled a gap in the retail market, then largely dominated by multiple stores, which sold endless racks of identically styled mainstream fashion, and the individual, but prohibitively priced dressmaker shops and department stores. The lively atmosphere and short runs of up-to-the-minute clothing sold in Bazaar appealed to the wealthier sections of the fashion-hungry youth market. Quant designed, and initially made, all the clothing she sold. Business boomed, and she soon sought the help of outworkers to make up her fashions.

In 1961 another boutique, also called Bazaar, was opened in Knightsbridge. Two years later Quant was exporting to America and moved into quantity production with her Ginger Group. In 1964 she started to design for Butterick patterns, which enabled her desirable styles to reach a wider and less well-off market. From 1965 Quant further expanded by arranging for numerous licensees to produce a wide variety of goods including cosmetics, stationery, toys, bed-linen, spectacle frames and even wine – all endorsed by her familiar daisy motif.

Mary Quant's name is most often associated with the introduction in 1962 of the mini-skirt, although the French *couturier* COURRÈGES also claims the credit for this. As the decade progressed the mini-skirt became increasingly shorter, reaching an unprecedented thigh level by 1967. The spin-offs to the hosiery trade were obvious, and Quant soon branched into this area, producing brightly coloured and textured stockings and tights. Quant designed multi-purpose clothing which, for the first time, could be worn at any time of the day or night. She also popularized mix 'n' match separates, designed to complement each other. Her adventurous young customers were dressed in high-waisted tweed suits, Norfolk jackets trimmed with fox fur, hipster trousers, skinny-rib jumpers, black leather coats and long boots. She also introduced wet-look rainwear, made from polyvinyl chloride (PVC), a wartime product which had never before been used for fashion. Her "baby doll" look included gym slips, schoolgirl pinafore dresses and knickerbockers. In her autobiography she states that at this point "sex appeal was the number one priority". A more sustaining unisex look was introduced in 1966. Quant broke down the traditional boundaries of gender dressing and put women in dungarees.

Quant's clothing was designed in reaction to the corseted styles of the 1950s, and, like CHANEL, she claimed to have liberated women's bodies. Her clothing has often been described as cheap, but in fact it was so only in relation to couture prices. It was certainly way beyond the reach of the majority of teenagers, who bought imitations of her popular styles in boutique chains.

Quant was at the peak of her profession during the 1950s and 1960s, when her fashions were seen as representing modernity and progress for women, although this was much debated by the end of the decade. She set the styles worn by teenagers all over Europe and America, and was also largely responsible for establishing London as a centre of fashion in the 1960s and the King's Road as the focus of the most adventurous youth fashion – a reputation which it has continued to enjoy to the present day. Today Quant operates from small London workrooms. Mary Quant Ltd no longer undertakes any manufacturing, but instead a number of designs for licensees.

Mary Quant.

Mary Quant, houndstooth-check shirtwaist dress, available in Butterick paper patterns, summer 1964.

RABANNE Paco b.1934   Spanish

Futuristic fashions, especially plastic and metal body jewellery from 1966.

Rabanne's mother was the leading seamstress of the *couturier* BALENCIAGA. In 1938 both families fled to Paris, to escape the Spanish Civil War. There, Rabanne studied architecture at the Ecole des Beaux Arts from 1952 to 1964. He then designed fashion accessories – handbags, shoes, jewellery and embroideries – on a freelance basis for BALENCIAGA, DIOR and GIVENCHY.

He launched his famous body jewellery in the spring of 1966, when he opened his own house. These garments, designed for the Space Age, were made from chain-mail (now much used by VERSACE), plastic and metal discs and tiles, which were held together with wire. Many of his experimental fashions were welded and moulded and combined unusual materials. His winter 1968/9 collection included ostrich-plume dresses with aluminium bodices. He also designed in silver leather and paper.

Rabanne's daring and highly dramatic fashions enjoyed much media coverage, and were purchased by the wealthy young.

RACE Ernst 1913–63   British

BA, Antelope and Springbok chairs.

Race trained as an architect at the Bartlett School of Architecture, London, and after the Second World War he designed furniture. His style was linear and sparse, but its roots were in 18th-century neo-classical forms rather than in the harsher geometry of mainstream European modernism. His most famous designs include his first, the BA chair, made in 1945 from cast aluminium, which has become one of the few English furniture design classics of this century.

His other well-known designs are the Antelope chair (1951) which, like his Springbok chair (1951), was of steel rod construction, the Flamingo easy-chair (1959) and the Sheppey settee-chair (1963). He did some work for ISOKON and contract design work for the P&O Orient lines, the Royal Netherlands Lines and the University of Liverpool Medical School.

RAMS Dieter b.1932   see page 192

RAMSHAW Wendy b.1939   British

Finely crafted jewellery.

Ramshaw trained in illustration and fabric design and is a self-taught jeweller. Her collections of rings, often grouped together on lathe-turned miniature acrylic minarets, created a great deal of interest in modern jewellery circles in the early 1970s. Her career has progressed steadily in Europe and the USA, but during the late 1970s and early 1980s her careful, extremely well crafted precious-metal work was overlooked in the general rush to award plaudits to the "new jewellers" who opposed, or said they opposed, the élitist values of precious metals.

Ramshaw persisted. Her work is now rich in the variety of its shapes and diverse in terms of scale and conception. Some of her most beautiful works are large gold or silver neckpieces.

She has experimented with performance work, and produced ranges of paper jewellery and used plastics and new composite materials such as Colorcore. Now that it is once more fashionable to admire finesse and the values of skill, her work is exerting a renewed influence.

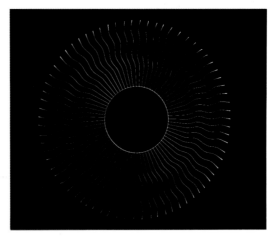

Wendy Ramshaw.

Wendy Ramshaw, Rays of the Sun necklace, silver gilt, 1989.

RAND Paul b.1914   American

Graphics consultant to major corporations including IBM.

A native New Yorker, Paul Rand studied at Pratt Institute and Parsons School of Design in the early 1930s, and later at the Art Students League (under

R

George Grosz) in 1939. He began his career during America's great "magazine renaissance"; in 1937, at the age of 23, he became art director of *Esquire* and *Apparel Arts* magazines. Breaking away from the magazine traditions of narrative illustration and symmetrical page layout, Rand developed the "visual dynamics" of the page. Type, layout and imagery acquired a new expressiveness and energy through his use of colour, texture, collage, montage and visual contrasts.

From 1941 to 1954 he was art director for the William H. Weintraub advertising agency, and his collaborations with the copywriter Bill Bernbach pioneered a relationship between design and copy that eventually developed into today's "creative team" approach to advertising. Rand produced designs for a wide range of advertisers and publishers, and works from this period still stand as some of the finest examples of US advertising and editorial design.

Throughout these early years, Rand was heavily influenced by the European art movements (Cubism, Constructivism, De Stijl, the BAUHAUS, etc.), and he has been widely acknowledged as having introduced their visual vocabulary into American design. But he also drew inspiration from the American culture, and developed this mixture into a highly recognizable personal style.

In the 1950s he was drawn into trademarks and corporate design, and the work he did as graphics consultant for IBM had a seminal influence on the development of the concept of "corporate image" over the following decades. He designed the IBM logotype and associated alphabet, and many graphics applications over the coming years, including stationery, annual reports, signage, packaging, advertisements, publications, etc. plus a "Design Guide" containing design guidelines. He also acted as consultant to other major corporations such as Westinghouse (1960), United Parcel Service (1961) and the American Broadcasting Company (1962).

A further contribution to the design world has come in the form of writing and education. Rand initially expressed his design philosophy and attitudes in the book *Thoughts on Design*, published in 1947 (and with an introduction by E. McKnight KAUFFER). It contained reflections, or essays, on the principles governing advertising design, as well as providing many examples of Rand's work to date and was regarded for many years after as a classic text. A revised version entitled *Paul Rand: A Designer's Art* (Yale

University Press) was produced in 1985. The educational world has benefited not only from his writings and his professional example, but also from his teaching: since 1956 he has been a professor of graphic design at the Yale School of Art and Architecture.

REID Jamie b.1940   British

graphic designer

Art direction for the Sex Pistols rock group; promotion of Punk movement.

Jamie Reid's graphic work for the Sex Pistols rock group in the 1970s became the visual representation of the Punk movement in Britain; it also created a street-graphics revolution that has had a phenomenal influence on commercial graphic design ever since.

Jamie Reid and Malcolm McLaren, one of the founders of Punk, met while attending art school in the London suburb of Croydon. Both became involved in the art and politics of the Situationists, a group of European artists and intellectuals who encouraged modern society's passive consumers to "interact and participate", thereby developing the creative possibilities of new city culture (1957–72). The Situationists staged anarchic events, and employed the graphic forms of advertising, comics and graffiti in collages and other artworks.

In 1970 Reid set up his own art/politics project in Croydon: a community paper called *The Suburban Press*. Artworks he created under the name of the Press in the early 1970s included posters, mixed-media collages, and a range of (now famous) subversive stickers, carrying slogans such as "This week only – This store welcomes shoplifters" (apparently flyposted on major department stores in Central London); "Save Petrol, Burn Cars" and "Keep Warm This Winter, Make Trouble". He also made use of torn paper, cut-up "ransom-note" lettering, and recycled imagery – and later transferred all of these techniques (along with some of the actual imagery) to his work for the Sex Pistols.

Although Punk was initially an art movement, it became a part of broader youth culture through the creation of the Sex Pistols rock group in 1975, with Malcolm McLaren as their manager and Jamie Reid as their art director. Reid designed all their graphic requirements (posters, record sleeves, T-shirts, etc.) until the group's end in 1979. Much of the group's notoriety was due to Reid's designs (often subject to court cases over the use of bad language, etc.).

Paul Rand, logo for Next Inc., 1986.

Paul Rand, poster for IBM, 1982.

Jamie Reid.

R

In graphic terms, his work for the Sex Pistols provided Punk with an anarchic new visual language, typified by the cut-out ransom lettering; the bright, brash colours of supermarket packaging; crude type and photo-reproduction; and chaotic "stick-it-down-anywhere" layout. His use of do-it-yourself graphics created a surge in street publishing and Punk fanzines.

Reid himself returned to fine art (his paintings have been exhibited internationally), while still continuing to work in graphics. He joined the design consultancy Assorted Images in 1986, and graphic projects from the 1980s have included the title credits for the film *Letter to Brezhnev*.

RHODES Zandra b.1942 — British

fashion and textile designer

Printed and painted silk and chiffon garments.

Zandra Rhodes trained in lithography and printing at Medway College, then studied textiles at the Royal College of Art, graduating in 1964 at the peak of the pop revolution. Greatly influenced by this movement, and the work of the painter Roy Lichtenstein in particular, she designed a paper wedding dress which retailed at 1s 4d (7 new pence). Paper clothes enjoyed a brief vogue in 1967: paper was the ultimate symbol of expendability in clothing.

She formed her own fashion house in 1968, and has since become famous for her fine chiffons and silks, screenprinted and painted by hand, which she produces in soft watery colours. Her designs have largely been inspired by her travels and historical research. For example, her Japanese travels produced the theme of lilies, America resulted in a collection which featured cacti and cowboys, and Kenya, zebra motifs. Other themes that regularly appear are art deco motifs, zigzags, feathers, shells and amoeba-like flowers. She also features words, such as "lilies" on her lily prints. Throughout her career many of her garments have been based on the continuing appeal of the kaftan, and she has often created dresses with handkerchiefs.

In 1977 Rhodes received much publicity for her startling, contrasting Punk-inspired garments, which upgraded and romanticized this street fashion into the luxury world of couture. Her top-price, silk-jersey evening dresses were made in black, creams and shocking pink, and were adorned with safety-pins incongruously covered with tiny seed pearls, chains and carefully contrived holes and slashes.

Zandra Rhodes, patchwork jacket, autumn/winter 1983–4.

Dieter Rams, electric desk fan for Braun.

RAMS Dieter b.1932 — German

industrial designer

Electrical appliances for Braun.

Dieter Rams, whose name is inseparably entwined with that of BRAUN, the electrical appliance manufacturer, is regularly described as the most important industrial designer of post-war Germany. He has many imitators, and there is even a mimeographed Rams fan magazine called *Der Braun-Sammler* 1-9.

His education included carpentry, followed by an architecture and art course at the Wiesbaden School of Art. His career began with the architectural practice of Otto Apel, who also collaborated with SOM (Skidmore, Owings and Merrill), the famous American architectural firm who were then working on commissions in the post-war reconstruction in West Germany.

Rams joined Braun in 1955 and subsequently became its head of design, collaborating early on with Hans GUGELOT, who had become head of the department of production at the Hochschule für Gestaltung (School of Design) in Ulm (see ULM). This collaboration was important to Rams because the design philosophy at Ulm stressed utility and rationalism. Gugelot, 12 years Rams' senior, was a mentor who taught that a product should function well and display its function without ornamentation.

Later Rams was also to teach at Ulm and the Rams-Braun/Gugelot–Ulm aesthetic has acted as the dominant rival to Italian design. Speculation as to why post-war West Germany was so rigorously clean in its design must include consideration of the new nation's determination to seek a tangible honesty in *everything*. Rams is regarded, as is Gugelot, as having picked up the baton of enlightenment that had been wielded

Dieter Rams, heater for
Braun.

Dieter Rams, film projector
for Braun.

at the BAUHAUS before that institution was closed by the Nazis in 1933. The rational and easy-to-use products that Braun manufactures are fully representative of the design ideology of functionalism.

Rams/Braun products can become collectors' items: the SK4 radio and record player, nicknamed "Snow White's Coffin" (1956), the H1/H2 fan-heater (1959) and the CSV 250 amplifier (1966) are examples. More recent work includes the ET 55 pocket calculator (1981) and the Atelier hi-fi stack (1987), designed with Peter Hartewein.

The depth of debate that Rams and his school of thought have generated in the 1980s among European designers is considerable because he and the Ulm School philosophy did not fit in with pluralism, postmodernism and the fashionable 1980s concepts of individuality and niche marketing. Obviously Rams and Braun made use of the 1980s microchip technology, but they did not see it as giving them a licence to turn design into art. Interestingly enough, Rams shares with Ettore SOTTSASS (in design terms an antagonist of Rams, Braun and Ulm) a belief in serving human needs, but Rams sees design as creating instruments for people, not images of society.

Rams works for other clients apart from Braun. In 1986 he began working with FSB, manufacturers of door handles, and the managing director has said of the collaboration: "The work with Alessandro MENDINI was great fun, but with Rams it was unbelievably strenuous. He questioned everything and criticized everything, absolutely terrible, but he was absolutely right. This is perhaps reflected in the fact that Mendini has one page in our new catalogue and Rams 24."

And Rams himself, talking not about FSB but about manufacturers in general, is surprising in his demands. He says that a firm should never give a designer a blank cheque and is, indeed, critical of what he calls the "profligate benevolence often practised by American firms". He says a company needs competent staff of its own, expert in their work and expectations – designing is a dialogue, a team effort, not an act of individuality. Rams *is* very particular: he made Braun enact exhaustive trials to find the best layouts for the pocket calculators; after all, he asked, what form should a calculator's keys take? Concave or convex?

Rams dislikes excess: "Good design is the least possible design. To leave out everything that is unimportant, and thus to emphasize what is important, is for me one of the crucial principles of design."

Rams apparently believes in good design in an absolute sense, and absolutism is a doctrine that many other designers, most notably Ettore Sottsass, have long rejected. The acclaim that Rams has won was matched in the 1980s by a hostility from a younger generation of designers who found the Rams-Ulm axis too stifling.

Ironically, as this generation in turn reaches middle age and a new set of young Turks arrive, it is possible that the discretion of Rams, his demanding scepticism and his rigour will suit minds concerned less with ego and more with environmental good manners and conservatism. Rams and Sottsass can both claim they were right – Rams because his style is appropriate once more, Sottsass because he can simply and correctly say that history has turned again in Rams' favour.

In the end the defining characteristic of Rams is not his beliefs about what good design is, but that he remains thoroughly consistent to those beliefs, whereas Sottsass's tendency is to go with the flow. Both approaches work, therefore both are tenable.

Dieter Rams, electronic
hand-held pocket calculator
for Braun.

R

RIE Lucie b.1902   Austrian

`potter`

Studio pottery.

Rie trained in fine art at the Kunstgewerbeschule in Vienna. Her first experience in pottery was from the country potter Michael Powolny. She enjoyed success as a potter in the 1930s and was well known in Europe, but not in Britain. Hence, on her arrival in London in 1938, as a refugee from the anti-semitism of Austria, she had to begin her career anew.

Lucie Rie, thrown stoneware bottle, 1979.

Bernard LEACH did not understand her work. One of the problems was, as George Wingfield Digby pointed out, "that she was a metropolitan potter doing studio wares", and thus not a quasi-traditionalist. She found a friend in a fellow refugee, the German Hans COPER, although this fruitful relationship did not begin until 1946.

Rie's work ranges from domestic ware, such as coffee services in the late 1950s, to sharply controlled small bowls with turned feet and sometimes a bright green or yellow glaze or a pink, petal colour. One of her characteristic decorative devices is sgraffito, often done in the form of cross-hatching. A number of her vases stand about 34cm (14in) high and have swollen bellies, long necks and wide-rimmed, concave brimmed tops. Sometimes these are covered in white tin glaze, with a volcanic pockmarked surface.

Rie's work, with its rejection of functionalism, is an example of the craft aesthetic as one of opposition to that of technology and industrialization.

RIETVELD Gerrit 1888–1964   Dutch

`architect and designer`

Schroeder House, Utrecht.

Rietveld trained as a cabinetmaker but became an architect and designer. He began his career as an architect by designing the furniture for a pioneering concrete house by the architect Robert van t'Hoff. In 1917 Rietveld designed a wooden chair which was made from 15 lintels and a plank each for the back and seat. It displayed neither cabinet-making nor fine woodworking craftsmanship. By 1918 a version of the chair was lacquered, the lintels were black with yellow ends, the back was red and the seat was blue. Rietveld may have been influenced in part by Piet Mondrian's grid-like primary coloured abstract paintings, and in part by Theo van Doesburg, a painter and writer with

Gerrit Rietveld, Red-Blue Chair, painted wood, 1917-18.

whom Rietveld collaborated.

Rietveld was really a craftsman rather than a designer, or rather he designed through making things. The Russian artist and designer El LISSITZKY, who in 1926 visited the Rietveld-designed Schroeder House of 1924 commented: "He does all with models, feeling things with his hands; and therefore his product is not abstract. One cannot judge such works by photographs, since by photographs we see only a view and not the life of the form."

The Schroeder House, Rietveld's most important commission, was commissioned by Mrs Truus Schroeder-Schrader, and the historian Paul Overy tells us she was credited in early articles with being the joint designer.

Of his work and its relationship to utility, Rietveld said: "Function is an accidental, casual need that will change with the time and indeed always changes in the course of time." That understanding of function as process, as something which alters with the flux of change, applies to the Schroeder House, which was designed with change in mind.

ROBINEAU Adelaide Alsop 1865–1929   American

`art potter`

Masterworks in porcelain, including the "Scarab Vase"; editorship of *Keramic Studio*.

Adelaide Alsop was born in Middletown, Connecticut, where she taught herself to paint on china, a craft she learned mostly from books. In her twenties she taught china-painting in Minnesota, and in the 1890s she studied with American Impressionist William Merritt Chase in New York. She married French-born Samuel Robineau in 1899, and in the same year the couple and a partner bought the journal *China Decorator*, changing the name to *Keramic Studio*.

In 1901 the Robineaus settled in Syracuse, upstate New York, where Adelaide experimented with various pottery techniques and glazes, as well as with the curvilinear shapes of art nouveau that appeared in *Keramic Studio* along with the more popular, traditional Beaux-Arts forms and patterns. The Robineaus built a workshop and kiln in 1903, and for a time, following several weeks of study with English-born studio potter Charles F. Binns at Alfred University (also in upstate New York), Adelaide devoted herself to making porcelain, a world apart from the neater, more "ladylike" art of china-painting. She threw and glazed her own vessels, and fired them at extremely high temperatures, with the final results – and one hallmark of her *oeuvre* – often delicate, thin-walled pieces with exquisite crystalline qualities, like blossoms of frost on pale-hued grounds.

The couple tried their hands at mass-producing Adelaide's designs, but they did not translate well into large quantities, so the production of cast vessels, which were then painstakingly hand-decorated, was considered a failed venture. Adelaide returned to crafting individual pieces, and her masterworks were widely admired by critics, winning awards both at home and abroad. The so-called "Scarab Vase", which took some 1,000 hours to produce (during her two-year stint at the short-lived University City Pottery in St Louis), helped her win the Grand Prize at the 1911 Turin exhibition. An exquisite showpiece, the tall ovoid vase was decorated overall with stylized scarab beetles on a lustrous white body, and was distinguished too for its lacy openwork, another Robineau speciality (and extremely difficult to achieve in porcelain). Some early pieces, such as the Viking vase of 1905 with its earth-toned glazes, were in the Arts and Crafts mode.

Adelaide Robineau's later works concerned themselves less with highly decorative, European-influenced patterns and more with simpler Oriental and Mayan motifs, or just with colour shadings, void of decoration altogether. Crackled glazes entered her repertory as well, though most of her output was dominated by crystalline surfaces. From 1919 she taught at Syracuse University.

Adelaide Alsop Robineau, Crab Vase.

RODCHENKO Alexander 1891–1956   Russian

graphic and industrial designer

Leading figure in Russian Constructivist movement of the 1920s.

In the wake of the 1917 revolution, Russian Constructivism emerged in the 1920s as one of the primary movements in art and design. Welcoming the machine age, Russian artists and designers were intent on building, or constructing, a new society. For the new "proletariat" they created everyday products and utility items that were modern and functional, and which embraced an abstract aesthetic pioneered by the European Cubists and Futurists. The graphics of the era also employed this avant-garde aesthetic. A visual language developed consisting of structural emphasis, geometric form, spatial dynamics and minimal colour – and possessing a boldness and vitality that was filled with optimism for the new Soviet future.

Rodchenko was one of the founders and leading figures of the Constructivist movement. The son of a stage property-maker, he entered the Moscow avant-garde art scene in 1915/16, producing three-dimensional spatial constructions, and line studies on canvas; by 1920 he had already given up easel painting and notions of "pure art" to devote himself to the Constructivist interests of industrial design and the applied arts. From 1921 onwards he concentrated on graphic and typographic design, and produced a body

Alexander Rodchenko, sketch for the state merchant air service, 1923.

R

of work that has continued to have a major influence on the graphic world. His range was extremely broad, and his most famous designs include covers, illustrations and layouts for the Constructivist journal *LEF*(Left Front of the Arts, 1923–5) and its successor *Novyi LEF* (New LEF, 1927–8); film posters for *Kino Glaz* (Dziga Vertov, 1923–4), Sergei Eisenstein's *Battleship Potemkin* (1925) and others; advertisements for foods, goods and state services – often in collaboration with his friend, the poet Mayakovsky, as copywriter (1923–5); as well as numerous designs for the books of Mayakovsky, among them the cover and text illustrations for the poem *Pro Eto* (About This, 1923), where Rodchenko first employed photomontage.

From 1924 Rodchenko also began working as a photographer, incorporating his own photographs into his montage work and developing his distinctive use of oblique camera angles and dynamic close-up views. Once the 1930s arrived, however, the climate in the Soviet Union changed in favour of Social Realism; Stalin outlawed abstract art and design in 1932, and the Constructivist movement became fragmented. Yet Rodchenko continued to work in photojournalism for *USSR in Construction* and other magazines, and also executed designs for books and periodicals with his other great collaborator, his wife, the versatile artist and textile designer Varvara Stepanova. By the 1940s Rodchenko's career as a book designer was over, but he continued to produce photographs and other graphic work until his death in Moscow in 1956.

ROGERS Richard b.1933   see right

ROLLS-ROYCE founded 1904   British

Exclusive, hand-built luxury cars.

The name of Rolls-Royce is synonymous with British traditions of exclusive, hand-built excellence and classical, if not staid, design. The firm was founded in 1904, when an agreement was signed between Frederick Henry Royce, an electrical engineer from an impoverished background, and the Hon. Charles Stewart Rolls, an aristocratic car racer and the first undergraduate at Cambridge to own a motor-car. Through the agreement Royce produced four different models, including a six-cylinder, 30-horsepower luxury car, selling at £890, with the distinctive radiator grill designed by

Charles Stewart Rolls.

ROGERS Richard b.1933   British

Pompidou Centre; Lloyd's Building.

Richard Rogers was born in Florence and brought up in Italy and England. He trained at the Architectural Association under Peter SMITHSON and at Yale University, America, under Paul Rudolph.

On his return to Britain Rogers formed a partnership with Norman FOSTER and the two designed the Reliance Controls Factory, Swindon, Wiltshire (1965). This was Rogers' first foray into building in the industrialized style known as high tech. The single-storey building was designed as a long horizontal slab faced with metal panels. The steel girder frame was exposed on the outside. Rogers and Foster acknowledged that their design had been influenced by Peter and Alison Smithson's Hunstanton School in Norfolk.

The Rogers/Foster partnership was eventually dissolved, and Rogers teamed up with the Italian Renzo Piano to work on the Pompidou Centre, Paris (1972–7), a commission which had been won in a competition. The arts centre was outrageous and daring in design, and was placed in the heart of old Paris at the Place Beaubourg. Resembling an enormous machine, the building was devised by Piano and Rogers to offer large gallery spaces inside while, set within a metal frame, they put escalators, air-conditioning and electrical ducts and plumbing pipes on the outside. The five-storey rectangular block of metal and glass glistens, and dashes of colour are added by the use of coloured pipes.

On a smaller scale, but constructed in a similar way, was the Inmos Factory, Newport, Wales (1982), formed of a long low slab. The Rogers hallmark can be

Richard Rogers, Pompidou
Centre, Paris, 1972–7
(below and left).

Richard Rogers, Lloyds Bank
Building, London, 1979–86
(above and left).

seen in the central spine of ducts, pipes, wires and metal trusses which run outside and above the building. When the Prince of Wales opened it, he is reported to have said: "Well, Mr Rogers, it looks as though the engineers got their way this time."

In the late 1970s Rogers won the most important commission of his career – the design of the Lloyd's Building in the City of London (1979–86). The shimmering silver and glass building pokes its head above the surrounding City office blocks and stands like an enormous 300 ft mechanical cathedral. The rugged skyline is composed of six towers, and in the middle is the arched glass skylight or "nave" which caps the building's full-height atrium. Also on top are the blue cranes used during construction, which Rogers decided to retain. Scaling the external walls are series of horizontal and vertical steel pipes, steel corkscrew staircases and clear glass lift "pods". The building is at its most breathtaking at night, when it is bathed in electric blue light.

Commenting on his aims, Rogers said: "Our intention in the design of the new Lloyd's building has been to create a building which would link and weave together both the over-simplified 20th-century blocks and the richer, more varied architecture of the past. Approaches to buildings in cities are often along narrow streets, so they can be seen obliquely. Lloyd's is designed to be approached on the diagonal and viewed in parts. As the viewer approaches the building, the form gradually unfolds."

The building was given a mixed reception by critics and suffered some technical teething problems, and its staff found it difficult to work in; however, its success with the public was clear when it rapidly became established as a major tourist attraction.

R

Frederick Henry Royce.

Royce himself. Rolls guaranteed to take all Royce's production, with the proviso that the name used should be Rolls-Royce. Royce's technical brilliance ensured that the cars were smooth, quiet and reliable. Although Rolls was killed in a flying accident in 1910, the firm survived with the aid of a third partner, Claude Johnson, who oversaw its day-to-day running.

The 40/50, known later as the Silver Ghost, was produced between 1906 and 1925, and was replaced in 1926 by the Phantom. The famous symbol of Rolls-Royce, the winged female figure known as the "Spirit of Ecstasy", was introduced as the mascot on the radiator in 1911. Following Royce's death in 1933, the Phantom 111 of 1936 differed significantly from its predecessors, with its V12 engine and top speeds in excess of 100 mph, making it one of the most impressive luxury cars ever built.

During the Second World War the company concentrated on supplying the RAF with Merlin aero

Rolls-Royce radiator grille, with Spirit of Ecstasy mascot, introduced in 1911.

engines, a field in which the company had excelled since 1908. Civilian production resumed in 1946 with the Silver Wraith, followed by the sleek Silver Cloud and then the Silver Shadow series.

ROSENTHAL founded 1879   German

porcelain factory

Tableware designs, many in limited editions.

At the beginning of the 20th century the Rosenthal company, founded in Bavaria by Philipp Rosenthal, produced versions of art nouveau designs for its tableware ranges, and in so doing established itself as a company of contemporary design and style. In 1960 the company began opening "Studio Houses" throughout Europe to promote its work, and it has through the years commissioned designs from the

Rosenthal, china vase designed by Fritz Heidenrich and decorated by Klaus Bendixen, c.1950.

middle-brow end of the avant-garde. Many of its special design ranges are limited editions.

ROSSI Aldo b.1931   Italian

architect, furniture and product designer

Teatro del Mondo, Venice.

Aldo Rossi is an Italian post-modern architect, who draws his inspiration from traditional classicism. He embarked on his career in 1956 at the age of 25, when he worked with Ignazio Gradella and later, Marco ZANUSO. Although primarily an architect, he has turned his attention to design both as a journalist, editing *Casabella-Continuita* until 1964, and as a product designer. He was commissioned by the Italian steel company ALESSI to design a tea and coffee service in 1979 as part of its Programme 6, along with 10 other leading post-modern architects, including Robert VENTURI, Charles Jencks, Michael GRAVES and Richard MEIER. Rossi's design was based on his floating wooden and steel theatre, the Teatro del Mondo, Venice (1979), and the Campanile in St Mark's Square, Venice. The silver service is housed in a pedimented glass case, complete with clock and surmounted by a flag.

Rossi continued to use scaled-down versions of buildings for Alessi commissions, including the La Conica stainless-steel espresso coffee-makers (1984), with their turret-like forms. More recently Rossi has designed marble furniture for Logoni, including the classically-inspired Rilievo table (1986). However, he is essentially a post-modern architect and theorist and was appointed chair of architectural composition at Venice University in 1975.

ROWE Michael b.1948   British

Non-functional metal container ornaments.

Rowe is a graduate of High Wycombe College of Art and the Royal College of Art, London. He is currently (1990) head of the department of metalwork and jewellery at the Royal College, and co-author (with Richard Hughes) of *Patinating Metals* (Crafts Council, London). He has developed a series of non-functional metal container ornaments which bridge the abyss between design and art. They are objects very much of their time, exploring a domestic sculptural language that parallels exactly sculptural tendencies in postmodern product design. In his work the spirit of experimental design has passed from Milan to London.

RUHLMANN Emile-Jacques 1879–1933   French

furniture and interior designer

Outstanding furniture designer and *ensemblier*.

The master *ensemblier* in art deco Paris, Emile-Jacques Ruhlmann was born in the French capital, the son of François Ruhlmann, a wealthy and successful building and painting contractor originally from Alsace. He was in his father's employ while still a teenager, and took over the business in 1907, when Ruhlmann *père* died. The healthy finances of the Ruhlmann family allowed Emile-Jacques the freedom and luxury to design, and to make his ideas a reality: by 1913 his firm was exhibiting furniture to the public, such as a Macassar ebony *bergère* inlaid with his signature in ivory dots at the Salon d'Automne.

The numerous interior-design commissions Ruhlmann received in a period of approximately two decades, considered together with his triumphs at the 1925 Paris Exposition and other exhibitions and salons, and the number of publications devoted to his work, are an impressive testament to his significance in his own time (when he died at the age of 54, his design firm essentially died with him). Like the 18th-century *ébénistes* who worked for French royalty, Ruhlmann numbered among his clients the *crème de la crème* of both the society and business worlds. Apart from private commissions, he designed furniture, furnishings, and interiors for restaurants, civic buildings, and ocean liners, even a cinema and stage set.

Without doubt, Ruhlmann was the leading interior designer and *ensemblier* – that is, creator of entire room ensembles, from floor to ceiling, ashtray to settee, and other objects in between – who was working in the opulent, high-style art deco vein in Paris in the 1920s, and he was the greatest furniture designer as well, from 1923 employing the finest cabinetmakers and other craftsmen to produce his magnificent commodes, cabinets, beds, chairs, sofas, tables, desks and so on. In Ruhlmann's boudoirs, bathrooms and bedrooms, his salons and dining rooms, even his conference rooms and ballrooms, there always existed a rich, elegant unity of materials, colours and shapes, and a sensitivity for the architectural and functional details – mouldings, lighting fixtures, curtains, carpets – which are so important in the overall conception of a room. No detail, big or small, aesthetic or technical, escaped Ruhlmann's eye.

Although Ruhlmann was not designing for industry or for mass production *per se*, some of his smaller objects, such as the table lamps and mirrors, were available to the public (those who could afford them, that is). He also designed some porcelain that was made by the Sèvres manufactory. But his foremost creations were one-of-a-kind furniture objects, showpieces such as corner cabinets and sideboards sheathed with exotic-wood veneer. Desks and dressing tables had inlaid tops of shagreen or sharkskin, and the so-called Elysée sideboard, shown at the 1920 Salon d'Automne, had a front veneered in amboyna wood and an overall pattern of ivory bubbles; its chased-bronze lock by Foucault depicted allegorical figures representing night and day.

Emile-Jacques Ruhlmann, macassar ebony bedroom suite and wool carpet, 1920s.

SAARINEN Eero 1910–61 — Finnish

General Motors Technical Centre; TWA's Kennedy Terminal; Dulles Airport.

Eero Saarinen, son of the architect Eliel Saarinen (1873–1950), was brought up in the United States and studied in Paris and at Yale. His building designs varied greatly in style, displaying influences from the cubic-style work of MIES VAN DER ROHE to the organic, flowing shapes achieved in concrete by LE CORBUSIER at the Ronchamp chapel.

The influence of Mies van der Rohe is clearly seen in Saarinen's designs for the General Motors Technical Centre, Warren, Michigan (1948–56) – a project he completed with his father. The centre was composed of a series of buildings including an engine-testing centre, a generating station, an auditorium, an administrative block and restaurant. The structures, set in a landscaped park, were arranged around a rectangular, 22-acre lagoon above which rose a peculiar 132 ft, shining steel water-tower in the shape of a globe on slender legs. Most of the buildings were long, low-rise slabs incorporating expanses of plain brick and glass curtain walls. The latter, in typical Miesian style, were divided into grids of square glass panes.

Shortly after this project Saarinen worked on another Miesian-style block – the Bell Telephone Company Laboratories (1957–62) at Holmdel, New Jersey.

At almost the same time, and yet executed in a completely different style, came the curvilinear concrete TWA Terminal at Idlewild (now JFK) Airport (1956–62). The influence of Le Corbusier's Ronchamp chapel (1950–4) is obvious both in the use of reinforced concrete as the main structural material and of bold curves in the design. It is fitting for an airport that the terminal resembled a great mythical bird with broad outstretched wings. Saarinen said that his aim was "to design a building in which the architecture itself would express the drama and specialness and excitement of travel".

Immediately after this Saarinen received a commission (constructed after his death) for the Dulles Airport (1962–4) at Washington, DC. While the design was a little more restrained than that of the TWA terminal, the sculptural theme continued. The rectangular building was given a curved roof, raised high along one side of the building.

Saarinen's employment of different styles provides a barometer of contemporary fashion – some-

thing for which he felt no need to apologize. Indeed, he once declared: "I am a child of my period. I am enthusiastic about the three common principles of modern architecture: function, structure and being part of our time."

Eero Saarinen, TWA Terminal at Kennedy Airport, New York, 1956–62.

SAINT LAURENT Yves b.1936 — French

Inventive and flamboyant designs, sophisticated tailoring (since 1962).

Born in Algeria, in 1954 Saint Laurent entered the International Wool Secretariat design contest, which he won with a design for a black cocktail dress. As a result he was introduced to Michel Brunhoff, then editor of French *Vogue*, and enrolled for a pattern-cutting course in Paris. A few weeks later he was introduced to Christian DIOR, who employed him. In 1957 Saint Laurent took control of the design at the house of Dior, following the early death of his mentor. In the following year his first collection, featuring the trapeze look, was a great success. Subsequent collections, however, were not so successful and he was compelled to leave the company when he was called up to fight in the Algerian war. In his absence he was replaced by Marc Bohan, and on his return he sued the house of Dior for the loss of his job and opened his own house in 1962.

During the 1960s Saint Laurent was the greatest iconoclast in Paris fashion, as he searched for a style to reflect the contemporary student political unrest and Left Bank influences. Artists and artistic movements have exerted a continuing influence on his work. One of his most popular and widely copied looks,

Yves Saint Laurent, homage to Braque evening dress, summer 1988.

the Mondrian look, inspired by the De Stijl painter Piet Mondrian, was launched in 1965. Pop art inspired his 1966 collection, a Surrealist influence has also been evident in some of his designs, and his 1979 collection paid tribute to the work of Picasso.

As early as 1966 Saint Laurent became aware of the potential of the ready-to-wear market and established his Rive Gauche boutiques, projecting the new fashion ideal for the young and rich. He also realized that fashion was turning towards informality and casualness, and his 1970s day wardrobe relied on sophisticated blazers, trousers and shirts, while his evening wear has consistently been exciting, glamorous and elegant. His diversification into accessories, perfume and even bed-linen has spread his flamboyant influence over a wide range of goods. During the 1960s he created costumes for a number of stage productions, including Roland Petit's ballets, and for films such as Buñuel's *Belle de Jour*.

Yves Saint Laurent.

SANDBERG Willem 1897–1984   Dutch
museum director, graphic designer, artist and writer

Director of the Stedelijk Museum in Amsterdam (1945–62) and designer of their posters and catalogues.

Willem Sandberg's importance spans the international art, design and museum worlds. He initially studied art in Amsterdam and then during the 1920s travelled widely in Europe, whereby he came into contact with some of the great art and design innovators of that time (Otto NEURATH and the Isotype team, the BAUHAUS, etc.). In 1937 he was appointed Curator of Modern Art for the Stedelijk Museum in Amsterdam. But from the start of the Second World War he played a significant role in Dutch resistance activities, followed by a two-year period in hiding.

After the War, in 1945, he was appointed director of the Stedelijk Museum. Under his directorship, the museum became world-renowned for its painting and sculpture collection, which he expanded substantially, and its innovative exhibition techniques and lively presentation. In addition, Sandberg designed many of the Stedelijk's posters and exhibition catalogues, and developed a widely recognized style that incorporated rough textures (for example, brown wrapping paper, newsprint and torn edges), and his own distinct handling of typographic style and language – for he was also a writer of letters, books

Willem Sandberg, design for the Stedelijk Museum in Amsterdam, 1935.

and poetry. Much of this was pioneering work for its time, and his influence on the design and typographic world, consequently, has been enormous. He also introduced the world to the art and typographic experiments of the Dutch printer H. N. WERKMAN (killed during the war), who had a profound influence on Sandberg's own life and work.

Having retired from the Stedelijk in 1962, Sandberg continued to serve on advisory committees for the Israel Museum in Jerusalem, the Pompidou Centre in Paris, and various museums and societies in the Netherlands, and before his death received many awards for his immense contribution to the Dutch and international cultural scene.

SAPPER Richard b.1932   German
industrial designer

Tizio lamp for Artemide; coffee-maker for Alessi.

Sapper was born in Germany but his designs have a distinctly Italian flavour. He studied a variety of subjects at the University of Munich, including engineering, economics and graphics. His first work as a designer was for Mercedes-Benz in Stuttgart.

S

In 1957 Sapper began working in Milan with Gio PONTI and Alberto Rosselli and in 1959 he joined the design department of La Rinascente stores. Sapper is best known for the products he designed in partnership with Marco ZANUSO with whom he worked for over 20 years (from 1961). These include a series of products for Brion Vega: the Doney 14 television (1962), folding radio (1965) and the Black television (1969). The Black television started an enduring trend in black consumer products.

Sapper and Zanuso also worked on furniture together, including one of the first injection-moulded polyethylene chairs for Kartell in 1963.

In 1972 Sapper designed the Tizio lamp for Artemide, a low-voltage, counter-weighted task light which has proved one of his most popular products. The other is the widely acclaimed espresso coffee-maker for Alessi (1979). Sapper has also designed a three-tone whistling kettle for Alessi (1984) that has become a cult object.

His other products include clocks for Lorenz and Artemide, and since 1980 Sapper has been product design consultant to IBM. He has also worked on experimental vehicles for Fiat and on pneumatic structures for Pirelli.

SARPANEVA Timo b.1926   Finnish

designer in glass and other media

Glass and ceramic designs in association with numerous Scandinavian and other companies, particularly the Iittala glass factory.

One of the premier names in Scandinavian design since the 1950s, Sarpaneva received his initial artistic training in draughting and graphics. Like his compatriot Tapio WIRKKALA, he attended Helsinki's Central School of Industrial Design, from which he graduated in 1948, and where he was to teach textile design and printing from 1953 to 1957. In 1949 he won second prize in a design competition sponsored by the Riihimäki glassworks, and a year later he became associated with the Iittala glass factory, for whom he still designs.

The list of companies for which he has provided designs is long, impressive and international, as is the variety of media he has worked in: among other things, he was art director at the Porin Puuvilla cotton mill (1955–6); he created cast-iron cooking vessels and wrapping paper for W. Rosenlew (1959–63); and he designed *ryijy* rugs for Villayhtymä Oy (1960–2), candles

for Juhava Oy (1963), metalwork for both Primo Oy (1964) and Opa Oy (1970), and plastics for Ensto Oy (1988). In the late 1980s he also created glass for Corning in New York and Venini in Italy, and since 1970 he has designed Studio Line porcelain and other objects for ROSENTHAL AG of West Germany.

Sarpaneva's contributions to both textile design and actual production methods have been highly significant, most of his work in this field taking place in the late 1960s and 1970s, for such firms as Tampella, Finlayson Forssa and Ab Kinnasand. Most notably he devised a technique whereby designs could be printed on both sides of a fabric at the same time. Just as innovative and exciting were his advances in glass making; one such was the part-blown, part-cast method developed at Iittala in the early 1960s, wherein glass sculptures were cast into a wooden mould, part of which was burned in the process, thus producing a unique work of glass art. The moulds were re-used in their ever-altering forms, and some were even displayed by Sarpaneva as individual sculptural works.

The results of Sarpaneva's long-term association with Iittala glass are without doubt his most acclaimed works. Among the singular, outstanding masterpieces he created for them were the Lansetti sculptures (designed in 1952), whose bold, simple form – like a clear-glass teardrop encasing a pearl of opaque-white glass – has become an icon of Scandinavian design. Radically different in feel, but no less arresting, were the one-off sculptural pieces in the mid-1960s Finlandia series, such as Purkaus (Eruption). Sarpaneva designed useful ware as well as sculptural pieces, for instance his vertically fluted, rough-surfaced Festivo candlesticks (designed in 1967 and still in production), and his award-winning stacking bottles of 1959.

Recent years have seen Sarpaneva's work develop even further: the simple shapes of the Jurmo series of vases serve as backgrounds for mysterious landscape-like designs. More recently, the mid-1980s Claritas series of free-blown vessels has comprised substantial yet exquisite pieces offsetting black, silver and opaline elements with colourless glass and even suspended air bubbles.

In 1962 Sarpaneva set up a design office of his own, and throughout his long career he has received worldwide recognition, from medals at Milan's Triennale, to an International Design Award from the American Institute of Interior Designers, to an honorary doctorate from the Royal College of Art in London.

Timo Sarpaneva, Orkidea sculptures for Iittala Glass, 1953.

SASON Sixten 1912–69   Swedish

Car design (for Saab).

Sixten Sason, who trained first as an artist and then as an engineer, was an important Swedish industrial designer who was instrumental in helping the Swedish aircraft company, Svenska Aeroplan Aktiebolaget (Saab), diversify into car production at the end of the Second World War. The first Saab was designed to be a mass-production small car which could be built using aircraft production technology. The characteristic shape of the original Saab 92 is not attributed to Sason, but to the engineer Gunnar Ljungström. Sason, who was Saab's technical illustrator, developed Ljungström's concept for the Saab 92, but later Saabs – the Saab 96 and Saab 99 – were his own responsibility. The Saab 99, produced in 1969, was sketched out in 1960; its wedge shape was advanced for its time.

Sason was a versatile designer. Following his successes with Saab, he worked as a consultant designer on a number of other projects, notably the single-lens reflex Hasselblad camera in 1949, and vacuum cleaners for the Swedish Electrolux Corporation.

Sixten Sason, the first Saab, Model 92, designed in 1947, produced in 1949.

SCHEID Karl and Ursula b.1929 and 1932   German

Modern German ceramics of great visual and tactile appeal.

They each attended F.T. Schroeder's ceramics class at the Lehrwerkstätte für bildende Kunst in Darmstadt, Karl from 1949 to 1952, Ursula from 1952 to 1954. Since 1956 they have had their own workshop in Budingen-Dudelsheim. The Scheids are in the modern German pottery tradition of producing finely wrought pots which are subtly glazed. Pieces with relief decoration are by Karl, while the somewhat more rounded, not so sharply angled forms (apart from simple dishes and bowls) are by Ursula. The appeal of their work is to the eye and the hand – they are like attractive fruits.

SCHIAPARELLI Elsa 1890–1973   see page 204

SCHLUMBOHM Peter 1896–1962   German

Glass water kettle and Chemex coffee-maker, both in Pyrex.

By the time he died in the USA in 1962 Dr Schlumbohm held over 300 patents for inventions, and he is quoted as saying: "Inventors are original, non-compromising pioneers; designers are parasitic politicians." (*Design Since 1945.* Philadelphia Museum of Art, 1983). He made his mark first in refrigeration; then, in 1941, he produced the hourglass-shaped Chemex coffee-maker made from Pyrex glass, and formed a company to manufacture it. In 1949 he invented the Pyrex glass water kettle.

Victor PAPANEK says of Schlumbohm that he was able to find better, more simple and usually non-mechanical ways of doing things. The Chemex has been much copied, whilst the water kettle boils water faster because of its configuration – its design is the consequence of applied physics, not style. As Papanek also notes, everything that Schlumbohm designed was also reasonably priced.

SCOTT Douglas 1913–90   British

London Transport Routemaster bus.

Scott trained as a silversmith at the Central School of Arts and Crafts in London. In 1936 he joined Raymond LOEWY's London design office, then the only professional multidisciplinary design studio in Britain. Under the Loewy aegis Scott redesigned the Aga cooker and collaborated on the design of refrigerators and vacuum cleaners for Electrolux. The studio was closed in 1939. During the Second World War Scott worked for the aircraft manufacturer De Havilland, specializing in metallurgy and quality control. After the war he designed a number of industrial products, such as

SCHIAPARELLI

Elsa Schiaparelli, ceramic drum buttons, probably from her music collection, autumn 1939.

SCHIAPARELLI Elsa 1890–1973   Italian

fashion designer

Novel and Surrealist-inspired fashion and textiles (1936–9).

Schiaparelli received no formal design training but was educated in philosophy. She moved to Paris in 1920 and entered the fashion business six years later when a jumper she designed herself and wore to a society dinner was much admired by the other guests, who asked for copies. Schiaparelli had been inspired by the roughly textured jumpers knitted by the Armenian peasant women living in France. The design was black, with the *trompe-l'oeil* effect of a crude white patterned bow around the neck. In contrast to the ubiquitous Garçonne Look of the day, Schiaparelli designed her jumper to end at the waist, rather than the hips. Orders soon flooded in for these unusual garments, and in 1928 Schiaparelli, who had secured a workforce of Armenian women knitters, opened a shop called Pour Le Sport to sell them. She also featured jumpers with white collar and tie, and X-ray-effect rib designs. She opened her own couture house one year later, in 1929.

    Schiaparelli became one of the most successful Parisian *couturiers* of the 1930s. Parisian *couturiers* were generally well supported by the French textile manufacturers and Colcombet, one of the leading textile magnates, satisfied Schiaparelli's requests for unusual fabrics with designs featuring musical scores, tree bark and newspaper clippings (about herself). He also produced the much-publicized rose-coloured cellophane which Schiaparelli made up into an evening dress for her daring and wealthy American client, Mrs Harrison Williams. Schiaparelli also created and named

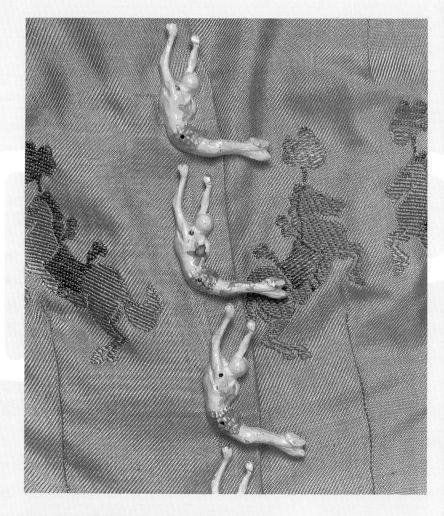

the vibrant colour "shocking pink". Her perfume, launched in 1938, was also named "Shocking". Schiaparelli had its bottle made to the exact proportions of the hour-glass figure of Mae West, the famous Hollywood film star. She was the first designer to exploit the zip (first patented in America by W. Litcomb Judson in 1893) as a decorative device, featuring them in contrasting colours to her garments from about 1935.

    Schiaparelli is most famous for her Surrealist fashions, from 1936. Surrealism was a confrontational art movement which aimed to change society by forcing its viewers to question their own perceptions of reality. The Surrealists featured images of paradox and dreams in their paintings, and the imagery and devices they employed greatly influenced fashion photography and illustration from the mid- to late 1930s, but Schiaparelli was one of the few *couturiers* directly to use them in their clothing. The basic styling of Schiaparelli's garments conformed to the lines of

Elsa Schiaparelli, circus jacket with embroidered motifs and ceramic acrobats, winter 1938.

Elsa Schiaparelli, *trompe l'oeil* jumper, designed 1926.

Elsa Schiaparelli, Tears evening dress, 1938.

1930s fashion: it was the decorative embellishments which she applied to these – and her millinery and accessories – which exploited Surrealist motifs and devices. She was assisted in her search for novelty by leading Surrealist painters of the day.

In 1937 Schiaparelli designed a fashionable, full-skirted, formal white evening dress, which defied convention because it had a large red lobster, complete with sprigs of parsley, splattered across the skirt. The image of the lobster greatly appealed to the Surrealists because it changed from its natural green-brown colour when under the sea to a bright red once cooked; they were fascinated by this type of transformation. Salvador Dali also designed a cover for a telephone receiver in the form of a lobster (about 1933) and Schiaparelli featured lobster buttons in her 1938 collection.

Dali combined forces with Schiaparelli to create many of her garments, accessories and shop interiors. Schiaparelli, in return, dressed Dali's wife Gala free of charge. Dali provided the inspiration for her much publicized Shoe hat of 1936, which was made in black velvet with a shocking pink heel. He also collaborated with her to produce her Tears dress in 1938. This fashionably shaped evening dress was made in pink silk crêpe with a print which gave the illusion of the dress being torn, with shreds of fabric hanging down. This challenged traditional notions of respectability and the formality of evening wear. Dali also dyed a stuffed bear shocking pink and put drawers in its stomach for the eccentric British collector, Edward James, who lent it to Schiaparelli to stand in her shop.

Schiaparelli also worked with Jean Cocteau and Christian Bérard, who designed unusual embroideries for her garments. Schiaparelli was also famous for the understated, elegant garments which she designed for her less adventurous clientele, but even these were often treated in a Surrealist manner in the fashion press. André Durst, Cecil Beaton and Hoyningen Heune photographed her models surrounded by coils of rope, which hurtled into oblivion, and posed them in front of cracked mirrors, which distorted their image. Christian Bérard illustrated her models floating on tasselled curtain swags and standing, isolated, on beaches dominated by oversize shells.

During the late 1930s Schiaparelli's collections were designed in themes. In 1937 she produced a music collection, in which the textiles and accessories incorporated musical iconography. In the winter of 1938 she produced a circus collection. This included textiles with clown prints designed by Bérard, circus-horse embroideries by LESAGE, acrobat-shaped buttons and cone-shaped clown hats. Her pagan collection featured insects, caterpillar clasps, foliage, fruit and flowers. Her astrology collection, in the spring of 1938, incorporated the signs of the zodiac and beautifully embroidered night skies by Lesage.

Schiaparelli's jewellery and accessories have also become legendary. Buttons were made in the shape of padlocks, peanuts, spoons, can-can dancers, four-leaf clovers, lips, hands and eyes. These last three items, displaced from the rest of the body, appeared in many Surrealist paintings. Her bags were made to resemble telephones and birdcages. She designed clear plastic necklaces embedded with black plastic bugs and flies. Surrealism has remained a potent source of inspiration to fashion designers, especially in the 1980s.

Schiaparelli left France in 1940 and moved to America for the duration of the Second World War. She re-opened in 1945 and retired in 1954.

S

navigational equipment for merchant ships and battery-testing units for the British Army.

The period between 1945 and the early 1960s was especially fruitful, because he worked extensively for London Transport, designing coaches and buses. He did not design on his own (London Transport had, as it has now, its own design teams), but he led the way on several innovations, including the RF Observation Coach (1948), and the prototype Routemaster London bus of 1953. This led to the design that Scott is most famous for, the 1959 London Routemaster bus, for years one of the most potent symbols of London. Scott's designs for the London Fire Brigade (the AEC Regent fire engine, 1953) and for the telephone service (telephone pay boxes, 1963) have remained in service for decades. His work has involved the design of petrol service stations, aircraft seating, heavy industrial machinery and kitchen and bathroom equipment.

Douglas Scott, Routemaster bus for London Transport, 1957.

SEYMOUR POWELL founded 1984   British

`product design consultancy`

Domestic products for Tefal; motorcycle designs for Norton.

Seymour Powell is a relatively young British design consultancy which has nevertheless made its mark with projects for international clients such as Tefal, Yamaha, Norton, ICI, Clairol and Philips.

The consultancy was formed in 1984 by Richard Seymour and Dick Powell. Seymour had trained as a graphic designer at the Central School of Art and the Royal College of Art, and went on to spend six years working in advertising. Powell had studied industrial design at Manchester Polytechnic and at the Royal College of Art, and worked for six years as a designer before teaming up with Seymour.

They describe their style of design as "soft tech", which means that they play down the technological sophistication of the products they work on and create a softer, often more rounded shape. This is particularly evident in the domestic products they have designed for Tefal, the first of which, the Freeline jug-kettle, was launched in 1987. Seymour Powell has since designed a sandwich-maker, a coffee-maker and a deep-fat fryer for Tefal.

Seymour Powell has also worked on two motorcycle projects for the British company Norton. The Commander, a paramilitary bike for the police and army, was launched in 1987. The second bike, the P55

road-bike, is a highly original design with an almost totally enclosed body. The idea, according to the designers, was to give it an image "more like a Porsche", rather than a racing bike.

A number of Seymour Powell's designs rely on a substantial input of engineering expertise, but both designers believe that the artistic input in styling a product is just as important. They see styling as a vital part of their work. It is styling which can endow a product with what they call the "X-factor".

Seymour Powell also undertake speculative projects which have attracted widespread attention. These include the skeletal and distinctive Blackhawk Stutz guitar and the motorized bicycle wheel, which effectively turns a bike into a moped.

SHIU-KAY Kan b.1949   Hong Kong

`lighting designer`

Innovation in lighting design.

Shiu-Kay Kan was born in Hong Kong. He trained as an architect at Central London Polytechnic and the Architectural Association and then worked for the British high-tech architects Foster Associates and Italian retailers FIORUCCI. In the mid-1970s he established his own lighting design firm, SKK Lighting and launched the Kite Light as the first product, which proved a tremendous success. Since then he has led British technical and formal innovation in lighting design.

SKK experimented with new technology, particularly the low-voltage fittings so much in demand in the field of retail design. During 1983–8 SKK developed the futuristic Mobile Robotic Light. This consists of two horizontal wires which can span a room and along which the mobile lighting unit, carrying two spotlights, can be remotely driven. SKK now runs its own retail outlet as well as a consultancy for contract interior-lighting schemes.

SINCLAIR Clive b.1940   British

`industrial designer`

Miniaturized electronic goods, including the first pocket calculator and the ZX80 computer.

Sir Clive Sinclair's chief contribution in the field of design has been the miniaturization of electronic goods. Born in Richmond, Surrey, Sinclair left school at 17 to work as a technical journalist. In 1962 he founded

Sinclair Radionics to sell radio and amplifier kits by mail order. His greatest early innovation was the world's first pocket calculator, which he launched in 1972. The Executive calculator won acclaim from design experts for its sleek, black plastic casing and went on display at the Museum of Modern Art, New York. Sinclair's next innovation was the miniature television, introduced in 1977. This was quickly followed by the launch of the Black Watch, a revolutionary timepiece in moulded black plastic with a five-digit LED display

To rescue flagging finances after the commercial failure of the Black Watch and increasing competition in the pocket calculator market, Sinclair decided to produce an affordable and easy-to-use home computer. The ZX80 was launched in 1980; costs were kept to a minimum with the use of a television set for a monitor and cassette player as program and data store. Two years later came the equally affordable Spectrum range with colour graphics, used mainly for games-playing in the home.

Sinclair's biggest marketing tragedy was the C5, introduced in 1985. The small, electronically powered car was perhaps ahead of its time, coming before concern about the environment had become a popular issue. In 1986 Sinclair founded the Cambridge Computer Company to concentrate on research.

Clive Sinclair, pocket calculator, designed 1972.

SITE founded 1970 — American
architecture and environmental art practice

Environmental art projects; known for jokey visual puns.

SITE grew out of an artistic debate whose protagonists were the writer and artist Alison Sky and the sculptor James Wines, who met in 1965. They rejected conventional distinctions between the arts, the isolation of artists from the mainstream of modern public life and the idea that art is a special activity. They advocated a return to a tradition of architecture as art, and used the term "De-Architecture" to describe their opposition to the Modernist Movement, which lacked all cultural relevance because of its dependency on technical formalist design.

The organization SITE (Sculpture in the Environment) was formed in 1970 and worked on a number of environmental art projects. Their breakthrough came with commissions for a series of shopping centres. The first was "Peeling Project" (1971–2), which was followed by "Tilt Showroom" (1976–8) and

"Intermediate Facade" (1974–5).

While their work is radically anti-modern in its overriding concern with the cultural meaning of architecture, SITE rejects the post-modern attempt to make architecture relevant by historical and metaphorical allusion. Despite appearances to the contrary, SITE is not part of the Deconstructionist movement and does not see architecture as a formal language. Instead, Wines claims that their iconography derives from Jungian ideas about the unconscious.

During the 1980s SITE's programme has been applied to many retail projects, exhibition and public spaces. It is the humour which may be found in their work which clearly appeals to commercial clients, as in their floating McDonald's restaurant (1983). But Wines feels that the "very simple and iconic ideas of the 1970s" set the stage for all subsequent work.

SITE, Best Products Notch Showroom, Sacramento, California, 1977.

SMART DESIGN founded 1979 — American
design consultancy

Corning eyeglasses, Copo tableware, Knoll International accessories.

Based in New York City, Smart Design is exemplary of the new generation of American design consultancies. Its founders, Davin Stowell and Tom Dair, graduates of Syracuse University, and Tucker Viemeister, a graduate of New York's Pratt Institute, established Smart Design after leaving college without passing through the customary apprenticeship with another consultancy.

Smart Design represents a third force in American design, more informal than the now traditional offices that continue to work under great names such as Henry DREYFUSS and Walter Dorwin TEAGUE, but without the European affinities of some other practices, such as that of Morison Cousins in New York or many of the industrial designers who serve the

S

Silicon Valley computer industry.

With a loose hierarchy and happy-go-lucky attitude, the firm resembles a design school studio more than a conventional consultancy. Its designers are equally adept at design for high-volume consumer products or temporary installations for downtown galleries. Smart Design specializes in industrial and consumer products, product graphics, packaging and corporate identity.

Among its best designs are a range of melamine tableware in bright colours and patterns for Copco and a continuing series of eyewear for Corning Optics that runs from high tech to high fashion.

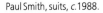

Paul Smith.

SMITH Paul b.1946   British

fashion designer

Modern and colourful classics for men.

Paul Smith's father was a general outfitter, and he in turn became involved in the rag trade at the age of 15, when he helped a friend to open and run a clothing shop. He opened his own shop in 1970. During this period he was instrumental in the formation of Brown's, which formed an outlet for young and creative as well as established British and international clothing designers in London. Three years later he left to form his own collection, and became designer and managing director of Paul Smith Ltd.

Smith has consistently placed emphasis on style and comfort, imbuing classical designs with bold and subtle pattern, colour and wit. His design sources are varied: his spring/summer 1990 collection combines eclectic inspiration from ethnic cultures, the Englishman abroad and 1960s bohemianism. Although he designs for men, many Paul Smith garments are also worn with enjoyment by women. Smith has always designed all his clothes and has established close connections with manufacturers.

There are six Paul Smith shops in England, five of which are in London. In addition to Smith's clothes, these also house a selection of modern accessories and small household objects – watches, jewellery, glassware and sculpture. The traditional styling and layout of his shops has been copied by numerous retailers of fashion. His clothes also enjoy great popularity in Japan, which supports 40 Smith shops, all of which are styled on the model of the British shops. This has involved the export of an entire chemist's shop interior from Sheffield and a chocolate shop from Newcastle.

Paul Smith, suits, c.1988.

SMITHSON Peter and Alison founded 1950   British

architectural firm

Hunstanton School; Economist Building; Robin Hood Gardens.

The husband-and-wife team, Peter (b. 1923) and Alison Smithson (b. 1928), formed a professional partnership in 1950 and were at the vanguard of the post-war British architectural movement known as the new brutalists. The brutalists admired the work of LE CORBUSIER and considered it important to use materials in an "honest" way – for example, by leaving concrete rough and unpainted. The designs too were kept plain, based on simple rectangles and squares and incorporating no ornamentation.

The couple were members of a number of radical, left-wing intellectual groups such as Team Ten, the 20th Century Group and the Independent Group which despised cultural snobbery, revelled in the popular culture of advertisements and pop music and explored – through paintings, photographs and philosophy – the rough grain of post-war urban living.

The Smithsons' early work has been highly influential, not least in inspiring modern school design and in municipal housing. Immediately after the Second World War, when Britain's bomb-damaged towns and cities were being rebuilt, the couple rejected prevalent ideas on the creation of garden cities and became fascinated with finding a new style of city development – something they called "Urban Re-identification".

Their early designs, such as the competition entry for a block of flats at Golden Lane in the East End (1952), showed the influence of Le Corbusier's Unité d'Habitation in Marseilles (1947–52); it was designed, like the Unité, to incorporate wide walkways lined by flats at each floor. The Smithsons declared that it was possible to recreate working-class street life on each storey above ground, calling the idea "street decks". Golden Lane was never built, but the idea was eventually adopted and built by Lynn, Smith and Nicklin at Park Hill in Sheffield (1961).

The Smithsons' first major project to be completed was the innovative Hunstanton School in Norfolk (1949–53). The series of buildings broke away from the traditional idea of designing a school building around a central play yard. The flat-roofed, rectangular blocks of one, two and three storeys drew inspiration from the work of MIES VAN DER ROHE with the incorporation of exposed, welded steel frames, precast

Peter and Alison Smithson,
The Economist Building,
London, 1962–4.

Peter and Alison Smithson,
The Economist Building,
London, 1962–4.

concrete slabs, plain brick walls and bands of windows formed from square panes of glass.

Moving away from the public sector, their next major commission was for the Economist Building (1962–4) in London's St James's Street. Here the Smithsons faced the difficult task of designing a contemporary building for a predominantly 18th-century street. The solution was the construction of three towers of different heights linked by a piazza.

The buildings were finished in honey-coloured stone to tone with the rest of the street. The plan of the three structures explored the Smithsons' ideas of building in clusters, which they saw as the way forward for cities of the future.

They returned to designing mass housing at the Robin Hood Gardens project in Poplar (1968–72). The two snaking, multi-storey walls of flats stood on either side of a small landscaped park. Here, at last, they succeeded in building the street decks first conceived, almost 20 years earlier, for Golden Lane.

SOM founded 1936 — American

architectural firm

Lever House; Marine Gunnery School; Sears Tower; Haj Terminal; Rowes Wharf.

The American architects Louis Skidmore (1897–1962) and Nathaniel Owings (1903–1984) became partners in 1936 and were joined by John Merrill (1896–1975) in 1939. Theirs has been one of the most successful partnerships in producing large numbers of corporate office buildings.

SOM specializes in huge commercial premises and built its first major commission, Lever House, New York (1951–2), at a time when America's economy was well on its way to recovery following the Depression and the Second World War. It is one of the earliest

John Merrill, Nathaniel Owings and Louis Skidmore of the SOM partnership.

glass-cased skyscrapers. Such was the success of the building that the design was adopted as a standard corporate style.

The MIES VAN DER ROHE influence and the availability of increasingly sophisticated materials were demonstrated at the Marine Gunnery School, Great Lakes, Illinois (1954). Designed as a huge shed, the rectangular box was given a smooth finish in square panes of dark glass.

One of SOM's most famous commissions was for the Sears Tower in Chicago (1971). Constructed again as a glass-covered steel frame, it was built at the same time as New York's World Trade Center, designed by Minoru Yamasaki. The contest to be tallest was won by the Sears Tower which stands, at 1450 ft, 100 ft higher than the World Trade Center.

The Company continues to operate despite the deaths of its founding partners, and, together with more glass-clad skyscrapers, has completed unusual designs for the Haj Terminal, Jeddah (1981–2), and Rowes Wharf, Boston, Massachusetts (1985–7).

Skidmore, Owings & Merrill, John Hancock Center, Chicago, 1970.

S

SONY founded 1946   Japanese

Sony Walkman personal stereo system.

Sony is one of Japan's best known companies in the West being synonymous in Western eyes with two key elements: high-tech electronics and good design. This achievement is to the credit of Sony's inspired chairman, Akio Morita. Unusually for Japanese businessmen, Morita has encouraged a high personal profile, and has been nicknamed "Mister Transistor" by the world's press.

The Sony Corporation started with a group of 20 people in 1946. From this modest start in the uncertain conditions of post-war Japan, Sony developed into an international company with the reputation of a quality brand leader. Morita and his partner, an engineer called Masaru Ibuka, moved quickly in 1952 to secure the American patent rights to a new invention, the transistor. In 1954 Morita developed the first transistor radio in Japan and in 1957 moved to America. During the following five years he revolutionized the company's selling methods, employing the well-known advertising agency Doyle, Dane, Bernbach, who had worked on the legendary Volkswagen campaign. The first move was to change the original company name of Tokyo Tsushin Kogyo Kabushika Kaisha to Sony.

The first Sony product to catch the public's eye (in 1959) was the TV 8-301, the first all-transistor portable television with an 8-inch screen. Since then televisions have become a key product for the company, and in 1968 it followed up the 8-301 with the first version of the famous Trinitron range, now an obligatory accessory for the designer home. The company's most famous product, however, was developed in 1979, a personal stereo system called the Sony Walkman. This product has become the archetypal Japanese success story.

Sony Walkman II.

SOTTSASS Ettore b.1917   see page 212

SOWDEN George J. b.1942   British

Furniture and interiors for Memphis.

George Sowden was the only British designer to make a substantial contribution to the radical Memphis Group of Italian designers. Born in Leeds, England, he trained as a designer at Cheltenham College of Art from 1966 to 1968, after which he founded his own furniture design business. In 1970 he moved to Milan to work as a computer design consultant for OLIVETTI, where he came into contact with Ettore SOTTSASS. Sowden was one of a group of young, adventurous designers whom Sottsass chose to work with when he formed the Memphis Group in 1981. The Group's mixture of 1950s revivalism and witty, colourful designs galvanized the Italian design scene. Sowden created furniture and interiors for Memphis and his research into decorated surfaces inspired the Luxor wardrobe, which he showed at the second Memphis exhibition of 1982. This piece had a bold, screenprinted pink and blue pattern on the door and his later experiments in interior design used similar contrasting patterns in pastel shades.

George J. Sowden, Palace chair for Memphis, 1983.

George J. Sowden, stainless steel fruit bowl for Bodum, 1987.

Sowden successfully translated such flat patterns into three-dimensional forms with designs for tableware. The Swiss company of Bodum commissioned a stainless steel fruit bowl from Sowden in 1987 which has amoeboid shapes decorating the rim and rectilinear cut-outs around the base, providing a touch of post-modern wit. Sowden now works as an independent consultant designer, often in partnership with Nathalie du PASQUIER.

SPEER Albert 1905–81   German

Work for Hitler and the Third Reich.

Speer trained under Heinrich Tessenow and at the age of 29 became Hitler's personal architect.

Hitler disliked much of the modern architecture which was being constructed in Germany during the early 1930s, particularly the flat-roofed, cubic-

Albert Speer, German Pavilion at Paris World Exhibition, 1937.

shaped houses, decrying it as un-German and as a product of Communism. However, while there was no official Nazi doctrine on architecture, Hitler's megalomania led him to commission enormous classical-style buildings which he considered the most appropriate forms in which to express visual evidence of his power.

Speer indulged Hitler's fantasies and created the settings for much Nazi pageantry. Among his first designs were those for Nuremberg – a complex consisting of a German Stadium to hold 405,000 people (commenced 1937), a large square to accommodate 540,000, the Marzfeld parade ground (700 × 900 m) and the Zeppelinfeld Stadium for the Nuremberg rally of 1937. Each structure was to be built entirely of stone.

The German Stadium was intended to stand to the glory of the German nation and to impress the world. It was half completed at the outbreak of the Second World War and was built on a plan some 540 m long by 445 m wide. The raked arena seating rose 90 m high. The designs were borrowed from the Panathenaic stadium of ancient Athens, with a temple-like colonnaded entrance reached by a flight of wide steps.

The Zeppelinfeld was also built on a massive scale and had as its focus a grandstand, its design drawing on the styles used by the ancient Egyptians, Babylonians, Greeks and Romans. Also in 1937 came the construction of Speer's German Pavilion at the Paris World Exhibition, with its great stone tower, entered by a long flight of steps and topped by an eagle with outstretched wings.

The following year saw the building of Speer's New Chancellery in Berlin, which has since been des-

troyed. This again was a showy set-piece and an exercise in intimidation intended to reflect Hitler's great power. It was built in just 18 months. Visitors entered by the column-flanked portal set in the Courtyard of Honour and then had a 200-yard walk passing through a vestibule, a mosaic room, round hall and long, gaudily decorated marble-lined corridor before reaching Hitler's salon and office.

One of Speer's last projects, in collaboration with Hitler, was the redesigning of Berlin. Work was never begun, but models show a city based on ideas taken from Paris, ancient Rome and Washington. There was to be included a wide, central avenue with a triumphal arch in Hitler's honour and a great domed hall, the largest in the world, as its focal point.

Speer became minister for armaments and munitions between 1942 and 1945. He was sentenced to 20 years in jail at the Nuremberg Trials for his use of slave labour. In 1969 he published his memoirs, entitled *Inside the Third Reich*.

SPENCE Basil 1907–76   British

architect

Coventry Cathedral; Household Cavalry Barracks.

Sir Basil Spence trained in Edinburgh and spent his early career designing country houses in Scotland. However, after the Second World War he had the opportunity to design on a large scale when he won the 1951 competition to design a new cathedral at Coventry.

Spence's new cathedral, consecrated in 1962, was built alongside the war-damaged ruins of the old, Gothic-style structure. In the optimistic atmosphere of post-war Britain there was a strong desire to escape from traditional designs and build in new styles. The experimentation extended to ecclesiastical buildings, and Coventry Cathedral was to stand as a symbol of a new, progressive Britain.

Spence made few attempts to make his new cathedral harmonize with the old. It was designed as a square mass, with little traditional detailing. It was, however, constructed of the same pale red Holington stone as its neighbour. The interior walls were faced with concrete and coarse-textured plaster, and the ceiling canopy was of criss-crossed concrete ribs; the diamond spaces in between were filled with wooden pyramids. The altar was in textured concrete.

In the spirit of cathedral-building in the Middle

Sir Basil Spence.

▶ page 214

SOTTSASS

Ettore Sottsass, adjustable typist's chair from Serie 45 office furniture for Olivetti, 1973.

SOTTSASS Ettore b.1917   Italian

architect, product and furniture designer

Founder of the Memphis design co-operative.

Ettore Sottsass was the most fashionable designer of the 1980s, successfully balancing a variety of roles as ageing *enfant terrible*, serious design consultant, sage, sceptic and philosopher. He is an enterprising entrepreneur, an opportunist and an artist. He was born in Innsbruck, Austria, the son of an architect, studied at Turin Polytechnic, from which he graduated in 1939; he went into the army, became a prisoner of war and survived to begin his career.

Sottsass's first job was as an interior designer, but he worked also for the Fiat carriage works in Turin. He joined the architectural practice of Giuseppe Pagano in 1945, but left to set up his own studio in Milan in 1946 and continued to work as a freelance designer and architect, specializing in interiors and exhibition design. He also worked on housing projects for the INA-Casa scheme, part of the Marshall plan for the postwar reconstruction of Northern Italian towns.

After a brief period in New York in 1956 working for George Nelson, the American furniture designer, Sottsass returned to Italy where, in 1957, he began working as a consultant to OLIVETTI; his designs from this period include the Tekne 3 electric typewriter and the Praxis 48. Meanwhile, he was still pursuing interests in the broader field of arts and design including sculpture, painting, ceramics, jewellery, lithographs and designs for scarves.

Signs of a radical departure in Sottsass's work from the prevailing Italian design ethic (championed by designers such as Gio PONTI and Marcello NIZZOLI), which was cool, chic and geared to affluent living,

came in 1965 with the furniture he designed for Paltronova. This was the first evidence of what came to be known as anti-design, the movement which developed throughout the 1960s.

The politics and motivations of Italian design are fluid: when a phrase such as "anti-design" entered the design vocabulary, it was not always clear who or what was being opposed. Sottsass is too clever to be pinned down, but if he is clearly opposed to anything, then it is to what he sees as the dogma of the rationalist West German school of design, as, for example, in the work of Dieter RAMS.

Anti-rationalist design in Italy was inspired by pop art and by *arte povera* and performance art; it was based on an interesting argument coined by Sottsass and taken up by other Italian designer-philosophers such as Andrea Branzi. This was that there is no such thing as *good* design, or rather, what is good is what the majority of the public likes. Consequently, if the public likes cocktail bars with padded furniture, then padded furniture is good design.

This does not mean that the new-wave Italian designers who followed Sottsass and Branzi into majority taste design necessarily liked it or endorsed it. What they tended to do was "quote" from kitsch or popular culture. Thus they both embrace popular taste and keep their distance from it, because quoting someone does not entail agreeing with that person. For an early example of Sottsass quotation there is his celebrated design for a typist's chair for Olivetti (Sistema 45, 1968), which is alleged to refer to Mickey Mouse in the design of the chair's feet.

In the late 1970s and 1980s Sottsass and his associates were busy devising confections which referred to lower-middle-class Italian taste and working-

Ettore Sottsass, Esamesa
bench, marble.

class American kitsch, and mixing it all up in a cocktail that included classicism, neo-classicism, modernism, post-modernism and, of course, ad-hocism. It does not matter if you do not understand the "isms" – these were part of the insider game of Italian design. Sottsass is both the great insider of Italian designer cliques and a populist identifying with the public. His genius is in playing *both* teams.

Sottsass has all the contradictions about taste, design and consumerism tied up. To the question "What *is* design?" he says: (1) design has to be as near as possible to the need a society has for an image of itself. (2) Design must follow the changes in history. In other words, Sottsass does not believe in static absolutes in design: even the notion of classical design is thrown into confusion, because "classic" implies "unchanging", and Sottsass believes design must and does change as we and our culture change. When pressed to discuss hierarchies in design, Sottsass spun the question back onto the interlocutor like a champion Frisbee thrower: "I don't understand why pyramids are better than Burmese straw huts."

On the contentious matter of the designer's role in encouraging waste he remarked: "If society plans obsolescence then the only possible enduring design is one that deals with that obsolescence."

In 1979 Sottsass joined STUDIO ALCHYMIA in Milan. Alchymia became known for its brightly coloured, patterned and playful furniture, conceived as a part of the experimentation into alternative design.

In the following year, with a group of similarly-minded individuals, including Michael GRAVES and Arata Isozaki, Sottsass set up MEMPHIS, a co-operative manufacturing furniture, ceramics and lights in the same post-modernist vein as Alchymia, which it super-

seded. Sottsass has said that he believes Memphis to be the signature design of the 1980s. The influence of Memphis was felt worldwide, and while its designs were produced only in limited editions, its style had enormous appeal to designers and design critics, and this appeal, mediated through the conservative thinking of marketing executives, influenced the design and decoration of consumer goods in the mid-to-late 1980s. Sottsass provided the arguments for designers to play around, for his logic is, as ever, incontestable, if you take him on his own ground: "A table may need four legs to function but no one can tell me that the four legs have to look the same."

Ettore Sottsass, Console
table, marble.

Sir Basil Spence, Coventry Cathedral, 1954–62.

Ages, Spence commissioned a number of works by eminent British artists; the great window of the baptistery was designed by John Piper, and a tapestry depicting Christ was designed by Graham Sutherland. Five pairs of abstract stained-glass windows, by Graham Clarke, Keith New and Lawrence Lee, were set into the two walls flanking the altar.

During the 1960s Spence also worked on designs for the new Sussex University at Stanmer Park, outside Brighton, and on the Abbotsinch Airport Terminal Building, Glasgow (1964–6).

Among his last commissions was the Household Cavalry Barracks in Knightsbridge (1970). This complex of heavy, slabbed concrete has received much criticism and was described by the late Norman Parkinson, photographer, as "a monstrous concrete mess". However, it also had admirers such as Sir Nikolaus Pevsner, who described it as "a very impressive achievement".

Knighted for his work as President of the RIBA, Spence received many awards including the Grande Medaille d'Or of the French Academy of Architects.

Erik Spiekermann at MetaDesign, type specimen booklet, 1987.

SPIEKERMANN Erik b.1947 — German

graphic and typographic designer

Author of *Rhyme & Reason: a Typographic Novel.*

When hot-metal typesetting gave way to new technology in the 1970s (via photosetting and digital typesetting), Erik Spiekermann emerged as a bright, young spokesman for the new typographic era. While others fretted about the damning influence and unlimited freedom of the new computerized systems, Spiekermann remained respectful of old traditions and scholarship, but dedicated to the creation of new standards and a new type aesthetic. Over a decade later, he has become an internationally renowned typographic authority, praised not only for his achieve-

ments as a graphic designer and type designer, but also for his writing and lecturing.

Spiekermann was born in Stadthagen, West Germany, and studied History of Art and English at Berlin's Free University in the late 1960s. During the 1970s he lived and worked in London (and at times in Berlin), teaching at the London College of Printing and other British schools, and working as a freelance designer in both cities along the way. In 1977 he produced his first type designs for H. Berthold AG – LoType, Block and Berliner Grotesk. By 1981 he had settled in Berlin, where he has been based ever since. His first book, *Ursache & Wirkung: ein Typografischer Roman*, was published in 1982; the English version, *Rhyme & Reason: a Typographic Novel*, in 1987.

In the mid-1980s Spiekermann became consultant to H. Berthold AG; designed a corporate typeface for Deutsche Bundespost; and formed his own design studio, MetaDesign, which now specializes in corporate design and complex design systems for clients all over the world, including Apple Computers, Adobe Systems, Berthold and others.

Spiekermann has written numerous articles on all aspects of visual communication; his books, however, deserve special mention. *Rhyme & Reason* has reputedly sold over 25,000 copies since it was first published. A handbook for typographic enthusiasts, it offers an entertaining introduction to typography for beginners, while also providing insights and "fine-tuning" hints that are more likely to be appreciated by professionals. The second book, published in German in 1989 and also written for students, is titled (in English) *All I've always wanted to know about type & typography but never dared to ask*.

Erik Spiekermann is a member of the Typeface Review Board of ITC (International Typeface Corporation) in New York; a member of the Board of Directors of the ATypI (Association Typographique Internationale); and belongs to numerous other professional associations and institutions.

STABLER Harold 1872–1945 — British

silversmith and metalwork and pottery designer

Designs in metalwork, ceramics and other media, encompassing both Arts and Crafts and Modern movements.

The long, distinguished career of Harold Stabler began in the Arts and Crafts mode and continued through to

Erik Spiekermann at MetaDesign, printed ephemera for Berthold mid-to late 1980s.

Erik Spiekermann.

the age of modernism, and throughout the 50 or so years he devoted to the arts, he created an amazing variety of highly praised objects, both unique and mass-produced, in several media and markedly different styles. Born in Levens, Westmorland (now Cumbria), Stabler studied woodworking, stone-carving and metalworking at the Kendal School of Art, then taught metalworking at the Keswick School of Industrial Art, the Cumberland (Cumbria) craft school. Stabler became a full-time director at Keswick by about 1898, but left soon after to join the Liverpool University Art School's department of metalworking. Early in the 1900s he taught at the Sir John Cass Technical Institute (Stabler became its Art School's head in 1907, a post he held until 1937). In addition, he was a teacher at the Royal College of Art from 1912 to around 1926.

The range of media Stabler was involved in included ceramics, hand-wrought silver, glass and graphics (posters for the London Underground, for which he also created decorative tiles). With his wife, he produced exquisite silver and enamel jewellery and other bejewelled objects.

It was in his varied metalwork that his outstanding design abilities, as well as technical virtuosity, were best manifested. His adaptability to modern production methods after the First World War was in marked contrast to his previous hand-crafted pieces, but a logical step after his helping to found the Designs & Industries Association in 1915. This largely resulted from his growing dissatisfaction with the Arts and Crafts exhibitions he had long participated in and his contact with the 1914 Deutscher Werkbund Exhibition

in Cologne. He had attended that landmark show with Ambrose Heal and the two, together with Harry Peach, W.R. Lethaby and others, set up the DIA to promote higher standards of design, to promulgate co-operation between design and industry and, in general, to give the modern designer a better name and more visibility. Stabler threw himself whole-heartedly into designing for industry, but did not wholly forsake his creations of specially commissioned, unique pieces.

One of Stabler's most interesting excursions into modern metal production was his 1930s association with the Sheffield stainless-steel manufacturer, Firth Vickers. Firth Vickers commissioned Stabler to provide them with a series of prototypes with etched and applied ornament, desirous as they were of introducing British companies to the product. The Cumberland tea set Stabler designed in 1938 was still in production in the 1950s.

Deservedly, Stabler received much critical and public acclaim over the years. Among his honours, in 1936 the Royal Society of Arts named him one of its first 10 Designers for Industry (along with Eric GILL, H.G. Murphy, Keith MURRAY and others). Indeed, he was one of the few designers of the late 19th and early 20th centuries who effectively and uncompromisingly straddled the Victorian era Arts and Crafts Movement and the forward-thinking Modern Movement.

STAM Mart b.1899   see BREUER

STARCK Philippe b. 1949   French

industrial designer, particularly of furniture

Tubular and pressed-metal furniture for Driade.

Philippe Starck is best known for his metal furniture designs but during the late 1980s he broadened his output to include consumer goods, interior design and architecture.

Starck began his professional career working with Pierre CARDIN. He came to wide public notice early in the 1980s by designing furniture for President Mitterrand's private suite in the Elysée Palace. Starck progressed to produce tubular and pressed-metal furniture designs for the Italian company Driade. These designs include the Tippy Jackson folding table in varnished iron (1982); the Von Vogelsang chair (1984); and the Titos Apostos folding table (1985).

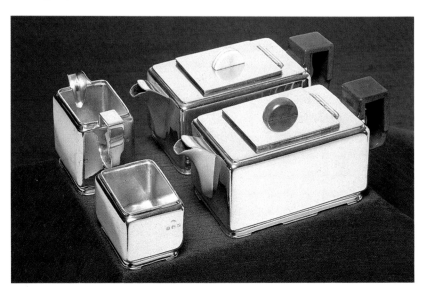

Harold Stabler, silver tea set with wood and ivory finials, made by Adie Brothers Ltd. of Birmingham, 1935.

S

Philippe Starck, stackable chairs in polymer and steel rod for Kartell in Milan.

His furniture tends to be insect-like, thin and made from pressed metal, and to rest on three legs rather than four. Good examples of Starck's attenuated style are the 1987 designs for Driade, especially the Insecte chair and the Joe Ship table. His non-furniture commissions have included work for Renault (he was commissioned to design a special "edition" of the Espace motor car); he has also designed television sets, a wrist-watch and a cigarette lighter.

Starck's ventures into architecture and interior design, which began with the Elysée Palace, have been consolidated in Tokyo. His first commission in Tokyo was for the interior of the Manin Restaurant (1987). One walks across a steel bridge which spans the restaurant, and enters the dining area by descending a spectacular staircase which cascades down two storeys to the ground floor. The furniture, designed by Starck, was produced by CASSINA, Japan.

The 1990s began with the realization of Starck's first architectural designs in Tokyo. He was commissioned by the Asahi Beer Company to produce a headquarters building. The top of the building is crowned with an extraordinary gold-coloured horn-like appendage which weighs 360 tons, is 43 metres long and looks like a stranded abstracted whale. The building itself is in black granite, the windows are like portholes and the interior features another Starck restaurant with a precipitous staircase. The second of Starck's Tokyo buildings, called Nani Nani, also opened in 1990 – although it is basically an office block, it is covered in a ribbed copper sheath, making it look like a cross between a giant mollusc and a warrior's helmet.

Deyan Sudjic, the design critic, has drawn a convincing parallel between Philippe Starck and Raymond LOEWY. Both are French, both are superb showmen, both are in love with America. Starck is quoted as saying: ". . .it's perhaps that American influence which has shaped my work, to the extent that I work instinctively, and above all fast. I can design a good piece of furniture in 15 minutes. . ." (*Blueprint*. April 1987).

STERN Robert A.M. b.1939   American

architect and author

Prolific New York post-modern classicist.

On completing his studies at Columbia and New York in 1965 Stern became a designer with Richard MEIER. In 1969 he set up his own practice with John Hagan and since 1972 has been principal of Robert A.M. Stern architects. He has held professorships at Yale and Columbia and has represented America at the Venice Biennales of 1976 and 1980.

He is as prolific a writer as designer and his name is inextricably linked with the polemics of post-modernism. His earlier work made classical allusions in a modernist context. The Westchester Residence (1974–6) is in the Le Corbusian syntax of Richard Meier. Subsequently, Stern has moved toward an eclectic post-modernism which he has defined in terms of three characteristics: contextualism, applied ornament and historical reference. He has become known for a series of exclusive country houses for wealthy New Yorkers which draw on a stylistic recapitulation of the history of American domestic architecture up to and including the innovations of Frank Lloyd WRIGHT, such as the residence at Millneck (1981–2).

Stern can be seen evolving toward a post-modern classicism, expounded in his book *Modern Classicism* (1989). His Observatory Hill Dining Hall (1982–4) for the University of Virginia, Charlottesville, exemplifies what Stern calls a "modern traditional approach that stresses the importance of cultural and physical context". Actually the design is a wrapping for an existing modern building; the particular classical style was obviously adopted in deference to Thomas Jefferson's campus buildings, also at Charlottesville. Point West Place, Framingham, Massachussetts (1983–5) is a large project in which Stern attempts to use the classical language of architecture to "dignify" a speculative office development.

STIRLING James b. 1926 British

architect

Leicester University Engineering Building; Cambridge History Faculty; Southgate Estate, Runcorn; Neue Staatsgalerie, Stuttgart; Clore Gallery extension of the Tate Gallery, London; Mansion House Square, London.

After being educated at Liverpool University, James Stirling set out as an architect with the aim of injecting new life into modern English building, which he felt had reached a state of stagnation immediately after the Second World War. The influence of LE CORBUSIER can clearly be seen in his early work, such as the Ham Common housing of 1957 which he designed with his partner James Gowan. Stirling and Gowan also worked together on the Leicester University Engineering Building (1959–63). Here the architects explored the use of industrialized materials usually found in the construction of factories such as red engineering tiles, light fixtures and large glazing panels. Stirling used an original way of designing at this time: instead of producing the usual drawings of side elevations, he opted for a bird's eye view – an axonometric drawing – to show the complex arrangement of the structure and the layout of the internal spaces.

Later, in the mid-1960s, Stirling worked alone on the Cambridge History Faculty (1965–7). Again he employed industrialized off-the-peg parts for the design, which was focused around the reading room. Shortly afterwards came a horseshoe-shaped student residence at Oxford University, called the Florey Building (1967–71). While the designs were greeted

James Stirling, Clore Gallery extension to the Tate Gallery, London, 1982–7.

with enthusiasm, the practicality of Stirling's buildings was questioned because of the acoustic problems and the leakage of water through ill-fitting glazing.

With his reputation still growing, in the late 1960s Stirling was asked to design municipal housing at the Southgate Estate in Runcorn New Town. The densely-packed warren of low-rise, slab-shaped blocks, providing over 1,300 homes, was threatened with demolition in 1989 because of the acute state of decay. Stirling was much criticized, but defended himself by saying that the estate was designed to fulfil the corporation's brief.

Stirling's most successful building to date is undoubtedly the Neue Staatsgalerie in Stuttgart (1977–84), designed with Michael Wilford. This large building, often referred to as Germany's Pompidou Centre, is composed of a circular open-air sculpture court surrounded by a sequence of single-height galleries which flow from one to the next.

Back in Britain, Stirling designed the Clore Gallery extension to the Tate Gallery in London (1982–7) and in the late 1980s a major building at Mansion House Square. The latter provoked much discussion, not simply on the grounds of its design, but because its construction could also mean demolition of listed buildings. Intended as an alternative to the proposal to build a MIES VAN DER ROHE glass tower, Stirling's idiosyncratic art deco-style design for the No 1 Poultry site at the junction of two roads was described by the Prince of Wales as resembling "a 1930s wireless".

STÖLZL Gunta 1897–1983 German

textile designer

Highly original weaver and most prominent woman teacher at the Bauhaus.

Gunta Stölzl studied weaving at the Munich School of Arts and Crafts from 1914 to 1919. She was among the first students at the BAUHAUS, joining the weaving workshop in the autumn of 1919. The experimental approach to materials (which owed something to war shortages) and aesthetic enquiry of the Weimar Bauhaus fired Stölzl. As a result of the number of painters on the teaching staff and the level of artistic debate between them, textile design at the Weimar Bauhaus was directed towards one-off pictorial works. Influenced by the paintings of Paul Klee, Stölzl's early works for Sommerfeld House proved her skill at mastering formally complex compositions on the loom.

After passing her journeyman's examination, Stölzl went on an external weaving course and joined Itten at the Mazdaznan headquarters in Herrliberg to run a small weaving workshop. She returned to the new Bauhaus at Dessau in 1925 and was made the exclusive head of department in 1926. Under her supervision the workshop adopted a more professional, systematic approach. Work was orientated towards industrial production as well as creative research. Materials, including aluminium and cellophane, were tested for performance and experimentation was seen as a method of research for preparing samples for manufacture. Equally capable of creating strong individual pieces and samples for mass production, Stölzl proved to be one of the finest weavers of her time.

STRAUB Marianne b.1909 · Swiss

textile designer, weaver

Development of Welsh textiles; designs for London Transport and British Rail seats.

Born in Amriswil in Switzerland, Marianne Straub studied weaving at the Kunstgeweber Schule in Zurich where she was taught by an ex-BAUHAUS pupil. The Bauhaus philosophy of production had a formative impact on her and was the motivating factor behind her decision to become a designer for industry. She followed this decision singlemindedly, serving a brief apprenticeship as a technician in a Swiss weaving factory before going to Bradford Technical College to study industrial weaving. She was only the third woman ever to have attended the college. In 1933 she introduced herself to Gospels, the craft weaving workshop in Sussex established by Ethel Mairet. The research at Gospels into the quality of weaving with hand-spun and hand-dyed yarns greatly enriched Straub's formal vocabulary.

As a consultant designer to 72 woollen mills in Wales on behalf of the Rural Industries Commission (1934–7), Straub revitalized their flagging production and became one of the leading proponents of modernist weaving in Britain. She compensated for the coarse quality and drab colours of Welsh yarns with an imaginative use of weave structure, and soon the Welsh mills were producing tweeds for prestigious firms such as Gordon Russell Ltd., Austin Reed and Hardy Amies.

She then became head designer, and later manager, for Helios fabrics, where she set a design precedent by experimenting with hand weaves for mass production.

The mechanization of screenprinting in the 1950s subdued the visual role of woven materials, but Straub's cloth gained a great deal of exposure – on the seats of tubes, buses and trains. Her designs for the more upmarket Tamesa range were much sought after by designers and architects and were used on ships such as the *Queen Mary* and the *QE2*.

STRAUSS Levi 1829–1902 · German

fashion designer

Designer of denim working clothes.

Although Strauss lived most of his life in the 19th century, his influence upon international dress in the 20th century has been profound.

Strauss arrived in California at the peak of the gold-mining rush of the 1850s. Recognizing the need for tough and durable clothing, he made trousers for the miners from a heavy brown tent canvas. A few years later he was introduced to denim, which he used thereafter. Strauss called his utilitarian trousers "waist-high overalls". In 1872 he added pockets to his design and took out a patent to protect it. One year later he went into business with a tailor, Jacob Davis, who suggested introducing copper rivets at the stress points, for added strength. In 1873 they stitched the now famous double arcuate design on the back pocket, and in 1886 the "Two Horse Brand" leather patch was added to the waistband.

During the late 1880s production was expanded to include linens, corsets and umbrellas. In 1890 Levi Strauss and Co. was formed, and the company assigned lot numbers to each of its products during the next few years – the waist-high overall was given the now legendary number 501. In 1908 production was expanded into denim bib 'n' braces and other functional clothing; in 1910 children's garments were added; belt loops were introduced in 1922, and the familiar red tab trademark was added to the back right-hand pocket in 1936.

During the Second World War, Levis were restricted to those undertaking war work in America. By the 1950s demand outstripped supply as they were promoted by Hollywood stars, and Levis' sales, along with those of their competitors, reached a peak during the 1970s, when jeans became mainstream fashion.

Levi Strauss, tough trousers for miners, c.1860s.

Bill Stumpf, Ethospace office systems, for Herman Miller Inc., 1986.

STUMPF Bill b.1936   American

industrial designer

Systems furniture for offices.

Stumpf graduated in industrial design at the University of Illinois and in environmental design at the University of Wisconsin. He is known for his systems furniture for offices. Stumpf was research director (design) and a vice-president of Herman Miller from 1970 to 1973. He subsequently formed a design partnership with Donald Chadwick (Chadwick, Stumpf and Associates). Stumpf was voted as designer of the 1970s by the American Industrial Design magazine. He has won many awards and his famous designs include the Ergon chair (first version, 1966) and the Ethospace office system (1985). The Chadwick/Stumpf partnership is a fruitful one; they avoid recondite philosophy, but have introduced into office design a mixture of practical engineering and the humane. In Ethospace, the latest of the Chadwick/Stumpf systems designs for Herman Miller, the possibilities exist for making the office almost domestic and in the Equa chair (developed 1979–84) the imagery is organic. It is a philosophy of being modern and scientific and also homespun.

SULLIVAN Louis H. 1856–1924   American

architect

Refinement of the concept of the steel-framed skyscraper.

After a disjointed training at MIT (1872), briefly at the Ecole des Beaux-Arts in Paris (1874) and in Philadelphia, Sullivan went to Chicago in 1875. It was at that time being reconstructed after a disastrous fire in 1871.

In 1879 Sullivan became an assistant to Dankmar Adler, becoming a partner in 1881. In 1886 they designed the massive and complex auditorium building in Chicago (1887–9), which used a steel-frame structure, but with a load-bearing masonry exterior of Romanesque design. However, in the celebrated Wainright Building, St Louis, Missouri (1890–1) and Guaranty Building, Buffalo, New York (1894–6), they adopted a full skeletal construction clothed in an aesthetically convincing masonry skin.

Sullivan had been a pupil of Le Baron Jenney, who had taken the first steps in the development of the skyscraper, made possible by the invention of the elevator in the 1850s and 60s in New York, and he was aware of the need to develop a suitable vocabulary for skyscrapers. In *The Tall Office Building Artistically Considered* (1896) he wrote of the need to emphasize the verticality of the building. Sullivan was also gifted in inventing quasi-abstract ornament which, like his pupil Frank Lloyd WRIGHT, he conceived "organically".

After the end of his partnership with Adler, Sullivan was involved in the design of several façades, notably the Carson Pirie Scott & Co. Department Store, Chicago (1899–1904), which has a strong horizontal rhythm to emphasize the selling floors. This was his last commercial project, and thereafter his work became more monumental and his decoration more rhetorical and highly decorated as in The National Farmers Bank, Owatonna, Minnesota (1907–8).

Louis Sullivan, Carson Pirie Scott & Co. Building, Chicago, 1904.

TALLON Roger b.1919 — French

industrial designer

Pioneer of independent design consultancy.

French industry was slow to accept industrial design as a profession in its own right, and it was only in the 1970s that design consultancy became truly independent of manufacturing companies. Tallon was one of the pioneers who made this possible.

In 1953 he became director of research for Technes. He designed cameras for SEM (1957 and 1961), a coffee-grinder for Peugeot 1957–8 and a typewriter for Japy in 1960. From 1957 to 1964 he was a consultant designer to General Motors, who produced Frigidaire refrigerators. He has produced a furniture range using polyester foam, and lighting designs for the German lighting manufacturer, Erco. Tallon is a consultant designer for the French railways (SNCF) and worked on the Corail locomotives. He has also designed machine tools and scientific equipment.

TEAGUE Walter Dorwin 1883–1960 — American

design consultant

Distinctive streamlined design.

In 1926 Walter Dorwin Teague became the founder-director of what was arguably the United States' first industrial design office. He was part of an élite group of designers, including Raymond LOEWY and Norman BEL GEDDES, whose work and approach helped to re-shape the consultant design profession not only in the United States but internationally. These consultancies began their pioneer work in the years of the Depression, when design was seen as a vital way of stimulating economic growth.

Teague's list of blue-chip clients became legendary and included Ford, Westinghouse and Kodak, for whom he designed the classic 1933 Baby Brownie camera. In line with his contemporaries, the house style was the distinctive streamlining that has come to be known as Machine Age. The style reached its apogee in the New York World's Fair of 1939, in which Teague was closely involved, designing several of the pavilions. The timing of the fair was, to say the least, unfortunate, and its impact was reduced by the onset of war.

Teague's approach to design received wider recognition with the publication in 1940 of his best-selling book *Design This Day. The Technique of Order in the Machine Age*. After the war Teague worked in

Walter Dorwin Teague, locomotive.

collaboration with his assistant Frank de GIUDICE; their best-known project was the interior design of the Boeing 707. Teague lived to become an elder statesman of American design and received many awards, as well as becoming the first President of the American Society of Industrial Designers.

TERRY John Quinlan b.1937 — British

architect

Newfield House; Waverton House; Richmond Riverside.

Quinlan Terry was trained under Peter SMITHSON in the modern architectural style largely created by LE CORBUSIER, Frank Lloyd WRIGHT and Walter GROPIUS. However, he cast aside the cubic shapes, flat roofs and concrete of the modernists to work in a traditional idiom based on the classical styles of ancient Greece and Rome.

Two major houses, Waverton House, Moreton-in-Marsh, Gloucestershire (1979–80), and Newfield at Mickley, Yorkshire (1980–1), were built in the style of Palladian villas based on a symmetrical design and incorporating arches, rectangular windows, finials, balusters, friezes, porticoes and slate roofs.

His largest commission was for the develop-

Quinlan Terry, Richmond Riverside Development, Surrey, 1986–9.

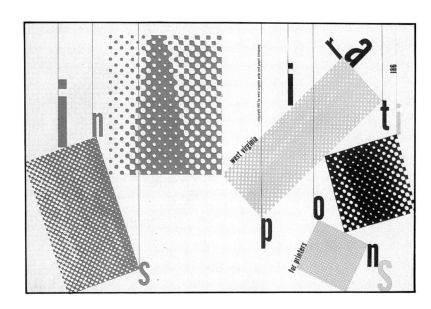

ment of riverside land at Richmond upon Thames, Surrey (1986–9). To replace a large river-front of dilapidated buildings, Terry designed a mixture of Georgian-style structures. The effect, although entirely classical in style, is of an area which has been constructed over several decades and designed by a number of architects. However, behind the façades lie entirely modern offices.

Terry, at the vanguard of the classical revivalists in Britain, has been criticized for producing a historical pastiche at Richmond which was described by the art historian Sir Roy Strong as "Disneyland Georgian".

Bradbury Thompson.

THOMPSON Bradbury b.1911 — American

graphic designer and magazine art director

Design of *Westvaco Inspirations for Printers* and the *Washburn Holy Bible*; design of over 90 US stamps.

Kansas-born Bradbury Thompson was one of America's famed "first generation" art directors. He was art director for *Mademoiselle* magazine in New York from 1945 to 1959, and for *Art News* (and its yearly issue, *Art News Annual*) from 1945 to 1972. He has also designed or redesigned formats for some three dozen other magazines (his formats for *Smithsonian* and *Harvard Business Review* are still intact).

One of his most famous publication projects was the design of *Westvaco Inspirations for Printers* (1938–62), a series of periodicals published by the West Virginia Pulp and Paper Company as a showcase for its papers. Thompson turned it into an avant-garde design exercise, and pushed the creative use of type, graphic techniques and printing processes to new limits (as in the printing of repeated images in separate process colours to suggest motion, the use of die-cuts and split-duct printing). Intended as an inspiration to printers, the Westvaco periodicals were also an inspiration to designers, containing experiments in simplifying the alphabet (such as dispensing with the use of capitals), as well as unconventional approaches to typographic styling and the effects on readability (for example, setting text in capitals and devising new ways of starting sentences and paragraphs).

Another well-known project was Westvaco's American Classic Book Series, which presented limited-edition volumes of classic literature (by Benjamin Franklin, Edgar Allan Poe and others) to Westvaco's friends at Christmas. Starting in 1958, it allowed

Thompson to display his mastery and love of book design for 26 volumes, over 26 years. His greatest contribution to book design, however, came in the form of the three-volume *Washburn Holy Bible*, published in 1979 after 10 years in preparation. In the *Washburn Bible* Thompson unlocked the traditional constraints of the Bible format, and rendered the text in a manner of style and phrasing that was more suited to the rhythms and logic of language, story-telling and comfortable reading.

In addition, Thompson has designed more than 90 stamps – which makes him the most prolific of all American stamp designers – and he has served on the faculty of Yale University School of Art since 1956.

Bradbury Thompson, design for the *Inspirations for Printers* series of periodicals, 1951.

THUN Matteo b.1952 — Austrian

industrial designer

Designs for computer-aided manufacturing.

Matteo Thun studied architecture at the University of Florence. He was a founder member of the Memphis group. He runs an architectural and design practice in Milan and is Professor of Product Design at the School of Applied Arts in Vienna.

He has designed tableware, storage systems, ceramics and lighting. He is especially skilled in designing for computer-aided manufacturers, especially in pressed and stamped metal.

Thun has coined the expression "the Baroque BAUHAUS" – it describes the thinking in the philosophical area that lies between the ULM University of Industrial Design and the Memphis-led Milan salon of urban

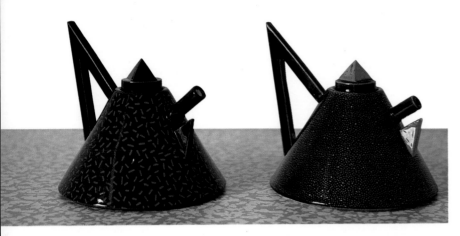

Matteo Thun, porcelain teapots for Memphis, 1983.

20th-century Baroque (Memphis designs are garishly painted, using 1950s revival patterns and relying heavily on an art deco style). In 1986 Thun said he was searching for images that would succeed "in communicating the sense of well-being" that he believes can be bred out of the Milan-versus-Ulm scuffles. But more recently (see *Design Now*, Prestel, 1989) he said: "In our culture a mechanism of formal turbulence is making itself felt: stable, ordered, regular, symmetrical forms are being succeeded by unstable, unordered, irregular, unsymmetrical forms."

TIFFANY Louis Comfort 1848–1933   see page 224

TIGERMAN Stanley b.1930   American

architect

Controversial, post-modern Chicago architect.

Tigerman attended MIT and, after receiving his architectural degree from Yale in 1961, started his own practice in 1964. He has held many academic appointments and published a number of books. As well as being an important influence on Chicago architecture since the 1970s, he has also built in Canada, West Germany and Bangladesh.

He became widely known in the 1960s for futuristic "mega-structure" projects such as Instant City (1966), representing a final development of the technological and functional thinking of the Modern Movement. Subsequently, however, Tigerman moved to consider architecture of mainly cultural rather than technological significance. He is famous (some would say infamous) for a series of expressive and personal buildings which make use of metaphor, such as the Hot Dog House (1975–6) and the euphemistically named Daisy House (1976–7), whose plan and elevation are

derived from the male and female genitalia. He has also caused controversy by the paradoxically brightly coloured library for the blind. Reactions to his work is mixed, and he has been described as "an attention-seeker" and "an architectural humorist". In common with some other American architects, Tigerman seems to find the cultural significance and meaning of architecture as important as the built form.

Latterly, Tigerman has turned to a jokey, but for him sober, interpretation of the classical tradition, notably in the Hard Rock café, Chicago (1985) and the One Pool House, Chicago (1987).

TINLING Teddy 1910–90   British

fashion designer

Sportswear, especially tennis clothing.

Tinling worked for the Lawn Tennis Association at Wimbledon from 1927 to 1931, when he opened his own London fashion house. For the following six years he successfully dressed the wealthiest Court circles in luxurious couture clothing. In 1937 he changed direction, channelling his creativity into the specialist, and largely neglected, area of sports clothing. Tinling combined his knowledge of couture fit and detail with his earlier experience of tennis requirements to create functional, unique and decorative clothing for the world's leading tennis players. While he designed womenswear for various sporting events, it is his tennis designs which have aroused the greatest interest.

Tinling revolutionized the design of tennis clothing, which had traditionally been all-white, by introducing colour – first as a trim, and then in entire garments. Solid colour was not permitted to be worn for major events until 1972, when the US Open Championships unexpectedly relaxed the rules. Tinling hurriedly remade Wendy Overton's dress in peach, and this was the first all-coloured dress worn in a championship event. From the start he made much use of synthetic fibres, such as rayon, and from 1956 he used silicone-based, stain-repellent finishes for his sportswear. Tinling introduced fashion and novelty into an area of clothing unaccustomed to such treatment. The frilly pants he designed for Gussie Moran in 1949 were considered very daring. His garments were embellished with ribbon, appliqué work, embroidery, cut-work, braid, silver Lurex, sequins and rhinestones. One of his most novel designs was made for Maureen Connolly in 1954; it featured appliquéd furry poodles

Teddy Tinling, printed cotton playdress and matching men's shirt worn with linen shorts, 1950s.

experience and a lecture-hall filled with laughter (and that despite interpreters, for he speaks only Polish).

In addition to his output of posters, he has received equal recognition for his book designs, and his satirical drawings and illustrations, including a collection entitled *Book of Complaints* (1961).

Henryk Tomaszewski, theatre poster for *Hadrian VII*, 1958.

with rhinestone eyes. In 1975 he sold his British business and moved to Philadelphia, where he worked until his death in 1990.

TOMASZEWSKI Henryk b.1914   Polish

poster artist, graphic designer and illustrator

Professor of Graphic Design, Warsaw Academy of Fine Art.

Since its post-war beginnings in the 1940s, the undisputed father of the "Polish poster school" has been Henryk Tomaszewski. A legend in his own time, he has taught or influenced nearly every poster artist emanating from Poland during that time – mainly through his classes at the Academy of Fine Art in Warsaw, where he has been Professor of Graphic Design since 1955. On viewing his work, it's easy to see why, for he is a grand master of the art of simplicity – able to draw a world of emotion and meaning out of one isolated object (like a shoe), or a skinny, nervous line. His status at the Academy is regal: stories abound of the adoration of his students, who present him with flowers and sit at his feet. His personality is equally famous – a curious mixture of joker, intellectual, authoritarian, and wit. Anyone lucky enough to witness a lecture appearance on one of his rare visits abroad will admit to a magical

TOTAL DESIGN founded 1963   Dutch

multi-disciplinary design group

Sign system for Schipol Airport; corporate identity scheme for Dutch Post Office (PTT).

Amsterdam-based Total Design was founded in 1963; it was the first large multi-disciplinary design group in the Netherlands, and has remained for almost 30 years a major name in the Dutch design establishment. The founders included the industrial designer Friso Kramer and graphic designers Wim Crouwel and Benno Wissing (also an architectural designer), as well as two accounting and management members. Graphic designer Ben Bos joined soon after, and by the late 1960s the group had grown to around 40 members.

They were known for cool, restrained graphic and informational design, marked by an analytical

▶ page 226

TIFFANY

Louis Comfort Tiffany, iridescent Millefiore vase.

Louis Comfort Tiffany, art nouveau floor lamp.

TIFFANY Louis Comfort 1848–1933　American
glass, ceramics, jewellery and interior designer

Master of decorative art nouveau glass, particularly lamps, vases and stained-glass windows; founder of own firm.

An outstanding name in late 19th- and early 20th-century American design, whose works were also admired and honoured in Europe, Louis Comfort Tiffany created his own distinctive version of art nouveau in the early 1900s in various media and his name is still widely known today as a result of the resurgence of interest in art nouveau since the 1960s.

The son of New York jeweller and silversmith Charles Louis Tiffany, Louis Comfort Tiffany sailed to Europe at the age of 17. Determined to be an artist, upon his return home the next year Tiffany took a class at the National Academy of Design. Then he returned to Paris to study with Leon Bailly (1868), and in 1870 he embarked on a North African trip which was to help shape his painting style and, in terms of his decorative artworks, his love of exotic, colourful detail.

After his return to New York in 1870, his interest in the decorative arts took firm root and he began working with glass soon afterward.

In 1877 Tiffany – along with stained-glass designer John La Farge, sculptor Augustus Saint-Gaudens and painters George Inness, Thomas Eakins, Albert Ryder, John Singer Sargent and James Abbott McNeill Whistler – formed the Society of American Artists, which was committed to exhibiting new trends in national art. In 1879 he set up Louis C. Tiffany and Associated Artists, a professional interior-decorating firm whose partners included Candace Wheeler, Samuel Colman and Lockwood de Forest.

The decorating company was amicably dissolved in 1883, with Tiffany now spending most of his time experimenting with, designing and producing glass, which mostly included stained-glass windows, made of lustre, mottled and opalescent glass segments, not just the traditional coloured pieces. In 1885 the newly incorporated Tiffany Glass Company was founded.

In the 1890s Tiffany's superb stained-glass windows (made at his Corona, New York, factory, set up in 1893), as well as his iridescent Favrile glass *objets*, the first vase of which was made around 1895, were offered both at home and abroad. German-born entrepreneur Siegfried Bing, whose Paris shop gave the art nouveau style its name, sold Tiffany glass on an exclusive basis (he also sold Liberty metalwork and William Morris fabrics). Tiffany glass was displayed at various international exhibitions to great acclaim. Bing was largely responsible for Tiffany's runaway success in Europe, and for the 1895 opening of his new Paris gallery he enlisted such major artists as Bonnard, Sérusier, Toulouse-Lautrec, Vallotton and Vuillard to design windows which were then made by Tiffany. To many, Tiffany glass became synonymous with art nouveau, and an unrivalled market success, with numerous competitors, both European and American (including Durand, Loetz, Quezal and Steuben) jumping on the bandwagon and imitating his Favrile glass.

In addition to glass in many guises, Tiffany also designed and produced jewellery, leaded-glass lamps, mosaics, furniture, pottery, metalwork, ecclesiastical objects and textiles, largely in his nature-inspired, quasi-exotic style. In 1902 Tiffany became artistic director of his father's firm (the elder Tiffany had died that year), contributing unique designs for "art jewel-

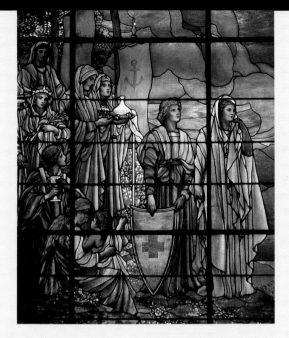

Louis Comfort Tiffany, section of a three-panelled window in the American Red Cross Headquarters, Washington, D.C., 1918; design by Frederick Wilson.

Louis Comfort Tiffany, Zinnia lamp.

lery"; that same year his own ever-expanding and diversifying multi-media firm became known simply as Tiffany Studios. Until the time of the First World War, Tiffany was a highly visible and active "mover and shaker" and stylemaker in the New York art world, not to mention one of its leading party hosts, but in 1919 he semi-retired and then in 1928 he left Tiffany Studios altogether; the firm survived until 1932. He spent most of his time from around 1920 in his lavishly designed and decorated Long Island, New York, estate, Laurelton Hall. Here he also set up a retreat for talented young artists – who had been named Tiffany Fellows by the Louis Comfort Tiffany Foundation he had generously established in 1918.

Although it is close to impossible to single out specific Tiffany pieces, some of his lighting devices deserve a mention, many of which were extraordinarily difficult to produce, and consequently exorbitantly priced. One such was the Cobweb Lamp of about 1904, its shade a network of lacy webs interspersed with floral blossoms, its base a bronze armature whose stems alternate with mosaic-tile panels decorated with yet more colourful flowers. The Squash Lamp of about 1906 has a simple patinated bronze base, yet it is moulded with vines and blossoms of the squash plant, vividly hued leaves which comprise the shade, and squash-shaped blossoms the six Favrile-glass globes, making an utterly harmonious, as well as functional, *objet d'art,* which casts a warm, multi-coloured aura.

Tiffany's many stained-glass windows – for churches, private homes, exhibitions – alone could have comprised the impressive output of one man's life, but they were just one aspect of his vast oeuvre. He experimented with new types of opalescent glass, with innovative ways of mixing colours, all in order to attempt to translate nature's splendours into what he called "the speech of stained glass". Critics have even deemed some of his early windows harbingers of American Abstract Expressionism – quite a striking comment when you consider the medium he was working in. Unlike medieval stained-glass artisans, who painted *on* glass, Tiffany wanted actually to paint *with* glass, the art of which he became the supreme master, paving the way for later 20th-century stained-glass artists whose work was unabashedly, undeniably modern.

Total Design, corporate design for the Dutch postal services (PTT).

approach and by love of geometry and the grid. Total's main projects in the 1960s included the sign system for Amsterdam Schipol Airport (the first comprehensive sign system at any airport) and, from 1964 onwards, Wim Crouwel's poster and catalogues for the Stedelijk Museum in Amsterdam. In 1967 Wim Crouwel designed his famous New Alphabet: a set of letterforms suitable for CRT (cathode-ray tube) composing systems, consisting solely of horizontal and vertical lines, with each character having an equal width. Other projects included one of their largest commissions, a complete corporate identity scheme for the Dutch Post Office (PTT) carried out in the late 1970s.

Throughout its history, Total has continued to explore the use of new technology: in the earlier years, with Wim Crouwel's New Alphabet and the design of *The Joy of Knowledge* encyclopedia, which pioneered book design by computer, and in recent years in its spirited typographic compositions.

TSCHICHOLD Jan 1902–74 German–Swiss

typographer and graphic designer

Spokesman of the New Typography; later active in book design.

Tschichold was not himself a member of the BAUHAUS, but was certainly party to the New Typography movement that emanated from that particular school of modernism (as practised by Bauhaus teachers László MOHOLY-NAGY and Herbert BAYER) as well as from the constructivist El LISSITZKY. Following in their footsteps, he refined the New Typography in practice, and also acted as spokesperson for the movement.

Tschichold came from Leipzig, although work

and interests soon led him to Berlin and Munich during the 1920s. In October 1925 he published an article in the German trade journal *Typographische Mitteilungen* which introduced the work of El Lissitzky and served as his own manifesto of modern typography. Through further articles in trade journals, he expounded the virtues of the New Typography – its strict functionalism, the use of sans serif typefaces (stripped of all decoration), and the dynamic qualities of asymmetric layout. But most importantly, he demonstrated its principles by constructing a method by which printers and compositors could apply the principles of the New Typography to their daily work. His first book, *Die Neue Typographie* (1928), was a veritable textbook for the new movement. Fleeing the Nazis, he left Germany for Basle in 1933, and there he published *Typographische Gestaltung* (1935).

He was at the same time a skilled practitioner, and produced a wide range of typographic work. But as the Second World War approached, he moved away from modernism and the New Typography he had advocated for so long (apparently associating it with Fascism), and returned to a classical, and symmetrical, typographic style. From that time on, he made a major contribution to book design, notably through his three-year stay (1947–9) in London, when he redesigned both the internal and external design of Penguin Books for Allen Lane, as well as through consultancy work for Swiss and German publishers. He continued to practise and write on typographic matters until the early 1970s.

Jan Tschichold, poster for the exhibition *The Professional Photographer*, 1938.

ULM Hochschule für Gestaltung founded 1951   German

school for designers

Formative influence on leading designers.

The Hochschule für Gestaltung at Ulm in West Germany was the innovative school for designers which replaced the BAUHAUS after the Second World War. Set up by Inge Aicher-School in 1951, in memory of family members killed by the Nazis during the War, it had as its first director Max BILL, who had been a Bauhaus student and promoted the concept of clean, functional design during his five years at Ulm.

During the later 1950s the notion that design had a theoretical context became current under the new director, the Argentinian Tomas Maldonado (b. 1922). Students spent over one quarter of their time at Ulm learning about ergonomics, sociology, economics and psychology to arrive at a systematic rather than inspirational approach to the design process. The Ulm professors deplored the increased affluence of the West, in which design satisfied the desires of the consumer rather than real needs. This critique of the capitalist system by Maldonado and his colleagues, former Ulm student Giu Bonsiepe (b. 1934) and Claude Schnaidt (b. 1931), and the tenacity of the various debates led to the demise of the school in 1968.

UNIT ONE founded 1933   British

group of modernists in various media

Furtherance of the Modern Movement.

Unit One was an association of sculptors, painters, architects and critics founded to further the cause of modernism in Britain. The driving force was the British painter Paul Nash; other members included Barbara Hepworth and Henry Moore (sculptors), Ben Nicholson, John Bigge, Edward Burra, Frances Hodgkins and Edward Wadsworth (painters), and Wells COATES and Colin Lucas (architects).

The group was based at the Mayor Gallery in London where it exhibited for the first, and only, time in April 1934. The exhibition attracted notoriety in the press because of the radicalism of Nicholson's abstract works. It was accompanied by a book, *Unit One: The Modern Movement in English Architecture, Painting and Sculpture*, published by Cassell and edited by the leading modernist critic, Herbert Read. It consisted of artists' statements with illustrations of their work, and is important in design terms as it used the typography and layout of earlier BAUHAUS books.

Unit One disbanded in 1934 as a result of disagreement among its members over the nature of abstraction, but it marked an important moment in the history of modernism in Britain.

UTZON Jorn b.1918   Danish

architect

Sydney Opera House.

Utzon studied at the Academy of Art, Copenhagen, under Steen Eiler Rasmussen. He was greatly influenced by the modern architects Gunnar ASPLUND of Sweden and the Finn Alvar AALTO, both of whom he worked for.

In his early career Utzon travelled to Mexico, the Far East and North Africa. He was fascinated by the flat-roofed mud houses of Morocco, which inspired him in his Kingo housing project at Birkehoj, Zeeland (1963). The small-scale development was based on a series of L-shaped cubic houses with courtyards. He then went on to design a church at Bagsvaerd, outside Copenhagen (1969–75), whose rather harsh and forbidding exterior, in a series of cubes and rectangles, belied the tranquil interior.

Utzon's greatest achievement was the design of the Sydney Opera House (1956–73) – a commission he won through an international competition. Inspired by the ships of Sydney harbour, he envisaged a bold sculptural structure composed of a series of enormous interlocking billowing white "sails". Commenting on the design, Utzon said: "If you think of a Gothic church you are close to what I have been aiming at... looking at a Gothic church, you never get tired, you will never be finished with it... the interplay of light and movement makes a living thing."

Construction was fraught with problems, not least of which were the acoustics, which underwent numerous modifications. These problems proved to be extremely expensive to solve and caused building costs to leap. National lotteries were run to raise additional funds, but economies and changes were introduced which Utzon found too compromising, and which led to his resignation from the project before it was finished.

Technical problems have continued to emerge. However, despite the setbacks, the building stands as an inspirational civic monument of great originality. It has become one of the strongest symbols of Australia.

Jorn Utzon, Sydney Opera House, 1956–73.

VALENTINO (Valentino Garavani) b.1932   Italian

Dramatic and decorative evening wear and precise, tailored daywear.

Valentino studied at the Accademia Dell'Arte in Milan and the Chambre Syndicale de la Haute Couture in Paris. He then remained in Paris, working for Dessès from 1950 to 1955 and for Laroche from 1955 to 1959, when he returned to Italy to open his own couture house in Rome. He showed his first collection in 1960 and within two years had achieved international attention for his glamorous and sophisticated, Hollywood-influenced, evening wear and for his bold, precise tailoring. In 1966 he introduced the V motif which is characteristic of his clothes and accessories.

In 1967 Valentino presented his famous no-colour collection – produced entirely in whites, creams and buffs – which provided a dramatic contrast to the psychedelic colouring which dominated that year. Defiant rather than subtle, Valentino's subsequent collections have become known for their bright colours and recurrent use of floral-motif fabrics and petal shaping. His textiles have also been regularly influenced by artistic movements: in 1969 he produced dramatic op-art designs, in 1972 he used Matisse colouring and in 1973 he featured art nouveau decoration and inspiration from the painter Gustav Klimt. In 1969 he brought out his Miss V ready-to-wear collection for women, and his ready-made menswear appeared in 1972 under the name of Valentino Uomo.

The international couture trade revived in the late 1970s as a result of British and American conservatism and the new Middle East market. Valentino was at the forefront of this trend, designing opulent and glamorous evening wear. His international franchises include the styling of an Alfa Romeo car.

VAN DE VELDE Henri 1863–1957   Dutch

Hotel Bloemenwerf, near Brussels; Grand Ducal School of Arts and Crafts, Weimar; Werkbund Exhibition Theatre, Cologne.

Born into a wealthy family, the son of a chemist, Henri van de Velde first set out as a painter, influenced greatly by the Pointillists. However, in the late 1800s his admiration for Ruskin, Morris and VOYSEY persuaded him to turn to design.

At the end of the 19th century he designed his own family home, the Villa Bloemenwerf (1894–5) at Uccle, near Brussels. He designed everything from the crossbred Arts and Crafts/Flemish building to the furniture, silver and cutlery; he even designed his wife's clothes, and is reputed to have advised her on the colour co-ordination of food to be served. He was an idealist, believing that it was possible to reform society through the design of the environment, and proclaimed: "Ugliness corrupts not only the eyes, but the heart and mind."

The house was admired by his friend Toulouse-Lautrec, and also by the businessman Siegfried Bing, who invited van de Velde to design ornate interiors for his Parisian shop, the Maison de l'Art Nouveau.

He is noted for introducing the art nouveau style to Dresden in 1897, with the design of a room at the Dresden Exhibition. In 1901 he completed another art nouveau interior for the imperial barber Haby in Berlin, where he took the radical step of exposing water pipes, gas conduits and electrical ducts.

Having acted as consultant to the crafts industries of the Grand Duchy of Saxe-Weimer since 1901, five years later he became director of the new Grand Ducal School of Arts and Crafts in Weimar, and set about remodelling it along the lines of MACKINTOSH's Glasgow School of Art, where tuition was given in workshops rather than in studios. Walter GROPIUS took over from van de Velde in 1919 and renamed the school the BAUHAUS.

In his early modernist concrete Werkbund Exhibition Theatre at Cologne (1914) he set out to test the idea that such a communal building could attract the attention of the "common man". In fact it missed its mark, and was patronized largely by a cultural élite.

Valentino, evening wear, summer 1986.

Henri van de Velde, two views of the Weimar School of Arts & Crafts, 1911.

V

VAN DOREN Harold 1895–1957   American

industrial designer

Plastic scale for Toledo Scale Company, Ohio.

Harold Van Doren was one of America's earliest industrial designers. He introduced design into the production process at a time when industrial artists (graphic designers in advertising) were the only "creatives" to get near manufacturers.

Although Van Doren was an American, born in Chicago, his family were Dutch, and Harold went to Europe to study languages. In Paris he worked in the Louvre, and when back in the USA he became assistant at the Minneapolis Institute of Arts. However Van Doren was frustrated by the passive role he was playing in the remarkable development of America's modern age; he left Minneapolis and founded his own design consultancy in Philadelphia.

Van Doren was a designer in the American mould; he rejected outright the moral high ground of the European functionalism and threw himself into the "streamline" style symbolic of America's new age. Arguing against the modernists – those who sought a single rational aesthetic in the new technological age – Van Doren pointed out that it was impossible to find an "honest shape" for products such as vacuum cleaners, which had no natural form.

Unlike the modernists, Van Doren had no interest in using design to create a new social order; he used it as a tool in the process of production. In his opinion styling was a means of selling products by appealing to consumer taste, and an understanding of new materials and processes was a means of exploiting new commercial opportunities.

During the Depression years of the 1930s Van Doren benefited from manufacturers' efforts to hold a market share with attractively styled products, working on restyling exercises for Philco refrigerator and cooker ranges. One of Van Doren's best-known products was for Toledo Scale Company, Ohio. It was originally cast in metal, but Van Doren designed a scale in a new thermosetting plastic resin, thereby reducing the number of fitted parts from 12 to eight. Toledo subsequently became one of the first major users of lightweight, large-scale plastic mouldings.

In 1940 Van Doren wrote a book, *Industrial Design: a Practical Guide,* a hands-on guide to working with new materials and production techniques and managing industrial design projects. He was also one of the founders of the Society of Industrial Designers.

VENINI Paolo 1895–1959   Italian

glass designer

The leading name in 20th-century Italian glass.

The diverse output and deserved fame of the ever-progressive Murano glassworks are chiefly due to one man, Paolo Venini. A Venetian who studied law in Milan, Venini gave up the legal profession in 1920 to devote himself to the medium of glass. He bought into the Murano glass factory run by Giacomo Cappellin in 1921 (Andrea Rioda and Vittorio Zecchin were also partners in the business), and by 1925 he was sole owner of the now renamed Venini & Company. By the time of the 1923 Monza Biennale Venini had presented the public with his clear, transparent or softly tinted goblets, vases and other vessels, their forms decidedly unfussy and eminently functional.

But Venini did not abandon the tried and true techniques of his esteemed Murano predecessors while experimenting with wholly new materials and production and decoration methods. By the 1930s he had revived the old techniques of making decorative *latticino, millefiori* and other kinds of glass, and developed such new types as *vetro pulagoso* (clear, with

Venini Handkerchief vase, designed by Fulvio Bianconi, c.1955.

condensed air bubbles) in 1928, *vetro corroso* (clear with a corroded-like texture) in 1933, *vetro sommerso* (bubbled, with an exterior casing of clear glass) in 1934 and *vetro inciso* (a layer of clear glass over a core of tinted glass). By the mid-1930s Venini was experimenting with novel, asymmetrical forms, the best-known of which is probably the handkerchief vase, some of its folds blithely pointing upward and the entire piece – which was often vertically striated – resembling a hankie blown aloft by the wind.

In the 1940s Venini was the leading maker of coloured glass, including both tableware and purely decorative pieces, throughout Europe as well as in Italy. The latter pieces – boldly striped, outrageously shaped, internally decorated with lacy filigree, dense trelliswork or undulating ribbons – have become highly collectable, for their colours and patterns, their virtuosity and their sheer, unalloyed beauty.

Throughout his long, productive career Paolo Venini continued to experiment, continued to borrow from the past and plunge into the present and unknown. He further added to the prestige and success of the company by hiring outside artists, both Italian and foreign, to provide him with designs. Among those who worked for Venini at one time or another were Gio PONTI (from 1927), Carlo Scarpa (from 1932) and, in the 1950s, Franco Albini, Eugene Berman, Ken Scott and Massimo VIGNELLI.

Venini himself remained the glassworks' principal designer until his death. Tobia Scarpa, Tapio WIRKKALA and Timo SARPANEVA are just a few of the designers hired since 1960 to create Venini glass, and of course the factory still flourishes today; the name Venini remains synonymous with the highest-quality 20th-century art glass.

VENTURI Robert Charles b.1925 see page 232

VERSACE Gianni b.1946 Italian

fashion designer

Fine tailoring and leatherwear.

Versace's mother owned a boutique and ran a dressmaking business, and he grew up knowing how to cut and sew. He left his mother's business in 1972 and designed freelance, first for Florentine Flowers and then for labels such as Genny, Complice, Callaghan and Mario Valentino. Versace gradually evolved his rich and

Paolo Venini, fluted glass bowl, c.1950.

sensuous style and gained a reputation for producing complex and technically skilled designs. In 1978 he presented his first women's ready-to-wear collection and the following year introduced his menswear. Versace is a true originator and many considered him to be the creative force of Milan.

Versace is greatly respected for his tailored menswear, unstructured jackets and leather blouson jackets. A less expensive range of menswear is marketed under the label Update. His body-conscious women's daywear is largely based on the ease of his men's clothing. He is noted for combining incongruous materials such as leather and silk. In 1982 he discovered a method of manufacturing a metallic mesh as pliable as silk jersey, and his 1983 and 1984 collections featured embroidered mesh.

For his knitwear and embroidery designs, Versace derives inspiration from the leaders of modern art and the classicism of ancient Greece. His clothes display contrasting moods – romantic and aggressive, masculine and sensuous – and the simplicity of his shapes often belies their sophistication. His use of deep, rich tones contrasts with the predominant black and white. Above all, Versace is admired for his talent at cutting, mostly on the bias, and draping of fabric.

VIGNELLI Massimo b.1931 Italian/American

graphic designer

Founder of Vignelli Associates in New York.

Massimo Vignelli and his wife Lella, an architect, are the husband-and-wife team credited with introducing restrained, European fashion and taste to America in the 1970s. Both born and educated in Italy, they married in 1958 and, after a brief period of study in America, set up their Office of Design and Architecture in Milan in 1960. They returned to America in 1965 and (with others) co-founded the renowned international corporation of Unimark, which collapsed due to over-expansion. Then in 1971 they established Vignelli Associates, based on such European traditions as design diversification and elegance achieved through economy of means. With Massimo handling the graphic side and Lella heading the furniture and product design branch, they became one of New York's most successful design firms and the range of their projects has been spectacular – from books to buildings, and just about everything in between.

Massimo's most distinguished projects have

Gianni Versace, beaded and embroidered jacket with circus motifs, autumn 1989.

Massimo Vignelli, publicity design for the Venice Biennale, 1964.

included a sign system for the New York City subway in 1966, the re-design of the New York City subway map in 1972, and the graphics system for the Washington Metro in 1976. For his National Parks Service Publication Program he received the First Presidential Design Award, presented by Ronald Reagan in 1985. He has also made a significant impact in the areas of periodical design (with the magazine *Skyline* perhaps receiving the most publicity) and packaging design for the likes of Saks Fifth Avenue and Bloomingdale's. But of even greater import is the weight and status of the Vignelli empire, for both Massimo and Lella, in their commitment to a "total design" philosophy, also teach, write, lecture, serve on juries and boards, and for the past two decades have made a vital contribution to American attitudes and standards in design.

VIONNET Madeleine 1876–1975   French

fashion designer

Bias-cut dresses of the 1920s and 30s.

Madeleine Vionnet was apprenticed into the dressmaking trade at the age of 12 in her home town of Aubervilliers. She also trained in the London tailoring

establishment of Kate Reiley and in the Paris houses of Callot Soeurs and Jacques Doucet. On completing this lengthy training she opened her own house in Paris in 1922. Four years later she introduced her now famous streamlined bias-cut garments. A bias cut is achieved by cutting across the grain of the fabric, which enables it to fall into smooth drapes. To facilitate this new cut, Vionnet commissioned double-width material, which had not previously been available. This body-moulding cut was launched at a time when the contrasting, loose-fitting Garçonne Look was at its peak. By the 1930s the bias cut was widely used for women's garments and was also worn and promoted by Hollywood's leading actresses, which further enhanced its popularity. Vionnet usually worked with plain, dark and neutral-coloured fabrics, although she made an exception with her favourite rose-pink and sometimes included evening wear decorated with embroidery and dazzling rhinestones. She also enjoyed making garments from transparent fabrics, which were worn over shifts.

Vionnet was also famous for her fluid classical styles, which were similar to those produced by Madame Grès, and she too showed her clothing without distracting accessories. Many of her garments were made in one piece, without fastenings, and were designed to be put on over the head. Vionnet originated the halter neck and softly draped cowl necklines, which fell in loose folds across the bodices of her garments. Both of these have been much used to the present day. Her handkerchief dress, made from four squares of fabric which were sewn to hang in points at the hem, has also been much copied.

The mid-to-late 1930s witnessed a brief revival of Victorian-style furnishing and fashion. Vionnet was at the forefront of this vogue in Paris, featuring among her collections hooped and corseted crinoline and bustle dresses. Vionnet retired in 1939.

VOLKSWAGEN founded 1938   German

car manufacturer

"Beetle", most popular car ever produced.

The Volkswagen "Beetle" was designed by Ferdinand Porsche in the early 1930s for the German motorcycle manufacturers NSU and Zundapp, who wanted to create an affordable, small car with popular appeal. Adolf Hitler adopted the plan as part of his *Volk* propaganda campaign. This entailed promoting only

Madeleine Vionnet, scalloped cotton dress with embroidered detail, c.1927.

▶ page 234

VENTURI

Robert Venturi, Chestnut Hill, house designed for his mother, Philadelphia, 1962–4.

VENTURI Robert Charles b.1925   American

Important exponent and major theoretician of post-modern design; author of *Complexity and Contradiction in Architecture*.

Robert Venturi has had great influence on architectural thinking and design through buildings and, more especially, through his writing, in particular *Complexity and Contradiction in Architecture* (1966), which has been a classic text. It is an important critique of modernism and the only polemic written by a practising architect since LE CORBUSIER'S *Toward a New Architecture*.

Venturi graduated from Princeton in 1950 and spent time with the firms of Oskar Stonorov and Eero SAARINEN (1950-4). The latter drew upon the industrialism-classicism of MIES VAN DER ROHE, but Venturi later spent two years (1956–8) with the practice of Louis KAHN, who was moving toward a freer, more idiosyncratic late modernism. In 1954–6 he was awarded a fellowship at the American Academy in Rome, where his consciousness of the classical tradition was deepened. The academic link continued when he was appointed to the faculty of the University of Pennsylvania in 1957, and from 1965 to 1970 he was professor of architecture at Yale University.

He first set up on his own in 1958, and his present practice dates from 1964. In 1967 he married Denise Scott Brown, who later joined the practice, which became the familiar Venturi Rauch and Scott Brown. The Venturis are very close professionally and their production should be seen as joint works.

It was in the well-known house which he designed for his mother in 1961 that the main themes of Venturi's work emerge. The interior is a free plan of irregularly shaped spaces. The exterior has a symmetricality drawn from a reference to a classical pediment. Otherwise there is a mixture of modern industrial and classical elements: industrial sash windows and applied classical detail, for example the symbolic arch above the entrance.

Venturi's literary output, especially his books *Complexity and Contradiction in Architecture* (1966) and later *Learning from Las Vegas* (1972), has had great impact. The first book presaged the so-called "crisis of modernism" and presented a wide-ranging and systematic critique of modernist principles which is central to Venturi's work.

Venturi argues that while the "great modernists" applied consistent design principles, post-modernists have to seek diversity. He suggests that much architecture is complex and, subjectively, he *likes* complexity, richness and ambiguity. The Modern Movement drew its force from a set of universal aesthetic theories and from machine production. Venturi suggests that architecture should be responsive to different local contexts, cultures and tastes. It is this pluralism which is central to his position.

He lays great stress upon symbolism and decoration in architecture precisely because it enables the designer to produce this kind of variety. In the modern economy building methods have indeed, to a large extent, become universal. We live in a world which is both smaller and more interdependent but, as can be seen from the crisis of modernism, people like diversity and are keen to retain cultural identities. Symbolism and decoration enable this to be achieved through a building. Venturi suggests that function/structure and symbolism/decoration should be allowed to go their

Robert Venturi, two views of the model for the Sainsbury Wing extension, National Gallery, London, begun 1988.

own ways – "allowing function to be truly functional, as it couldn't be, ironically, when form followed function in the old modern days".

Venturi claims that modern technique and historical symbols rarely harmonize, so that symbolism is almost always false and redundant. But this does not matter because "we see differently" and do not expect there to be harmony. This irony is seen in his use of cut-outs that represent classical details in his house in New Ash (1978) and in Franklin Court (1972), where a frame symbolizes a whole building!

Venturi also suggests that, rather than buildings being mainly an expression of their function, they should communicate through their decoration. Buildings which are shaped like their functions Venturi calls "ducks", and says that one of the chief sources of interest to the Modern Movement was the arrangement of spaces – but this was often not functional. He advocates simple functional space planning with decoration on the outside: "decorated sheds, not ducks".

This thinking has also led Venturi to suggest a definition of architecture as "a shelter with decoration on it". As far as the content of the decoration is concerned, the early work was concerned with the way in which a building could communicate through symbolism, and in *Learning from Las Vegas* he analysed commercial roadside buildings as a form of applied symbolism in the same way as he had previously treated classical symbolism.

The latter work, however, picks up a theme first seen in the extension to the Allan Memorial Art Museum (1973) which uses historically derived abstract decoration. A similar use of decoration is seen in the Molecular Biology Building, Princeton (1983–5) and the Best Products Showroom (1977).

While Venturi is associated with the architectural movement of post-modernism, he is critical of much of what he sees as its indiscriminate revivalism and borrowing of historic details, and clearly he does not see why decoration should be confined to classical detailing. He admires the achievement of the early modernists, but believes their principles are no longer relevant – buildings must reflect their period. However, he rejects the label of "populist" and sees himself as belonging to the classical tradition – it is just that the rules have changed!

Perhaps Venturi's most important and certainly his most public commission has been for the National Gallery extension in London (begun 1988). The design embodies Venturi's thinking, fitting into its context but being recognizably "modern". It echoes many of the features, first seen in his mother's house, of shallow classical detail applied to the exterior of a building which otherwise is conceived in a non-formal way. The design also contains another quite specific level of irony in the way it acknowledges the main National Gallery, since the classical detail clusters in the corner adjacent to the old building and then fades out to leave an almost totally *undecorated shed*.

Robert Venturi, house in New Castle, Delaware, 1978.

V

German, vernacular art and design to appeal to the grassroots majority. Hitler renamed the Volkswagen the *KdFwagen* after the Nazi "Strength Through Joy" (*Kampf durch Freude*) organization for recreation.

Prototypes were first produced at the Daimler-Benz factory in 1937, and featured the familiar rear mounted, flat four, air-cooled engine and streamlined profile. Work on a new factory at Wolfsburg began the following year, where production was to be based on the American method as developed by Henry Ford.

The VW Beetle was the most popular car ever manufactured, gaining cult status among the young during the 1960s. However, its very popularity spelt disaster for the VW company who, by the early 1970s, could no longer rely on this outdated design as their major source of income. Toni Schmucker, the managing director, hired Giorgio GIUGIARO and his firm Ital Design to create a new, small car. The Volkswagen Golf of 1974 was the first of the popular sporty hatchbacks to captivate the European market, and revitalized Volkswagen's fortunes.

VON ETZDORF Georgina b. 1955   British

textile, fashion, furniture and product designer

Exclusive prints in various media.

Georgina von Etzdorf is one of the most enduringly successful, and perhaps more conservative, designers to survive from the British art-based print revival of the early 1980s style boom. The rapid development of her career, from printing designs in her parents' garage to establishing a shop in London's Burlington Arcade, was one of the success stories of the 1980s.

Georgina von Etzdorf's training at Camberwell School of Arts and Crafts gave her a sound grounding in traditional craft production techniques, while encouraging an individual painterly approach to pattern. On leaving college she encountered the perennial difficulty of selling her patterns as a freelance designer in Britain, and so set up as a designer-maker. From her original line of exclusive, high-quality prints on silk, von Etzdorf and her partners, Jonathan Docherty and Martin Simcock, have gradually expanded their business to include fashion, ceramics and furniture.

Her prints derive from an eclectic combination of influences from museums and the countryside, rather than from the fashion market. She is inspired by painters such as Paul Klee and Richard Burra, and takes her bright palette from 19th-century Indian miniatures. By issuing no more than three patterns a year Etzdorf ensures that her designs are of a consistently high quality. With their large repeats, finely drawn patterns and painterly surfaces, they express her feeling for craftsmanship. Etzdorf is one of the few British textile designers to be admired by the Italians.

VOULKOS Peter b. 1924   American

potter

Innovative figure in modern studio ceramics.

Peter Voulkos studied painting at Montana State University, graduating in 1949; he then studied for a master's degree in ceramics at California College of Arts and Crafts, and graduated in 1952. In 1951 he began working at the Archie Bray foundation in Montana with the resident sculptor, Rudy Autio. Voulkos was one of six artists in the Ceramic Sculpture exhibition (1981–2) at the Whitney Museum of American Art.

Much has been made of Voulkos the sculptor by those who want ceramics to be accepted as a fully-paid-up member of the fine art area, but still Voulkos's most significant contribution has been to the history and living tradition of pottery.

Voulkos has been an important teacher and exemplar for younger clayworkers, but many have been misguided by the seeming ease with which he works. The followers of Voulkos have often interpreted the generous roughness of his volumes as "clumsiness".

Voulkos has pushed modern studio ceramics well away from functional utilitarian work and, in a sense, walloped the vessel into asymmetrical, primeval "statements" of the artist's mood and temperament – although many people regard this kind of explanation (applied in general to abstract expressionism) as incoherent wishful thinking.

Peter Voulkos, thrown, wood-fired stoneware bowl, 1981.

VOYSEY Charles F. Annesley 1857–1941   British

architect

Highly influential English domestic architect and designer, associated with the Arts and Crafts movement but seen as a precursor of modernism.

Voysey set up on his own in 1882, although his first house was not built until 1888; in the meantime, he worked on commissions for furniture and fabrics. By 1890 his architectural practice was well established, and there followed about 40 houses developing the highly artful use of the traditional English vernacular

also seen in the works of Webb, LUTYENS and Shaw. Voysey, however, is notable for his use of simple volumes, plain rough-cast stucco with slate roofs, and for arranging his windows in horizontal groupings.

It is widely agreed that Broadleys, Lake Windermere (1898) is his best house. It demonstrates the innovations which were being made in the space planning of the Anglo-American house and is as original as anything which Frank Lloyd WRIGHT was producing. Indeed, after 1900 Voysey's name was better known internationally than Wright's, through the work of M.H. Baillie Scott, who went further in developing the free-style plans suggested by Voysey.

As an equally active designer of wallpaper, fabrics and furniture he avoided the medievalism of the Arts and Crafts movement and welcomed the machine as an aid to production, while in his architecture he avoided ornamentation.

The First World War brought to an end the era of "dreamlike English country houses". In the inter-war period he built almost nothing at all. However, his style was adopted by the speculative suburban developments of the time because its rural and domestic symbolism was so powerful.

But the double irony of Voysey's career was that the inter-war generation of modernists saw him, with his use of simple undecorated volumes, as a precursor of modernism (of which he did not approve). It was on the basis of this perception that he was awarded the RIBA Gold Medal in 1940.

C. F. A. Voysey, oak chair, 1906–09.

C. F. A. Voysey, wallpaper designs.

W

WAGENFELD Wilhelm b.1900   German

Designs in glass, metalwork and other media.

Wagenfeld is one of the most versatile, influential and committed industrial designers of the century, having worked in metal, ceramics, glass, lighting and plastics, taught at the BAUHAUS and in Berlin, exhibited and been honoured throughout the world and remained a firm believer in the altruistic role of the designer in society, to that end concentrating on mass-produced, generally inexpensive objects. Likewise, he has always retained close contact with industry, with the workers who have brought his designs to fruition.

      Wagenfeld was born in Bremen, where he served an apprenticeship in the draughting office of a silver factory and studied at the Kunstgewerbeschule. He attended the Drawing Academy (Staatliche Zeichenakademie) in Hanau in 1919 and in 1922 he entered the Bauhaus at Weimar, first studying metalwork under László MOHOLY-NAGY, then himself teaching from 1926 to 1929, the year he left to work as an independent designer (and later to teach in Berlin, from 1931 to 1935). In addition to the modernist lamps, teapots, gravy-boats and other Bauhaus metal wares produced by the firm of Walter & Wagner of Schleiz in the 1920s, Wagenfeld designed for the medium of glass, and by the 1930s he was involved more with glass and ceramics than with metal. The Jenaer glassworks and Vereinigte Lausitze glassworks produced his goblets, jugs, vases and other useful ware (the former still makes a heat-resistant tea service of his design), and he was also involved with designing publicity for the VLG, as well as being their art director from 1935 to 1942. He created plain, functional porcelain in the 1930s for the Fürstenberg and ROSENTHAL factories, taught industrial design at Berlin's Hochschule für Bildende Kunste from 1947 and in 1950 moved to Stuttgart, where he set up a design studio, Werkstatt Wagenfeld. Since the 1950s he has designed, among other things, appliances for Braun, lighting for Lindner in Bamberg and Peill & Putzler in the Rhineland, plastic plates and utensils for Lufthansa airlines, glass, cutlery and other metalwork for the Württembergisches Metallwarenfabrik in Geislingen and more porcelain for Rosenthal. One of his early Bauhaus table lamps, of 1923–4, a crisp geometric model in glass and chromium-plated metal (designed in collaboration with K.J. Jucker) was reproduced in the mid-1980s by Tecnolumen. From 1958 he was the co-editor of the magazine, *Form*.

Wilhelm Wagenfeld, stainless steel tableware for Württembergisches Metallwarenfabrik (WMF), 1952–4.

      Wagenfeld has primarily been concerned with function, economy and simplicity, and with bringing good design to the masses. This has been the overriding interest of his long, distinguished career – one which has brought him numerous commissions and distinctions, including several prizes at the 1937 Paris Exposition Internationale des Arts et Techniques and at the Milan Triennale.

WALLIS Sir Barnes Neville 1887–1979   British

R80 airship, Wellington bomber.

Sir Barnes Wallis is popularly known for inventing the "bouncing bomb", used in a successful attack on the Möhne and Eder dams in May 1943 and immortalized in the film *The Dam Busters*. However, his work in the field of airship and aircraft design was far more significant. After leaving school at 17 he was apprenticed at the Thames Engineering Works and then at J.S. White's shipyard at Cowes. He was then appointed chief designer for the R9 airship project at Vickers, which was completed in 1916. Wallis continued with his design work on airships after the First World War, designing the revolutionary R80, which first flew in 1920. Wallis abandoned the conventional cigar shape and introduced an innovative streamlined form, making this the fastest airship to date.

      In 1928 Wallis turned to aircraft design at Vickers Aviation, where he developed the geodesic structure for biplane fuselages. This robust but lightweight framework was the result of his airship work and consisted of a slim, intersecting spiral structure surrounding the four main longitudinal supports. This framework allowed for a more streamlined fuselage and wing construction and was used in Wallis's designs for the Wellesley bomber. Just before the outbreak of the Second World War, Wallis developed the twin-engined Wellington bomber, renowned for its durability under attack; 12,000 were produced during the war. Wallis spent the post-war years as head of a special research department at Vickers Aviation until 1971, but his main contribution had been made during the Second World War.

Barnes Wallis, Vickers-Wellington bomber, 1940.

David Watkins.

WATKINS David b.1940   British
jeweller and sculptor

Precise, often abstract jewellery and sculpture.

Watkins studied sculpture at the University of Reading; he was a jazz musician and is currently Professor of Jewellery and Metalwork at the Royal College of Art, London. He has digested all the formalist principles of De Stijl, but over a period of 25 years he has produced work which is very much his own. His work has two dominant characteristics: spareness of line and of volume, and precision workmanship or engineering. The pieces are frequently large and abstract and his neckpieces dominate a wearer, although not to the extent that his explorations of the body as jewellery did during the 1970s, when he produced works that framed the whole torso.

There is a great richness in the precision of this work and sometimes there is a sensuousness through the unexpected combinations of materials – such as paper, metal and gold leaf. He often uses bright colour, and the 1980s saw a successful series of jazzy, colourful, erratic and futuristic neckpieces.

Watkins has completed garden sculptures for Leeuwarden in the Netherlands and for Kowloon Park, Hong Kong, and has designed a centrepiece for The Silver Collection in Britain. He set up a partnership with Wendy RAMSHAW in 1970. He has used computer-aided design and computer-aided manufacturing alongside handwork for a number of years, and expects to expand his use of these tools in the 1990s.

WEDGWOOD founded 1759   British
pottery manufacturer

Employment of named designers.

Towards the end of the 19th century the famous pottery founded by Josiah Wedgwood at Burslem, Staffordshire, began to employ named designers such as Walter CRANE and C.F.A. VOYSEY, and to publicize the fact that it was doing so. In the 1930s Susie COOPER, Keith MURRAY, Eric Ravilious and John Skeaping also began doing work for the company. Since the Second World War the company has flirted with named designers, but it has mainly followed a quasi-traditional approach, updating classics from the 18th and 19th centuries. It has developed modern decorated ranges, but has tended to follow rather than lead public taste.

WEIL Daniel b.1953   Argentinian
architect and industrial designer

Unconventional industrial designs.

Daniel Weil trained as an architect in Buenos Aires before coming to Britain to study industrial design at the Royal College of Art from 1978 to 1981. It was while at the RCA that Weil met Gerard Taylor, with whom he now works in partnership in London.

The work which first brought Weil attention was the series of digital clocks, radios and lights which he designed from 1981 for Parenthesis. Encased in soft, pliable plastic, these appliances are brightly coloured, with all their workings revealed. Weil has always questioned the conventions of product design, and his approach has made him a controversial figure in the design world. Many have called his products art objects, but Weil maintains that he is an industrial designer, and that his designs could be mass-produced. His work, after all, does not rely on crafted elements, but on commercially produced components and everyday objects (such as his clock, which incorporates a

Daniel Weil.

W

Daniel Weil, Bag radio,
1981.

length of stainless steel cutlery and two wine-glasses).

Weil and Taylor together have worked for a variety of international clients, including retail projects for Esprit in Australia (in association with SOTTSASS Associati), ALESSI in Bari and French Connection. They have also designed office furniture for KNOLL International, a domestic residence in Belgravia, London, and domestic furniture and lighting for Anthologie Quartett (West Germany).

WEINGART Wolfgang b.1941   German

graphic designer and typographer

Typography instructor at the Basle School of Design in Switzerland; posters and book jackets.

Wolfgang Weingart started teaching at the Basle School of Arts and Crafts in 1968, and was soon hailed as the *enfant terrible* of Swiss typography. Situated in the epicentre of the (by then) tired Swiss graphics movement, Weingart incited a visual revolution and introduced a radical new teaching approach. He rejected the movement's rigid constraints, but at the same time retained the qualities of the Swiss tradition that he liked (emphasis on structure and visual order, a preference for sans serif type, and so on). The Basle School became famous all over again (this time for being radical, not restrictive).

His impact on the educational scene was phenomenal, particularly in the USA. The initial spark was provided when, in the early 1970s, he gave lectures at leading design schools in the USA, and the transatlantic link continued when he conducted typography workshops for the Yale University Summer School in Brissago, Switzerland. But a slower, more silent connection, and perhaps the most effective, has been provided by the American (as well as European) students of the school in Basle who then returned home to spread the word or, as in the case of the US West Coast designer April GREIMAN, used the experience to create their own new directions and movements. Weingart's teaching has been regarded by many as the foundation of the 1970s New Wave graphics movement in America, and continued to be influential in the "typographic revolution" that followed on both sides of the Atlantic in the 1980s.

Weingart's posters and book jackets have won many Swiss government awards. He founded two magazines, *TV/Communication* and *Typographic Process*, and has collaborated on projects with the periodicals *Typographische Monatsblätter* and *Visual Language,* in the course of which he produced some of his most memorable compositions (including a cover design for *VL* that centred on the statement "No idea for this fucking cover today"; a brazen act in 1974 and an aberration in the light of Swiss tradition). His book *Projects,* based on his teaching at Basle, was published by Arthur Niggli in 1980.

W

WELLINGTON Irene 1904–84 — British

Richly decorated calligraphic work.

Irene Wellington trained under Edward Johnston at the Royal College of Art, London, in the 1920s. As well as being a calligrapher, she was an accomplished illustrator and embellished her calligraphic work with heraldry, medieval horsemen, flowers, birds and animals. She admired Johnston greatly and agreed with his emphasis upon simplicity in penmanship. But the hallmark of her own work is its complexity: much of it was done in the period following the Second World War, when geometrical outlines and starkness were in fashion. In her complexities there is immense richness. Her output was considerable, much of it done to commission, often for formal and ceremonial occasions of state and government. One of her masterpieces is a calligraphic collage, *Alphabetical Fragments*, which demonstrates her fluency as a calligrapher, mastery of drawing and fine sense of composition.

A book in Wellington's honour, *More Than Fine Writing,* was published by Pelham Books in 1986.

WERKMAN H. N. 1882–1945 — Dutch

graphic and typographic designer and printer

"Druksels" (experimental compositions).

The typographic art of Hendrik Werkman was brought to the public eye in a major retrospective at the Stedelijk Museum in Amsterdam not long after his death in 1945. It was organized by Willem SANDBERG, whose own work owed much to Werkman.

Werkman lived and worked in Groningen in Northern Holland. He earned a living by running a small jobbing press, printing stationery and ephemera for local businesses, in the period after the First World War. He began to produce oil paintings in his spare time in 1917, and soon expanded this activity into his print workshop. Over the next three decades he created experimental compositions called "druksels" in which he used printing ink, hand rollers, wood-letters and metal type in a painterly fashion to create print-collages of great emotion and sensitivity. (Although referred to as "druksels", meaning "prints", they were for the most part one-off images.)

Werkman existed outside the radical art movements of De Stijl and Constructivism, although he was in contact with and influenced by both. From 1923 onwards, he also published his own periodical entitled *The Next Call* (producing 10 issues in all), which contained his own typographical experiments and texts. He sent the journal all over the world, to friends or in exchange for other avant-garde journals, thereby keeping in touch with the international scene.

Werkman was arrested and executed by the Nazis in April 1945, only a few days before the liberation of Groningen. Much of his work was seized and destroyed at the time; only about half of his creative output survives.

WESTWOOD Vivienne b.1941 — British

fashion designer

Unconventional and cult fashions.

Westwood studied at Harrow Art School for one term only, before leaving to train as a primary-school teacher. From this unlikely background, Westwood dominated the fashion headlines throughout the 1970s and continues to be a major force in British fashion. Almost single-handedly, Westwood injected a fresh and lively impetus into the flagging British fashion industry during the early 1970s.

With her partner Malcolm McLaren, Westwood opened her now legendary clothing shop at 430 King's Road, London, in 1971. With Westwood's intuitive creativity and McLaren's business acumen, the partnership was instantly successful. Initially named Let It Rock, their shop sold 1950s revival teddy-boy styles. In 1972 it changed its name to Too Fast to Live, Too Young to Die, selling James Dean-style, loosely-cut denim jeans and capped-sleeve T-shirts. Again renamed in 1974, Sex sold fetishistic and theatrical rubber and leather garments. It was, however, Seditionaries, as it was renamed in 1976, which became the first punk clothing shop, and which generated the most publicity. It sold predominantly black slashed and torn garments covered with multiple zips, sloganned T-shirts which were designed to shock, mohair jumpers and bondage trousers with "bum flaps", loin-cloths or kilts. Westwood and McLaren dressed the well-off punks, but their style was widely copied.

In the spring of 1981 Westwood changed her shop name and her style again. World's End started selling a softer "pirate" style, which was championed by the New Romantic pop stars such as Adam Ant. In 1982 she produced her Buffalo collection, which took

Vivienne Westwood, womenswear, autumn/ winter 1984–5.

W

the folk dress of the Appalachians as its inspiration. In this year she also introduced 1950s-style, satin bras, which were worn over her dresses. In 1983 she parted company with McLaren. In 1985 she introduced the mini-crini to counteract the triangular, shoulder-padded Dynasty look.

Many of Westwood's fashions have initially been derided, but they have subsequently been much copied and appeared, in less extreme guises, in the High Streets.

WIRRKALA Tapio 1915–80 — Finnish
craftsman and designer in glass and other media

Decorative and commercial glass designs with sculptural qualities; long-time association with Iittala glassworks and other companies.

From the time he won first prize for his design in the 1946 Iittala glass competition, Tapio Wirkkala was one of the most prolific, versatile and innovative Scandinavian designers in the post-war period. Born in Hanko, Finland, Wirkkala was a sculpture student at Helsinki's Central School of Industrial Design from 1933 to 1936, later serving for a time as its art director (1951–4). He became a designer for the Iittala glassworks after winning the 1946 contest, and was to be associated with the firm until his death. He was, however, employed on a freelance basis by numerous other domestic and foreign companies from the 1950s, among them Raymond LOEWY in New York (1955–6), ROSENTHAL AG in West Germany (1956–85), VENINI glass in Italy (1959–85), and Christofle silver in France, as well as three Finnish businesses, the cutlery company

Tapio Wirkkala, Kantarelli vases for Iittala Glass, designed in 1946.

Hackman, the lighting manufacturer Airam and the maker of wooden objects, Soinne & Kni. He even designed currency notes for the Bank of Finland.

Wirkkala's primary role, though, was as chief designer for Iittala, and it was under his guidance (aided by the design skills of Timo SARPANEVA, who joined the firm in 1950 and is its senior designer to the present day) that the glassworks, which had been founded in 1881, became the premier maker of both art and useful glass in Finland, as well as the recipient of much international acclaim.

Ever true to his training as a sculptor, Wirkkala imbued many of his glass designs with organic, sculptural qualities, making the resultant objects so much more than utilitarian vases or bowls; indeed, many were accepted on their own as decorative works of art, and marketed as such. His creations were mostly made of clear, colourless glass, such as the elegant, organic Kantarelli (Chanterelle) vase of 1946. In contrast to the light, almost wispy, wind-blown quality of Kantarelli, in 1950 he designed the heavy-walled, jagged Jäävuori (Iceberg) and Jääpala (Iceblock) vases, both inspired by the frozen forms of Lapland. Still with an icy theme, the glass sculptures called Paaderin Jää (Paader's Ice), named after a lake in Lapland, were made in 1962; the series won a Gold Medal at the Milan Triennale.

Among his commercial wares, glasses and pitchers often featured bas-relief textures reminiscent of frost, ice or condensation; such a tactile surface marks the well-known machine-mould-blown bottles he designed for Finlandia vodka (in production since 1978, but designed nearly a decade earlier). Less evocative of a cold climate was his 1970 Coreano dish for Venini glass, which featured a bold design of a snail-shell-like swirl.

Wirkkala achieved considerable recognition via the exhibitions he organized and designed for Finland that were presented abroad. In 1981 he even designed an entire museum devoted to glass, the Riihimäki Glass Museum, located on the premises of the huge Finnish factory.

WOLF Henry b. 1925 — Austrian–American
graphic designer

Art direction for the magazines *Esquire* and *Harper's Bazaar* and *Show*.

In America the 1950s was the Golden Decade that gave birth to a new consumer society of which the most

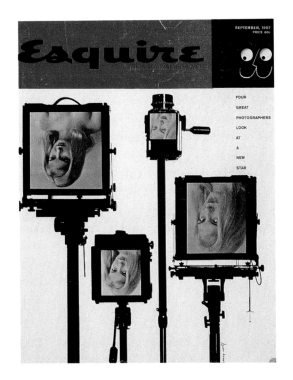

Henry Wolf, cover design for
Esquire magazine, 1957.

Wolf was an outstanding and influential member of the second generation of US magazine art directors (following on from first-generation masters, such as Alexey BRODOVITCH, with whom he studied design and photography; Dr M. F. Agha; Paul RAND and others). Both generations helped to establish magazine art direction as a specific graphic design area at which the USA excelled and received worldwide applause. Wolf himself was responsible for numerous magazine covers and advertisements, all of which bore his distinctive mark: experimental (and sometimes surreal) use of photographic images, Magritte-inspired collage effects, and lively typography. He also broke away from the bland, sleek commercial art norm by commissioning artists and photographers (Ben Shahn, Leonard Baskin and others) not usually associated with magazine work – a truly rebellious approach in that era of tight conformism.

WOODMAN Betty b.1930   American

potter

"Pillow" pitcher.

Betty Woodman studied at the New York State College of Ceramics, Alfred. Her domestic wares, such as cups and saucers, have generous form and decoration, and the success of all her works rests in the fact that people want to hold and use them. "One of Woodman's best-known forms is the 'pillow'-pitcher; this is frequently decorated very loosely and it gives the sensation that, if you were to jab at it, it would deflate. The sensation is heightened by the stiffness of the pitcher's neck compared to its billowing body." (*New Ceramics*, Peter Dormer.)

important propagators were advertisement-carrying glossy magazines such as *Look* and *Life*, *Fortune* and *Esquire*. These delivered news, lifestyles, Hollywood gossip, and the ethic of "buy, buy, *buy*", right to the consumer's doorstep. The magazines of the 1950s provided the commercial and informational "glue" that held together the vastly spread-out populations of America and formed their perception of the world (and America's pre-eminent position in it), as well as their tastes and values.

Henry Wolf was a central figure in the world of commercial art during this magazine heyday. Born in Vienna, he studied in France, emigrated to America in 1941 and continued to study in New York at the School of Industrial Arts. He worked in an art studio (1945–7) and an advertising agency (1947–51), and as an art director for the US State Department in 1952. He was then engaged as art director of *Esquire* magazine ("the magazine for men") from 1952 to 1958, *Harper's Bazaar* from 1958 onwards, and *Show* magazine from 1961 to 1966. He later undertook art direction for various agencies and concerns in New York, until in 1971 he started Henry Wolf Productions for photography, film and design. Since 1957 he has taught in New York's best-known visual arts institutions, including Cooper Union, the School of Visual Arts and the Parsons School of Design.

Betty Woodman,
earthenware wheel-thrown
vessel on tray, 1983.

Frank Lloyd Wright, exterior view, Falling Water, Bear Run, Pennsylvania, 1937–9.

Frank Lloyd Wright, interior view, Falling Water, Bear Run, Pennsylvania, 1937–9.

WRIGHT Frank Lloyd 1869–1959   American

architect

One of the most important American architects of the 20th century; exponent of "Organic Architecture".

Wright was one of the world's most original architects. He was a flamboyant personality embodying many of the contradictions of modern America. He spent two years studying engineering, but otherwise was self-taught, and read widely. He was greatly influenced by Emerson's individualism and optimism. Wright's professional life lasted for close to 70 years, and shows a remarkable creativity and diversity. He produced a huge oeuvre of drawings, essays and lectures. Wright himself believed that his diverse achievements were unified by his belief that he was creating an "organic architecture". Wright's creativity is not matched by systematic thought, and it is difficult to say what he means by this. In his Princeton Lecture of 1930 he finally produced 50 different definitions!

After a brief spell in the office of a minor architect practising in the traditional shingle style, Wright really began his architectural career in 1888 when he entered the practice of Louis SULLIVAN, the greatest American architect of the period, best known for his Chicago skyscrapers with inventive, quasi-art nouveau "organic" decoration.

Both Sullivan and Wright were seeking a form of decoration and architecture which would be appropriate for the new civilization of America. Wright was put in charge of the domestic commissions, producing the Charnley House (1891–2) and the Winslow House (1893), both symmetrical "boxes" with bands of Sullivanesque decoration. He had designed a house for himself in 1889 which showed Japanese influence. Wright was dismissed in 1893 for working on "bootlegged" private commissions and he subsequently developed his own distinctive language in buildings such as River Forest Golf Club (1898), and especially in the Warren Hickox House (1900), which gave the name to the Prairie Style, after a magazine article called "A Home in a Prairie Town". The well-known Robie House was designed in 1909. Wright was very proud of having "broken the box" – his plans were typically split-level, open-plan or double-height, features which were to have immense ramifications in 20th-century interior design. The plans were often T-, X- or L-shaped; this stemmed from Wright's intense feeling for geometry, which may have been acquired by playing with wooden blocks, part of the Froebel educational method.

Wright's non-domestic works were equally forward-looking, and possibly more influential in Europe at the time. Both the Larkin Administration Building, Buffalo, New York (1904) and Unity Temple Church, Chicago (1906) have sculptural monumental exteriors and are top-lit. The Unity Temple features pre-Mayan-type ornament and represents Wright's continuing attempt to find a suitable ornament for the democratic modern age.

His immediate post-Prairie phase was identified by Wright himself as "baroque", and consisted of two works, the Midway Gardens, Chicago (1913–4), which develops to an extreme the geometricity of his earlier work, and the Imperial Hotel, Tokyo (1915–22), which again shows Wright's fondness for semi-abstract ornamentation. This theme was indeed taken up in a series of Californian houses, the most famous of which is the Millard house (1923), whose organically con-

Frank Lloyd Wright, Great Workroom of S. C. Johnson Building, Racine, Wisconsin, 1936–7.

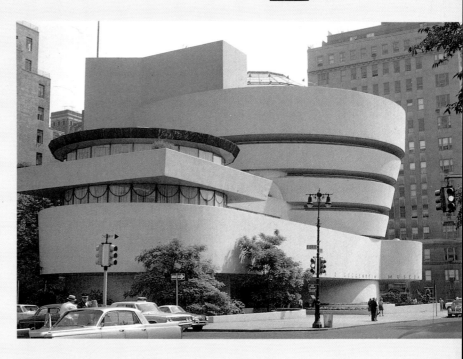

Frank Lloyd Wright, Guggenheim Museum, New York, 1946–59.

ceived decoration (Wright said it was "of" the surface, not "on" the surface) further removed its architect from the development of European modernism.

By 1936 it might be assumed that Wright's career was ended, but in this year he produced two of his most original works. The S.C. Johnson Administration Building (1936) has an interior of non-functional mushroom-shaped columns, uses circular shapes and profiles, and, like many of Wright's buildings, it turns its back on the city. The house, Falling Water (1936) has been interpreted as a spectacular affront to the international modern style. It exploits the expressive potential of reinforced concrete; the house is cantilevered from a natural rock outcrop like a natural form in an "organic" manner, "like a twig from a branch".

The late 1930s also saw the development of another element in Wright's disparate thought. He had originally coined the term "Usonia" to refer to the new democratic culture which would emerge in America. He further envisaged, in his book *The Disappearing City* (1932) and his Broadacre City proposal of 1935, that this future would consist of an idealized devolved city. There was no practical scheme to realize these proposals, and such ideas did little more than encourage the drift toward American suburbia. Nevertheless, Wright also applied the name Usonia to a series of moderate houses which he designed for the rest of his career. Another significant theme which was developed – and differentiates him from European modernism – was the relation of architecture to landscape and natural environment. His own "organic" winter home, Taliesin West, was begun in 1938 and was followed by Pauson House (1940).

But it was exploration of geometry which was to dominate his work until the end of his life. He was interested not only in the cubic forms of his early domestic work but also in forms based on triangular geometries, on the circles he had used before and also spirals. These geometries were used with success in the Bartesville Tower (1953–5), in which two geometries interlocked to form a counterpoint of forms which also worked practically to produce double-height areas and stairways. However, Wright became increasingly constrained by these geometries and he increasingly came to conceive projects in very formal and superficial terms. The Grady Gammage Memorial Auditorium (1959–66) had appliqué decoration, which the early Wright would have dismissed as "unorganic". There has been much controversy as to whether the spiral form of the Guggenheim Museum (designed 1943–6) is appropriate for a picture gallery. There was also an element of Sci-Fi vulgarity in many of the latter projects, notably the Marin County Civic Center (1959–64). There were a variety of fantastic projects for urban schemes and a skyscraper a mile high.

Wright is more difficult to judge than other modern architects because of his search for an organic architecture. As can be seen, it is difficult to say what this means, how it could be realized or to what extent it was embodied in his work.

Clearly, the idea of nature was in many ways central to Wright and it is possible that, for various reasons connected with the changing attitudes toward nature and technology, Wright's work will become even more relevant.

W

WRIGHT Russel 1904–76   American

ceramics, furniture, glass, and metalwork designer

Gifted and prolific designer of primarily domestic furnishings and objects including American Modern dinnerware.

Russel Wright was committed to offering the American public "good design" at reasonable prices, and many of his simple, handsome and affordable household accessories proved extremely popular. Born in Lebanon, Ohio, Wright moved to New York City in 1920. He studied for a year or so at Princeton University, where his association with a theatrical group put him into contact with Norman BEL GEDDES, a stage-set designer soon to become a leading industrial designer. From around 1924 Wright began working as a theatre-set designer himself, but by 1927, the year of his marriage to Mary Small Einstein, also his lifelong professional partner, he had turned his interest to the applied arts.

By 1931, Wright had started to design (and produce) his thoroughly modern "useful wares", first chrome-plated steel and spun-pewter accessories, then spun-aluminium wares. He extended this range to include tureens, ice buckets and various other vessels, serving pieces, even lamps, most of which were part of what he called the American Modern line, made by Wright's own company. One of Wright's most exciting designs was the chromium-plated pewter cocktail shaker of about 1931, a Machine Age icon which was essentially a metallic sphere centring two thick metallic cylinders. A critic commented that its sleek, simple shape was "indicative of the speed of our age".

By far the most famous American Modern product designed by Russel Wright was his dinnerware: subtly coloured (in bean brown, coral, sea-foam blue, granite grey, cedar green, etc.) and gently curving plates, cups and saucers, bowls and a wide assortment of serving pieces. They proved a phenomenal success, with some 80 million pieces being produced between 1939 and 1959. In the 1940s Wright created flatware, glassware and even table linen to complement the dinner-ware. The soft, flowing lines also characterized subsequent Wright designs in other media, including the so-called Pony Skin armchair (made in 1934 for his own use), whose sculptural form foreshadowed the biomorphic chairs and sofas of the 1960s, by craftsmen such as Wendell CASTLE and Sam Maloof.

Russel Wright, American Modern dinner service, designed in 1937.

Wright's best-known furniture, however, was mass-produced by Conant-Ball from 1935 and was also a part of the American Modern range. Unlike most furniture of the time, which was veneered, Wright's designs were largely of solid maple, either with a reddish tint or the popular bleached "blond", and their shapes were plain, straightforward and blocky, often with soft, rounded edges.

Wright also offered the public a Modern Living line, wherein furniture, lamps, floor covering, curtain fabric – basically all the components of a room – could be purchased in one place, a service heretofore limited to a wealthy clientele who could afford an interior designer. After an exhibition of BAUHAUS design at the Museum of Modern Art in New York in 1938, Wright grandly conceived the somewhat nationalistic and chauvinistic American Way line, which included works by Raymond LOEWY, Walter Dorwin TEAGUE, Gilbert Rohde, himself and other American designers. In 1940 the American Way was set in motion, but distribution and quality-control problems, as well as the Second World War, put a stop to this endeavour in 1942.

In the late 1940s and 1950s, Wright continued to design furniture, glassware and ceramics. He created Flair glassware for Imperial Glass Corporation of Bellaire, Ohio, in 1949, and a year later he designed the 50-piece Easier Living furniture line for Stratton, as well as a popular folding chair in plywood for Samsonite. In 1951 he and his wife wrote *A Guide to Easier Living,* and also in the 1950s Wright was involved with a US State Department project to encourage and advise small cottage industries in the Third World. This in turn put him in touch with Japanese firms, for whom he designed over 100 different products in the mid-1960s. In 1967 he gave up design to work as a consultant for the National Parks Service.

YAMAMOTO Yohji b.1943   Japanese

fashion designer

Oversize, unstructured black garments.

Yamamoto graduated in law from Japan's Keio University in 1966. He attended the Bunka College of Fashion and worked freelance before forming his own company in 1972. His first collection was shown in Japan in 1976. He established himself in Paris in 1981, alongside Rei KAWAKUBO, Kansai Yamamoto and other Japanese designers, who then launched their revolutionary, understated, oversize garments onto the catwalks of Paris.

Yamamoto has gained a reputation for being a design purist and an intellectual recluse. His garments reject the female shape and are notable for their long, loose styles, textured weaves, additional flaps, straps and pockets, asymmetrical detailing, misplaced sleeves, adjustable waists and knotted shapes. Ninety per cent of his clothing output is made in black – he says that bright colours quickly bore him. Yamamoto eschews fleeting styles and fashion novelty, aiming instead to create more enduring designs. He derives much of his inspiration from travelling. His Summer 1985 collection was influenced by the nomads of the North African desert, and diamond patchwork fabric featured in his collections following a trip to India. Like most Japanese designers, he makes no evening clothes – his garments are designed for all times of day.

Yohji Yamamoto, womenswear and menswear.

YAMASAKI Minoru b.1912   American

architect

Pruitt-Igoe estate, World Trade Center.

Born in Seattle, Minoru Yamasaki studied in Seattle and New York. Yamasaki's building designs first hit the headlines in 1972 when a series of his public housing tower blocks at the Pruitt-Igoe Estate, St Louis (1953), were blown up. Such was their unpopularity with local people that the council decided the flats were uninhabitable. The few remaining residents were re-housed and the towers destroyed.

Minoru Yamasaki, World Trade Center, New York, 1970–4.

The Pruitt-Igoe estate was composed of 33 identical 11-storey blocks containing almost 3,000 apartments. They had been poorly made, were densely populated, and soon fell into disrepair. Initially just three central blocks were felled, but by 1980 all 33 had been razed to the ground.

The demolitions had wide repercussions, and were particularly significant in Britain, where many post-war council blocks had become very unpopular with their residents. As a result of the demise of the American towers, some blocks were destroyed in British cities.

Yamasaki's career took a long time to recover. However, after designing a number of undistinguished office blocks, he was commissioned to build the impressive World Trade Center in New York (1970–4).

The twin towers, in the heart of Manhattan's financial district, measuring 1350 ft (412 metres) high, have sheer sides encased in glass. They are extremely popular with tourists.

ZANUSO Marco b.1916　　　　　　　　Italian

architect and industrial designer

Use of new materials in industrial design.

Marco Zanuso, who studied architecture at Milan Politecnico, is a significant figure in post-war Italian design because he has exploited new materials and production processes. His Lady chair (1951) was designed in response to a new material from Pirelli – foam rubber. The Lambda chair (1962) was another experiment, this time with enamelled sheet metal.

Zanuso worked with German-born designer Richard SAPPER on another chair that used new materials – the polyethylene child's stacking chair for Kartell. One of his earliest experiments in furniture design was with tubular-steel-frame chairs in 1948. His long working relationship with Sapper resulted in such products as the Doney and Black televisions for Brion Vega and the Grillo telephone.

Zanuso has designed sewing machines for Necchi and Borletti and kitchen scales for the French company Terraillon. He has continued to practise architecture and has designed industrial plants for OLIVETTI, IBM and Necchi. He has also taught at Milan Politecnico, and for two years (1947–9) he was editor of the design magazine *Casabella*.

ZAPF Hermann b.1918　　　　　　　　German

type designer, calligrapher and book designer

Typeface designs and calligraphy.

Hermann Zapf was born and educated in Nuremberg; he studied calligraphy privately, from manuals by Edward Johnston and Rudolf Koch, and then worked at Paul Koch's Haus zum Fürsteneck type workshop in Frankfurt. In the late 1930s he was introduced to the Stempel Foundry in Frankfurt and began his career in type design.

He produced an initial blackletter typeface in 1941 but his career was then interrupted by the Second World War. It was in the post-war climate, when German printers and founders were rebuilding factories damaged by bombing, that roman typefaces were needed for re-stocking. Zapf produced Palatino (1949), based on classical Italian letterforms and one of his most popular typefaces. There followed such famous faces as Melior (1952), designed as a newspaper face, and Optima (1958), the "serifless" roman. His type designs number over 250, including family

variations and titling fonts, and span the developments in technology over the past 50 years, moving from hot-metal, to film, to digital type design.

Zapf's earlier hot-metal work was created for the Stempel or Linotype foundries. With the arrival of film composition and computerization he produced designs for the International Typeface Corporation in the 1970s (Zapf Book, 1976; Zapf International, 1977; and Zapf Chancery, 1979), and in the 1980s became involved in digital type design, including work with Stanford University's Donald Knuth on the Metafont design programme.

He has also produced a number of outstanding portfolios and books on typographical design and lettering, which include *Manuale Typographicum* (Frankfurt, 1954), *About Alphabets* (Frankfurt and New York, 1960), and *Typographische Variationen* (Frankfurt, 1963).

ZEISEL Eva b.1906　　　　　　　　Hungarian

ceramics designer

Elegant and functional designs in ceramics and other media for industry.

The Hungarian-born Eva Stricker Zeisel worked as a designer at the Kispester earthenware pottery in Budapest, followed by stints at several German potteries from 1927 to 1932. She spent part of the 1930s in the Soviet Union, and became an art director in the Central Administration of the Glass and China Industry of the USSR, based in Moscow. In the 1920s and early 1930s, many of Zeisel's designs reflected the prevalent modernist taste and were decorated with geometric motifs.

Zeisel emigrated to the United States in 1937, where she proceeded to teach at the Pratt Institute of Arts in Brooklyn (1939–53) and at the Rhode Island School of Design in Providence (1959–60), as well as to

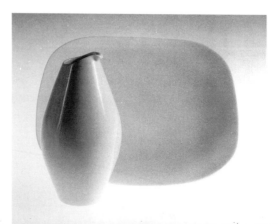

Eva Zeisel, tray and creamer from Museum service, made by Castleton China, 1941–5.

design ceramics and, to a lesser extent, other objects for industry; some of her earliest American designs were for Riverside China and Bay Ridge Specialty. In 1946 the Museum of Modern Art in New York presented the exhibition Modern China by Eva Zeisel, which featured the classic 1941–5 porcelain service commissioned by the Museum and Castleton China, Inc., of New Castle, Pennsylvania. Elegantly curved and eminently functional, the plates, bowls, cups, jugs and other pieces in the Museum service, which was available in stark white, were continuations of the simple, organic designs Zeisel and other European designers had begun to create before the Second World War, and among the first of many such undecorated, single-colour services to appear throughout America in subsequent years.

By the end of the 1940s, Zeisel was firmly established as one of the premier designers for industry working in the United States. In 1953 she was honoured with a Senior Fellowship by the National Endowment for the Arts, and her work was the subject of a travelling North American exhibition in 1984.

ZEPPELIN Count Ferdinand von 1838–1917   German

designer

Airships and aerodynamic technology.

Count Zeppelin was born at Constance, Baden, and served in the Franco-Prussian War. Between 1897 and 1900 he constructed the first rigid airship or dirigible balloon which became known by his name, and set up a factory for its production at Friedrichshafen.

The realization is now growing that the technology and engineering employed had a considerable input into the techniques employed in later 20th-century architecture. Some idea of their importance to modern technology can be gauged by the brief Count Zeppelin set for the construction of the first steel shed in 1909. To prevent the internal temperature from fluctuating excessively, the roof covering and walls were constructed from materials with low heat conductivity. The gable ends, which also functioned as doors and had to be lightweight, were steel-framed and clad with galvanized metal sheet lined with cork with an insulating air layer between the two surfaces.

All these demands forced new research into ventilation, temperature control and metallurgy. There were other demands as well: the military wanted airship hangars that could be taken apart and

reassembled, and the airship manufacturers wanted to standardize parts for economy. Both requirements advanced prefabrication techniques considerably. The Zeppelin Company also pioneered other developments, such as the use of the wind tunnel. Thus when Paul Jarray began testing automobile designs in the company wind tunnel in the early 1920s, he evolved some principles about streamlining that were taken up by car designers and manufacturers.

ZWART Piet 1885–1977   Dutch

graphic and industrial designer

Typography, photography and industrial design.

The work of Piet Zwart still has a significant influence on students of typography. He created one of the most inspired and lively new approaches to typography this century, derived from the love of architectural structures and the pure forms of De Stijl, but injected with the vigour and expressiveness of Dada, not to mention his own sense of humour and imagination.

Having studied general arts and crafts, Zwart spent most of his early career involved in three-dimensional design, working in offices concerned with architecture, furniture and interiors. It was not until 1921, while assisting the Dutch architect H. P. Berlage, that he produced his first advertisement designs. By 1925, then aged 40, he was beginning to concentrate on typography, particularly designing ads and catalogues for Nederlandsche Kabelfabriek (cable works) at Delft. By the late 1920s, photography was increasingly evident in his advertising work for NKF as well as his designs for the Post Office, including booklets and stamps. (After 1928, the photographs he used in his designs were his own; he was also his own copywriter.) Perhaps part of the magic of his concoctions was that they revolved, by and large, around seemingly bland industrial concerns such as flooring manufacturers, printers, and of course, cable works (for which he designed the amusing typo-classic, Hot Spots).

He continued to produce graphic work throughout the 1930s (and three decades beyond that), but in the mid-1930s he made a significant return to industrial design when he developed the Bruynzeel kitchen, composed of individual matching units and now seen as a forerunner to the modern fitted kitchen.

Piet Zwart, promotional design for a firm handling rubber flooring, c.1922.

BIBLIOGRAPHY

GENERAL

Anscombe, Isabelle *A Woman's Touch, Women in Design from 1860 to the Present Day* (Viking Penguin, 1984).

Arwas, Victor *Art Deco* (Academy Editions, 1980 and Harry N. Abrams, Inc., 1980).

Banham, Reyner *Design by Choice* (Academy Editions).

Bayley, Stephen *In Good Shape* (Design Council).

Bayley, Stephen *The Conran Directory of Design* (Conran Octopus, 1985).

Bayley, Stephen, Garner, Philippe and Sudjic, Deyan *Twentieth Century Style and Design* (Thames & Hudson, 1986).

Blanca, Oscar Tusquets *The International Design Yearbook 1989/1990* (Thames & Hudson, 1989).

Brunhammer, Yvonne *Art Deco Style* (St. Martin's Press, 1984).

Clark, Robert Judson, ed. *The Arts and Crafts Movement in America 1876–1976,* exhibition catalogue (Princeton University Press, 1972).

Design Since 1945, exhibition catalogue (Philadelphia Museum of Art, 1983).

Dormer, Peter *The Meanings of Modern Design* (Thames & Hudson).

Forty, Adrian *Objects of Desire – Design and Society 1750–80* (Thames & Hudson, 1986).

Heskett, John *Contemporary Designers* (St. Janus Press, 1985).

Hillier, Bevis *The Style of the Century* (Herbert).

Hiesinger, Kathryn B. and Marcus, George H. eds. *Design Since 1945,* exhibition catalogue (Philadelphia Museum of Art, 1983).

Morgan, Ann Lee, ed. *Contemporary Designers* (Macmillan Publishers, 1948).

The International Design Yearbook 1986/1987 Ambasz, Emilio, ed. (Thames & Hudson).

The International Design Yearbook 1987/1988 Starck, Philippe, ed. (Thames & Hudson).

The International Design Yearbook 1988/1989 Isozaki, Arata, ed. (Thames & Hudson).

Jervis, Simon *The facts on file Dictionary of Design and Designers* (Penguin, 1984).

McQuiston, Liz *Women in Design: A Contemporary View* (Trefoil Publications, 1988).

Pulos, Arthur J. *The American Design Adventure* (MIT Press, 1988).

Rowland, Kurt *A History of the Modern Movement: Art, Architecture, Design* (Van Nostrand Reinhold, 1973).

Sparke, Penny *An Introduction to Design and Culture in the Twentieth Century* (Allen & Unwin, 1986).

Sparke, Penny *Design in Context* (Bloomsbury, 1987).

Sparke, Penny *Italian Design* (Thames & Hudson, 1987).

ARCHITECTURE

Banham, R *Theory and Design in the first Machine Age* (Architectural Press, 1960).

Frampton, Kenneth *Modern Architecture: a critical History* (Thames & Hudson, 1980).

Glancey, Jonathan *New British Architecture* (Thames & Hudson, 1989).

Jencks, Charles *Modern Movements in Architecture* (Penguin, 1973).

Jencks, Charles *The Language of Post Modern Architecture* (Academy Editions, 1977).

Jencks, Charles *Late-Modern Architecture* (Academy Editions, 1980).

Pevsner, N. *Pioneers of Modern Design* (Penguin, 1949).

Sterne, Robert A. M. *Modern Classicism* (Thames & Hudson, 1988).

Venturi, R. *Complexity and Contradiction in Architecture* (Museum of Modern Art, 1966).

Massey, Anne *Twentieth Century Interior Design* (Thames & Hudson, 1990).

DECORATIVE ARTS

Bayer, Patricia and Waller, Mark *The Art of René Lalique* (Bloomsbury, 1988).

Becker, Vivienne *The Jewellery of René Lalique,* exhibition catalogue (The Goldsmiths' Company, 1987).

Dormer, Peter *The New Ceramics* (Thames & Hudson).

Dormer, Peter and Turner, Ralph *The New Jewellery* (Thames & Hudson).

Eatwell, Ann *Susie Cooper Productions,* exhibition catalogue (Victoria & Albert Museum, 1987).

Klein, Dan and Bishop, Margaret *Decorative Art 1880–1980* (Phaidon Press, 1986).

Opie, Jennifer Hawkins, ed. *Scandinavia: Ceramics & Glass in the Twentieth Century* (Victoria & Albert Museum, 1989).

Wentworth-Shields, Peter and Johnson, Kay *Clarice Cliff* (L'Odeon, 1976).

White, Colin *The Enchanted World of Jessie M. King* (Canongate Publishing, 1989).

FASHION

Beaton, Cecil *The Glass of Fashion* (Weidenfeld and Nicholson, 1954).

Coleridge, Nicholas *The Fashion Conspiracy* (Heinemann, 1988).

Haye, Amy de la *Fashion Source Book* (Macdonald, 1988).

Milbank, Caroline Reynolds *Couture: The Great Designers* (Stewart, Tabori and Chang, 1985).

Wilson, Elizabeth and Taylor, Lou *Through the Looking Glass* (BBC Books, 1989).

GRAPHICS

Graphic Communication through Isotype, introduction by Professor Michael Twyman, exhibition catalogue (University of Reading, 1975).

Graphic Design in America: a visual language history, essays by Mildred Friedman et al, exhibition catalogue (Walker Art Center and Abrams, 1989).

McQuiston, Liz *Graphic Design Source Book* (MacDonald Orbis, 1987).

Olins, Wally *Corporate Identity* (Thames & Hudson).

Remington, R. Roger and Hodik, Barbara, J. *Nine Pioneers in American Graphic Design* (MIT Press, 1989).

Spencer, Herbert *Pioneers of Modern Typography* (Lund Humphries, 1969).

Speikermann, Erik *Rhyme & Reason: a typographic novel* (Berthold, 1987).

Thompson, Philip and Davenport, Peter *The Dictionary of Visual Language* (Bergstrom and Boyle Books, 1980).

INDUSTRIAL AND PRODUCT

Aldersey-Williams, Hugh *New American Design* (Rizzoli, 1988)

Brand, Steward *The Media Lab* (Viking Penguin, 1987).

Heskett, John *Industrial Design* (Thames & Hudson, 1980).

Loewy, Raymond *Industrial Design* (Fourth Estate).

Lucie-Smith, Edward *A History of Industrial Design* (Phaidon, 1983).

McCoy, Michael and Katherine, eds. *Cranbrook Design* (Rizzoli, 1990).

Papanek, Victor *Design for the Real World* (Thames & Hudson).

Pulos, Arthur J. *American Design Ethic, A History of Industrial Design* (MIT Press, 1983).

INDEX

CREDITS

Abbreviations
c = centre
t = top
b = below
r = right
l = left

p11 Telegraph Colour Library
p12 Telegraph Colour Library
p14 Architectural Association c J Beckett
p15 Canon
p16 Lawrence & Beavan
p17 Raymond Loewy International Inc
p18 Gert Dumbar
p19 Topham
p20 Mary Evans Picture Library
p21 Anthony d'Offay © Daniel Blau
p22 Phillipe Starck
p23 Kodak Museum at the National Museum of Photography
p24 Topham
p25 Telegraph Colour Library
p26 Architectural Association © V. Bennett
p27 Peter Dormer
p29 Anthony d'Offay
p30 Martin Trelawny
p31 Aviation Picture Library
p32 Austin Rover
p33 Telegraph Colour Library
p36 r Niall McInerney
p37 t Santi Caleca
p38 Architectural Association © P. Collymore
p39 t Massachusetts Institute of Technology bl Design Council br Hardy Amies Ltd/Snowden
p40 tl Mark Houldsworth tr Peter Dormer
p41 bl Peter Dormer cr Niall McInerney
p42 cl, bl Niall McInerney cr Architectural Association © F Penagos
p43 Design Museum
p44 cl Laura Ashley plc tr Dan Branch
p45 Peter Dormer
p46 c Peter Dormer tr Rien Basen cr Peter Dormer
p47 Victoria and Albert Museum
p48 all House of Balmain
p49 Bauhaus-Archiv © Lucia Moholy
p50 r Quaker Oats
p51 l BFI r American Telephone and Telegraph
p52 l Bauhaus-Archiv r Vintage Magazine Company

p53 cl, bl Professor Freidrich Becker tr Peter Dormer br Niall McInerney
p54 tc Design Council br Design Council
p55 l Design Museum r Peter Dormer
p56 l John Jesse/Irina Laski r Peter Dormer
p57 c RIBA r Design Council
p58 l Niall McInerney m Architectural Association c C. Nino r Onno Boekhoudt
p59 both Bruno Monguzzi/Studio Boggeri
p60 l Fiat Auto (UK) Ltd r Angelo Hornak
p61 tl Braun AG bl Sheila de Bretteville
p62 l Peter Dormer r Vintage Magazine Company
p63 m Neville Brody r Carol Burtin-Fripp
p64 both Carol Burtin-Fripp
p65 m Roberto Capucci r Corning Museum of Glass
p66 l Victoria and Albert Museum r Michel Boutefeu
p67 l Peter Dormer both Cartier Archive
p68 Vintage Magazine Company
p69 l Vintage Magazine Company r Peter Dormer
p70 cl Design Museum bl Peter Dormer
p71 l Hulton Picture Company m, cr, br Niall McInerney
p72 Chermayeff & Geismar Ass.
p73 l Citroen SA The Telegraph Colour Library
p74 Christie's Colour Library
p75 l Bridgeman Art Library r Christie's Colour Library
p76 l Architectural Association both H. Cook
p77 tl Zanotta bl, tr Jasper Conran
p78 Victoria and Albert Museum
p79 l Peter Dormer r Corning Museum of Glass
p80 Peter Dormer
p81 l Victoria and Albert Museum r Kathy McCoy
p82 l Peter Dormer
p84 tl Peter Dormer bl Metropolis Designs Ltd
p85 l Harper's Bazaar © Daniel Fallot tc, br Niall McInerney bm ADAGP Willy Maywald
p86 both Design Museum
p87 both Gert Dumbar
p88 Christie's Colour Library © DACS 1985
p89 Design Museum

p90 Hulton Picture Company
p91 Design Museum
p92 Niall McInerney
p93 tr Peter Dormer br Salvatore Ferragamo
p94 l Woodhead Public Relations r Gerda Flockinger
p96 l Foster Associates photo A Ward r Foster Associates photo Richard Davis
p97 l Peter Dormer r Foster Associates photo Ian Lambert
p98 Design Museum
p99 RIBA
p100 Orrefors Glasbruk
p101 l Chloe Alexander r Niall McInerney
p102 Architectural Association © D. Crompton
p103 l Frederick Gibberd Coombes & Partners r National Portrait Gallery
p104 bl, tr Givenchy m Fiat Auto (UK) Ltd br Milton Glaser Inc
p105 Vintage Magazine Company
p106 Grapus
p107 l Peter Dormer tr Michael Graves photo William Taylor br SPADEM 1985
p108 l April Greiman photo Taylor King c April Greiman r Victoria and Albert Museum
p110 l Hochschule fur Architektur und Bauwesen r Braun AG
p111 Orrefors Glasbruk
p112 bl, tr Katharine Hamnett bm Niall McInerney
p113 l Norman Hartnell m Hartnell Picture Company
p114 Vintage Magazine Company b KLM
p116 tl Angelo Hornak
p117 tr Honda br Architectural Association © A Higgott
p118 l Michael Hopkins m, r Richard Horden Associates
p119 r Niall McInerney
p120 both Design Museum
p121 all Austin Rover
p122 b RIBA t Niall McInerney
p123 both Royal Copenhagen
p124 Eva Jiricna
p125 t Aviation Picture Library bm, br both Angelo Hornak
p126 i-D Magazine
p127 t i-D Magazine b Aurum Press
p128 l Niall McInerney r Lynn Franks
p129 Gustavsberg
p130 l Architectural Association © P. Cook tr, br Niall McInerney
p131 l London Transport Museum r Niall McInerney
p132 Niall McInerney

p133 both David King
p134 t Tadema Gallery photo Eileen Tweedy b Niall McInerney
p135 John Jesse/Irina Laski
p136 l John Jesse/Irina Laski r Porsche
p137 Royal Copenhagen
p138 all Peter Dormer
p139 Niall McInerney
p140, 141 all Galerie Moderne
p142 tl Platon Antoniou bl Angelo Hornak r Niall McInerney
p143 l Crafts Council r Vintage Magazine Company
p144 l Gebrüder Thonet r Deidi von Schaewen
p145 Deidi von Schaewen
p146 Fay Sweet
p147 reprinted with permission of U&lc, The International Journal of Type and Graphic Design
p148 Vintage Magazine Company
p149 t David King b Vintage Magazine Company
p150 tr Design Museum
p151 l Rosenthal r Architectural Association © C. Limpert-Peers
p152 Glasgow School of Art
p153 Peter Dormer
p154 t Gorham Inc. cr Paddy Timmins br Peter Dormer
p155 Corning Museum of Glass
p156 tl, bl Peter Dormer r Sally Hunter
p157 both Sally Hunter
p159 t Architectural Association © A Minchin b Design Museum
p160, 161 The Hearst Corporation, courtesy of Harper's Bazaar
p162 l, c David Mellor r Design Council
p164 l Design Museum r RIBA
p165 both Angelo Hornak
p166 Niall McInerney
p167 tl Niall McInerney bl, r Moggridge
p168 l David King r Niall McInerney
p169 t Peter Dormer b Niall McInerney
p170 tl Niall McInerney bl Jean Muir photo Gemma Levine r Niall McInerney
p171 l Vintage Magazine Company r by courtesy of the Wedgwood Museum Trustees, Barlaston, Stoke-on-Trent, Staffordshire, England
p172 Otto & Marie Neurath Isotype Collection, Department of Typography & Graphic Communication, University of Reading
p173 tl Design Museum tr Necchi br Olivetti

p174 l Bridgeman Art Library tr Design Museum br Peter Dormer
p175 Camera Press
p176 all Olivetti
p177 Kolbjorn Ringstad
p178 Peter Dormer
p180 t Architectural Association c A Higgott bm, cr Pentagram
p181 Peter Dormer
p182 t Bella & Ruggeri b Michael Peters
p183 Zanotta
p184 Angelo Hornak
p185 l Victoria and Albert Museum c Mary Evans Picture Library tr, br ET br ET Archive © DACS 1985
p186 t Porsche bm Design Museum br Janine du Plessis
p187 t Janine du Plessis b Architectural Association © G Smythe
p188 bl Christie's Colour Library tr Karl Eric Steinbrenner cr Vintage Magazine Company
p189 tr Mary Quant br Camera Press
p190 l Wendy Ramshaw r David Banks
p191 tl Paul Rand bl Vintage Magazine Company r Jamie Reid
p192 l Niall McInerney r Design Museum
p193 tl Design Council b Braun AG
p194 l Peter Dormer r BPCC Aldus Archive
p195 l Everson Museum c Courtney Frisse r Design Museum
p196 l Rolls-Royce r Valerie Bennett
p197 tl Angelo Hornak tr, br Richard Einzig/ARCAID
p198 l Rolls-Royce r Ian McKinnell © Crucial Books r Rosenthal
p199 Christie's Colour Library
p200 t Angelo Hornak b Niall McInerney
p201 l Niall McInerney r Vintage Magazine Company
p202 Iittala Glass
p203 both Design Museum
p204, 205 all Victoria and Albert Museum
p206 A Jones © Crucial Books
p207 l Design Museum r Architectural Association SITE
p208 both Paul Smith
p209 l Skidmore, Owings & Merrill c Architectural Association R Whitehouse r Angelo Hornak
p210 l Design Museum c, r both Peter Dormer
p211 l RIBA r Basil Spence Partnership

p212 Olivetti
p213 both Ultima Edizione
p214 l Architectural Association J. Alleyne r Erik Spiekermann c Steven Heller
p215 Victoria and Albert Museum
p216 Peter Dormer
p217 Angelo Hornak
p218 Levi Strauss
p219 l Peter Dormer r Angelo Hornak
p220 t Design Museum b Architectural Association Hazel Cook
p221 l Bradbury Thompson r reproduced by Baseline Magazine published by Esselte Letraset Ltd
p222 Matteo Thun
p223 l Hulton Picture Company
p224 l Bridgeman Art Library/Haworth Art Gallery r Sotheby's
p225 l American Red Cross r Christie's Colour Library
p226 l Total Design r Vintage Magazine Company
p227 Topham
p228 bl, br Architectural Association A. Higgott tr Valentino
p229 Corning Museum of Glass
p230 l Corning Museum of Glass r Niall McInerney
p231 l Vintage Magazine Company r Victoria and Albert Museum
p232, 233 all Venturi, Scott Brown
p234 Doyle Dane Bernbach Ltd
p235 l Peter Voulkos c both Design Council r BPCC/Aldus Archive
p236 WMF
p237 l David Watkins c Hulton Picture Company r Wolfgang Neeb
p238 l Design Museum
p239 Niall McInerney
p240 Iittala Glass
p241 l Vintage Magazine Company r Betty Woodman
p242 both Andrew Higgott
p243 l RIBA r Kamlesh Parikh
p244 Musée des Arts Decoratifs de Montreal
p245 t both Niall McInerney b Angelo Hornak
p246 Musée des Arts Decoratifs de Montreal
p297 Design Museum